Ferruccio Busoni as Architect of Sound

Ferruccio Busoni as Architect of Sound

ERINN E. KNYT

OXFORD
UNIVERSITY PRESS

OXFORD
UNIVERSITY PRESS

Oxford University Press is a department of the University of Oxford. It furthers the University's objective of excellence in research, scholarship, and education by publishing worldwide. Oxford is a registered trade mark of Oxford University Press in the UK and certain other countries.

Published in the United States of America by Oxford University Press
198 Madison Avenue, New York, NY 10016, United States of America.

The publisher gratefully acknowledges assistance from the General Fund of the American Musicological Society, supported in part by the National Endowment for the Humanities and the Andrew W. Mellon Foundation.

Library of Congress Cataloging-in-Publication Data
Names: Knyt, Erinn E., author.
Title: Ferruccio Busoni as architect of sound / Erinn E. Knyt.
Description: [1.] | New York : Oxford University Press, 2023. |
Includes bibliographical references and index.
Identifiers: LCCN 2022040686 (print) | LCCN 2022040687 (ebook) |
ISBN 9780197625491 (hardback) | ISBN 9780197625514 (epub)
Subjects: LCSH: Busoni, Ferruccio, 1866–1924—Criticism and interpretation. |
Music—20th century—History and criticism. | Music and architecture.
Classification: LCC ML410.B98 K593 2023 (print) | LCC ML410.B98 (ebook) |
DDC 780.92—dc23/eng/20220823
LC record available at https://lccn.loc.gov/2022040686
LC ebook record available at https://lccn.loc.gov/2022040687

DOI: 10.1093/oso/9780197625491.001.0001

1 3 5 7 9 8 6 4 2

Printed by Integrated Books International, United States of America

For My Father

Contents

List of Figures, Examples, and Tables

Figures

Examples

Tables

Acknowledgments

This book would not have been written without support from numerous scholars, colleagues, friends, and family members. I appreciate advice from colleagues at the University of Massachusetts Amherst, including Evan MacCarthy, Ernest May, Marianna Ritchey, Emiliano Ricciardi, Jason Hooper, Brent Auerbach, Gary Karpinski, Chris White, and Salvatore Macchia, some of whom listened to presentations or read chapter drafts. I am also thankful for encouragement from George Barth, Karol Berger, Anna Maria Busse Berger, Sandra Graham, Tom Grey, Heather Hadlock, Stephen Hinton, and Christopher Reynolds. I am particularly indebted to my editor, Norman Hirschy, for his advice and counsel, and to my anonymous readers for their valuable suggestions. This project would not have been as complete without assistance locating obscure letters, documents, and scores from people at the following institutions: Archives et Musée de la Littérature (Kosta Siskakis), Archivio storico comunale (Paola Furlan), Bauhaus-Archiv (Erika Babatz), Bildarchiv Foto Marburg (Annette Otterbach), Fotoatelier Louis Held (Stefan Renno), Klassik Stiftung Weimar (Christiana Herrgott, Evelyn Liepsch, and Sabine Walter), Kurt Weill Foundation (Dave Stein), Library of Congress (Paul Allen Sommerfeld), Mills College (Janice Braun), Paul Sacher Stiftung (Felix Meyer, Michèle Noirjean, and Heidy Zimmermann), San Francisco Conservatory of Music (Jeong Lee), Staatsbibliothek zu Berlin (Jean-Christophe Gero and Marina Gordienko), Stanford University (Leif Anderson, Ray Heigemeir, Jerry McBride, Tim Edward Noakes, and Larry Scott), The Rudolph Ganz Papers (Lisa Schoblasky), University of California at Berkeley (Dean Smith), University of Massachusetts Amherst (Erin Jerome and Anne Moore), Yale University Library (Jake Fewx and Jonathan Manton), and Zentralbibliothek Zürich (Heinrich Aerni). I am also grateful to the following people for sharing their memories about Egon Petri: Lois Brandwynne (University of California at Davis), Ken Bruckmeier, Daniell Revenaugh (d. 2021), and my former piano teacher, Julian White (d. 2006), who studied with Petri and spoke of him often during lessons. Special thanks are also due Benjamin Ayotte for his typesetting of the examples, to Timothy

DeWerff for his copyediting, and to Colleen Wetzel for her assistance in procuring sources.

This book would not have been possible without the generous support of a Faculty Research Grant from the University of Massachusetts Amherst. I would also like to thank my parents and parents-in-law for their support while traveling to archives. The unexpected loss of my father in December 2021 deserves special mention, and I am dedicating this book to him. Finally, I would like to express my deepest gratitude to my husband Eric, and to my children, for their patience as I worked on book drafts and went on numerous trips to archives and libraries.

Introduction

Ferruccio Busoni and Architecture

Deep and quiet, the pillars of rock begin to sound
—Adam Oehlenschläger, *Aladdin* (1808)[1]

While approaching death in spring 1924, Ferruccio Busoni (1866–1924) reportedly confessed to his pupil Gottfried Galston that it had been his dream from his youth to become an architect rather than a musician. However, as the son of two musicians, his path in life had seemed predetermined:

> I wanted to become an architect, but how was it possible? The course was already fixed by the continuous directions, teachings, commitments, and models offered by my father—a clarinetist—and my mother—teacher of piano![2]

[1] [Die Felsensäulen fangen an tief und leise zu ertönen.] Adam Oehlenschläger, *Aladdin oder die Wunderlampe: Ein dramatisches Gedicht in zwei Spielen* (Amsterdam: Kunst und Industrie, 1808), 560. Quoted in Busoni, *Piano Concerto, BV 247* (Leipzig: Breitkopf und Härtel, 1906), 294.

[2] [Mein Wunsch ging dahin, Architekt zu werden. Aber wie sollte das kommen. War doch der Weg festgestellt durch die steten Unterweisungen, Lehren, Bemühungen und Vorbilder, die mir der Vater—Clarinettist—und die Mutter—Klavierlehrerin—ständig lieferten! So waren ja die Gleise gelegt und befestigt, und mein Schicksalsrad rollt sicher und unverrückbar in dieser Richtung.] Busoni, quoted in Gottfried Galston, diary entry of March 29, 1924, *Kalendernotizen über Ferruccio Busoni*, Taschenbücher zur Musikwissenschaft 144 (Wilhelmshaven: Florian Noetzel, 2000), 30. Busoni elaborated about his desire to become an architect in a memoir recorded by his friend, the architect Henry van de Velde. Van de Velde remembers that Busoni particularly disliked being promoted as a child prodigy—and it was in those instances that he most strongly hoped to switch to the field of architecture: "Busoni explained that when he felt an insurmountable reluctance to be shown to the public and the European Court as a child prodigy, such a passion for architecture arose in him, that he was ready to renounce music and to devote himself to architecture." [Im Anschluss an eine diskrete Bemerkung seiner Frau erklärte Busoni, dass als ihn eine unüberwindliche abneigung ergriff, dem Publikum und den europäischen Höfen als Wunderkind vorgeführt zu werden, eine solche Leidenschaft für die Architektur in ihm erwachte, dass er bereit war, auf die Musik zu verzichten, um sich der Architektur zu widmen.] Henry van de Velde, *Geschichte meines Lebens*, ed. Hans Curjel (Munich: R. Piper and Co., 1962), 392–99/503.

Ferruccio Busoni as Architect of Sound. Erinn E. Knyt, Oxford University Press.
DOI: 10.1093/oso/9780197625491.003.0001

Although Busoni never realized his dream of designing buildings, he became an architect of sound. Numerous references to architecture in his writings and letters reveal his fascination with architectural design, and he translated this knowledge into unconventional and multi-dimensional ways of sculpting sound and organizing pitches. An architectural mindset became scaffolding for the ways he approached music. Influencing elements from form to acoustics, harmony, color, treatment of the musical language, and timbre, his fascination with architecture led to compositional and interpretive experimentation.

While examining ways architecture inspired him, this book provides a long overdue assessment of Busoni as composer and arranger. When scholars mention him, they frequently note discrepancies between his compositional practice and his aesthetic theories. This book posits that Busoni was not only a radical thinker, but also an innovative and significant composer. Developments during the twentieth century included new means of pitch organization, the spatialization of sound, the expansion of formal structures, a new emphasis on tonal color, and novel treatments of the musical language. Busoni participated in these trends by writing pieces that feature sound radiating from different directions, montage formal structures, and the free use of all twelve pitches of the chromatic scale. When altering the music of others in live performances or in notated scores, Busoni modified the pitches, structure, and tone color to reflect his own ideals and the acoustic possibilities in the concert halls built during his lifetime. Thinking about the physicality of sound and the space it occupies expanded Busoni's ideas about music organization, about tones and timbres, and about the spatial possibilities of music.

Busoni was fascinated by aspects of dimension and space, factors obvious in relation to buildings, which possess visible mass, but less so with music, where the materials are invisible; nevertheless, they still take the form of sound waves that can fill rooms and emanate from different directions. In 1907, Busoni compared different art forms, such as architecture, sculpture, poetry, painting, and music. He concluded that music was unique in its immateriality and abstractness, calling sound waves "sonorous air" that floats in space:[3] "This child [music]—*it floats on air!* It touches not the earth with its feet. It knows no law of gravitation. It is well-nigh incorporeal. Its material

[3] Busoni, *Sketch of a New Aesthetic of Music*, trans. Th. Baker (New York: G. Schirmer, 1911), 4.

is transparent. It is sonorous air."[4] While the other art forms took up physical space, and according to Busoni, imitated nature mimetically, music was more abstract and could travel freely: "Even the poetic word ranks lower in point of incorporealness. It [music] can gather together and disperse, can be motionless repose or wildest tempestuosity; it has the extremest heights perceptible to man—what other art has these?"[5] That said, these waves could be translated into physical symbols that take up space on paper (if imperfectly), according to Busoni, and they emanate from physical beings and objects when they are conceived, delivered, and received.

Thinking about sound and the space it occupies expanded Busoni's ideas about music organization, about tones and timbres, and about the spatial placement of sounds. And while some of his abstract notions of music and space transcended any physical boundaries, as he cried that music is "free ('frei')," some of his ideas about spatialized *Tonkunst* were more tangibly realized in relation to architecture.[6] Busoni's creative activities were informed by the study of buildings and floor plans as well as by the ideas of contemporary architects, such as Henry van de Velde and members of the Weimar Bauhaus. His approach to form resembles *Jugendstil* art and architecture in the 1910s and Bauhaus art, theater, and architecture in the 1920s. He drew architectural diagrams to describe his structural conception for pieces and the space they occupied. These diagrams represent a departure from linear notions of form as possessing a beginning, middle, and end. In some of his operas, architecture determined spatial aspects of the music and staging. In his arrangements, he imposed his own ideas about architectural shape on compositions of others to create unique structures. He also enlarged textures in the compositions of others to fill the large new concert halls in which he performed.

Even despite the importance of architecture for Busoni's work, scholars have only touched upon the topic lightly.[7] Through close readings of his

[4] Busoni, *Sketch of a New Aesthetic of Music*, 4. [Das Kind—es schwebt! Es berührt nicht die Erde mit seinen Füssen. Es ist nicht der Schwere unterworfen. Es ist fast unkörperlich. Seine Materie ist durchsichtig. Es ist tönende Luft. Es ist fast die Natur selbst. Es ist frei.] Busoni, *Entwurf einer neuen Ästhetik der Tonkunst* (Wilhelmshaven: Florian Noetzel, 2001), 12.

[5] Busoni, *Sketch of a New Aesthetic of Music*, 5. [Selbst das dichterische Wort steht ihr an Unkörperlichkeit nach; sie kann sich zusammenballen und kann auseinanderfliessen, die regloteste Ruhe und das lebhafteste Stürmen sein; sie hat die höchsten höhen, die Menschen wahrnehmbar sind—welche andere Kunst hat das?] Busoni, *Entwurf*, 13.

[6] Busoni, *Sketch of a New Aesthetic of Music*, 4.

[7] Antony Beaumont, for instance, has written about the connection between Busoni's architectural sketches and the Piano Concerto, BV 247. Beaumont, *Busoni the Composer* (Bloomington: Indiana University Press, 1985).

writings, music, and recordings, this book provides the first comprehensive view of how architecture informed his composition and performance approaches. In the process, the book reveals continuity among his activities as composer, arranger, performer, and thinker. At the same time, it reveals connections between music and architecture.

This book also addresses Busoni's historiographic significance as a composer. Uncertainty about how to situate Busoni historically has led to neglect of his music in general. As Carl Dahlhaus has observed, he, along with one of his mentees, Jean Sibelius, does not fit easily in any historiographic categories. He cannot be clearly considered as either a progressive or a traditionalist: "Composers as Jean Sibelius and Ferruccio Busoni, undoubtedly belonged to the modernists—as they were understood at that time, but were afraid to take the final step towards new music; for critics unable to make an aesthetic judgment without first ascertaining their historical significance, they ended up in an aesthetic 'no-man's land' by failing to conform to historiographical formulae."[8]

Part of the confusion about Busoni's historiographic significance can be attributed to the fact that he never broke with earlier musical traditions even as he wrote about and explored experimental ideas. That makes it difficult to understand his works in relation to much of the discourse about modernism in music.[9] Many of Busoni's contemporaries were also critical of the composer for his Janus-faced interest in and reliance on historical styles and tonality and his seeming failure to implement all of his radical aesthetic ideals. Arnold Schoenberg, for instance, was surprised by Busoni's compositions, expecting a more direct break with past musical traditions based on his novel ideas about the future of music. On September 4, 1910, Schoenberg wrote to Busoni, requesting to see some pieces that more fully implemented his vision for new music: "And now something which I have long been meaning to ask

[8] [Komponisten wie Jean Sibelius und Ferruccio Busoni, die zweifellos der Moderne—wie man sie damals verstand—angehörten, sich jedoch scheuten, den Schritt zur Neuen Musik zu vollziehen, gerieten für eine Kritik, die kaum noch ästhetisch zu urteilen vermochte, ohne sich des geschichtlichen "Stellenwerts" einer Erscheinung zu vergewissern, dadurch in ästhetisches Niemandsland, dass sie sich den historiographischen Formeln entzogen.] Carl Dahlhaus, *Die Musik des 19. Jahrhunderts: Mit 75 Notenbeispielen, 91 Abbildungen und 2 Farbtafeln*, Akademische Verlagsgesellschaft Athenaion (Wiesbaden: Laaber Verlag, 1980), 309.

[9] Michael Levenson, for instance, has described modernism as involving new treatments of the tonal language and instruments, disunities, and experimentation, These were topics Busoni was interested in, wrote about, and practiced. Yet, these notions described by Levenson were often associated with historical rupture and a break with past traditions, such as tonality, which Busoni never wanted to do. Michael Levenson, "Introduction," in *The Cambridge Companion to Modernism*, ed. Michael Levenson (Cambridge: Cambridge University Press, 1999), 3.

you. I would like to know some other works of yours. Those which actually put into practice what you have promised in your pamphlet [*Sketch of a New Aesthetic of Music*]."[10] At the same time, Daniel Grimley has contended that, in spite of the fact that Busoni promoted the music of Carl Nielsen in Berlin, Nielsen "always seems to have had more respect for Busoni as a pianist than as a conductor or composer."[11] Even Sibelius considered many of Busoni's compositions more traditional than his own works.[12]

In addition, while recent scholars have recognized the importance of Busoni's ideas, they have not always given the same weight or attention to finding congruence between his compositions and his ideas. John Williamson, for instance, has written a compelling article about the uniqueness of Busoni's vision of the musical work, but his writings focus predominantly on Busoni's aesthetic writings, as opposed to his compositions.[13] Martina Weindel has similarly written a very thorough text that focuses primarily on Busoni's aesthetics.[14] While comprehensive studies of Busoni's compositions by Antony Beaumont and Larry Sitsky have done much to spread knowledge about his compositional output, they have primarily focused on the valuable activities of cataloguing, documenting, and analyzing his most important compositions, rather than in showing continuity between Busoni's visionary ideas and his compositional practice.[15] More recent studies have focused on issues of continuity between his ideas and musical practice, such as Paul Fleet's study on phenomenology in the music and

[10] Arnold Schoenberg, letter of September 4, 1910, in *Ferruccio Busoni: Selected Letters*, ed. Antony Beaumont (New York: Columbia University, 1987), 408.

[11] Daniel M. Grimley, *Carl Nielsen and the Idea of Modernism* (Woodbridge, Suffolk: Boydell Press, 2010), 192. Grimley supports his statement with a quote from a diary entry of 1891. He does not provide additional assessments of Busoni from Busoni's maturity. Nielsen dedicated his Symphony no. 2 "The Four Temperaments," op. 16, to Busoni. Busoni was instrumental in having the piece performed in Berlin on November 5, 1903, by the Berlin Philharmonic Orchestra (with Nielsen conducting).

[12] Jean Sibelius, entry of June 13, 1912, in *Dagbok: 1909–1944*, ed. Fabian Dahlström, Skrifter utgivna av Svenska litteratursällskapet i Finland 681 (Helsingfors: Svenska litteratursällskapet i Finland, 2005), 141.

[13] John Williamson, "The Musical Artwork and Its Materials in the Music and Aesthetics of Ferruccio Busoni," in *The Musical Work: Reality or Invention?*, Liverpool Music Symposium, ed. Michael Talbot (Liverpool: Liverpool University Press, 2000), 187–204.

[14] Martina Weindel, *Ferruccio Busonis Ästhetik in seinen Briefen und Schriften*, ed. Richard Schaal (Wilhelmshaven: Heinrichsofen-Bücher, 1996). Albrecht Riethmüller has also explored Busoni's aesthetics, but primarily in relation to specific music examples. While primarily exploring the ambiguous boundaries between transcription, arrangement, and compositions, as well as Busoni's theories of *Junge Klassizität*, Riethmüller does not emphasize Busoni's experimentation with the more experimental aspects covered in this book. Albrecht Riethmüller, *Ferruccio Busonis Poetik*, Neue Studien zur Musikwissenschaft 4 (Mainz: Schott, 1988).

[15] Beaumont, *Busoni the Composer*; Larry Sitsky, *Busoni and the Piano: The Works, the Writings, and the Recordings*, Distinguished Reprints 3, 2nd ed. (Hillsdale, NY: Pendragon Press, 2009).

aesthetics of Busoni, or Tamara Levitz's study on Busoni's Berlin master class (1921–1924).[16] However, this is just a beginning to scholarly discourse about a complex and varied topic.

Given that Busoni's music did not easily fit within constructed historiographic models, it is not surprising that there is not even a single mention of Busoni in most major music history textbooks. When scholars mention his importance, it is usually in relation to his aesthetic ideas. Richard Taruskin, for instance, who is one of a few to even mention Busoni in histories of music, writes about him on two separate pages in his six-volume *The Oxford History of Western Music*, where he called him both a pianist and composer. Yet he noted that even though Busoni envisioned tripartite divisions of tones, "he made no move at all toward implementation."[17] Taruskin also notes his activities as a composition teacher in Berlin from 1921 to 1924, where he taught Weill, and briefly mentions his mentorship of Schoenberg.[18] Yet not a single one of his compositions was discussed.

Busoni was thus not understood well by his own generation, because he was trying to reconcile musical traits associated with the traditions he knew and the experimental future he envisioned in a time when many of his contemporaries were either hanging on to tradition and looking to a new future with fear (as Hans Pfitzner), or else seeking to break with some past traditions to usher in a new future (as Schoenberg).[19] His compositions have also not received the attention that they deserve in recent scholarship. Vânia Schittenhelm has claimed, however, that Busoni's musical activities and his ideas were not irreconcilable.[20] As Schittenhelm points out, much of the confusion over the relative merits of Busoni's compositions comes from searching for a break with the past and with tonality rather than for experimentation with other factors; these include an experimentation with sound, an exploration of new ways of organizing music, an expansion of the musical language

[16] Paul Fleet, *Ferruccio Busoni: A Phenomenological Approach to His Music and Aesthetics* (Cologne: Lambert Academic Publishing, 2009); Tamara Levitz, *Teaching Young Classicality: Busoni's Master Class in Composition, 1921–1924* (Frankfurt: Peter Lang, 1996).

[17] Richard Taruskin, *Music in the Early Twentieth Century*, Vol. 4 of *The Oxford History of Western Music* (New York: Oxford University Press, 2010), 286. While it is true that he never composed pieces with microtonal divisions, he did commission instruments that did, and he inspired his students and followers to try them. For more information, see Erinn Knyt, *Ferruccio Busoni and His Legacy* (Bloomington: Indiana University Press, 2017), 107.

[18] Taruskin, *Music in the Early Twentieth Century*, 539.

[19] Vânia Schittenhelm, "The Dangerous Issue of Modern Music in the Controversy between Busoni and Pfitzner," *Electronic Musicological Review* 2:1 (October 1997), http://www.rem.ufpr.br/_REM/REMv2.1/vol2.1/The_Dangerous_Issue.html (accessed August 7, 2019).

[20] Schittenhelm, "The Dangerous Issue of Modern Music."

without rejecting tonality ("metatonality"), and an expansion of the many varied timbral and registral hues.[21] While he did not manage to successfully implement all of his ideas in his compositions, such as the use of microtones or electronic sounds (sometimes due to limitations in instruments and technology), he did implement some of them, such as an expansion of the musical language, and a new exploration of space and sound. In the process he helped create a significant, interesting, and innovative body of works.

Busoni's works can be understood and contextualized in relation to recent scholarship that has expanded notions of musical modernism beyond an experimental treatment of the tonal language and ruptures with the past.[22] Julian Johnson has claimed that there does not need to be a perception of a single narrative characterized by hard divisions between "conservative and progressive camps."[23] He maintains that there was actually a "co-existence and interaction of diverse stylistic practices, which, on closer inspection, begin to show some remarkable similarities."[24] Several other scholars have also recently identified multiple modernisms by differentiating between continental European modernism and slightly different approaches employed by Nordic and British composers, in particular. They have, for instance, written about Sibelius, Nielsen, and Edward Elgar, among others, placing them within discourse about a plurality of styles characterized in many cases, by modification of past traditions in new ways.[25] As Jenny Doctor has shown, in Great Britain, and even into the post–World War I era, traditionalisms and experimentation existed side by side. She argues that music of the era can sometimes include "modifying" traditions, not just "overturning" them.[26]

21 Fleet has used the term "metatonality" to describe Busoni's approach. See Fleet, *Ferruccio Busoni*.

22 For a survey of uses of the term "modernism," see Susan Stanford Friedman, "Definitional Excursions: The Meanings of Modern/Modernity/Modernism," *Modernism/Modernity* 8:3 (2001): 493–513. See also Matthew Riley, "Introduction," in *British Music and Modernism, 1895–1960*, ed. Matthew Riley (Burlington, VT: Ashgate, 2010), 1–11.

23 Julian Johnson, *Out of Time: Music and the Making of Modernity* (New York: Oxford University Press, 2015), 7–8. For more scholarship about the topic, see also Karol Berger, *Bach's Cycle, Mozart's Arrow: An Essay on the Origins of Musical Modernity* (Berkeley: University of California Press, 2007); Karol Berger, Anthony Newcomb, and Reinhold Brinkmann, eds., *Music and the Aesthetics of Modernity: Essays* (Cambridge, MA: Harvard University Department of Music, 2005); John Butt, *Bach's Dialogue with Modernity: Perspectives on the Passions* (Cambridge: Cambridge University Press, 2010).

24 Johnson, *Out of Time*, 7–8.

25 See, for instance, James Hepokoski, *Sibelius: Symphony No. 5* (Cambridge: Cambridge University Press, 1993); J. P. E. Harper-Scott, *Edward Elgar, Modernist* (Cambridge: Cambridge University Press, 2006); Grimley, *Carl Nielsen and the Idea of Modernism*.

26 Jenny Doctor, "The Parataxis of 'British Musical Modernism,'" *Musical Quarterly* 91:1–2 (Spring/Summer 2008): 89–90/110. In this quote, Doctor is also drawing from scholarship by Peter Childs, *Modernism* (London: Routledge, 2000), 4.

Grimley has also similarly described aspects of modernism in music as characterized by fragmentation and instability that ultimately leads to regeneration and change, such as in the music of Nielsen.[27]

Although the scholars mentioned above have recently sought to create multivalent and pluralistic accounts of modernism in music that move beyond notions of rupture with the past as well as beyond musical autonomy and elitist exclusivity or esotericism, Busoni's place has yet to be established or discussed in detail.[28] Moreover, the scant scholarly discourse about Busoni and modernism still focuses on aspects of his musical writing that is tied to the past, as opposed to his equally interesting quests to modify the traditions he venerated in order to write new and experimental music.

Walter Frisch, who is one of the few to discuss Busoni in relation to musical modernism, has also called for many alternate understandings of modernism, even within the works of European continental composers. As Frisch notes:

> Most accounts of Austro-German music from about 1885–1915, or roughly from the death of Wagner until the start of World War I, still tend to focus on chromaticism and atonality as the barometers of emergent modernism. Only more recently have we begun to understand that early modernism was a many splendored thing, not restricted to late Mahler, Schoenberg and his pupils, and Strauss through *Elektra*.[29]

He sought to broaden the concept in a number of ways, including in describing one modernist approach that does not reflect a rupture with the past. This concept of "historicist modernism" is in line with a notion of modifying tradition, as opposed to rejecting it. Frisch describes "historicist modernism" as "music written around 1900 that derives its compositional and esthetic energy not primarily from an impulse to be New, but from a deep and sophisticated engagement with the music of the past."[30] At the same time, he views "historicist modernism" not as nostalgia for the past, but as

[27] Grimley, *Carl Nielsen and the Idea of Modernism*, 237.

[28] Björn Heile and Charles Wilson, "Introduction," in *The Routledge Research Companion to Modernism in Music* (London: Routledge, 2019), 1.

[29] Walter Frisch, "Reger's Bach and Historicist Modernism," *19th-Century Music* 25:2–3 (2001): 296.

[30] Walter Frisch, *German Modernism: Music and the Arts* (Berkeley: University of California Press, 2005), 139.

the use of musical techniques from the past as a way to create some distance from late romantic styles.

Although Busoni is of mixed Italian-German heritage, Frisch discussed him in his book on German modernism and has called Busoni a "historicist modernist." In doing so, he grouped Busoni together with other continental German or Austrian composers such as Johannes Brahms and Max Reger. He has observed that even in Germany, "technically advanced language and a clear sense of moving away from the past" is only a part of musical modernism.[31] Frisch argues that composers such as Brahms, Reger, and Busoni used techniques of the past to serve original approaches toward musical language. Frisch was particularly interested in how these composers alluded to Bach, not in a retrogressive way, but as muses as they adapted older styles for a new age, even as Bach was seen as restorative in an era of decadence and extravagance. As examples, Frisch cited the final movement of Brahms's Symphony no. 4 in E minor, op. 98, and numerous pieces by Reger, including his Variations and Fugue on a Theme of Bach, op. 81.

Unlike Neoclassical music, where evocations of the past are frequently alienated from newer defamiliarized treatments of the musical languages, this "historicist modernism" approach allows the past to be part of the present in a continuous way, and without a sense of rupture. Frisch specifically notes that in the Variations and Fugue on a Theme of Bach, op. 81, Reger composes in such a way that it not only acknowledges the past, but also introduces a kind of fragmentation and temporal layering that "composes out the distance" between the composers and eras.[32]

Drawing on Albrecht Riethmüller's analyses of Busoni's music, Frisch also describes the appearance of his concept of "historicist modernism" in the third movement of Busoni's Violin Sonata no. 2, BV 244 (1900), which is a set of Beethovenesque variations featuring Bachian chorale motifs. He also notes Busoni's use of the fugue and chorale in the *Fantasia contrappuntistica*, BV 256, as indicative of "historicist modernism."

While Frisch's discussion of Busoni's position in musical modernism is a valuable and much-needed start to considering Busoni's place in historiographic narratives, it also limits the discussion to one aspect of Busoni's approach and to a narrow part of Busoni's output. Part of the limitation is caused by the scope of Frisch's project, which focuses on music composed

[31] Frisch, *German Modernism*, 4.
[32] Frisch, "Reger's Bach and Historicist Modernism," 312.

before 1915, and thus misses some of Busoni's more mature and experimental approaches during and after World War I until the time of his death in 1924. In addition, Frisch's emphasis on the Bach connection necessarily leaves out other important aspects of Busoni's compositional style, including his interest in contemporaneous ideas about new instruments, new scales, and general musical experimentation, as well as on his simultaneous allusions to Mozart. In focusing on a few pieces, and on historical connections to Bach, Frisch presents only a limited view of Busoni's compositional activities, one that emphasizes his connections to the past, as opposed to his equally strong experimental side. It obscures his interest in experimenting and modifying tradition in new ways to evoke a new future of music characterized by unique approaches to form, timbre, color, and space.

This book builds upon Frisch's ideas by presenting a broader view of Busoni's compositional activities as not only intimately connected to history (and not just the music of Bach), but also as closely aligned with a contemporary interest in experimentalism and in finding new ways to combine the materials of music in relation to other art forms. In doing so, it presents a more comprehensive portrait of the composer's compositional interests. It shows that even if Busoni did not call for a rupture from previous eras, as many early twentieth-century composers did, he still contributed to other related ideals of fragmentation, a bringing together of the arts, an expansion of the tonal language, an exploration of new formal structures, and an enlargement of space, color, and sound. In the process, it presents Busoni's approach as multifaceted, and situates Busoni's idiosyncratic musical voice among the plurality of musical modernisms that is beginning to be discussed.[33]

Moreover, it shows that Busoni's approach was firmly rooted in a contemporaneous interest in blending the arts in the early twentieth century. As Daniel Albright has already revealed, there was a tendency of the arts to lean toward each other in the early twentieth century.[34] Albright maintains that both temporal (i.e., poetry and music) and spatial (i.e., painting and

[33] It is possible that Busoni's mixed Italian-German heritage contributed to his idiosyncratic approach to modernism, but that topic is beyond the scope of this project. For more information about Busoni's heritage, see Knyt, "Ferruccio Busoni and the Liceo musicale di Bologna: Transnationalism and Italian Musical Culture," *Music and Letters* 99:4 (November 2018): 303–26; Martina Weindel, "Ferruccio Busoni und der Nationalismus," in *Italian Music during the Fascist Period*, ed. Robert Illiano (Turnhout: Brepols, 2004), 283–99.

[34] See, for instance, Daniel Albright, *Untwisting the Serpent: Modernism in Music, Literature, and Other Arts* (Chicago: University of Chicago Press, 2000); Albright, *Putting Modernism Together: Literature, Music, and Painting: 1872–1927*, Hopkins Studies in Modernism, ed. Douglas Mao (Baltimore: Johns Hopkins University Press, 2015).

architecture) art forms collided and combined in modernist music and art in unprecedented ways to form new "panaesthetic whole[s]."[35] He goes on to state that "on the one hand [they] retain their distinctness; on the other hand, they collapse into a single spatiotemporal continuum, in which both duration and extension are arbitrary aspects."[36] Albright contends that this "collaboration among several arts is at once a labyrinth and a thread that needs to be followed."[37] He convincingly describes many varied ways the arts collide in the modernist era through specific case studies of numerous artists, authors, and painters, including Kurt Weill, one of Busoni's pupils, who explored intersections between *gestus* and music. Yet Albright's text could not possibly cover every example, and it did not mention similar approaches in the works of Weill's teacher, Busoni, a lacuna this book hopes to fill.

Busoni explores resonances between art forms that forge unique intersections between artistic autonomy and social functionality, between form and content, between space and time, and between known history and the unknown future and experimentation. In bringing together different art forms, he was very much part of his era. Yet even if Busoni joined other contemporaneous composers in exploring interactions between the arts to inspire new compositional approaches, the specific architectural-musical thinking of Busoni was unique and contributed to an idiosyncratic view of music with respect to the relationship between form and material, in particular, but also in relation to issues of artistic autonomy and ontology. In particular, he argued for the uniqueness and independence of music as an art form, but at the same time insisted that it was informed by the human ideas and experiences of the creator. In this, he forged a middle ground between notions of absolute musical autonomy and extra-musical ideas.[38]

35 Albright, *Untwisting the Serpent*, 33.

36 Albright, *Untwisting the Serpent*, 33.

37 Albright, *Untwisting the Serpent*, 33. For additional literature on modernism, see Christopher Butler, *Early Modernism, Literature, Music, and Painting in Europe, 1900–1916* (Oxford: Clarendon Press, 1994); Joseph Straus, *Remaking the Past* (Cambridge: Cambridge University Press, 1990); Rebecca Walkowitz, *Cosmopolitan Style: Modernism Beyond the Nation* (New York: Columbia University Press, 2012); Carol J. Oja, *Making Music Modern: New York in the 1920s* (Oxford: Oxford University Press, 2000); Matei Călinescu, *Five Faces of Modernity: Modernism, Avant-Garde, Decadence, Kitsch, Postmodernism* (Durham, NC: Duke University Press, 1987); Jürgen Habermas, *The Philosophical Discourse of Modernity*, trans. Frederick Lawrence (Cambridge, MA: MIT Press, 2000); Richard Taruskin, *The Danger of Music and Other Anti-Utopian Essays* (Berkeley: University of California Press, 2008); David Roberts, *The Total Work of Art in European Modernism*, Signale: Modern German Letters, Cultures, and Thought (Ithaca, NY: Cornell University Press, 2011).

38 For more information, see Knyt, "Ferruccio Busoni and the Absolute in Music: Nature, Form, and *Idee*," *Journal of the Royal Musical Association* 137:1 (May 2012): 35–69.

In order to document the resonances between the art forms Busoni explored, this book clarifies the extent of Busoni's interest in architecture as well as his exposure to philosophers, architects, architectural historians, and musicians that were also interested in related topics. In addition, it documents his interactions with Henry van de Velde and faculty members at the Bauhaus to reveal fascinating cross-disciplinary exchanges of ideas. It also shows how these interactions impacted his novel ideas about space, timbre, and form as a composer and as an arranger of the music of others. It highlights his exploration of overtones, terraced sound, an expansion of timbral possibilities, and structural form. Through architectural analogies, the composer moved beyond a three-dimensional notion of music as harmony and melody moving in time. He pioneered a multi-dimensional view of music inspired by architecture that led to concepts of organized sound, structural and assemblage forms, omnidirectional theater, and unlimited tonal, registral, and harmonic colors and hues. In practice, he envisioned ways that musical sound could fill up physical spaces, and he emphasized color and timbre through terraced approaches to pedal and dynamics.

In the process, Busoni not only had a major influence on the spatialized music of the next generation of composers and performer-composers, such as Edgard Varèse, Stefan Wolpe, Wladimir Vogel, Egon Petri, and Kurt Weill, but also anticipated many of the textural, spatial, collage, and spectral experiments that were yet to come. As this book suggests, the long-term impact of his ideas on musical theater and opera, on the expansion of means of musical organization, and on the enlargement of concepts of sounds and colors reveals that he participated in the modernism of his own generation even as he played a more prominent role in the multivalent developments of music than previously understood.

Overview of Chapters

Throughout five chapters, this book explores the multiple ways architectural space, form, and design impacted Busoni's compositional style and experimentation. In the process it elucidates some of the more original aspects of his creative output, including the expansion of tonality, the spatialization of sound, and multi-dimensionality of form. In this way it also adds to ever-broadening scholarship on the topic of a melding of art forms in the era of modernism. In doing so, it reassesses Busoni's position in the historiographic narrative and in relation to current discourse about a plurality of modernisms in music.

Chapter 1 documents Busoni's extensive knowledge of architectural styles through analyses of letters, essays, drawings, and other documents, some unpublished. His connections with architects at and beyond the Weimar Bauhaus also indicate a rich exchange of ideas. In addition, this chapter documents how the composer's use of architectural metaphors, such as Gothic architecture in reference to Bachian polyphony, and Hellenic architecture in reference to Mozartian clarity of form, participated in and expanded upon ideals of his age. In particular, it shows that he not only mentioned these metaphors, but also used them to inform some of his original aesthetic theories, such as *Young Classicality*, which blended Gothic and Hellenic ideals to generate a visionary music of the future characterized by melodiousness, as intersections of independent voices create new harmonies, scales, and textures. The chapter explains Busoni's metatonal approach not as retrogressive, but as an expansion of the diatonic tradition. It also reveals ways Busoni realized these ideals in his *An die Jugend*, BV 254, and his *Fünf kurze Stücke zur Pflege des polyphonen Spiels*, BV 296, some of which were performed at the Bauhaus exhibition in Weimar in 1923.

Chapter 2 unveils Busoni's evolving approach to musical structure. Through close readings of letters, drawings, programs, memoirs, and sketches in conjunction with analyses of Busoni's compositions, this chapter reveals how architecture provided Busoni with ideas about how to move beyond traditional formal models to create new structures. Busoni sought inspiration in natural and architectural forms in the early 1900s; in the 1910s he created architectural montage structures. In the 1920s, his structures also included the fragmentation and combination of small discrete forms in a cubist manner. Furthermore, the chapter documents how architectural principles provided Busoni with ideas about how to move beyond traditional formal models to achieve these new structures. In two pieces, the Piano Concerto, BV 39 (1906), and the two-piano version of the *Fantasia contrappuntistica*, BV 256b (1922), Busoni illustrated his conception of the compositional structures with architectural drawings. In these and other instances, specific architectural styles were catalysts for his idiosyncratic formal approaches. Furthermore, the chapter reveals parallels between Busoni's ideas and those at the Weimar Bauhaus. In particular, it shows similarities between Oskar Schlemmer's "ambulant architecture" in the *Triadisches Ballet* and Busoni's textural layering in *Arlecchino*, BV 270, as well as between the Haus am Horn at the Bauhaus, where the square became a fundamental shape that was recombined in numerous ways to create the larger structure, and the combination of small forms into larger structures in Busoni's *Doktor Faust*, BV 303. In the process, the chapter reveals how a blending of ideals from different art forms led to an idiosyncratic approach to form and how shared early twentieth-century artistic ideals spanned across disciplines.

Chapter 3 discusses Busoni's spatialization of sound. It delineates his knowledge about physical space and architectural multi-dimensionality, documenting how it influenced his decisions about timbre, placement of instruments, and dramaturgy. His compositions from the 1910s and 1920s feature sound radiating from different directions, textural layering, and evocations of depth and height through a play with register, timbre, acoustics, and time. Many of his aesthetic ideas were based on metaphysical notions of inaudible sound in the universe that he translated into spatialized audible sound using the model of physical space in architectural buildings. For instance, Busoni re created the sounds associated with particular architectural building styles, such as cathedrals. He also posited novel theories about how music could encircle a stage and envelope listeners as it emanated from different locations simultaneously (i.e., below the stage, behind the stage, above the stage, in front of the stage, etc.). Architectural drawings for novel theatrical spaces, such as a triple stage opening inspired by Henry van de Velde, or a multilevel stage area, although never realized, informed his ideas about spatial instrument placement and inspired simultaneity of musical textures in *Doktor Faust*.

Chapter 4 documents the role Busoni's architectural conceptions played in his arrangements of the music of other composers in response to the reverberant and large concert halls erected during his lifetime. It specifically delineates how he shaped other composer's pieces aurally into monumental and multi-dimensional sound structures. "Colossal," "monumental," and "architectural" are common metaphorical descriptors for Busoni's interpretations, which featured the use of arm weight, the back, and the whole body. These descriptors were also commonly applied to those of the emerging Russian School, in particular, Anton Rubinstein, due to his lengthy concert programs and massive tone. Yet Busoni also arranged and re created pieces, such as J. S. Bach's "Goldberg Variations," altering them structurally according to his idiosyncratic conceptions that have been compared to architecture in terms of scope and structure. Similarly, he grouped together romantic miniatures by Chopin and Liszt into monumental cycles, by playing complete sets of preludes, etudes, or other pieces without break, while creating an overall shape to the pieces. The chapter reveals that Busoni also evoked architectural features and multi-dimensional sounds when he avoided the popular practice of fine nuance and linear playing in favor of a terraced approach, characterized by sudden changes in tempo, color, and touch. This created an aural impression analogous to structural blocks and multi-dimensionality even as he altered other's compositions in real time. In addition, he enriched chords and added octave doublings to provide aural height and depth.

Chapter 5 documents the lasting importance of Busoni's compositions, arrangements, and teachings about architecture for his mentees. This chapter primarily traces his influence on the mentees he invited to the Bauhaus exhibition of 1923, Egon Petri, Wladimir Vogel, Kurt Weill, and Stefan Wolpe. This "field trip" proved to be a climactic moment for Busoni's closest mentees and composition master class pupils, helping them solidify their understanding of his teachings about spatial forms and sounds. Soon thereafter, Vogel started composing pieces that explored textural means of organization as well as spatialized sounds in choral ensembles and polyphonic speech choirs. He explored aural space in terms of register and timbre. Weill's mixed-genre multi-dimensional montage forms based on a notion of *Urform* stem from Busoni's formal teachings and were based on Busoni's own operas. Moreover, Wolpe pioneered spatial approaches to music, including geometric pitch relations. At the same time, Petri also adopted a terraced approach and further cultivated Busoni's notions of architectural shape and sonorous color in his re creations of others' music. As the chapter reveals, Busoni's teachings about music also influenced the work of film artist Hans Richter and visual artist Henrik Neugeboren, who cite his views about musical counterpoint as impacting the direction of their art. Yet, as the chapter shows, Busoni's earlier composition mentees, that is, those he mentored prior to the Berlin composition master class (1921–1924), such as Varèse, also assimilated Busoni's ideas about spatialized sound, thereby revealing continuity in his teachings. Varèse's most obvious melding of spatialized sound, architectural space, and music was his *Poème électronique*, composed in conjunction with Le Corbusier and Iannis Xenakis for the Brussels World Fair in 1958. However, he wrote spatialized music long before that, and, as this chapter reveals, Busoni was a primarily catalyst for this.

In documenting the ways Busoni foresaw and propagated an interest in spatialized sound, multi-dimensional forms, and metatonal treatments of the tonal language, this book not only reassesses his importance as a composer, but also reveals ways that multidisciplinary understandings and multi-artistic collaborations impacted music development in Busoni's era. In the process, it provides a long overdue assessment of Busoni's musical creations and the impact of his compositional style on his students, even as it expands knowledge about the development of twentieth-century music, thereby adding more layers to gradually expanding notions of pluralistic musical modernisms in the early twentieth century.

1
The Cathedral of the Future and *Young Classicality*

> There is also a Gothic art of music and J. S. Bach is the master cathedral builder in music.
>
> —Ferruccio Busoni, 1910[1]

Architectural styles and spaces were fundamental to Ferruccio Busoni's ideas about music from his youth to his maturity.[2] Busoni (1866–1924) made general connections between physical architectural spaces and music; he also equated specific styles of architecture metaphorically with certain composers, especially Gothic architecture with Johann Sebastian Bach and Hellenic architecture with Wolfgang Amadeus Mozart. He likened Bach to a cathedral builder whose successors were mainly Germanic and French. He cited Bach's ornamentation that is intimately connected to the larger structure as being characteristically Gothic, and he also mentioned elaborate polyphony in which "continuing basses, figurations, themes, and imitations intersect, mesh, cross, and continuously spin out."[3] Likewise, he compared Mozart's symmetrical phrasing and solid forms to Hellenic architecture that is characterized by simplicity, purity, and youthfulness.

[1] [Es gibt auch eine gotische Kunst der Töne und J. S. Bach ist der Dombaumeister in der Musik.] Ferruccio Busoni, "Die 'Gotiker' von Chicago [1910]," in *Von der Einheit der Music*, ed. Joachim Herrmann and Max Hesses, Handbücher der Musik 76 (Berlin: Max Hesses Verlag, 1956), 133–34.

[2] I am grateful to Paola Furlan (Archivio storico comunale, Bologna), Kosta Siskakis (Archives et Musée de la littérature), Jean-Christophe Gero (Staatsbibliothek zu Berlin), and Martina Gordienko (Staatsbibliothek zu Berlin) for help locating archival sources for this chapter. An early version of this chapter was presented to the New England Chapter of the American Musicological Society, to the University of Massachusetts Musicology and Music Theory Lecture series in April 2018, and to the Nineteenth-Century Studies Association Annual Conference in March 2021. I am thankful to audience members for their helpful comments and suggestions.

[3] [Kontinuierenden Bässe, Figurationen, Themata und Repliken, wie sie sicht durchschneiden, ineinandergreifen, Kreuzen und sofort während welchsende, notwendig entstehende Akkordkombinationen bilden], Busoni, "Die 'Gotiker' von Chicago," 135.

Ferruccio Busoni as Architect of Sound. Erinn E. Knyt, Oxford University Press. © Oxford University Press 2023.
DOI: 10.1093/oso/9780197625491.003.0002

Busoni's association of Bach with Gothic architecture was part of a Romantic trend idealizing the mysterious and the metaphysical. The nineteenth century was marked by renewed interest in Gothic cathedrals and in their restoration.[4] Associations of Gothic literature and paintings with the otherworldly also fascinated nineteenth-century authors and coincided with their notions of a *Kunstreligion*.[5]

The Gothic remained a symbol of perfection in modernist artistic circles as late as the 1920s, such as for students and faculty members at the Weimar Bauhaus. In addition, during the first decades of the twentieth century, Mozart simultaneously became a model for burgeoning Neoclassical movements across the arts, with Hellenic art, with which Mozart was metaphorically connected, serving as a symbol of youthfulness, simplicity, and rejuvenation.[6]

Yet as this chapter reveals, Busoni's knowledge of architecture went beyond the idealized metaphorical notions of many of his contemporaries. He avidly studied real Gothic cathedrals and images of Hellenic temples, in addition to other historical and contemporaneous architectural styles.[7] His interactions with contemporary architects and with faculty at the Weimar Bauhaus suggest shared modernist ideas about a future of art characterized by a merging of different art forms. This informed his unique approach to music composition; fascination with architectural styles inspired Busoni to translate those styles into music in nuanced and idiosyncratic manners. He brought together spatialized and temporal art forms in unique ways.

Through analyses of letters, essays, and scores, this chapter reveals that architecture, including both knowledge of real buildings and metaphorical associations with music, inspired some of Busoni's innovations as a composer

[4] For instance, building on the Cologne Cathedral began in 1248, but construction stopped in 1560, and the building was left incomplete. Construction resumed in 1840, and the cathedral was completed in 1880, when Busoni was about fourteen years old.

[5] See, for instance, Katherine Bergeron, *Decadent Enchantments: The Revival of Gregorian Chant at Solesmes* (Berkeley: University of California Press, 1998).

[6] Some of these ideals were also embodied in the *Jugendstil* movement. For more information about the *Jugendstil* movement, see Andrew McCredie, ed., *Art Nouveau and Jugendstil and the Music of the Early 20th Century,* Adelaide Studies in Musicology 13 (Adelaide: Miscellanea Musicologica, 1984). These architectural styles were described in some detail in the writings of Wilhelm Worringer. See Worringer, *Form Problems of the Gothic,* Authorized American Edition (New York: G. E. Stechert and Co., 1910), https://archive.org/details/formproblemsofth00worruoft/page/n49/mode/2up (accessed September 22, 2020).

[7] An example of Neoclassical architecture in Berlin that was significant for Busoni is the Staatstheater, which Busoni describes visiting. Busoni, letter of May 30, 1921, to Edward Dent, in *Ferruccio Busoni: Selected Letters,* ed. Antony Beaumont (New York: Columbia University Press, 1987), 335.

and arranger. To do so, it documents Busoni's knowledge of architectural styles. In addition, it reveals ways his evocation of architectural metaphors expanded upon ideals of his age, while simultaneously informing some of his original theories about music, such as *Young Classicality.* In practice, knowledge of architecture informed his approach to both form and content. It led to his expansion of tonality through the use of new scales and harmonic plurisignificance deriving from polyphony. In his maturity, Busoni's music was characterized by what he describes as a "neo-Gothic" approach that chromatically expanded upon quasi-Baroque sequences and counterpoint coupled with a neo-Hellenic attention to solid formal structures. The result is abstract and economic architectural music. Finally, this chapter analyzes how Busoni realized these ideas in *An die Jugend*, BV 254, and in *Fünf kurze Stücke zur Pflege des polyphonen Spiels*, BV 296. In the process, the chapter describes Busoni's indebtedness to architectural models and metaphors for musical and idealistic inspiration; it also presents his resultant approach that embraced new scalar and harmonic approaches without rejecting tonality as an innovative alternative to atonality and serialism. It not only calls for a reassessment of Busoni's importance for the historical evolution of compositional treatments of the musical language, but also contributes new knowledge about ways interdisciplinary knowledge and ideals informed music composition in the early twentieth century.

Busoni's Knowledge of Architecture

Knowledge of architecture, fostered by a study of the designs and floor plans of buildings he visited, informed Busoni's compositions. Conversations with architects also influenced how he shaped sounds. As a child, Busoni created sketches of buildings to study their design.[8] A letter to his father provides one memoir of his early architectural drawings:

> I am getting up early and profiting from the coolness of the morning to go out and sketch some "views" of Trieste. Today I began to copy the church of the Schiavoni, which is a beautiful ["bellissimo"] building ["edificio"] in

[8] For more information about Busoni's drawing ability, see Herbert Günther, *Künstlerische Doppelbegabungen*, expanded ed. (Munich: Heimeran, 1960).

Moorish style ["stile Mauro"] and also perhaps one of the most beautiful ["capi"] pieces of architecture in Trieste.[9]

The use of the Italian word "capi" in the letter suggests not only beauty, but also Busoni's youthful assessment of the quality of the architecture. It indicates that Busoni believed the building held a chief position among architectural accomplishments in Trieste.

His drawings became more detailed as he matured. This is evident in his pencil drawing of a cathedral on the back of an envelope on a letter he received from Max Reger in 1895. It features turrets, spires, side buildings, and recessed passageways, even if the combination of Gothic spires combined with Romanesque semi-circular (as opposed to pointed) arches seems imaginative. Reger's discussions of Bach's music in the letter evidently inspired the sketch (see figure 1.1).

In an even more detailed drawing of a Gothic structure of an unknown date, Busoni sought to illustrate the relationship between ornamentation and structure; this is evident in the carefully sketched details, including filigree above the windows and a fountain next to the building. Although the original appears to be lost, it was reproduced and published in 1960.[10]

Busoni's knowledge of architecture came not only from observing and drawing masterpieces, but also from studying images in the beautifully illustrated books that he owned. At the time of his death, his personal Berlin library contained multiple volumes of architectural prints and drawings that he studied in detail, such as Thomas George Bonney's book *Cathedrals, Abbeys and Churches of England and Wales*, which has detailed descriptions and numerous photographs of ornate churches.[11] His copy of Julien Guadet's

[9] Busoni, letter of May 29, 1881, to his father, in Busoni, *Selected Letters*, 9. The alternate name for the church is the La Chiesa di San Spiridione. [Mi alzo presto per approfittare del fresco della mattina per uscire, dove disegno delle "vedute di Trieste." Oggi ho cominciato a copiare la Chiesa dei (!) Schiavoni che è un bellissimo edificio in stile Mauro (morscho) e forse anche uno dei più bei capi d'architettura di Trieste.] Martina Weindel, ed., *Ferruccio Busoni: Lettere ai genitori* (Rome: Ismez, 2004), 47.

[10] Günther, *Künstlerische Doppelbegabungen*, 26. Günther stated that the drawing belonged to Gerda Busoni, but it is unclear where the original drawing is today; it is not in his Nachlass at the Staatsbibliothek zu Berlin.

[11] For a list of the books Busoni owned at the time of his death, see Max Perl, *Bibliothek Ferruccio Busoni: Werke der Weltliteratur in schönen Gesamtausgaben und Erstdrucken, illustrierte Bücher aller Jahrhunderte, eine hervorragende Cervantes- und E.T.A Hoffmann-Sammlung, Bücher mit handschriftlichen Dedikationen, ältere und neuere Literatur aus allen Wissensgebieten, Musik; Versteigerung Montag, den 30. und Dienstag, den 31. März 1925* (Berlin: Max Perl Antiquariat, 1925), https://digi.ub.uni-heidelberg.de/diglit/perl1925_03_30/0017/text_ocr (accessed June 8, 2020); Thomas George Bonney, *Cathedrals, Abbeys and Churches of England and Wales*, 2 vols. (London: Cassell, 1896).

Figure 1.1. Busoni, sketch of a cathedral on the envelope from a letter by Max Reger of September 6, 1895, to Busoni. Staatsbibliothek zu Berlin, Musikabteilung mit Mendelssohn Arkiv, Preussischer Kulturbesitz, Mus. Nachl. F. Busoni, B II, 4053.

influential four-volume *Eléments et théorie de l'architecture* (1915) contained sketches and floor plans for gardens, commemorative monuments, galleries, and monumental buildings from many historical periods and geographical regions, including an Athenian temple and the more contemporary hôtel Salé in Paris.[12] When Busoni was ill in Berlin in 1924, Gottfried Galston

[12] Julien Guadet and Jean-Louis Pascal, *Eléments et théorie de l'architecture; cours professé a l'École nationale et spéciale des beaux-arts* (Paris: Librairie de la Construction Moderne, 1915).

brought him a copy of François Blondel's *Cours d'architecture* (Paris, 1675–1683) to cheer him up.[13] Other volumes in his collection featured architecture in Berlin, France, Italy, and around the world.

A handwritten list shows that he had access to many of these books during World War I, even though he had left most of his personal book collection in his Berlin apartment. He owned a substantial number of volumes in Zurich during World War I on diverse architectural styles ranging from medieval France, to ancient Rome, to the architecture of India, Germany, and Italy (see figure 1.2).[14] It is probable that he purchased most of the volumes while in Zurich; he wrote to Jella Oppenheimer about his frequent visits to used bookstores there: "I love to rummage in old bookstores—but by now I know every one of them, and the dealers are receiving no new deliveries from abroad."[15] The large number of books he acquired about architecture seems to indicate a special interest in the topic at the time. Moreover, he sent his collection back to Berlin after World War I. Although not all the books arrived safely, quite a few of those listed in his Zurich book collection are also included in the auction records listing his personal book collection after his death.[16] There were books by or about Eugène Viollet-le-Duc, James Fergusson, Guadet, Vitruvius, Canova, Auguste Rodin, and Andrea Palladio, along with texts about terracotta architecture and buildings in Berlin.[17] These books provide both large overviews of historical styles of architecture as well as more specialized and focused studies of buildings in specifical locales or times periods. Of these, Fergusson's text offers a comprehensive history of architectural styles, while the book on architecture in

[13] Galston, diary entry of April 26, 1924, *Busoni: gli ultimi mesi di vita. Diario di Gottfried Galston*, ed. Martina Weindel (Rome: ISMEZ, 2002), 52. See also Galston, *Kalendernotizen über Ferruccio Busoni*, ed. Martina Weindel (Wilhelmshaven: L. F. Noetzel, 2000). François Blondel and Simon de la Boissière, *Cours d'architecture enseigné dans l'Académie Royale d'Architecture* (Paris: Paris Auboin, 1675).

[14] Busoni, list of books in Busoni's Zurich book collection, Staatsbibliothek zu Berlin—Preußischer Kulturbesitz, Musikabteilung mit Mendelssohn-Archiv, N. Mus. Nachl. F. Busoni, H, 18, 5. The title page of Busoni's notebook states: "gegen 1000 Baende darstellen die Zürcher Bücher: Sammlung von F. Busoni 1915–1920" [About 1,000 volumes represented in the Zurich Book Collection of Ferruccio Busoni 1915–1920]. Some of the items on the list contain curious parallels to Busoni's own drawings. The Canova Mausoleum, for instance, bears some similarities to the middle image in the published drawing for his Piano Concerto, BV 247. Both feature a triangular shape with ornate figures in front of a recessed doorway, for instance.

[15] Busoni, letter of September 1917 to Jella Oppenheimer, in Beaumont, *Selected Letters*, 265.

[16] Tamara Levitz made this claim based a letter of October 25, 1920, from Busoni to his son, Rafaello Busoni. Levitz, "Teaching New Classicality: Busoni's Master Class in Composition 1921–1924" (PhD diss., University of Rochester, 1994), 57. I was unable to locate a letter of that date between the two in the Busoni Nachlass. She might be referring to the letter of October 24, 1920, Staatsbibliothek zu Berlin—Preussischer Kulturbesitz, Musikabteilung mit Mendelssohn-Archiv, N. Mus. Nachl. 4, 147.

[17] Max Perl, *Bibliothek Ferruccio Busoni*, 7–9; 20; 88; 107.

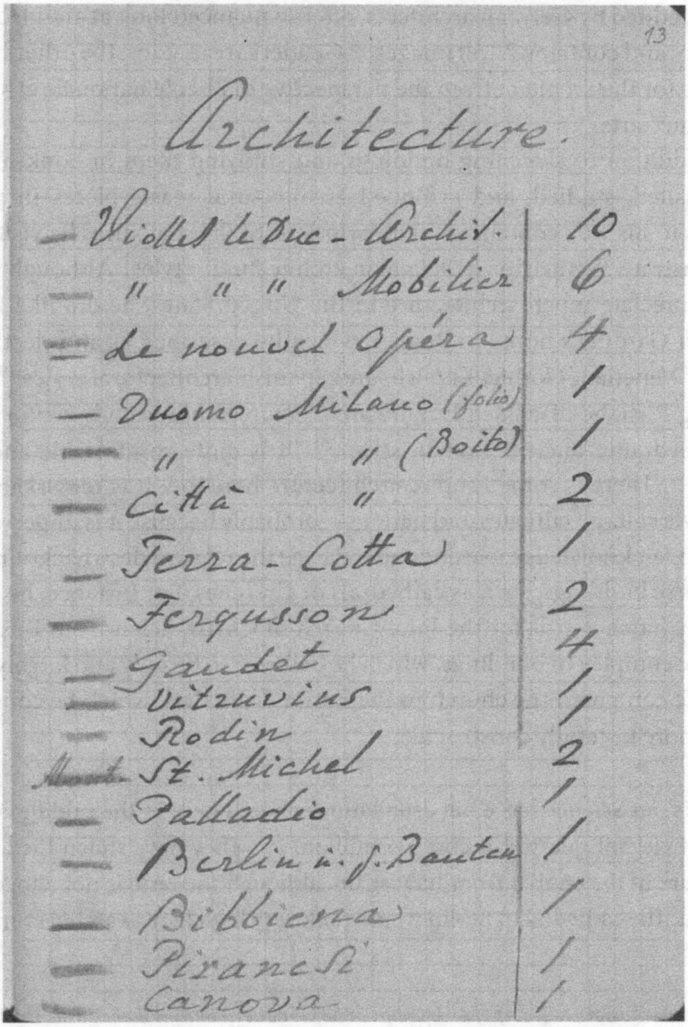
13
Architecture.
Viollet le Duc - Archit. 10
" " " Mobilier 6
Le nouvel Opéra 4
Duomo Milano (folio) 1
" " (Boito) 1
Città " 2
Terra-Cotta 1
Fergusson 2
Gaudet 4
Vitruvius 1
Rodin 1
St. Michel 2
Palladio 1
Berlin u. s. Bauten 1
Bibbiena 1
Piranesi 1
Canova 1

Figure 1.2. Busoni, list of architecture books in Busoni's Zurich book collection. Busoni, Sketchbook. Staatsbibliothek zu Berlin, Preussischer Kulturbesitz, Musikabteilung mit Mendelssohn Archiv, N. Mus. Nachl. F. Busoni, H, 18, 5, 13.

Berlin, edited by German architects, offers a nuanced look at architecture in that city and contains 2,150 images.[18] Guadet's treatise, on the other hand, is a guide for the architect from the perspective of l'Ecole nationale et spéciale des beaux-arts.

In addition to sketching buildings and studying them in books, Busoni also visited, studied, and critiqued architectural masterpieces in person. Letters to his wife contain vivid descriptions of the structures he visited and demonstrate familiarity with major architectural styles. Although he did not appreciate much architecture in the United States, he did like Isabella Stewart Gardner's home in Boston, which he described as an eclectic mixture of Venetian, Gothic, English, and Spanish architectural styles.[19] When visiting Riga, he discussed Empire architecture, a nineteenth-century trend patterned after ancient Roman styles:[20] "It is quite comfortable and quiet here. . . . There is some Empire architecture here too; it is remarkable how this style suits all climates and nations—probably because it is impersonal."[21] He also felt knowledgeable enough to judge the relative drawbacks or merits of diverse buildings, such as cathedrals or churches. For instance, he had especially harsh words for the First Church of Christ, Scientist in Boston, an eclectic complex of buildings, which he believed to be ugly and largely imitative. He compared the church to the Berlin Cathedral, which he considered to be more tastefully constructed:

> Christian Science has a big ostentatious church here in the middle of the most elegant quarter! It cost 1½ million! . . . They have stolen the architecture of the church from Italy again, although the taste is not altogether good. The cathedral in Berlin would rank very high here as architecture.[22]

[18] James Fergusson, *A History of Architecture in All Countries: From the Earliest Times to the Present Day* (New York: n.p., 1907); *Berlin und seine Bauten* (Berlin: Ernst, 1877).

[19] Busoni, letter of March 4, 1904, to Gerda Busoni, in Busoni, *Letters to His Wife*, trans. Rosamond Ley, Da Capo Press Music Reprint Series, ed. Roland Jackson (New York: Da Capo Press, 1975), 71.

[20] One of the most famous examples of Empire architecture is the Arc de Triomphe de l'Étoile in Paris.

[21] Busoni, letter of November 8, 1912, to Gerda Busoni, in *Letters to His Wife*, 210. [Es ist hier behaglich und still. . . . Einiges Empire giebt's auch hier; es ist merkwürdig, wie dieser Styl zu allen Klima's und Nationen paßt—wohl durch wein Unpersönliches.] Busoni, *Briefe an seine Frau*, ed. F. Schnapp (Zurich: Rotapel, 1935), 260–61, https://archive.org/details/BusonisBriefeAnSeineFrau/page/n296/mode/1up (accessed June 12, 2020).

[22] Busoni, letter of March 12, 1910, to Gerda Busoni, in *Letters to His Wife*, 160–61. [Die *Christian Science* hat hier eine grosse prunkhafte Kirche mitten in feinsten Viertel! 1½ Million! . . . Die Kirche ist übrigens wieder einmal von Italien gestohlen, wenn auch nicht gerade mit gutem Geschmack. Der Berliner Dom würde hier, als Architektur, einen hohen Rang einnehmen. Mann muss sich an so Etwas erinnern, um den Maasstab zürückzufinden.] Busoni, *Briefe an seine Frau*, 193.

Busoni's knowledge about architecture came from his extensive study not only of building exteriors, but also floor maps and interior spaces. This is evident in his description of the Palais Garnier, named after its architect, Jean-Louis Charles Garnier (1825–1898). He mentioned studying the building with respect to its architectural lines and structure, and he concluded that the form was a work of genius:

> I went round the opera house for half an hour yesterday and studied the plan of it. As far as I can say about architecture [Baukunst], I think the form genial [genius-like] and the execution of it masterly. The ground plan, above all, is grand; and it was a splendid idea to put this ground plan under Garnier's bust in the place of an inscription. Every line, which the walls follow, was put in its place with greatest certainty and clarity.[23]

In his descriptions of buildings, Busoni sometimes made direct connections to music, such as when he visited the famed Cologne Cathedral. It had been recently renovated, and he connected it to the music of J. S. Bach. In his description, Busoni alluded to its enormous height, towering over the surrounding buildings. He also mentioned its ornate complexity:

> We stopped two hours in Cologne. But unfortunately from 9:30–11:30. I only saw the Cathedral in silhouette; Cologne has the narrowest streets I know, and the Cathedral looks like Gulliver in Lilliput. I shall have time, on the way back, to study this Bach-like composition in architecture.[24]

Similarly, on a visit to London, he compared what he described as tasteful, but cautious architectural feats, such as the old Waterloo Bridge across the Thames, to a performance in which the performer is playing a piece of music

[23] Busoni, letter of August 14, 1912, to Gerda Busoni, in *Letters to His Wife*, 208. [Ich bin gestern eine halbe Stunde am das Opernhaus herumgegangen und habe den Plan studiert. So viel als ich über Baukunst sagen darf: ich finde die Form genial und die Ausführung meisterhaft. Vor Allem der Grundriss ist herrlich und es war ein prächtiger Einfall, dass man, under der Büste Garniers, anstatt einer Inschrift, diesen Grundriss setzte. Aber auch die Mauern zeigen nicht eine Linie, die nicht mit grösster Sicherheit und Klarheit hingestellt wäre. Die Dekoration ist allerdings schwer und konventionell.] Busoni, *Briefe an seine Frau*, 258.

[24] Busoni, letter of February 24, 1897, to Gerda Busoni, in *Letters to His Wife*, 20. [In Köln hielten wir zwei Stunden. Doch leider von 9½ bis 11½ Uhr. Vom Dom sah ich nur die Silhouette; Köln hat die engsten Strassen; die ich kenne und der Dom sieht aus wie Gulliver in Liliput. Beim Zurückfahren werde ich Zeit haben, den Bach der Architektur gründlich zu bestehen.] Busoni, *Briefe an seine Frau*, 11.

slowly and carefully but without spirit. Designed by John Rennie, with the assistance of George Dodd, the bridge featured nine arches covered in granite and decorated with Doric columns. Busoni considered the shape to be overly simple, repetitive, and lacking in vitality.[25]

The composer not only studied buildings, but also befriended architects and mingled with them, which led to important exchanges of ideas. When he was the director of the Liceo musicale di Bologna from 1913 to 1914, he oversaw architectural plans for the conversion of the Santa Lucia church into a concert hall for an orchestra.[26] Much of the planning took place from May to June 1914 and involved architects such as Luigi Corrini, engineers, and civic leaders. Unfortunately, with Busoni's permanent departure from Bologna in summer 1914 and a newly elected socialist government, the plan was not realized.[27] In addition, there were some objections to redoing the building, because of its historical value. It was originally constructed in 1623 and designed by architect Girolamo Rainaldi, who was famed for his Mannerist style.[28]

The composer also met with a network of intellectuals, composers, artists, writers, pupils, and architects in Zurich and Berlin that informed his views. Many of these came to his home during weekly "Black Coffee" hours that offered a salon atmosphere and rich exchanges of ideas.[29] Others visited Busoni privately as well.

In particular, he befriended contemporary architects, such as Henry van de Velde (1863–1957), who visited his residence in Zurich. Van de Velde was a Belgian architect and painter who was a pioneer of *Jugendstil* architecture and exerted a significant influence on German architects and architectural styles at the beginning of the twentieth century. He moved to Weimar in 1899, shortly before Busoni held his summer master classes there in 1900 and 1901, even if the two reportedly did not first meet until their joint

[25] The original Waterloo Bridge opened in June 1817 but closed in 1924 due to safety concerns. It was demolished in 1934. Busoni, letter of September 30, 1919, to Gerda Busoni, in *Letters to His Wife*, 267–68.

[26] The Liceo is now known as the Conservatorio Giovanni Battista Martini. For more about Busoni's time at the Liceo, see Knyt, "From Nationalism to Transnationalism: Ferruccio Busoni, the Liceo Musicale di Bologna, and *Arlecchino*," *Music & Letters* 99:4 (November 2018): 604–34.

[27] For more information, see the following documents: Bologna, Archivio storico comunale, PG 14421, 15404, 15723, and 15749.

[28] Mannerist architects feature irregular proportions and seemingly arbitrary placements of decorative features. This was a style that was popular from about 1520 to 1600.

[29] For more about these salon gatherings in Busoni's Berlin apartment, see Levitz, "Teaching New Classicality," 115–17. Busoni's gatherings usually took place on Thursdays when he was living in Berlin in the 1920s.

sojourn in Switzerland during World War I.[30] It was in Weimar that van de Velde founded the Großherzoglich-Sächsische Kunstschule Weimar, which preceded the Weimar Bauhaus.

Van de Velde, who moved to Switzerland in 1917, reportedly met Busoni there through Volkmar Andreae, a Swiss composer and conductor who was important for Busoni's career during World War I. A shared interest in both architecture and music served as a bond between the men. That said, both were evidently aware of each other's work long before they met, and Busoni, in particular, displayed an intimate knowledge of van de Velde's architecture. Van de Velde's memoirs note that Busoni could dialogue with him about it in detail. Busoni reportedly pointed out many parallels between van de Velde's architecture and his own music:[31]

> In his small, charming Zurich apartment, which he occupied during the war, we talked over a meal that Busoni's wife Gerda had served us, about the relationship between music—his art—and architecture—mine. The naturalness with which he portrayed and analyzed these relationships, which one cannot take seriously enough, the technical precision with which he spoke of my "metier," while I felt unable to find the appropriate words for his art, excited my highest astonishment. Following a discreet remark from his wife, Busoni explained that when he was overcome by an insurmountable reluctance to be presented to the public and the European courts as a prodigy, such a passion for architecture awoke in him that he was ready to give up music to devote to architecture.[32]

The two were also aware of each other's aesthetic writings. Van de Velde delved deeply into Busoni's *Sketch of a New Aesthetic of Music* (1907), while

[30] For more information about the summer master classes, see Knyt, "Franz Liszt's Heir: Ferruccio Busoni and Weimar," *Nineteenth-Century Music Review* 17:1 (May 2019): 35–67.

[31] Henry van de Velde, *Geschichte meines Lebens*, 2nd ed., ed. Hans Curjel (Munich: Piper, 1986), https://www.dbnl.org/tekst/veld006gesc01_01/index.php (accessed November 29, 2018).

[32] [In seinem kleinen, reizvollen Zürcher Appartement, das er während des Krieges bewohnte, unterhielten wir uns nach einem Essen, das uns Busonis Frau Gerda serviert hatte, über die Beziehungen von Musik—seiner Kunst—und Architektur—der meinigen. Die Selbstverständlichkeit, mit der er diese Beziehungen, die man nicht ernste genug nehmen kann, darstellte und analysierte, die technische Präzision, mit der er von meinem "Metier" sprach, während ich mich unfähig fühlte, die geeigneten Worte für seine Kunst zu finden, erregten mein höchstes Erstaunen. Im Anschluß an eine diskrete Bemerkung seiner Frau erklärte Busoni, daß, als ihn eine unüberwindliche Abneigung ergriff, dem Publikum und den europäischen Höfen als Wunderkind vorgeführt zu werden, eine solche Leidenschaft für die Architektur in ihm erwachte, daß er bereit war, auf die Musik zu verzichten, um sich der Architektur zu widmen.] Van de Velde, *Geschichte meines Lebens*, 396.

Busoni read van de Velde's treatise on architectural beauty, *Traité de la triple offense à la beauté,* which was originally published in German in Zurich in 1918. In his text, van de Velde argued that there were three things preventing beauty in art: an offense against nature, an offense against the human dignity of the creator, and an offense against reason.[33] Van de Velde claimed that art needed spirit, reason, and form to be great. Busoni expressed his delight at receiving the book and praised it, stating, "I find it interesting, just, very well written, and necessary."[34]

Busoni was also in contact with architects at the Bauhaus, who were known for their pioneering of the International Style of architecture. Although any documents revealing Busoni's first connections with the Bauhaus no longer seem to exist, Busoni must have discussed its predecessor, the Weimar School of Arts and Crafts, with van de Velde in Switzerland as early as 1917. Moreover, he was friends with Alma Mahler, who married Walter Gropius, the founder of the Bauhaus. Alma Mahler had begun an affair with architect Gropius in 1910, an affair which, after a hiatus from 1911 to 1915, eventually resulted in their marriage on August 18, 1915 (after Gustav Mahler's death).[35] Although Busoni's primary connection to Alma Mahler was initially established through Gustav Mahler, Alma Mahler continued to correspond with Busoni even after Gustav Mahler's death and after her marriage to Gropius.[36] Franz Werfel, Alma's third husband, with whom she began an affair in 1917 and married in 1929, was part of Busoni's close circle in Zurich during World War I as well.[37] Alma Mahler's long friendship with Busoni is indicated, for instance, in that she sent Busoni birthday wishes in 1916 in a joint letter from several others of Busoni's circle, some of whom attended the salon gatherings in his home, including Melchior Lector (painter), Oskar

[33] Van de Velde, *Die drei Sünden wider die Schönheit* (Zurich: Max Rascher Verlag, 1918).

[34] [Mon cher Maître, j'ai recú, avec une agréable surprise, le livre qui Traité de la "triple offense à la beauté." Je le trouve intéressant, juste, trés-bien écrit, et necessaire.] Busoni, letter of December 19, 1918, to Henry van de Velde, reproduced in van de Velde, *Geschichte meines Lebens*, 2nd ed., 397. The original is located at the Archives et Musée de la littérature in Brussels, Belgium.

[35] Gustav Mahler died on May 18, 1911.

[36] It is noteworthy that Alma Mahler also had an affair with Oskar Kokoschka from 1912 to 1914.

[37] For more about the life of Alma Mahler, see Karen Monson, *Alma Mahler, Muse to Genius: From fin-de-siècle Vienna to Hollywood's Heyday* (Boston: Houghton Mifflin, 1983); Cate Haste, *Passionate Spirit: The Life of Alma Mahler* (London: Bloomsbury Publishing, 2019); Donald Arthur, *Malevolent Muse: The Life of Alma Mahler*, trans. Oliver Hilmes (Boston: Northeastern University Press, 2015). Alma's affair with Werfel began in 1917 even if she did not marry him until 1929. For a list of Busoni's Zurich circle, see H. H. Stuckenschmidt, *Ferruccio Busoni: Chronicle of a European*, trans. Sandra Morris (New York: St. Martin's Press, 1967), 57. Other members of the Zurich circle included conductor Oskar Fried; poets Ludwig Rubiner, Ivan Goll, and Leonhard Frank; author James Joyce; as well as publishers and critics such as Paul Cassirer and Stefan Zweig.

Bie (artist, art historian, and musicologist), Gustav Brecher (conductor and composer), Rudolf Cahn-Speyer (conductor), Eugen Spiro (painter), Alfred Kerr (author), Johann Martin Kraus (composer), Georg Richard Kruse (author, conductor, and arranger), Otto Lessmann (composer), Adolf Paul (author), Ludwig Gurlitt (reform pedagogue), Hugo von Hofmannsthal (author), Hans Huber (composer), Margarethe Klinckerfuss (pianist), Artur Schnabel (pianist), Therese Behr (singer), Jakob Wassermann (author), C. Bechstein (piano manufacturer), and Steinway and Sons (piano manufacturer).[38]

Even if Busoni was in the United States and Switzerland during World War I, and thus not physically close to Alma Mahler, he was aware of Alma Mahler's new husband, Gropius, and would have become knowledgeable about his work through Alma Mahler before the establishment of the Bauhaus in 1919. Moreover, Gropius was one of the architects mentioned in Busoni's massive book about architecture in Berlin.[39] Busoni and Schoenberg corresponded briefly about Gropius and Alma Mahler as well during World War I, after Busoni, who was in Switzerland at the time, inquired how Alma Mahler was doing. Schoenberg mentioned Alma Mahler's marriage and described Gropius as "pleasant":

> Frau Mahler has married. Her husband, the architect Gropius, has been in the field as a lieutenant since the beginning of the war. He is a very pleasant fellow. There was a nasty disagreement between Frau Mahler (Gropius) and myself (for nearly a year), which has now been patched up, that is why I have so little news of her. But tomorrow I shall call on her and send her your best wishes.[40]

[38] Several letters from Alma Mahler written after Gustav Mahler's death can still be found in the Staatsbibliothek zu Berlin. These are as follows: "Reste der Busoni-Festschift 1916," Preussischer Kulturbesitz, Musikabteilung mit Mendelssohn Archiv, Mus. Nachl. F. Busoni B II 2943; Alma Mahler, letter of July 18, 1911, to Busoni, Preussischer Kulturbesitz, Musikabteilung mit Mendelssohn Archiv, Mus. Nachl. F. Busoni, B II 2942; Alma Mahler, letter of May 16, 1913, to Busoni, Preussischer Kulturbesitz, Musikabteilung mit Mendelssohn Archiv, Mus. Nachl. F. Busoni, B II 2943; Alma Mahler, letter of 1914 to Busoni, Preussischer Kulturbesitz, Musikabteilung mit Mendelssohn Archiv, Mus. Nachl. F. Busoni, B II 2944; Alma Mahler, letter of 1915 to Busoni, Preussischer Kulturbesitz, Musikabteilung mit Mendelssohn Archiv, Mus. Nachl. F. Busoni, B II 2946; Alma Mahler, letter of March 23, 1916, to Busoni, Preussischer Kulturbesitz, Musikabteilung mit Mendelssohn Archiv, Mus. Nachl. F. Busoni, B II 2945.

[39] *Berlin und seine Bauten*, 19, 597, https://babel.hathitrust.org/cgi/pt?id=mdp.39015086696369&view=1up&seq=783 (accessed October 13, 2020).

[40] Schoenberg, letter of January 30, 1917, to Busoni, in Busoni, *Selected Letters*, 421.

In addition, several of Busoni's pupils and members of his intellectual/artistic circle were or became involved with the Bauhaus, some upon Busoni's advice. His composition mentee, Stefan Wolpe, who worked with him in Berlin beginning in 1921, had studied at the Bauhaus as early as 1919.[41] Busoni also visited the Weimar Bauhaus in August 1923 and maintained contact with Bauhaus members through the final year of his life, 1924. In addition, his pupil Gisella Selden-Goth was involved with Bauhaus performances as early as November 24, 1920, as performer and composer. Two of Busoni's songs were also performed that night at the Bauhaus (*Lied des Mephistopheles*, BV 278a, and *Lied des Unmuts*, BV 21), with Wilhelm Guttmann as the singer and Selden-Goth at the piano.[42] Busoni must not have been present for that performance, but Selden-Goth sent Busoni a copy of the program with a handwritten note describing that the pieces were received well. Henrik Neugeboren, who studied piano and composition with Busoni in Berlin in the 1920s, likewise went on to study art at the Bauhaus beginning in 1928.[43] Neugeboren met Busoni through Egon Petri, with whom he studied piano at the Berliner Musikhochschule, and it was Busoni who was reportedly seminal for supporting his burgeoning interest in composition.[44] Moreover, it was Busoni's discussions of architecture and Bach that inspired some of his visual artwork as well.[45] Gerhart Hauptmann, an author and a friend of both Busoni and Alma Mahler, who received a Nobel Prize in literature in 1912, likewise became affiliated with the Bauhaus, even joining the Circle of Friends of the Bauhaus, a curatorship established in October 1924 that involved donating large amounts of money to the Bauhaus and issuing public

[41] Although considered the greatest art form at the Bauhaus, architecture was not covered regularly in the curriculum until 1927 due to budget constraints and due to its place at the end of the curriculum. However, preparatory formal principles borrowed from architecture were taught in all of the workshops. See also Austin Clarkson, "Stefan Wolpe and the Busoni Legacy," in *Busoni in Berlin: Facetten eines kosmopolitischen Komponisten*, ed. Albrecht Riethmüller and Hyesu Shin (Wiesbaden: Franz Steiner Verlag, 2004), 268; Thomas Gartmann, "Stefan Wolpe und das Weimarer Bauhaus: Ein Gästebucheintrag als Dokument der Wendezeit," *Zwitschermachine* 8 (2020): 70–77.

[42] Selden-Goth (1884–1975) appeared as pianist and composer on a Bauhaus Abend program dated November 24, 1920. Preussischer Kulturbesitz, Staatsbibliothek zu Berlin, Musikabteilung mit Mendelssohn Archiv, Mus. Nachl. F. Busoni, E, 1920, 19. Selden-Goth was not only a pianist and composer, but also wrote her own tribute to Busoni: *Ferruccio Busoni: Der Versuch eines Porträts* (Leipzig: E. P. Tal & Co., 1922).

[43] For more about Neugeboren, see Heinrich Poos, "Henrik Neugeborens Entwurf zu einem Bach-Monument (1928): Dokumentation und Kritik," In *Töne, Farben, Formen: Über Musik und die bildenden Künste—Festschrift Elmar Budde zum 60. Geburtstag*, ed. Elisabeth Schmierer et al. (Laaber: Laaber-Verlag, 1995), 45–57; Heinrich Neugeboren, "Eine Bach-Fuge im Bild," *Bauhaus: Vierteljahr-Zeitschrift für Gestaltung* 3:1 (1929): 16–19.

[44] Petri taught at the Berliner Hochschule from 1921 to 1926.

[45] See chapter 5 for more information about this topic.

statements in support of the institution. Busoni's friendship with Hauptmann extends back at least to 1908 and continued until Busoni's death.[46] In a letter of unknown date, but addressed from the Hotel Bristol in Zurich, Busoni ecstatically thanked Hauptmann for his play *Michael Kramer*, which he stated he had both read and watched. Busoni said thank you "from the bottom of my heart for the gift you have given your nation and your generation."[47] He also owned the complete writings of Hauptmann at the time of his death.[48] Hermann Scherchen, a conductor and a friend, also regularly socialized in Berlin with Busoni and promoted his music.[49] Scherchen's circle of friends who frequented his Berlin abode included members of the Bauhaus, such as Oskar Schlemmer, Wassily Kandinsky, and Walter Gropius, along with other members of the Busoni circle, including Hans Stuckenschmidt, Heinz Tiessen, Leo Kestenberg, and Stefan Wolpe, so there would have been a rich exchange of ideas. Scherchen seems to have been instrumental in inviting Busoni to the Bauhaus week in 1923, as evidenced by a letter from Busoni to his pupil Egon Petri discussing his program choice for the week: "At Scherchen's request, I have today written to *Gropius* in Weimar; have passed on your assent, together with your name and the programme."[50]

Busoni was also present at the Bauhaus exhibition in 1923, the year before he died.[51] Erich Mendelsohn (1887–1953), Frank Lloyd Wright (1867–1959), and Le Corbusier (Charles-Édouard Jeanneret, 1887–1965) were among the architects contributing to the exhibition. The Bauhaus was intent upon tearing down the walls between the arts—it aimed to bring the arts together utilizing the newest technology—something that Busoni also strongly supported—even if he would not have liked the emphasis on usefulness or mass production that they supported.

46 The first letter is dated March 25, 1908. Busoni, letter of March 25, 1908, to Hauptmann, Preussischer Kulturbesitz, Staatsbibliothek zu Berlin, Musikabteilung mit Mendelssohn Archiv, Signature 55 EP 1710. See Walter Gropius and László Moholy-Nagy, eds., *Bauhaus: Zeitschrift für Gestaltung* (Dessau: n.p., 1926).

47 [von ganzen Herzen zu danken für die Gabe, die Sie Ihren Nation und Ihrer Generation geschenkt.] Busoni, letter of unknown date to Gerhart Hauptmann, Preussischer Kulturbesitz, Staatsbibliothek zu Berlin, Musikabteilung mit Mendelssohn Archiv, GH Br NL A: Busoni, Ferruccio, 1–2, Bl.

48 Gerhart Hauptmann, *Gesammelte Werke in zwölf Bänden* (n.p.: Berlin, 1922). This is noted in Perl, *Bibliothek Ferruccio Busoni*, 46.

49 See Hermann Scherchen, *Aus meinem Leben* (Berlin: Henschel, 1984).

50 Busoni, letter of July 24, 1923, to Hermann Scherchen, in Busoni, *Selected Letters*, 368.

51 For more about the Bauhaus exhibit, see Michael H. Kater, *Weimar: From Enlightenment to the Present* (New Haven, CT: Yale University Press, 2014).

During the 1923 exhibition, there were lectures by Wassily Kandinsky (1866–1944) and Walter Gropius (1883–1969), exhibitions by painters and architects, and musical performances, including of Igor Stravinsky's *L'histoire du soldat*, which greatly moved Busoni. The exhibition also featured part of Busoni's *Fünf kurze Stücke zur Pflege des polyphonen Spiels*. Several of Busoni's close circle were present, including Scherchen, who conducted the concerts, and Ernst Krenek, who also had a composition performed at the exhibition.[52] Moreover, his interactions with members of the Bauhaus continued after the exhibition of summer 1923 (August 15–September 30), and included discussions about a performance of Busoni's *Arlecchino*, BV 270, in Weimar in 1924.[53]

Busoni's Writings about Architecture

Although Busoni displayed his knowledge of architecture in his letters, it is in his published essays that his theories about the relationship between architecture and music become most apparent. His early writings reveal that he considered the structural similarities between the two art forms to be significant. In his *Sketch of a New Aesthetic of Music* (1907), the composer described both musical composition and architectural design as multi-dimensional and organic.[54]

[52] For more about the relationship between Scherchen and Busoni, see Dennis C. Hutchinson, "Performance, Technology, and Politics: Scherchen's Aesthetics of Modernism" (PhD diss., Florida State University, 2003). Hutchinson has noted that Scherchen's house was also a musical center that was frequented by many of the Busoni's closest colleagues and pupils. He notes that Scherchen often invited the following: Ernst Krenek, Hans Stuckenschmidt, Heinz Tiessen, Leo Kestenberg, Artur Schnabel, Eduard Erdmann, Stephan Wolpe, Hans Jürgen von der Wense, Oscar Schlemmer, Wassily Kandinsky, and Walter Gropius.

[53] Paul Klee, Lily Klee, Wassily Kandinsky, Nina Kandinsky, Ise Gropius, and Walter Gropius, letter of February 1924 to Busoni, Staatsbibliothek zu Berlin—Preußischer Kulturbesitz, Musikabteilung mit Mendelssohn-Archiv, Mus. Nachl. F. Busoni B II, 2574. The letter suggests that Busoni was on friendly terms with Klee and Kandinsky, even if Gottfried Galston reports that Busoni did not like Klee's artistic style and was suspicious of Russians. Gottfried Galston, entry of May 25, 1924, in *Busoni: gli ultimi mesi di vita. Diario di Gottfried Galston*, ed. Martina Weindel (Rome: Ismez, 2002), 91.

[54] Busoni would have been familiar with the organic metaphor via the writings of Johann Wolfgang von Goethe and E. T. A. Hoffmann, among others. For more recent literature on the topic of organicism, consult the following sources: Ruth Solie, "The Living Work: Organicism and Music Analysis," *19th-Century Music* 4:2 (1980): 147–56; G. S. Rousseau, ed., *Organic Form: The Life of an Idea* (London: Routledge and Kegan, 1972); Holly Watkins, "Towards a Post-Humanist Organicism," *Nineteenth-Century Music Review* 14 (2017): 94–114; Watkins, *Musical Vitalities: Ventures in a Biotic Aesthetics of Music* (Chicago: University of Chicago Press, 2018); Eero Tarasti, "Metaphors of Nature and Organicism in the Epistemology of Music: A 'Biosemiotic' Introduction to the Analysis of Jean Sibelius's Symphonic Thought," in *Musical Semiotics Revisited*, ed. Tarasti

There are varied applications of the concept of organicism in the nineteenth century, but many are predicated on the notion that a work of art should seem to grow naturally, as opposed to being artificially constructed. In addition, it should contain germinal material that dictates the overall form and thereby contributes to a unity of the artwork. As Holly Watkins explains, eighteenth- and nineteenth-century thinkers were primarily concerned with morphological ideas of continuous growth or part-whole integration based mainly on models of plants or animals when discussing organicism, and these two ideals were sometimes difficult to reconcile.[55] Immanuel Kant, for instance, described organicism as self-maintaining and generating entities, in which internal processes convert energy into tangible matter. The parts of a tree and the whole form are thus related because the parts are dependent on the whole.[56] Goethe, however, clarified this reading, noting that organisms are actually pluralities.[57] G. W. F. Hegel, by contrast, privileges metaphors of animals over nature.[58] E. T. A. Hoffmann sought to bring together notions of growth and unity in his critique of Beethoven's Fifth Symphony (1810), in which he used a metaphor of "tree, buds and leaves, blossom and fruit as springing from the same seed," to compare to the "inner structure of Beethoven's music."[59] Eduard Hanslick likewise described music in organic terms as unity that arises out of the unfolding of music like the blossoming of a bud.[60]

In the early twentieth century, dynamic models of organicism based on gestalt psychology also developed.[61] Although predominantly dealing with visual topics, gestalt theorists nevertheless mentioned principles of human perception that were also applicable to music or other arts. They specifically observed the mind's ability to recognize similarities and organize them into

(Helsinki: National Semiotics Institute, 2003); Michael Marder, *Plant Thinking: A Philosophy of Vegetal Life* (New York: Columbia University Press, 2013).

55 Watkins, "Toward a Post-Humanist Organicism," 102.

56 Immanuel Kant, *Critique of Judgement*, trans. J. H. Bernhard (New York: Hafner Press, 1951), 217–18.

57 Johann Wolfgang von Goethe, *Collected Works*, vol. 12 (Scientific Studies), ed. and trans. Douglas Miller (Princeton, NJ: Princeton University Press, 1994), 58–64.

58 G. F. Hegel, *Philosophy of Nature*, trans. A. V. Miller (Oxford: Clarendon Press, 2004), 377.

59 E. T. A. Hoffmann, "Recension," *Allgemeine musikalische Zeitung* 12:40 (July 4, 1810): 634.

60 Eduard Hanslick, *On the Musically Beautiful*, ed. and trans. Geoffrey Payzant (Indianapolis: Hackett, 1986), 81.

61 Gestalt psychology is a branch of psychology dealing with the organizational tendencies of the mind. The theories are derived from principles found in Goethe, Immanuel Kant (1724–1804), and Ernst Mach (1838–1916), among others. See Bruno Petermann, *The Gestalt Theory and the Problem of Configuration* (London: Kegan Paul, 1932), 7.

mental groups. August Halm, for instance, believed disparate musical forms could be unified through the unfolding of a continuous melodic line through kinetic energy.[62] Like Halm, Ernst Kurth argued, in part, that unity of musical material could be created through endless and unsegmented melodies composed of interlocking motives that connected diverse textures, sections, or styles of music. According to Kurth, notes contained energy, and they form waves of sound that push the melody, generating movement and coherence to the next thought and to the larger structure. Kurth specifically discussed motivic types that function as tiny units of motion. The motives could be ascending, descending, or oscillating.[63]

In his writings from 1907, Busoni draws more heavily upon morphological theories of organicism, and refers to both the unfolding of the structure in relation to the content, and to the unity of the parts in relation to the overall form. When describing architecture, Busoni sought to reconcile notions of growth and unity by comparing the building process from the ground upward to the vertical growth of a plant. At the same time, he described architectural unity between the parts (i.e., windows and roof) and the overall structure:

> Architecture has its fundamental form, growth from below upward, prescribed by static necessity; window and roof necessarily provide the intermediate and finishing configuration; these are eternal and inviolable requirements.[64]

Similarly, he compared the structure of music composition as a state of tension between a structure and its constituent parts. In particular, he likened

[62] Some of Halm's most important texts include Halm, *Von zwei Kulturen der Musik* (Munich: G. Müller, 1913) and *Die Symphonie Anton Bruckners* (Munich: G. Müller, 1914). In the former work Halm articulates some of his fundamental views about musical unity, including his attempts at the integration of formal structures, such as that of the fugue and sonata, and his notions of the basic material of music.

[63] It is possible that Busoni might have been aware of Kurth's text, *Grundlagen des linearen Kontrapunkts Einführung in Stil und Technik von Bachs melodischer Polyphonie* (Bern: Drechsel, 1917). A selection of his writings has been translated into English and appear in the following source: Kurth, *Selected Writings*, ed. and trans. Lee A. Rothfarb, Cambridge Studies in Music Theory and Analysis (Cambridge: Cambridge University Press, 1991).

[64] Busoni, *Sketch of a New Esthetic of Music*, trans. Th. Baker (New York: G. Schirmer, 1911), 2–3. "Of the art" seems to have been added by Baker for clarity. For the text in German, see Busoni, *Entwurf einer neuen Ästhetik der Tonkunst*, ed. Martina Weindel, Taschenbücher zur Musikwissenschaft 145, ed. Richard Schaal (Wilhelmshaven: Florian Noetzel, 2001). [Die Architektur hat ihre Grundform, die von unten nach oben zu schreiten muss, durch statische Notwendigkeit vorgeschrieben; Fenster und Dach geben notgedrungen die mittlere und abschliessende Ausgestaltung; diese Bedingungen sind an ihr bleibend und unverletzbar.]

the growth of a musical motive into a complete and unified structure through a process of becoming or growth. In both music and architecture, the organic growth of the material leads to unique structures, and to clear relations between the smallest parts and the whole structure. However, in architecture, the tension between the constant state of becoming and the whole structure is not as pronounced as in music, with its temporal liquidity.[65]

There are also some parallels between Busoni's writings and those of his contemporaries in their description of architecture as organic.[66] The term "organic" was used frequently by Busoni's contemporaries in relation to architecture. Frank Lloyd Wright, for instance, began using the term around 1908 to describe architecture that was not only in tune with natural surroundings, but also unified from the smallest parts to the whole.[67] Similarly, Wilhelm Worringer, one of the foremost contemporary authorities on art and architectural history, wrote about the relationship between architecture and organicism, also including discussions of the role of human impulses in relation to form. It is possible that the paths of Busoni and Worringer might have crossed, since he was acquainted with members of Der blaue Reiter, with which several of Busoni's circle were also involved, including Schoenberg. Moreover, Worringer's two most important texts on the topic appeared around the same time as Busoni's writings, with his dissertation, *Abstraktion und Einfühlung*, appearing in 1907 and *Formprobleme der Gotik* appearing in 1911. In the latter text, Worringer described Classic architecture in organicist manners using language similar to Busoni's. However, while Busoni noted the more "static" nature of buildings, Worringer emphasized more dynamic notions of life, vitality, and growth in relation to certain types of architecture. While both authors wrote about the growth of the building upward, Worringer focused more specifically on Classical Greek architecture with its rounded pillars, likening them to tree trunks that push upward and that offer structural support. He viewed the rounded shapes and the peculiar use of the building materials as especially reflective of life:

> The thing that gives the column its expression is its roundness. This roundness immediately calls forth the illusion of organic vitality, firstly, because it

[65] Busoni, *Sketch*, 10–11.

[66] For more information about organicism and architecture, see Caroline van Eck, *Organicism in Nineteenth-Century Architecture: An Inquiry into the Theoretical and Philosophical Background* (Amsterdam: Architectura and Natura Press, 1994).

[67] Frank Lloyd Wright, *The Natural House* (New York: Bramhall House, 1954), 3. He introduced the term "organic" into his theories of architecture as early as 1908.

> directly recalls the roundness of those natural members that exercise a similar carrying function, especially in the tree trunk, that carries the head, or the stalk, that carries the blossom; secondly, however, the roundness in and for itself welcomes our natural organic sense without suggesting an analogous idea.[68]

Where Worringer differed most from Busoni was in his more nuanced exploration of different architectural styles. For Worringer, Gothic architecture, in contrast to Classic architecture, is inorganic, and artificially constructed because of its angular lines, sinuous ornamentation, and unnatural use of stone; buildings rise to celestial heights despite the weightiness of the material. According to Worringer, it is thus an expression of the supersensuous and spiritual, rather than the organic.

However, that is not how Busoni viewed Gothic architecture. He still considered it to be organic and as a model of both structure and unity. Busoni's views about Gothic architecture were more in line with others in Germany who viewed the Gothic as the epitome of *Kultur* and structure due to its integration of form and ornamentation. Bradley Brookshire has summarized these prevalent views during Busoni's lifetime:

> Bach, as a stand-in for Gothic art and culture, came to represent a protomodernist strand of particularly Germanic art, laudable for its severity, its weight, its structure, and, above all, its embodiment of organic unity and economy of means, particular regarding surface decoration. . . . In this way, Bach came to represent the fundamental concepts of Kultur and Bildung: i.e., organicism, integrity, abstraction, thoroughness, and deep spirituality.[69]

For Busoni, differences between organic and inorganic architecture had little to do with stylistic periods. Instead, they had more to do with the originality of a specific structure in relation to the material and content. They had to do with the unity between the parts and the whole. He specifically rejected mass-produced buildings constructed according to prescribed formulas and floor plans as inorganic, and with little thought about the integration of the material and the overall structure; this was an architectural approach that did

[68] Worringer, *Form Problems of the Gothic*, 78.

[69] Bradley Brookshire, "Edwin Fischer and Bach Pianism of the Weimar Republic" (PhD diss., CUNY, 2016), 182.

not become popularized until the 1920s even if it was already in play in the late nineteenth and early twentieth centuries, especially in the United States and Canada.[70] Busoni would have encountered mass-produced homes on his extensive concert tours of the United States in 1891–1894, 1904, 1910, 1911, and 1915.[71]

He similarly cautioned against music that was constructed based on repeatable formulas and patterned after traditional musical forms. Making the analogy explicit, he used the term "architectonic" ("architektonische") in a derogatory manner in 1907 in relation to music with metaphorical reference to mass-produced architecture. He criticized those creating forms based on past traditions rather than on unique themes, ideas, and materials:[72]

> Per contra, absolute music is something very sober, which reminds one of music-desks in orderly rows, of the relation of Tonic to Dominant, of Developments and Codas. Methinks I hear the second violin struggling, a fourth below, to emulate the more dexterous first, and contending in needless contest merely to arrive at the starting point. This sort of music ought rather to be called the "architectonic" ["architektonische"], or "symmetric" or "sectional," and derives from the circumstance that certain composers poured their spirit and their emotion into just this mould as lying nearest them or their time.[73]

Despite formal similarities, Busoni considered architecture to be inferior to music in 1907 because of what he perceived as its restricted ability to convey

[70] The Sears mail-order home kits that were available beginning in 1908 were some of the more popular models, but other lesser-known companies made similar kits in the nineteenth century as well. For more about kit homes, see Mike Jackson, "Assembly Required: A Brief History of Twentieth-Century Kit House Designs," *Architect: The Journal of the American Institute of Architects* (August 2, 2018), https://www.architectmagazine.com/practice/assembly-required-a-brief-history-of-20th-century-kit-house-designs_o (accessed September 23, 2020).

[71] Marc-André Roberge, "Ferruccio Busoni in the United States," *American Music* 13:3 (Autumn 1995): 295–332.

[72] For more about Busoni's views of absolute music, see Knyt, "Ferruccio Busoni and the Absolute in Music: Nature, Form, and *Idee*," *Journal of the Royal Musical Association* 137:1 (May 2012): 35–69. Busoni idealized something he called "the absolute in music," which lay on a spectrum somewhere between absolute and program music. He favored using human ideas and experiences to inform every element of music, including the form. These ideas then had to be translated into music.

[73] Busoni, *Sketch*, 6–7. [Absolut Musik ist dagegen etwas ganz Nüchternes, welches geordnet aufgestellte Notenpulte erinnert, an Verhältnis von Tonika und Dominante, an Durchführungen und Kodas. Da höre ich den zweiten Geiger, wie er sich eine Quart tiefer abmüht, den gewandteren ersten nachzuahmen, höre einen unnötigen Kampf auskämpfen, um dahin zu gelangen, wo man schon am Anfang stand. Diese Musik sollte vielmehr die architektonische heissen, oder die symmetrische, oder die eingeteilte, und sie stammt daher, dass einzelne Tondichter ihren Geist und ihre Empfindung in eine solche Form gossen, weil es ihnen oder der Zeit am nächsten lag.] Busoni, *Entwurf*, 15.

human emotions. His views changed over the next decade, however, as he evolved as a thinker. It is probable that he was influenced by the work of contemporary writers on architecture, especially in relation to burgeoning theories about its expressivity. Worringer, for instance, argued that architecture is an expression of mankind's artistic will and that its history is characterized by differing aims of expression in different stylistic periods; abstraction in Gothic architecture is an attempt to convey unseen spirituality, whereas realism in Classic architecture more clearly conveys the expression of the sensuous world:

> The history of architecture is not a history of technical developments, but a history of the changing aims of expression, of the ways and means by which this technique conforms and ministers to the changing aims through ever new and different combinations of its fundamental elements.[74]

Worringer's thoughts were likely informed by the earlier work of Heinrich Wölfflin, who described architecture in 1886 as a reflection of the human body, expressivity, and experience. Wölfflin taught at the University of Berlin from 1901 to 1912, so he was in Berlin at the same time as Busoni, who lived there from 1904 to 1913 and again from 1920 to 1924. Although it is unclear if they actually met, there are unmistakable parallels in their writings, and both also had connections through der Blaue Reiter.[75] Wölfflin specifically wrote about the relationship between human mood (*Stimmung*) and the visual appearance of space, structure, and ornament in architecture, as well as connections between the architectural object and the living human experience.[76] He examined how architectural objects can invoke visual impressions of lived experiences that in turn convey human expression. The internal structure thus becomes living by means of the experience of the person observing the building; as a result, architecture affects the body and psyche of the viewer expressively. As the body moves and enters the physical space, the visual impressions and the form contribute to emotional

[74] Worringer, 77. For a summary of information about the burgeoning views of expression and architecture, see Vlad Ionescu, "Architectural Symbolism: Body and Space in Heinrich Wölfflin and Wilhelm Worringer," *Architectural Histories* 4:1 (2016): 10.

[75] Martin Warnke, "On Heinrich Wölfflin," *Representations* 27 (1989): 179.

[76] See, for instance, Wölfflin, *Prolegomena to a Psychology of Architecture* [1886], in *Empathy, Form and Space: Problems in German Aesthetics, 1873–1893*, ed. Harry Francis Mallgrave and Eleftherios Ikonomou (Santa Monica, CA: Getty Centre for the History of Art and the Humanities, 1994), 149–90.

responses in the body. The *Lebensgefühl*, or vital feeling, to which Wölfflin refers indicates the connection of bodily movement in space and its response to its own form in relation to architectural structure. When the body is in congruence with the architectural form, there can be feelings of pleasure and harmony. As a result, there is a direct connection between the materials of architecture, such as form, gravity, and matter, the overall structure, and the physical body.

Van de Velde joined Wölfflin in searching for the expression of human emotions through pure structure in 1894 with his essay *Déblaiement d'art*, where he argued that structure itself could express human emotions and states of mind.[77] Moreover, James Fergusson, whose history of architecture Busoni owned, described the formal structures as capable of expression when artistically combined and melded with the material: "So it is with forms: the square and angular are expressive of strength and power; the curves of softness and elegance; and beauty is produced by effective combination of the right-lined with the curvilinear. It is always thus in nature."[78]

By 1916, Busoni also began to consider architecture not only as an organic art form in a morphological sense, but also in a dynamic sense, and as an expressive one on par with music. His developing ideas appear in an essay fragment penned in Zurich in spring 1916, entitled: "Thoughts about Expression in Architecture."[79] Some of his ideas bear striking similarity to Worringer's in that he acknowledged continuity between human expression and architectural design. He wrote in the essay fragment about his belief that architecture could not be reduced to mere form and matter and stated that it was just as expressive as other art forms: "Architecture [Baukunst] works with forms, basically no more and no less than all other arts. Throughout much of my life I believed the accepted thought that architecture [Architektur] works with forms 'exclusively.' "[80] He came to believe that architectural form could unite with content and be a facilitator for human expression; it could bear the vital imprint of its creator as much as

77 Van de Velde, "A Clean Sweep for the Future of Art [1894]," in *Symbolist Art Theories: A Critical Anthology*, ed. Henri Dorra (Berkeley: University of California Press, 1994), 122. The original title of the work is *Déblaiement d'art*.

78 Fergusson, *History of Architecture in All Countries*, 26.

79 Busoni, "Gedanken über den Ausdruck in der Architektur" [(fragment), spring 1916], in Busoni, *Von der Einheit der Musik* (Berlin: Max Hesses Verlag, 1922), 229–37.

80 [Die Baukunst arbeitet mit Formen, im Grunde nicht mehr und nicht weniger als alle übrigen Künste. Durch eine lange Zeit meines Lebens stark ich in der übernommenen Überzeugung, dass die Architektur mit Formen "ausschliesslich" arbeite.] Busoni, *Von der Einheit der Musik*, 229.

any other type of art. Consequently, it was just as capable as the other arts of evoking visceral reactions.

It might be significant that Busoni uses the term "Baukunst" in this passage. That term normally connotes building as an art form, as opposed to the more functional vision of building space for use. As Eduard von Hartmann explains, in a Kantian sense, it is also seen in a broader manner to encompass the complete building, including its internal furnishings, wallpaper, and decorations.[81] "Architektur" is thus a part of "Baukunst," but has a narrower definition that applies mainly the structural design and form.

In the essay, Busoni acknowledged two types of expression in architecture, one emanating from the building, and the other, the phenomenological response of the human viewer: "I would like to distinguish between two types of architectural expression. First, the building 'expresses' which is its purpose—second that it radiates expression in relation to the human mind."[82] Like Wölfflin, he thus sought that expressivity not only in the architectural object, but also connected it to human perception of the building. However, unlike Worringer, he did not see in it a human will that varied expressively in relation to historical era and architectural style. Instead, he took a more individualized approach, noting divergent emotional reactions in viewers in response to similar buildings even from the same era. To illustrate, he provided the example of two churches of the same size and style that elicited very different emotional reactions.[83] He attributed some of the difference to environment, including lighting and age, noting that stone buildings in London appear differently in color depending on whether they are facing north or south, for instance.[84] He also talked about the importance of age on the overall emotional effect, specifically citing Alfred Messel's use of sculptures and decorations on the neo-Gothic Wertheim Department Store on Leipziger Strasse in Berlin (1896–1906) that appeared already weathered to coincide with the overall affect of the building.[85]

[81] Eduard von Hartmann, *Ästhetik*, Eduard von Hartmann's Ausgewählte Werke (Berlin: Carl Duncker's Verlag, 1886), 462. This term [Baukunst] is rarely used by Busoni but was commonly used at the Weimar Bauhaus.

[82] [Ich möchte zwei Arten des architektonischen Ausdrucks unterscheiden. Zum ersten: dass das Gebäude "ausdrücke," welche seine Bestimmung sei.—Zum zweiten: dass es Ausdruck im Verhältnis zum menschlichen Gemüte ausstrahle.] Busoni, "Gedanken über den Ausdruck in der Architektur," 231.

[83] Busoni, "Gedanken über den Ausdruck in der Architektur," 233.

[84] Busoni, "Gedanken über den Ausdruck in der Architektur," 234.

[85] Busoni, "Gedanken über den Ausdruck in der Architektur," 234.

Busoni supported his developing beliefs about the expressivity of architecture with descriptions of his own experiences contemplating architecture:

> My question as to architecture was as follows: why two different, equally well-constructed buildings, held in the same style, exert a different effect upon me; the one warms me, the other cools? The question about which—in music—was already clear—finds its solution in this answer: it is the expression of acts, which decide the ultimate reason for every work of art. Architecture is, in its highest potency and effect, an art of expression.[86]

In particular, he noted that similarly structured buildings evoked divergent emotional responses based on the materials and the location, for instance. He concluded that, like music, architecture is able to "speak to the heart" too.[87]

Like Wölfflin, Busoni also described the synergy that needs to exist between the purpose of the building, the physical form of the people inhabiting the building, and the shape of the building. This also resembles the theories of Johannes Volkelt, on which some of Wölfflin's ideas were based. Volkelt argued that "the spatial form is interpreted in terms of movement and the effect of forces, in an activity that cannot in itself be called symbolic. . . . To interpret the spatial form aesthetically we have to respond to this movement vicariously throughout senses, share in it with our bodily organization."[88] Wölfflin, in a similar manner, connected the human body and movement, stating that "it is astonishing to travel through history and observe how architecture everywhere imitates the ideal of man in the form and movement of the body."[89]

Busoni echoed these thoughts when he implied that human form and movement are essential to being in congruence with architectural design. For instance, he claimed that houses should be built in primarily horizontal shapes, because of the way the human body moves through space. His views

86 [Stellte sich meine Frage zur Architektur in dieser Fassung: warum von zwei gleich gut konstruierten und in dem nämlichen Stile gehaltenen Gebäuden, eine verscheidene Wirkung auf mich ausgeübt verschiedene Wirkung auf mich ausgeübt werde; das eine mich erwärme, das andere kühl lasse? Die Frage, über die ich—in der Musik—schon vorher klar geworden, löste sich in dieser Antwort: es ist der Ausdruck der wirkt, und die im letzten Grunde für jedes Kunstwerk entscheidet. Die Architektur ist in ihrer höchsten Potenz und Wirkung eine Kunst des Ausdruckes.] Busoni, "Gedanken über den Ausdruck in der Architektur," 230.

87 Busoni, "Gedanken über den Ausdruck in der Architektur," 232–33.

88 Johannes Volkelt, *Der Symbol-Begriff in der neuesten Ästhetik* (Jena: Hermann Dufft, 1876), quoted in Wölfflin, *Prolegomena to a Psychology of Architecture*, 153.

89 Wölfflin, *Prolegomena to a Psychology of Architecture*, 183.

in 1916 thus also seem to be in line with those at the soon-to-be established Bauhaus, in that he sought congruence between form and function:

> It is most natural for people to move in a horizontal direction, which is why a dwelling house on a horizontal plan will be more natural than one that is built on the [concept of] height. . . . Just as a book aligns its form with the hand that holds it and with the eye that passes through its surfaces and symbols, so a house should also align itself with the shape and natural movements of people.[90]

Unfortunately, Busoni never completed his essay, which was also supposed to go into detail about architecture related to the theater and the church. Even so, the fragment that survives shows Busoni's evolving thoughts about architecture and his engagement with contemporary concerns about it. In particular, it reveals Busoni's new understanding about the expressive capabilities of architecture and its connectedness to human form and perception, which were topics of contemporary concern.

Busoni, Bach, and the Gothic Style

Busoni was thus fascinated with architecture from his youth, and he made a conscious effort to study buildings. He also interacted with contemporary architects, and some of his ideas about architecture reflected those of contemporary architecture historians. At the same time, Busoni was also influenced by philosophical thought about architecture and its metaphorical application to music. Architecture was popular as a descriptive metaphor in the nineteenth century, with authors familiar to Busoni, such as Arthur Schopenhauer and Goethe using it.[91] They likened music to liquid architecture and architecture

[90] [Dem menschen ist es am natürlichsten sich in horizontaler Richtung zu bewegen, deshalb wird ein Wohnhaus auf horizontalem Plan Naturgemäßer sein, als seines nach der Höhe angebautes. . . . So wie ein Buch sein Format nach der Hand richtet, die es halt, und nach dem Auge, welches seine Flächen und Zeichen durchläuft, so soll auch ein Wohnhaus nach der Gestalt und den natürlichen Bewegungen Menschen sich richten.] Busoni, "Gedanken über den Ausdruck in der Architektur," 236–37.

[91] See Johann Peter Eckermann and Margaret Fuller, eds., "Conversations with Goethe in the Last Years of His Life," trans. Margaret Fuller (Boston: Hilliard Gray, 1839); Friedrich Wilhelm Joseph Schelling, *Philosophie der Kunst* (Stuttgart: Cotta, 1859); Arthur Schopenhauer, *Parerga and Paralipomena: Short Philosophical Essays*, Vol. II, trans. E. F. J. Payne (Gloucestershire: Clarendon Press, 2001); Eduard Hanslick, *On the Musically Beautiful: A Contribution towards the Revision of the Aesthetics of Music*, trans. Geoffrey Payzant, based on the 8th ed. [1891] (Indianapolis: Hackett, 1986).

to music set in stone. Ruins were viewed as similar to musical fragments and ornamentation in music to architectural decoration. Particularly prevalent was writing about Gothic architecture and the music of J. S. Bach.

There is a direct connection between Bach and Gothic architecture in that the Thomaskirche where Bach worked in Leipzig had been renovated in a late Gothic style.[92] However, nineteenth-century thinkers primarily connected them metaphorically because of the spirituality and decorativeness of both Gothic art and Bach's music.[93]

The Gothic architectural style is most strongly associated with religious buildings where a balance of horizontal and vertical elements can be seen as symbolizing both earthly and spiritual realms, while the play with light through the inclusion of many stained-glass windows, often depicting biblical stories, adds to the analogy.[94] The pointed arches supported by flying buttresses enabled builders to create taller buildings than ever before, as the cathedrals reached upward toward the heavens. Many Gothic churches are chiastic in shape with a long nave and intersecting transept, thereby reinforcing the religious symbolism of the cross. Large towers and spires also add a vertical element and dominate the skylines in some cities. Impressive and lofty facades are designed to overwhelm worshippers with the vastness of God, while sublime intricacy, such as the pointed and arched doorways, flying buttresses, and ribbed vaults that are surrounded by elaborate moldings and decorative sculptures, represent God's complexity. There is also an intimate connection between the smallest parts of the building and the whole, in that

Busoni mentioned Schopenhauer and Goethe in his letters, and both authors were also included in his library at the time of his death. See, for instance, Perl, *Bibliothek Ferruccio Busoni*, 41–42 and 94.

[92] Thomas Braatz, "Johann Sebastian Bach's Performance Environment in the *Nikolaikirche* from 1723–1750," http://www.bach-cantatas.com/Articles/Nikolaikirche-Braatz.pdf (accessed June 21, 2017). General ideas about relationships between contemporaneous church music and architecture were long in circulation. Erwin Panofsky has recorded some of these and made the argument, for instance, that there are close correlations between Gothic architecture and Notre Dame styles of organum. Erwin Panofsky, *Gothic Architecture and Scholasticism* (New York: The World Publishing Co., 1967).

[93] For more information about the connection between J. S. Bach and Gothic architecture, see Heinrich Besseler, "Bach und das Mittelalter," *Bericht über die Wissenschaftliche Bachtagung, Leipzig 23 bis 26 Juli 1950* (Leipzig: C. F. Peters, 1951), 108–30; Duilio A. Dobrin, "A Comparison between Bach's Compositional Style and Gothic Architecture" (M.M. thesis, Ball State University, 1979); Bernd Sponheuer, "Reconstructing Ideal Types of the 'German' in Music," *Music and German National Identity*, ed. Celia Applegate and Pamela Maxine Potter (Chicago: Chicago University Press, 2002), 36–58.

[94] For more information about Gothic cathedrals, see the following sources: Roland Recht and Mary Whittall, *Believing and Seeing: The Art of Gothic Cathedrals* (Chicago: Chicago University Press, 2008); Karen Ralls, *Gothic Cathedrals: A Guide to the History, Places, Art, and Symbolism* (Lake Worth, FL: Ibis Press, 2015).

the stones are held together primarily by pressure. Removing one stone could lead to structural weakness or even collapse of the whole building. Worringer similarly argues that the type of construction spiritualizes Gothic buildings because of the way the material is used to construct the lofty edifices. In the process, the material, the form, and the function become one:

> Here the stone is apparently rid of all its material weight. Here it is only the vehicle of an unsensuous, incorporeal expression. In short, here it has become dematerialized. This Gothic dematerialization of the stone in favor of a purely spiritual expressiveness corresponds to the degeometrization of the abstract line, such as we indicated in the ornament, in favor of an identical expressional purpose. The antonym of matter is spirit. To dematerialize stone means to spiritualize it.[95]

An interest in Gothic architecture underwent a revival in Germany in the late eighteenth and nineteenth centuries in Germany. Numerous authors preceding Busoni metaphorically connected Gothic architecture and Bach, and the topic is still widely discussed today.[96] Frédéric Louis Ritter in 1883, for instance, equated the combination of intricate polyphony, harmonic complexity, and idealistic unity with the Gothic style. Ritter specifically highlights close relations between each part and the whole as representative of both Gothic architecture and Gothic music:

> Counterpoint, as I have already proved, is the production of the Northern German mind; and, like the Gothic style of architecture, each part of the complicated form is only understood in connection with the whole

[95] Worringer, *Form Problems of the Gothic*, 84.

[96] For more recent scholarship on the topic see Thomas Grey, "Metaphorical Modes in Nineteenth-Century Music Criticism: Image, Narrative, and Idea," in *Music and Text: Critical Inquiries*, ed. Steven Paul Scher (Cambridge and New York: Cambridge University Press, 1992), 93–117; Charles M. Joseph, "Bach the Architect: Some Remarks on Structure and Pacing in Selected Praeludia," in *Johann Sebastian: A Tercentenary Celebration*, ed. Seymour L. Benstock (Westport, CT: Greenwood Press. 1992), 83–93; Toomas Siitan, "Muusika: Elustunud arhitektuur?," in *Tekste modernismist. II: Muusika ja arhitektuur*, ed. Gerhard Lock, Maris Valk-Falk, and Saale Kareda (Tallinn: Scripta Musicalia, 2008), 11–19; Christoph Wolff, "Die Architektur von Bachs Passacaglia," *Acta Organologica* 3 (1969): 183–94; David Yearsley, *Bach and the Meanings of Counterpoint*, New Perspectives in Music History and Criticism (Cambridge and New York: Cambridge University Press, 2002). See also Isabella van Elferen, "The Gothic Bach," *Understanding Bach* 7 (2012): 9–20, http://www.bachnetwork.co.uk/ub7/UB7_Elferen.pdf (accessed May 8, 2018); Isabella van Elferen, *Gothic Music: The Sounds of the Uncanny*, Gothic Literary Studies (Cardiff: University of Wales Press, 2012); Ruth Tatlow, *Bach's Numbers: Compositional Proportion and Significance* (Cambridge: Cambridge University Press, 2015).

composition; and, though every one of these parts is brought to the greatest individual perfection, they all concur in the expression of one great thought, of one great idea. Like all Gothic art, this form reflects, in its variety of rhythm, in its richness of harmony, and its finish and perfection of workmanship.[97]

C. J. Becker, who discussed parallels between the spiritual appeal of Gothic art and the music of George Frideric Handel and Bach, likewise claimed in 1838 that music was closely related (metaphorically) to architecture in its spirituality, decoration, and vastness.[98] Becker similarly maintained that seeing the Strasbourg Cathedral was like seeing Bach's music set in stone. This was partly because of the multitude of decorations. Becker asserted that when he looked at the building, he did not see a form in stone, but instead, thought of Bach's music and "heard" it in his mind.[99]

These ideas about Bach's music, spirituality, and Gothic architecture connected to contemporaneous ideas about his music as being part of a *Kunstreligion.* As scholars have already noted, there was a notion of Bach's music as sacred, as possessing healing powers, and as divine.[100] In his biography of Bach, which Busoni owned, Albert Schweitzer, for instance, emphasized the spiritual in relation to Bach's music; he brought the connections back again to architecture when he claimed that Bach's music was not only spiritual, but also Gothic in its decorativeness and in the inseparable relationship between the smallest part and the larger structure: "Bach's music is Gothic. Just as in Gothic architecture the great plan develops out of the simple motive but unfolds itself in the richest detail instead of in rigid line, and only makes its effect when every detail is truly vital."[101]

97 Frédéric Louis Ritter, *The History of Music from the Christian Era to the Present Time* (Boston: Oliver Ditson, 1883), 150.

98 C. J. Becker, "Ideen über Baukunst und Musik [1838]," in *Music and Aesthetics in the Eighteenth and Early Nineteenth Centuries*, ed. Peter le Huray and James Day, Cambridge Readings in the Literature of Music (Cambridge: Cambridge University Press, 1981), 493–97.

99 Becker, "Ideen über Baukunst und Musik," 493–97.

100 See, for instance, Max Scheler, *Wesen und Formen der Sympathie* (Bonn: Friedrich Cohen Verlag, 1923), originally published under the title *Zur Phänomenologie und Theorie der Sympathiegefühle* (Halle: Niemeyer Verlag, 1913); Nicole Heinkel, *Religiöse Kunst, Kunstreligion und die Überwindung der Säkularisierung Frühromantik als Sehnsucht und Suche nach der verlorenen Religion* (Frankfurt am Main: Peter Lang Verlag, 2004); Brookshire, "Edwin Fischer and Bach Pianism of the Weimar Republic"; Walter Frisch, "Bach, Regeneration, and Historicist Modernism," in *German Modernism: Music and the Arts* (Berkeley: University of California Press, 2005).

101 Albert Schweitzer, *J. S. Bach* [1911], trans. Ernest Newman, vol. 1 (New York: Dover Publications, 2012), 363. Perl, *Bibliothek Ferruccio Busoni*, 73. Busoni owned first and second editions of this biography. For more about Schweitzer's views, see Wolf Kalipp, "Albert Schweitzer und seine Kultur der Orgel," *Musik und Gottesdienst* 4 (2011): 168–78.

Although Gothic architecture was seen by some in the early eighteenth century, such as by architect Christopher Wren, as inferior to the simpler, cleaner lines of Neoclassic art patterned after Greek ideals, that mindset was largely replaced by 1800 as Bach began to be viewed not only as spiritual, but also as a genius with divine inspiration, as a progenitor of great German art.[102] Goethe thought of him as the epitome of German genius.[103] That said, many scholars today see architectural design in Bach's music not just metaphorically in terms of its spirituality, but also in terms of more concrete musical characteristics, such ornamentation, line, and structure.[104] Others, such as Laurence Dreyfus, describe the music in spatial terms, just like spacious Gothic cathedrals.[105]

Busoni was familiar with metaphorical connections between the Gothic style and Bach's music, and used them himself, frequently equating Gothic architecture with Bach in concrete ways, such as in terms of decoration, spirituality, emotion, spatial aspects, and form. In a letter to Egon Petri, he described Bach's *Well-Tempered Clavier* as decorative Gothic art in its cleverness of variation: "In the case of Bach, as I said, this art of variation—controlled by feeling—is elevated to the level of Gothic decorative art."[106] In his notes to the *Well-Tempered Clavier*, book I, which was intended primarily as a performance edition, he likened the fugues in C major (book I) and E♭ minor (book I) to Gothic architecture and used diagrams to demonstrate.[107] The C major fugue, he suggests, forms a chiastic architectural shape with intersecting horizontal and vertical dimensions, with the internal development section featuring the most complex counterpoint exactly in the center of the composition (see figure 1.3).

Moreover, metaphorical ideas influenced Busoni's interpretation of Bach's compositions. For instance, in his recording of Bach's Fugue in C Major from book I of *The Well-Tempered Clavier*, Busoni brings out inner voices with such clarity that it creates a sense of aural multi-dimensionality—like

[102] See Sponheuer, "Reconstructing Ideal Types of the 'German' in Music," 48.

[103] Johann Wolfgang von Goethe, "On German Architecture," in *Goethe on Art* (Berkeley: University of California Press, 1980). 108.

[104] Naomi Waltham-Smith, "Disruptive Spatiality and the Experience of Recordings of Bach's Solo Cello Suites," *Current Musicology* 82 (Fall 2006); Grey, "Metaphorical Modes in Nineteenth-Century Music Criticism"; Joseph, "Bach the Architect," 83–93; Wolff, "Die Architektur von Bachs Passacaglia," 183–94; Yearsley, *Bach and the Meanings of Counterpoint*.

[105] Laurence Dreyfus, *Bach and the Patterns of Invention* (Cambridge, MA: Harvard University Press, 1996), 21, for instance.

[106] Busoni, letter of July 12, 1910, to Egon Petri, in Beaumont, *Selected Letters*, 108.

[107] Bach-Busoni, *The First Twenty-Four Preludes and Fugues of the Well-Tempered Clavichord* (New York: G. Schirmer, 1894), 7.

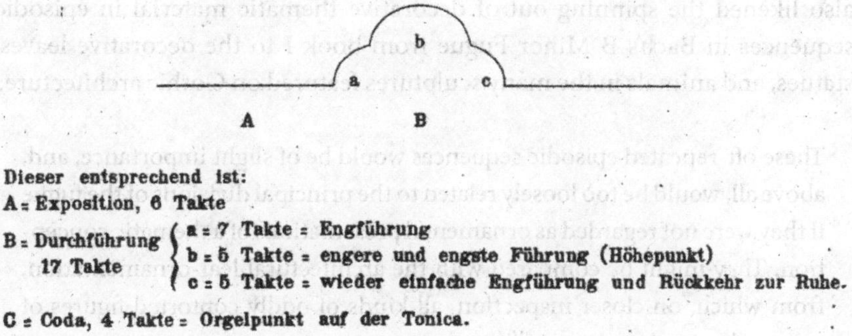
b
a
c
A
B
Dieser entsprechend ist:
A = Exposition, 6 Takte
B = Durchführung 17 Takte
a = 7 Takte = Engführung
b = 5 Takte = engere und engste Führung (Höhepunkt)
c = 5 Takte = wieder einfache Engführung und Rückkehr zur Ruhe.
C = Coda, 4 Takte = Orgelpunkt auf der Tonica.

Figure 1.3. Busoni, diagram related to the formal structure of the Fugue in C Major from J. S. Bach's *Well-Tempered Clavier*, book I.

bringing different angles into relief. At the same time, he creates a sense of architectural structure (clear contours), imposing it on Bach's unfolding arpeggios that under the hands of many performers seem to spin out without clear structural shape. Busoni creates an overall three-part ("chiastic") structure through changes in dynamics, touch, texture, and tempo (mm. 1–6, [7–13, 14–18, 19–23], 24–27). In Busoni's interpretation, the climax happens near the center of the piece when he increases dynamics up to that point; he then gradually slows the tempo and reduces the dynamics after the eighteenth measure. With control of color and touch, he brings the voices into relief to create different textures. For instance, beginning in the exposition, although all the entrances are audible, the four voices are similar in dynamic level. By contrast, beginning in measure 7, he creates the impression of a two-voice duet with accompaniment by bringing into relief the soprano and tenor voices in imitation followed by the alto and bass in duet.[108] The additional voices are subdued and treated as accompaniment.

Busoni likewise describes the E♭ Minor Fugue from book I metaphorically, claiming the climax ("upward striving") occurs at the end, thus likening the continuous sense of growth to an upward arching Gothic spire.[109] He

[108] Ferruccio Busoni, piano, Fugue no. 1 in C Major by J. S. Bach, from the *Well-Tempered Clavier*, book I, recorded February 27, 1922, London studios of British Columbia Records LP, International Piano Archives, IPA 104, 1976, https://www.youtube.com/watch?v=qySy5TnXP7g (accessed June 26, 2017).

[109] Bach-Busoni, *The First Twenty-Four Preludes and Fugues*, 7.

also likened the spinning out of decorative thematic material in episodic sequences in Bach's B Minor Fugue from book I to the decorative leaves, statues, and animals in the many sculptures featured on Gothic architecture:

> These oft-repeated episodic sequences would be of slight importance, and, above all, would be too loosely related to the principal divisions of the fugue if they were not regarded as ornamental presentations of a thematic conception. They might be compared with the architectural leaf-ornamentation, from which, on closer inspection, all kinds of oddly contorted figures of men and animals peep out.[110]

Moreover, in a general sense, Bach's polyphony seemed inherently Gothic in style in a metaphorical sense for Busoni because of the intersections of horizontal and vertical elements. He specifically compared the chiastic shape of many cathedral floor plans to Bach's polyphony in terms of the horizontal lines and the vertically moving motifs: "Thus, we see the idea of the horizontal (vertical) motifs, which are moving into the height (vertical), by means of a four-line art (horizontal). The sign of the cross, the ground plan to the cathedral!"[111]

Busoni, Mozart, and the Hellenic Style

If Busoni compared Bach's music to Gothic architecture, he also wrote about Mozart and Hellenic architecture. Ancient Greek architecture from the Hellenic Period (900–323 BC) has been praised for its play with light, as temples are often built on the peaks of hills where light reflects off the surface in different ways when the buildings are viewed from multiple angles (i.e., close up versus from below or far away, for instance). The marble surfaces are smooth, curved, fluted, or ornately sculpted in order to reflect

[110] Bach-Busoni, *The First Twenty-Four Preludes and Fugues*, 148. [Diese oft wiederkehrenden Zwischenspiel-Sequenzen würden eine zu geringe und vor allem zu lockere Beziehungen zu den Haupttheilen der Fuge haben, wenn man sie nicht als ornamentale Darstellungen eines thematischen Inhaltes interpretirte. Sie sind mit jener Blätter-Ornamentik vergleichbar, aus welcher sich bei nährer Betrachtung allerhand verschnörkelte Menschen und Thiergestalten entwickeln.] Bach, *Das wohltemperierte Klavier*, vol. 1, ed. Busoni, Joh. Seb. Bach Klavierwerke, ed. Busoni, Egon Petri, und Bruno Mugellini (Leipzig: Breitkopf & Härtel, 1894).

[111] [Also sehen wir den in die Höhe (vertical) strehenden Gedanken durch eine ihn dienende Vier-Linien Kunst (horizontal) zur entfaltung gebracht. Das zeichen des Kreuzes, der Grundriss zur Kathedral!] Johann Sebastian Bach, *Das wohltemperierte Klavier* II, ed. Busoni, Klavierwerke, ed. Busoni, vol. 4 (Wiesbaden: Breitkopf & Härtel, n.d.), 31.

the sun, casting shadows and changes in color with the changing light of day. Renowned for a style characterized by proportion in shape, columns, pediments, and entablatures, variations in the symmetry, such as columns that are slightly wider at the base, create the optical illusion of regularity. As a preferred building material, the white marble, so characteristic of Greek buildings has become a symbol of purity and youthfulness, even as tasteful ornamentation above the columns in the Ionian or Corinthian styles adorn the structures without obscuring them. Displaying intersections of vertical and horizontal elements of the columns and pediments, yet with very few right angles, for instance, the style is seen as analogous to Classical themes and melodies floating above the vertical harmonies.

Much like Gothic architecture, Greco-Roman art and architecture was also thought to represent perfection and the pinnacle of human civilization after Johann Joachim Winckelmann helped popularize that idea in the eighteenth century.[112] In his division of Greek art into four periods, and in his extreme veneration of the period, he brought attention to and knowledge about a period that had previously been little understood.[113] By Busoni's time, scholars like Worringer described Greek (or Classic) architecture as a high point in creativity. In his discussions about human impulses encapsulated in artistic works, he claimed that Greek sculpture and architecture was so outstanding, in part, because it exemplified a perfect and inseparable synthesis between human will and sensuous form:

> With classical man, the absolute dualism of man and outer world vanishes, and consequently the absolute transcendentalism of religion and art vanishes. The divine is divested of its other-worldliness; it is secularized, incorporated in the mundane.[114]

Another aspect that made Classic architecture so great, according to Worringer, was the treatment of form, which emphasizes and capitalizes upon the material nature of the marble of which it is composed even as the structure and outline are prominently displayed. It thus makes material and

[112] Johann Joachim Winckelmann, *Reflections on the Painting and Sculpture of the Greeks* (London: A. Millar and T. Cadell, 1767); Katherine Harloe, *Winckelmann and the Invention of Antiquity: History and Aesthetics in the Age of Altertumswissenschaft* (Oxford: Oxford University Press, 2013), xxii.

[113] Winckelmann, *Geschichte der Kunst des Altertums* (Dresden: In der Waltherischen Hof-Buchhandlung, 1764).

[114] Worringer, *Form Problems of the Gothic*, 39.

structure inseparable. He claims that "to emphasize the stone means to express architectonically. Since the essential quality of stone is weight, its architectonic employment is built up on the law of gravity."[115]

Music of the Classical era with relatively thin textures and simple melodies resounding over harmonic progressions metaphorically can be seen as resembling the balance of horizontal and vertical elements in Hellenic architecture. The relatively thin textures and short, concise movements also draw attention to the structure. The aural illusions of proportion and symmetry created out of varied repetitions resonate in the sonata forms and developing thematic material. Rhythmic variety exudes youthful exuberance, even as Classical harmonies with numerous modulations fill the pieces with ever-changing colors. Classical serenity is seen as relating to the controlled and natural expression of the Viennese masters.

Scholars from Busoni's time wrote about this metaphorical imagery, likening Mozart's music to Hellenic architecture, and Busoni was part of a revival of interest after Mozart's compositions lay in the shadow of Beethoven during the Romantic era. In 1903, W. F. Peters Jr., for instance, described Mozart's proportions, symmetry, textures, and attention to detail as Hellenic:

> Mozart was a Greek in his nature and, like the Greeks, his artistic sense was unerring: the lightness, grace, and divine beauty of the Hellenic temples are expressive of the Greek ideals. So Mozart's music has the proportion, the organic unity, and the symmetry of a Greek shrine.[116]

Mozart's compositions became connected with main characteristics also associated with Hellenic architecture, including "youthfulness," "serenity," "purity," "radiance," "timelessness," "religiosity," and "beauty." C. von Sternberg, for instance, described Mozart's melodies as chaste and serene: "The chastity and purity of Mozart's melody is what has caused his art to be called 'Hellenic,' and not altogether unjustly so."[117]

[115] Worringer, *Form Problems of the Gothic*, 83.

[116] W. F. Peters Jr., "Mozart; an Appreciation," *Yale Literary Magazine* 610 (October 1903): 8; Franz Eduard Gehring, *Mozart the Great Musicians*, ed. Francis Hueffer (London: Sampson Low, Marston, Searle, and Rivington, 1883), 110.

[117] C. von Sternberg, "Mozart's Genius," in *Musical Essays: Art, Culture, Education,* selected and reprinted from "The Etude" 1892–1902 (Philadelphia: Theo Presser, 1902), 273; see also Nicholas Till, *Mozart and the Enlightenment: Truth, Virtue, and Beauty in Mozart's Operas* (New York: W. W. Norton, 1992).

This veneration of Mozart and the Classical style was intimately connected to burgeoning ideals of Neoclassicism. Composers were not simply interested in Classical forms for their own sake, or because they were simpler and more beautiful, but rather, often, for the profoundly modernist reason of desiring a distilled version of expression that presented a reaction against the excesses of late Romanticism.[118]

Busoni continued these analogies, describing Mozart's music as simple, clear, youthful, and full of proportion, symmetry, and order; these are features he also considered closely related to Hellenic architectural ideals. Yet Busoni's idealizations about Mozart probably say more about himself and his own generation than they do about Mozart. His musings about the composer are less about Mozart representing purity and simplicity; rather, the references to youth and childlikeness were about seeking after a sense of immediacy or perhaps even naivety in the Schillerian sense that many believed had been lost in the twentieth century. The economy of expression that he praised in Mozart was about distillation, not about simplicity in a colloquial sense. Some of his descriptions about Mozart that depict his own ideals are presented in an essay about Mozart:

> Through the mastery and unusually beautiful treatment of form, Mozart's settings attain that peculiar aesthetic calm which (if in discussing western music the thought of a relationship with Hellenic art is at all allowable) might lead one to draw a parallel with Mozart's settings. . . . This is a procedure which Mozart knows how to employ in the most effective way: through the symmetrical relationships of his form, within separate pieces, as also in their relationship to one another through the architecturally organized building up of the orchestral period, and finally in that restraint in the mastery of beauty, even in the highest moments of tragedy and of the most violent passion.[119]

[118] For an overview of Neoclassicism in France and Germany, see Scott Messing, *Neoclassicism in Music: From the Genesis of the Concept through the Schoenberg/Stravinsky Polemic* (Rochester, NY: University of Rochester Press, 1988).

[119] Busoni, "For the *Don Giovanni* Jubilee [1887]," in *The Essence and Oneness of Music and Other Papers*, trans. Rosamond Ley (London: Salisbury Square, 1957), 111. [Kraft der Beherrschung unter der selten schönen Behandlung der Form gewinnt der Satz Mozarts jene eigentümliche ästhetische Ruhe welche verleiten könnte falls bei der abendländischen Musik der Gedanke an eine Verwandtschaft mit der hellenischen Kunst überhaupt statthaft wäre eine Parallele zwischen jenem (dem Mozart'schen Satze) und dieser zu ziehen. . . . Ein Verfahren, das Mozart auf das Wirksamste anzuwenden versteht; durch die ebenmässigen Verhältnisse seiner Form, sowohl innerhalb der einzelnen Stücke, wie auch der einzelnen Stücke zueinander; durch den architektonisch gegliederten Aufbau des orchestralen Satzes; endlich durch jenes Einhalten des Schönheitsmasses, selbst in

Busoni also made the connection explicit between Mozart and his own ideals of youthfulness in his *Sketch* when he cried out: “Mozart! The seeker and finder, the great man with the childlike heart.”[120]

Busoni made additional metaphorical references about Mozart and architecture throughout his aphoristic writings, including those he published in 1906 for the 150th anniversary of Mozart's birth. In particular, he mentioned the proportions in Mozart's music: “His proportions are astoundingly correct, but they can be measured and verified.”[121] Busoni also believed that Mozart achieved a perfect balance between horizontal and vertical elements (melody and harmony) through counterpoint resulting from song-like melodies.[122] He considered Mozart's music to be multi-dimensional in scope, just like the plastic arts and architecture, due to its many styles and textures: “His art is like a sculptor's masterpiece—presenting from every side a finished picture.”[123] Moreover, Busoni praised him for his economy of expression (“He can say very much, but never says too much”).[124] Despite moments of storminess, Mozart's music is joyful and youthful overall for Busoni, who stated: “Joy is his most outstanding feature; his smile decks with flowers even what is most unpleasant and His smile, which was so human, still shines on us transfigured.”[125] Yet it is not exuberant joy, but classic and serene: “If cheerful serenity and simplicity are characteristics of genius, Mozart possessed them in full measure. In fact, no one could lay claim to genius with greater justice than Mozart.”[126] The theme of youthfulness and naivety surfaces in Busoni's descriptions of Mozart as well: “He is young as a

den Momenten der höchsten Tragik und der heftigsten Leidenschaft.] Busoni, “Zum Don Juan-Jubiläum,” in *Von der Einheit der Musik* (Berlin: Max Hesses Verlag, 1922), 10.

120 Busoni, “Zum Don Juan-Jubiläum,” 7.

121 Busoni, “Mozart: Aphorisms [1906],” in *The Essence of Music and Other Papers*, 105. [Seine Masse sind erstaunlich richtig, aber sie lassen sich messen und nachrechnen.] Busoni, “Mozart-Aphorismen,” 79.

122 Busoni, “From the *Don Giovanni* Jubilee [1887],” 108–9.

123 Busoni, “Mozart: Aphorisms,” 104. [Einem Bildhauer-Meisterwerke gleich, ist seine Kunst—von jeder Seite gesehen—ein fertiges Bild.] Busoni, “Mozart-Aphorismen,” 78.

124 Busoni, “Mozart: Aphorisms,” 104. [Er kann sehr vieles sagen, aber er sagt nie zu viel.] Busoni, “Mozart-Aphorismen,” 79.

125 Busoni, “Mozart: Aphorisms,” 106. [Heiterkeit ist sein hervorstechender Zug: er erüberblümt selbst das Unangenehmste durch ein Lächeln.] Busoni, “Mozart-Aphorismen,” 79. The published English translation departs significantly from the German in the second part of this aphorism.

126 Mozart, “From the *Don Giovanni* Jubilee,” 109. [Wenn Heiterkeit und Naivität die Merkmale des Genies sein sollen, Mozart befass sie in vollem Masse; und in der Tat, kein anderer als Mozart könnte mit grössere Berechtigung auf den Namen “Genie” Anspruch machen.] Busoni, “Zum Don Juan-Jubiläum,” 6.

boy and wise as an old man—never old-fashioned and never modern, carried to the grave and always alive."[127]

Unlike Worringer, who considered Greek architecture to be sensuous, however, Mozart's music bordered on the religious for Busoni, who viewed his forms as transcendent: "His sense of form is also supernatural."[128] He also considered his approach to harmony as religious ("He is religious in so far as religion is identical with harmony").[129] Moreover, Busoni believed that Mozart did not merely imitate the Hellenic style, but that he also expanded upon it by blending it with ideals of his own age. He specifically praised him for a blending of "ancient" (presumably Grecian) architecture with rococo decoration: "In him the antique and rococo combine in perfect ways without resulting in new architecture."[130] He likened Mozart to the new classicism of Goethe and Gotthold Ephraim Lessing, stating that these authors achieved a perfect balance between form and content, just like Mozart. They did not separate the material from the form.[131]

Busoni, Skyscrapers, and a New Gothic Art

Busoni not only used architectural metaphors to describe the historical composers he most admired; he also used them in relation to contemporary musicians, such as Bernhard Ziehn (1845–1912) and his pupil, Wilhelm Middelschulte (1863–1943) of Chicago.[132] Ziehn wrote about expanding tonal possibilities and proposed having harmonies form from the intersection of individual lines, something Busoni later wrote about too. Busoni

127 Busoni, "Mozart: Aphorisms," 106. [Er ist jung wie ein Jüngling und weise wie ein Greis—nie veraltet und nie modern, zu Grabe getragen und immer lebendig.] Busoni, "Mozart-Aphorismen," 80.

128 Busoni, "Mozart: Aphorisms," 104. [Sein Formensinn is fast aussermenschlich.] Busoni, "Mozart-Aphorismen," 78.

129 Busoni, "Mozart: Aphorisms," 105. [Er ist religiös, soweit Religion identisch ist mit Harmonie.] Busoni, "Mozart-Aphorismen," 80.

130 Busoni, "Mozart: Aphorisms," 105. [In ihm verbinden sich Antike und Rokoko in vollendeter Weise, doch ohne eine neue Architektur zu ergeben.] Busoni, "Mozart-Aphorismen," 80.

131 Busoni, "From the *Don Giovanni* Jubilee," 108.

132 For more information about these composers and the Gothic tradition, see Enrique Alberto Arias, "Wilhelm Middelschulte's 'Kontrapunktische Symphonie' and the Chicago Gothics," *The Diapason* 94:6 (June 2003): 17–22; Marc André Roberge, "Ferruccio Busoni: His Chicago Friends, and Frederick Stock's Transcription for Large Orchestra and Organ of the *Fantasia Contrappuntistica*," *Musical Quarterly* 80 (1996): 302–31. For a summary of some of Ziehn's theories, see Severine Neff, "Otto Luening (1900–) and the Theories of Bernhard Ziehn (1845–1912)," *Current Musicology* 39 (1985): 21–41.

described this approach as neo-Gothic in that the polyphony of old is rejuvenated with new treatments of the tonal language:

> Both young masters in Chicago cultivate this high art [Gothic] with proper understanding; But will they be able to bring it back to life? Can anyone do it? The art of a different time?—One seeks to authentically overlay the Gothic fugue with rejuvenating colors and a great new harmony, which makes these independent of each other through the unrelentingly logical intervallic movement of the individual voices, and especially at the points where they meet, creating individualistic harmonies.[133]

Busoni pointed out that just as Bach was surrounded by lofty Gothic cathedrals, the two "Gothics of Chicago" were surrounded by awe-inspiring twenty-story high skyscrapers. Chicago, was, in fact, an early center of skyscraper construction, with the earliest steel-frame skyscraper built there in 1885. Although the earlier Gothic cathedrals were ornate, and many of the later skyscrapers were sleeker, both aspired upward and transcended previous architectural limitations due to new building techniques and materials. Gothic cathedrals were made possible by the discovery of the pointed arch, which facilitated greater height when coupled with the flying buttress, but skyscrapers reached higher than ever before, due to the use of steel rods, concrete, and glass in new ways. A similarity between both is the use of many windows.

Busoni's equation of skyscrapers with a new Gothic art was, again, part of his own contemporaneous mindset, although it is unclear where he acquired those ideas. Worringer, for instance, claimed a connection between Gothic cathedrals and skyscrapers in that both achieve a level of expression by means of the construction. In both cases, even despite differences in material, the form and the material are inseparable:

> Only modern steel construction has brought back a certain inner understanding of the Gothic. For in it people have been confronted again with

133 [Die beiden jüngeren Meister in Chicago pflegen diese hohe Kunst mit richtigstem Verständnis; ob sie aber vermögen, sie wieder lebendig zu machen? Ob das jemand überhaupt vermag? Die Kunst einer anderen Zeit?—Sie versuchen es redlich und legen über das gotische "Gefüge" die verjüngenden Farben einer grossen, neuen Harmonik, die durch rücksichtstlos-logische Intervallenführung der einzelnen Stimmen diese von einander unabhängig macht und namentlich an den Punkten, wo Sie zusammentreffen, auch eigenartige Akkordgebilde entstehen lässt.] Busoni, "Die Gothiker von Chicago, Illinois [1910]," in *Von der Einheit der Musik* (Berlin: Max Hesses Verlag, 1922), 134–35.

> an architectural form in which the artistic expression is supplied by the method of construction itself. Yet despite all outer relationship, an important inner difference is discernible. For in the modern case it is the material itself that directly encourages such structural one-sidedness, while the Gothic arrived at such ideas, not by means of the material, but in spite of the material, in spite of the stone.[134]

Busoni described the polyphonic art of these two men of Chicago metaphorically as a new Gothic art in which there is height and depth, but less ornamentation and an expansion of the tonal palette. It is an art in which there is an integration of material content and the overall form. The new tonal palette, in some ways, parallels the changes in construction materials:

> Everything is ingeniously arranged and structured in the richest confusion. One leads to the other, the highest organically develops from the lowest; everything is necessary to the whole, transparent in its peak, unshakable in its foundations, a bridge from the earth to the sky. Such is the Gothic, and the two men cherish this most exquisite flowering of human spirit in American Chicago, while around them surround buildings of twenty or more stories, broad and unadorned, signaling a new century in a new world.[135]

In terms of musical material, Busoni was particularly fascinated by the composers' use of new harmonic procedures, including plurisignificance and symmetrical inversion, procedures that facilitated tonally ambiguous music through varied chromatic material, thereby expanding the possibilities of tonality without breaking away from it completely. It was a way of embracing past, present, and future simultaneously.[136]

134 Worringer, *Form Problems of the Gothic*, 88.

135 [Alles ist sinnreich geordnet und im reichsten Gewirre rein gegliedert. Eines trägt das Andere, das Höchste entzweigt sich organisch aus dem Tiefsten; alles Einzelne zum Ganzen notwendig, spitzenhaft durchsichtig, unerschütterlich in Seinen Gründen, eine Brücke von der Erde zum Himmel. So ist die Gotik und zwei Männer pflegen diese auserlesenste Blüte menschlichen Geistes im amerikanischen Chicago, indes rings um sie steinerne Würfel von zwanzig und mehreren Stockwerken plump und schmucklos ein neues Jahrhundert in einer neuen Welt signalisieren.] Busoni, "Die Gotiker von Chicago, Illinois," 133.

136 For an explanation of their theories in relation to Busoni and his pupil Otto Luening, see Neff, "Otto Luening (1900–) and the Theories of Bernhard Ziehn (1845–1912)." See also John Becker, "Wilhelm Middelschulte, Master of Counterpoint," *Musical Quarterly* 14 (1928): 192–202; Winthrop Sargeant, "Bernhard Ziehn, Precursor," *Musical Quarterly* 19 (1933): 169–77. For an explanation of their relevance for Busoni, see Colin Davis, "'The New Harmony' of Ferruccio Busoni's *Fantasia Contrappuntistica*," *Journal of Musicological Research* 37:3 (July–September 2018): 239–73.

Figure 1.4. Photo of Ferruccio Busoni with Frederick August Stock, Wilhelm Middelschulte, and Georg Hütter, 1911. Dortmund, Atelier Neuhaus. Staatsbibliothek zu Berlin, Preussischer Kulturbesitz, Musikabteilung mit Mendelssohn Archiv, Mus. Nachl. F. Busoni, P I, 137.

As Paul Fleet has noted, Busoni's metatonal harmonic approach similarly came from the layering of melodic lines that "resist a tonal reading."[137] Although Busoni was already developing a metatonal approach on his own, discussions with Ziehn and Middelschulte in 1911 led to a significant change (see figure 1.4). Busoni described their influence in a brief essay penned in Chicago in 1911 that he intended for publication in *Signale* in Berlin. In his essay, Busoni describes four new harmonic approaches that include new harmonies built out of new scales, atonality (called anarchy by Busoni), a new key system, polyphony in which all the voices function independently, and symmetrical inversion. Of these, Busoni credits Ziehn with having shown him the last: "By symmetrical inversion of the harmonic order Bernhard Ziehn shows me the second way."[138]

[137] Paul Fleet, *Ferruccio Busoni: A Phenomenological Approach to his Music and Aesthetics* (Cologne: Lambert Academic Publishing, 2009), 112.
[138] Busoni, "The New Harmony," in *The Essence of Music and Other Papers*, 24. [Den zeiten Weg weist uns Bernhard Ziehn mit der symmetrischen Umkehrung der Harmoniefolgen.] Busoni, "Die neue Harmonik," in *Von der Einheit*, 159.

An important idea behind Ziehn's theories is that a pitch can belong to any number of chords or pitch collections, allowing for nontraditional progressions and tonal mutability. For instance, in the opening of Middelschulte's *Kanonische Fantasie über BACH und Fuge über 4 Themen von Joh. Seb. Bach*, each chord in the opening measures contains pitches that change function in the next (see example 1.1).[139] An A in measure 2 is the fifth of a D minor seventh chord. In measure 3, it is the third of an F♯ half-diminished seventh chord. In polyphonic passages, harmonies result from whatever pitches coincide, and pitches in different voices can function independently. Middelschulte's subsequent figurations, for instance, move through an array of collections as distant as B♭, D minor, B minor, and G major (see mm. 5–7, for instance), over a D pedal, a pitch that constantly changes significance and function.

In Middelschulte's work, chromaticism covers dense and thick textures, and the harmonic progressions are not traditional. Dissonances disrupt any sense of stability as the music is constantly in motion. Chromatic saturation creates moments of atonality that nonetheless never completely supplant tonality.

Busoni and *Young Classicality*

Given Busoni's use of architectural metaphors to describe the music of contemporary composers he admired, it is not surprising that he also used them to explain his own ideals too. Although combining neo-Gothic and Neoclassical ideals in a single building might seem like an unlikely choice, Busoni envisioned combining elements of each of these peak creative periods musically.

In particular, his aesthetic ideas recorded in the late 1910s and early 1920s allude to both Gothic and Hellenic metaphors to explain his mature aesthetic vision of *Young Classicality* ["Junge Klassizität"]; the latter draws upon metaphorical imagery associated in his own time with the Hellenic in terms of evocations of youthfulness and Classical form. For instance, he described ideal *Tonkunst* as possessing solid and unique formal structures; he described it as "the mastery, the sifting and the turning to account of all

[139] The "BACH" motive is composed of the pitches B♭-A-C-B.

Example 1.1. Middelschulte, *Kanonische Fantasie über BACH und Fuge über 4 Themen von Joh. Seb. Bach*, mm. 1–16.

Example 1.1. Continued

the gains of previous experiments and their inclusion in strong and beautiful ['feste und schöne'] forms."[140] Busoni envisioned unique structures that were not tied to *Formenlehre* traditions. He also idealized what he perceived as Hellenic simplicity and saw his artistic ideals not as regressing through such allusions to the past, but as rejuvenating and perfecting them.[141]

Busoni hoped for an art that would not only be "old and new at the same time," but also characterized by his own nostalgia for a simplicity and serenity of previous eras, as opposed to the romantic sensuousness he observed in the late nineteenth century.[142] He stressed in 1922 that the music of the future should be simplified, with fewer notes and less dense textures; he specifically mentioned Mozart as his model, criticizing one of his own earlier compositions, *Die Brautwahl*, BV 258, in the process:

> Should not music also try to express only what is most important with a few notes, set down in a masterly fashion? Does my *Brautwahl* with its full score of seven hundred pages achieve more than *Figaro* with its six accompanying wind instruments? It seems to me that the refinement of economy is the next aim after the refinement of prodigality has been learnt.[143]

He also emphasized proportion but introduced new understandings of the term, claiming it could relate to time (as opposed to phrasing), all types of contrasts, and key relationships. He also noted that proportion was an essential part of the structure of a composition:

> There are three kinds of proportion which surpass all the rest in importance: measurement in time, contrast in sound, and relationships in modulation. And three subordinate ones: movement, sequence of intervals, and atmosphere. . . . It is the form which first raises conception, intention, and

[140] Busoni, letter of January 1920 to Paul Bekker, in *The Essence of Music and Other Papers*, 20. This letter was first published as "Junge Klassizität," in the *Frankfurter Allgemeine Zeitung* (February 7, 1920). [die Meisterung, die Sichtung und Ausbeutung aller Errugenschaften vorausgegangener Experimente: ihre Hineintragung in feste und schöne Formen.] "Junge Klassizität," in *Von der Einheit*, 276–77.

[141] Busoni, letter of June 18, 1921, to his son [Rafaello Busoni], in *The Essence of Music and Other Papers*, 22–23.

[142] Busoni, letter of June 18, 1921, to his son [Rafaello Busoni], 21.

[143] Busoni, "Simplicity of Music in the Future [1922]," in *The Essence of Music and Other Papers*, 23. [Sollte nicht auch die Musik dahinstreben, nur das Wichtigste, mit wenigen meisterlich hingesetzten Noten auszusprechen? Erreicht den meine Brautwahl mit ihren 700 Partiturseiten mehr, als Figaro mit seinen sech begleitenden Blasinstrumenten? Das Raffinement der Sparsamkeit scheint mir das nächste Ziel, nachdem das Raffinement der Verschwendung gelernt worden ist.] Busoni, "Aufzeichnungen," in *Von der Einheit*, 288–89.

direction to the rank of a work of art. And inside the form, proportion is one of the strongest and most sensitive demands.[144]

Busoni's theory of *Young Classicality* draws not only on ideals of neo-Hellenic youthfulness, renewal, simplicity, and strength of form, but also on neo-Gothic ideals of polyphony. Busoni was calling for a new melodic art, a linear counterpoint, in which the intersections of independent voices would generate the harmonies, some new and dissonant, and also generate new textures, forms, and scales:

> With "Young Classicism" I include the definite departure from what is thematic and the return to melody again as the ruler of all voices and all emotions (not in the sense of a pleasing motive) and as the bearer of the idea and the begetter of harmony, in short, the most highly developed (not the most complicated) polyphony.[145]

Busoni's ideas bring to mind the theories of Ernst Kurth, who similarly described polyphony in 1917 as moving lines that generate harmonies through their congruence.[146]

Like the "new Gothics" of Chicago, Busoni envisioned using a new polyphony that expanded the possibilities of tonality. He described his ideas in an essay from 1922, in which he called for harmonic expansion through the natural coincidence of pitches, yet without a rejection of traditional tonality. He stressed that this new kind of polyphony could still display simplicity and did not need to follow traditional tonal harmonic progressions.[147] He called this new approach "polyharmony" [Polyharmonik], when pitches are freed

144 Busoni, "Proportion [1922]," in *The Essence of Music and Other Papers*, 33. [Es gibt deren drei überragende: der Masse in der Zeit, der Gegenüberstellung im Klange, der Beziehungen in der Modulation; und drei untergeordnete: der Bewegung, der Intervallenfolge, der Stimmung. Erst die Form erhebt Einfall, Gesinnung und Richtung zum Range des Kunstwerkes. Und innerhalb der Form ist die proportion eine der strengsten und empfindlichsten Forderungen. In einem weiteren bande, der von diesen Fragenhandeln soll, hoffe ich dem Leser wieder zu begegnen.] Busoni, "Von den Proportionen," in *Von der Einheit*, 357–58.

145 Busoni, letter of January 1920 to Paul Bekker, in *The Essence of Music and Other Papers*, 21. [Zur "jungen Klassizität" rechne ich noch den definitive Abschied vom Thematischen und das Wiedergreifen der Melodie—(nicht im Sinne eines gefälligen Motives)—als Beherrscherin aller Stimmen, aller Regungen, als Trägerin der Idee und Erzeugerin der harmonie, kurz: der höchst entwickelten (nicht kompliziertesten) Polyphonie.] Busoni, "Junge Klassizität," in *Von der Einheit*, 278.

146 Kurth, *Grundlagen des linearen Kontrapunkts Einführung in Stil und Technik von Bachs melodischer Polyphonie.*

147 Busoni, "Concerning Harmony [1922]," in *The Essence of Music and Other Papers*, 26–27.

from rules of traditional tonality.[148] That said, Busoni's music sounds very tonal, at times, and at others, bitonal, or atonal. Even in the tonal sections, however, he often uses tonality nontraditionally through his evocation of plurisignificance, ever-changing harmonic underpinnings, and chromatic variations to scales. The composer thus eventually took the expansion of tonality farther than Ziehn and Middelschulte.

Practically speaking, his proposed approach was metatonal. He called for using all twelve chromatic tones, yet without rejecting tonality. He believed that intersections of melodic lines would result in new harmonies when they intersected vertically. He had already been thinking about these ideas in the early 1900s. In 1907, for instance, he had proposed adding new and imaginative scales using chromatic coloration, such as C-D♭-E♭-F♭-G-A-B-C, or C-D-E♭-F♭-G♯-A-B-C, stating: "With this presentation, the unity of all keys may be considered as a kaleidoscopic blending and interchanging of twelve semitones within the three-mirror tube of Taste, Emotion, and Intention—the essential feature of the harmony of today."[149]

Busoni claimed that his new polyphony arose from a deep knowledge of Bach's contrapuntal practice, which he had learned in his youth. At the same time, he believed it continued in the same spirit, even as it explored greater independence of line and nontraditional harmonies and scales:

> One of the most valuable of these was the newly found harmony that can arise through independent polyphony. Thus, I had many tools in hand for the making of a good technical building. . . . I believed I was acting in accordance with the spirit of Bach, when I placed the latest possibilities of our present-day art in the service of his plan—as the organic continuation of his art—as he himself brought the latest possibilities of the art of his time to expression.[150]

[148] Busoni, "An Attempt at a Definition of a Melody [1922]," in *The Essence of Music and Other Papers*, 33. Busoni, "Aufzeichnungen," in *Von der Einheit*, 288.

[149] Busoni, *Sketch*, 30. [Mit dieser Darstellung dürfte die Einheit aller Tonarten endgültig ausgesprochen und begründet sein. Kaleidoskopisches Durcheinanderschütteln von zwölf Halbtönen in der Dreispiegelkammer des Geschmacks, der Empfindung und der Intention das Wesen der heutigen Harmonie.] Busoni, *Entwurf*, 50.

[150] Busoni, "Self Criticism [1912]," in *The Essence of Music and Other Papers*, 48. [Seit früher Kindheit habe ich Bach gespielt und Kontrapunkt geübt. Damals war es mir zu einer Manie geworden, und tatsächlich kommt in jedem meiner Jugendwerke mindestens "Fugato" vor. Nun fand ich mich wieder als Kontrapunktiker, wenn auch auf einem für mich durchaus neuen Standpunkt. Die ununterbrochene, versteckte Arbeit der natur hatte vieles in mir unbewusst gewirkt und ich wurde unvermiteter Errungenschaften gewahr, die innerlich gereist waren. Von diesen eine der

Decorative figurations led him to gradually discover his own new approach to the musical language through an expansion of sequences, counterpoint, and chromaticism. Busoni's contrapuntal writing thus displays polytonality at times, and some unconventional scalar systems, as well as tonal mutability and dense chromaticism.

Taken in the context of the burgeoning Neoclassical ideals of his generation, Busoni's theories of *Young Classicality* are very much a part of his time in their evocation of the past. Yet his idiosyncratic approach was also distinctly different from many of his contemporaries who relied on historical forms coupled with a defamiliarization of the musical language. Igor Stravinsky's Neoclassical works, such as the Octet or the *Symphony of Psalms*, for instance, are examples.

Busoni's goal, by contrast, was not to re create the musical forms of the past (e.g., fugues and sonatas), nor to return to tonal centers with added dissonance, but rather to create new and unique musical structures and new scales and harmonies using timeless compositional procedures with expanded musical materials. In drawing on Bach for inspiration, Busoni's practice resonates with Walter Frisch's concept of historicist modernism described in this book's introduction.[151] Rather than seeking after brand-new musical languages that ruptured from the past and presented as discontinuous and defamiliarized sounds, Busoni sought historical continuity. He drew upon past compositional procedures, such as counterpoint, to lead to the new harmonies and scales he envisioned. Yet as this chapter has shown, Busoni also looked to Mozart for inspiration about concision and proportion for his new musical experiments, and in the process envisioned his idiosyncratic approach of *Young Classicality* that differs from Frisch's "historicist modernism" concept that was based solely on Bach. One of the pupils from his Berlin composition master class, Wladimir Vogel, remembers Busoni making a distinction between forms, which needed to respond to the current age, and compositional approaches, which he

wertvollsten war die durch rücksichtslose Polyphonie sichs ich neu gestaltended harmonik. So hatte ich viele Werkzeuge in der hand zur Fertigung eines guten technischen Bauwerkes; . . . Ich glaubte im Geiste Bachs zu wirken, wenn ich die letzten Möglichkeiten unserer heutigen Kunst—als organische Fortsetzung der seinen—in den Dienst seines Planes stellate; wie ihm selbst die letzten Möglichkeiten der Kunst seiner Zeit zum Ausdruck wurden.] Busoni, "Selbst-Rezension," in *Von der Einheit*, 177–78.

151 See Walter Frisch, *German Modernism: Music and the Arts* (Berkeley: University of California Press, 2005).

considered timeless, in a conversation he had with him at the Bauhaus Exhibition in Weimar in 1923:

> One can write fugues today with the traditional means, or even with modern or atonal means, liberated from all inherited and obsolete harmony, tonal links, etc. . . . But there will still be something of an antique character about such a fugue . . . for the fugue is a "form." As such it is tied to its time, "transitory," whereas polyphony has no form but is a principle and as such timeless. . . . It is a free, contrapuntal process, linked to no traditional form and yet formed through the laws of equilibrium, proportion, deployment, intensification and termination.[152]

As Stephanie Probst has noted, Busoni's theories about this new polyphony that he already expressed in 1912 challenged common contemporaneous assumptions about music composition and Bach's German cultural legacy, even while they were expressive of ideas that were considered ideologically modernist. In particular, she notes that Busoni's favoring of the melody to create new harmonies went against what other more traditional theorists were considering, including August Halm, who privileged harmonic readings of polyphony and Bach's music.[153] Kurth expanded upon these views already espoused by Busoni in his 1917 *Grundlagen des linearen Kontrapunkts Einführung in Stil und Technik von Bachs melodischer Polyphonie*, but in his own way, with theories of linear counterpoint.[154] Although Kurth did not coin the term, he did popularize the concept. Yet while Kurth eventually distanced himself from more modernist interpretations of the ideas in 1927 when he restricted his theories to tonal contexts, Busoni's main purpose was to move beyond tonality and to expand harmonic and tonal possibilities. Moreover, the idea of freeing harmonic areas through the intersections of

[152] Wladimir Vogel, "Impressions of Ferruccio Busoni," *Perspectives of New Music* 6:2 (Spring–Summer 1968): 169.

[153] August Halm, "Über Ferruccio Busoni's Bachausgabe," *Melos* 2 (August 1921): 207–13, 239–44.

[154] Kurth, *Grundlagen des linearen Kontrapunkts Einführung in Stil und Technik von Bachs melodischer Polyphonie*. For more information, see Susanne Fontaine, "Ausdruck und Konstruktion: Die Bachrezeption von Kandinsky, Itten, Klee, und Feininger," in *Bach und die Nachwelt*, ed. Michael Heinemann and Joachim Lüdtke (Regensburg: Laaber Verlag, 2000), 396–426; Stephanie Probst, "Sounding Lines: New Approaches to Melody in 1920s Musical Thought" (PhD diss., Harvard University, 2018); Probst, "Pen, Paper, Steel: Visualizing Bach's Polyphony at the Bauhaus," *Music Theory Online: A Journal of the Society for Music Theory* 26:4 (December 2020), https://mtosmt.org/issues/mto.20.26.4/mto.20.26.4.probst.html (accessed April 13, 2021); Alexander Rehding, "(Mis)Interpreting Ernst Kurth" (MA thesis, Harvard University, 1995).

melodic lines was adopted by several members of Busoni's circle, including Paul Bekker and Ernst Krenek.[155]

Busoni's Architectural Music

If Busoni possessed a deep knowledge of architecture and was inspired by past historical styles, he was also alive at a time in which there was interest in cross influence between art forms. As Daniel Albright has noted, the arts tended to cross-pollinate each other in a variety of ways in the first decades of the twentieth century.[156] One example of this cross-influence can be observed in the *Jugendstil* movement, of which Busoni had firsthand knowledge through van de Velde.

Although the *Jugendstil* movement is primarily associated with the visual arts and architecture, it also borrowed from music, and in turn, influenced composers. It began around 1890 and was characterized in visual art by youthful energy, florid ornamentation, flowing lines, and asymmetry. The French analogue (Art Nouveau) has been widely associated with Debussy's music and Impressionism. Connections have also been made between this trend and Gothic ornamentation and asymmetrical lines as well as with Classical youthfulness and simplicity.[157]

Scholars have difficulty agreeing on the specific connection between visual aspects of *Jugendstil* and the music of Germany. Hans Hollander, for instance, admits a very broad array of late nineteenth- and early twentieth-century compositions ranging from Gustav Mahler and Richard Strauss to Alban Berg that display colorful orchestrations and fluid lines. Carl Dahlhaus, by contrast, does not consider it a viable category for understanding music.[158] Yet as Walter Frisch points out, there probably is a middle ground, and cross influence

155 For a reception of Kurth's treatise, see Rehding, "(Mis)Interpreting Ernst Kurth." See also Paul Bekker, "Kontrapunkt und Neuzeit," *Frankfurter Zeitung* (March 27, 1918); Nora Schmid and Lea Hinden, eds., Volltextbriefe zum Inventar Nachlass Ernst Kurth (Vers. 4.0) (Bern: University of Bern, Institut für Musikwissenschaft, 2007), http://www.musik.unibe.ch/dienstleistungen/nachlass_kurth/index_ger.html (accessed April 18, 2021).

156 Daniel Albright, *Untwisting the Serpent: Modernism in Music, Literature, and Other Arts* (Chicago: University of Chicago Press, 2000).

157 For more about the *Jugendstil* movement, see Walter Frisch, "Musik and Jugendstil," *Critical Inquiry* 17:1 (Autumn 1990): 138–61; Hans Hollander, *Musik und Jugendstil* (Zurich: Atlantis, 1975); Robert Münster, ed., *Jugendstil-Musik?, Münchner Musikleben 1890–1918* (Wiesbaden: Reichert, 1987); Jürg Stenzl, ed., *Art Nouveau, Jugendstil, und Musik* (Zurich: Atlantis, 1980).

158 Hollander, *Musik und Jugendstil*; Carl Dahlhaus, *Die Musik des 19 Jahrhunderts* (Laaber: Laaber-Verlag, 1980), 279.

between art forms was not uncommon at the time, especially for a composer like Busoni, who was so interested in other arts and their application to music.[159]

It is notable that the *Jugendstil* movement received a flurry of interest in the years surrounding Busoni's maturation; leaders of the movement assembled in 1907, debating how to reconcile decoration with industry and functionalism. They fostered experimentation and encouraged a synthesis of fine and applied arts, a *Gesamtkunstwerk* of architecture and visual art. As the movement evolved, color, form, and line developed into symbols and abstractions.

An important leader in making *Jugendstil* more abstract was van de Velde, He created art and architecture that featured sinuous lines deriving from natural forms that, nevertheless, still maintained an overall sense of pleasing form and proportion. Van de Velde claimed that he found his model for an abstract ornamental artistic style in music. One can only wonder which musical scores served as his models:

> It was the idea that lines are interrelated in the same logical and consistent way as numbers and as notes in music that led me to go in search of a purely abstract ornamental style, one which engenders beauty of its own accord and by means of the harmony of construction and the harmony of the regularity and equilibrium of forms which compose an ornament.[160]

In van de Velde's famous *Jugendstil* buildings (although van de Velde preferred the term "new style"), such as the Villa Hohenhof in Hagen, Germany, there is also congruence between form and content, where *Jugendstil* designs are external and internal (wallpapers, draperies, furnishings, ornamentation, and landscaping), while simultaneously focused on nature and geometric shapes.

It is not hard to observe similarities between the works of Busoni and van de Velde. Even if the two did not meet until Zurich, Busoni was aware of his architecture long before their meeting, and the shared ideals were part of their *Zeitgeist.* There are parallels in their shared abstract ornamental approach in the early to mid-1900s as a means of experimentation with new means of expression.[161] A favoring of slightly asymmetrical proportions

[159] See Frisch, "Music and Jugendstil," *Critical Inquiry* 17 (Autumn 1990): 138–61.
[160] Van de Velde, "Das neue Ornament [1901]," in *Zum neuen Stil*, ed. Hans Curjel (Munich: R. Piper, 1955), 94. Quoted in Frisch, "Musik und Jugendstil," 144.
[161] For a brief overview of van de Velde's vast output, including his textiles and bookbinding, see Ole W. Fischer, "Passion, Function, and Beauty: Henry van de Velde and His Contribution to European Modernism," in *West 86th: A Journal of Decorative Arts, Design, History, and Material Culture* 21:1 (Spring–Summer 2014): 142–48.

Figure 1.5. Photo of Henry van de Velde's Bloemenwerf House, c. 1895. An example of *Jugendstil.*

with gentle and inauspicious lines in which ornamentation was indelibly interwoven is common to both.

Van de Velde looked to music for an example of how to approach color even as he abstracted from gesture a sense of movement in his neo-Gothic decorative lines.[162] Moreover, he created a sense of symmetry out of constant variation. For example, van de Velde's Bloemenwerf House in Belgium of 1895 features a facade with three main sections and three near-triangular shaped roof peaks—each similar, but with slightly different lines and angles (see figure 1.5). Two sets of similar windows surround on each side a center door on the first floor, and a large display window on the second. On the second floor, the window on the left has decorative side shutters, while the window on the right, although similarly shaped, has protruding shutters over the top half of the windows. On the first floor, a single window on the right with only a left shutter balances a double window on the left—pleasingly similar, but different. The color scheme throughout was amaranth red, blue,

162 Van de Velde, "A Clean Sweep for the Future of Art [1894]," 122.

and green, which he described in musical terms as forming a "basic chord that recurred throughout the house."[163]

Busoni's *An die Jugend* (1909) can be seen as exhibiting some of these *Jugendstil* ideals as well, even as it brings the notion of rejuvenation and youthfulness to his work through explicit references to youth of the upcoming generation. It thus seems to draw upon Busoni's knowledge of contemporary architectural styles even as it relies on his burgeoning neo-Gothic ideas about musical language and harmony.

Upon learning of the title of Busoni's piece, *An die Jugend*, it is likely that at least some of Busoni's listeners would have thought of the *Jugendstil* movement.[164] The implicit suggestion is supported by the musical style. For instance, the opening number displays sinuous chromatic polyphony and florid lines even as it also simultaneously alludes to the music of Debussy and Bach. At the same time, the polyphony helps generate new harmonies through plurisignificance.

In addition, the title of Busoni's composition also explicitly refers to specific youth. Although the piece is too difficult from a technical perspective to be played by most children, it was composed with the younger generation in mind; Busoni dedicated each of the movements to his promising piano pupils: Book 1. Josef Turczyński (1884–1953), Book 2. Louis Theodor Gruenberg (1884–1964), Book 3. Leo Sirota (1885–1965), Book 4. Louis Closson, and Epilogue. Émile R. Blanchet (1877–1943).[165]

Finally, the title references Busoni's own desire for musical innovation. His writings, such as the *Sketch of a New Aesthetic of Music*, which he published in 1907, and in which he discussed the relatively young age of music, suggest the potential for musical innovation, experimentation, and growth.[166] He stated that he considered music to be the least developed of the arts with the greatest potential for change. He thought of music as free and unfettered, like a child, because of its ephemeral material (sound waves).[167] The evolutionary aspect in the metaphor is amply evident in that just as a child matures into a man, so music of the past should not be rejected, but rather, developed in new ways.[168]

163 Van de Velde, *Geschichte*, 113.

164 Busoni contributed to the journal *Pan* from 1911 to 1912 along with other authors, poets, and artists that were associated with the *Jugendstil* movement: "Routine," *Pan* 1:20 (August 16, 1911): 654–55; "Schönberg-Matinée," *Pan* 2:10 (January 25, 1912): 298; "Selbst-Rezension," *Pan* 2:11 (February 1, 1912): 327–30.

165 I was unable to definitively determine Louis Closson's birth and death dates.

166 Busoni, *Sketch*, 3.

167 Busoni, *Sketch*, 4–5.

168 Busoni, *Sketch*, 18.

The theme of youthful renewal is an important part of the composition, which comprises four short books and an epilogue; each is written with reference to another composer—yet each is reshaped according to Busoni's conception of the future of music. That Busoni drew upon and reworked styles of composers from the Baroque, Classical, Romantic, and contemporary eras demonstrates the historical lineage that the composer was connected to, and without any sense of rupture. It also shows that Busoni drew upon other composers beyond Bach, which Frisch focuses on exclusively in his discussion of historicist modernism.[169] Busoni included previously composed music—some quoted exactly, some paraphrased, and some merely alluded to—but transformed it according to his own imagination and ideals:

1. Preludio, fughetta ed Esercizio (allusions to Debussy and Bach)
2. Preludio, Fuga e Fuga figurata ("Studie nach J. S. Bachs Wohltemperiertem Klavier")
3. Giga, Bolero, e Variazione ("Studie nach Mozart")
4. Introduzione e Capriccio (Paganinesco) & Epilogo

The opening preludietto of *An die Jugend* illustrates Busoni's expansion of tonality in decorative *Jugendstil* lines. While it pays homage to Debussy in its use of pentatonic and whole tone collections, coupled with parallel fourth intervals and enriched Impressionist harmonies, the florid scalar passages and lines simultaneously reflect the decorative ideals of *Jugendstil* and neo-Gothic polyphony. Yet unlike many of Debussy's piano preludes, the piece lacks a descriptive title. Moreover, it resounds with textual transparency and simplicity.

The piece also creates new harmonies out of the neo-Gothic polyphony. Busoni considered Debussy to have made some progress in expanding tonality in "isolated passages" ["vereinzelten Momenten"].[170] Yet Busoni expanded scalar possibilities even farther, thereby creating a kaleidoscope of tonal colors. The piece begins and ends in A, yet the main body of the work features tonal ambiguity that results from the sinuous *Fortspinnung* lines. One technique he uses to create new harmonies is the reharmonization of scales using the technique of plurisignificance. For instance, a G♮ beginning in measure 3, coupled with the introduction of the melody note A in the

[169] Frisch, *German Modernism*.
[170] Busoni, *Sketch*, 29.

Example 1.2. Busoni, "Preludietta," *An die Jugend*, BV 254, mm. 1–12.

treble, and an expanding scalar range in the bass, creates ambiguity between tonal areas of A major, D major, and B minor (see example 1.2).

As Busoni mentioned in his *Sketch*, there is unexpected beauty in hearing scales supported by different harmonic areas: "you cannot avoid feeling a delightful surprise at the strangely unfamiliar euphony."[171] In addition, Busoni also used voice leading to migrate freely through tonal areas. For instance,

171 Busoni, *Sketch*, 30. [und man wird sich der angenehmsten Überraschung über den fremdartigen Wohllaut nicht erwehren können.] Busoni, *Entwurf*, 49.

in measures 10–12, he used chromatic pitch changes to implicate B minor, C minor, and E major. Finally, he used unconventional scale collections, such as the one in measures 11–12 (C, D, E, F♯, G, A, B♭, B) that hints at C hypodorian, with the chromatic B♭ inflection. Then there is a mysterious scale featuring a tritone in the middle with the appearance of the B natural in measure 12. Tonal plurisignificance and chromatic voice-leading contribute to enhanced tonal mutability beginning in measure 16 when the treble features two-note block intervals rather than single melodic pitches. Moreover, beginning in measure 18, Busoni included block parallel seventh intervals, as opposed to the more typical parallel octaves in impressionistic writing. This enhances the level of dissonance and the metatonal implications.

The ensuing fughetta, reminiscent of Bach, but chromatically extended, likewise features an expansion of tonality through plurisignificance and chromatic melodic writing (see example 1.3). The opening subject in C major is varied in measures 3–4 with the added modal inflection of E♭. Measures 5–6 present a sequential repetition at the third that brings the piece to G major before the dominant answer beginning in measure 7. Subsequent measures implicate harmonies as remote as D major and F minor (m. 11), for instance.

An die Jugend thus couples the florid lines characteristic of *Jugendstil* with polyphony in which the conflux of lines results in new harmonies. But Busoni's music of the 1920s went beyond that and more closely approached his vision of *Young Classicality* in bringing together not only innovative counterpoint, solid forms, and new harmonies, coupled with newfound concision and abstraction. This can be observed, for instance, in his *Sieben kurze Stücke zur Pflege des polyphonen Spiels*, published initially as a collection of five, and then six, and then seven short pieces, three of which he had premiered at the Bauhaus exhibition in 1923. These were performed together with Busoni's *Prélude et étude en arpèges*, BV 297, the Toccata (Preludio, Fantasia, Ciaccona, BV 287), and the Perpetuum mobile, BV 293. Since the composer was quite ill at the time, Egon Petri, Busoni's closest piano disciple, performed them for him in Weimar. The pieces demonstrate Busoni's expansion of the tonal language through polyphony coupled with his attempts to create unique ("solid and beautiful") forms. In addition, these pieces represent a new level of abstractness and economy of expression characteristic of many music compositions of the 1920s (see figure 1.6).[172]

[172] The pieces were composed between March and May 1923. They were later reissued in 1925 together with the Preludietto no. 1(from book I of the Klavierübung in five parts, 1st ed.) and the Andantino tranquillo no. 7 in the Klavierübung in ten books, vol. 9 (2nd ed.).

Example 1.3. Busoni, "Fughetta," from *An die Jugend*, BV 254, mm. 1–18.

On the surface, short piano pieces seem a curious choice for Busoni to bring to such a momentous celebration of the arts at the Weimar Bauhaus exhibition. The Bauhaus came about after the resignation in 1915 of van de Velde from the Grand Ducal School of Arts and Crafts in Weimar but was based on some of his ideas. Van de Velde's successor, Gropius, recommended by van de Velde himself, was an architect with a vision for bringing the arts together, like many modernists. After World War I, he merged two schools (the Weimar Art Academy and the Grand Ducal School of Arts and Crafts) to found the Staatliches Bauhaus in Weimar in

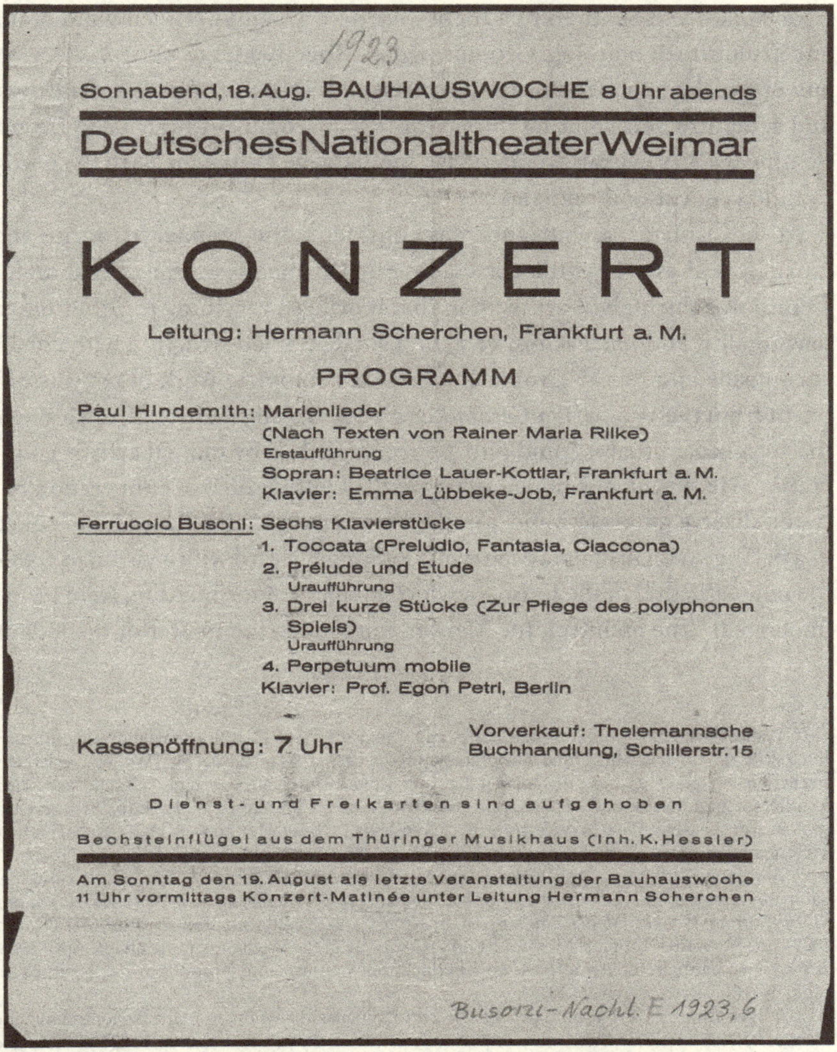

1923

Sonnabend, 18. Aug. BAUHAUSWOCHE 8 Uhr abends

DeutschesNationaltheaterWeimar

KONZERT

Leitung: Hermann Scherchen, Frankfurt a. M.

PROGRAMM

Paul Hindemith: Marienlieder
(Nach Texten von Rainer Maria Rilke)
Erstaufführung
Sopran: Beatrice Lauer-Kottlar, Frankfurt a. M.
Klavier: Emma Lübbeke-Job, Frankfurt a. M.

Ferruccio Busoni: Sechs Klavierstücke
1. Toccata (Preludio, Fantasia, Ciaccona)
2. Prélude und Etude
Uraufführung
3. Drei kurze Stücke (Zur Pflege des polyphonen Spiels)
Uraufführung
4. Perpetuum mobile
Klavier: Prof. Egon Petri, Berlin

Kassenöffnung: 7 Uhr

Vorverkauf: Thelemannsche Buchhandlung, Schillerstr. 15

Dienst- und Freikarten sind aufgehoben

Bechsteinflügel aus dem Thüringer Musikhaus (Inh. K. Hessler)

Am Sonntag den 19. August als letzte Veranstaltung der Bauhauswoche
11 Uhr vormittags Konzert-Matinée unter Leitung Hermann Scherchen

Busoni-Nachl. E 1923, 6

Figure 1.6. Program from the Weimar Bauhaus Week, August 18, 1923. Staatsbibliothek zu Berlin, Preussischer Kulturbesitz, Musikabteilung mit Mendelssohn Archiv, Mus. Nachl. F. Busoni, E, 1923, 6.

1919. Gropius envisioned that artists and craftsmen would together create the "building of the future"; this resembled the cooperation of historical craftsman guilds to build new architectural masterpieces in which the exterior and interior elements were related. He wanted all the arts together in one place and believed that there were no divisions between handicrafts and sculpture or painting. Gropius wrote: "Together let us desire, conceive, and create the new structure of the future, which will embrace architecture and sculpture and painting in one unity."[173] Gropius fittingly used Lyonel Feininger's "Cathedral" woodcut as a main image for the ideals of the newly founded college of design in 1919.[174]

At the Bauhaus, architecture was considered the premier art form, and music was given very little consideration. The manifesto stated that architecture was the highest art form in that it brings everything together into a new totality, an *Einheitskunstwerk*, or a single unified structure with coherence inside and out.[175] Gropius's vision of a complete work of art was different from the Wagnerian *Gesamtkunstwerk*, which emanated from a single mastermind, in that it could only be accomplished by mutual artistic cooperation. He specifically hoped to revive the Gothic spirit of cooperation between diverse guilds to build a unified masterwork. Like Busoni, he looked to a past age with nostalgia even while looking forward with a vision to create the new cathedral of the future in which all parts of the building were just as integrated: "The architect, the Meister vom Stuhl (the master of the lodge),

[173] Walter Gropius, "Bauhaus Manifesto and Program [1919]," http://mariabuszek.com/mariabuszek/kcai/ConstrBau/Readings/GropBau19.pdf (accessed May 8, 2018). [Wollen, erdanken, erschaffen wir gemeinsamen den neuen Bau der Zukunft, der alles in einer Gestalt sein wird: Architektur und Plastik und Malerei.] Gropius, Das Bauhaus Manifest [1919]," https://theoria.art-zoo.com/de/das-bauhaus-manifest/#:~:text=Wollen%2C%20erdenken%2C%20erschaffen%20wir%20gemeinsam,Walter%20Gropius%2C%20Weimar%2C%201919 (accessed Sept. 26, 2022).

[174] Magdalena Bushart, "Am Anfang ein Missverständnis. Feiningers 'Kathedrale' und das Bauhaus-Manifest," in *Bauhaus-Archiv Berlin/Museum für Gestaltung, Stiftung Bauhaus Dessau und Klassik Stiftung Weimar: Modell Bauhaus*, ed. by Hatte Cantz (Ostfildern: Kulturstiftung des Bundes, 2009), 29–32; Walter Gropius, Manifesto and Programme of the Weimar State Bauhaus, April 1919, https://www.bauhaus100.de/en/past/works/education/manifest-und-programm-des-staatlichen-bauhauses (accessed March 25, 2018).

[175] Walter Gropius, "Programm des Staatlischen Bauhauses in Weimar," Beinecke Rare Book and Manuscript Library, Yale University. https://collections.library.yale.edu/catalog/2107189 (accessed Sept. 27, 2022). This term was used in the Bauhaus manifesto to describe the ideal artwork and appears to have been coined at the Bauhaus: "The Bauhaus strives for the collection of all artistic creativity for the unification of all artistic disciplines—sculpture, painting, applied arts and crafts—to a new architecture as its inseparable components. The last, albeit distant, goal of the Bauhaus is the unified work of art (Einheitskunstwerk)—the great building—in which there is no boundary between monumental and decorative art." [Das Bauhaus erstrebt die Sammlung alles künstlerischen Schaffens zur Einheit, die Wiedervereinigung aller werkkünstlerischen Disziplinen—Bildhauerei, Malerei, Kunstgewerbe und Handwerk—zu einer neuen Baukunst als deren unablösliche Bestandteile. Das letzte, wenn auch ferne Ziel des Bauhauses ist das Einheitskunstwerk—der große Bau—, in dem es keine Grenze gibt zwischen monumentaler und dekorativer Kunst.] Gropius, Bauhaus Manifesto of 1919, quoted in *The Walter Gropius Archive: An Illustrated Catalogue of the Drawings, Prints, and Photographs in the Walter Gropius Archive at the Busch-Reisinger Museum, Harvard University*, Vol. 1, ed. John C. Harkness (New York: Garland Publishing and Harvard University Art Museums, 1990), xxi.

should gather around himself all like-minded workers from all professions in order to prepare the 'future cathedral of freedom' in a new living and working community in the spirit of the medieval guilds."[176] His ideal was of a building that not only had a skillfully formed shape, but that was unified inside and out from the largest design to the smallest details through the cooperation of different types of architects and artists:

> The ultimate aim of all visual arts is the complete building! To embellish buildings was once the noblest function of the fine arts; they were the indispensable components of great architecture ["Baukunst"]. Today the arts exist in isolation, from which they can be rescued only through the conscious, cooperative effort of all the craftsmen. Architects, painters, and sculptors must recognize anew and learn to grasp the composite character of building both as an entity and in its separate parts. Only then will their work be imbued with the architectonic spirit, which it has lost as "salon art."[177]

This *Einheitskunstwerk*, as it was called at the Bauhaus, was first embodied in a luxurious villa, the Sommerfeld House (1920–1921) built for Adolf Sommerfeld in Berlin and designed by Walter Gropius and Adolf Meyer. Everything was integrated, even if multiple people worked on different aspects of its design. Geometric forms in two or three dimensions as well as textures on wood and clearly defined angles served as unifying motifs throughout the house, including in the entrance door, the curtains, and the stairs. The overall architectural design appears to be an expansion of Frank Lloyd Wright's Prairie Houses. However, the emphasis on geometric shapes contrasts with Wright's more natural and irregular shapes. Decorations inside and out are inseparable from the building as a whole. Building was thus a social, intellectual, and symbolic activity. It reconciled previously diverse

[176] Gropius, Bauhaus Manifesto of 1919, xxi.

[177] Gropius, Bauhaus Manifesto of 1919, quoted in *The Theory of Decorative Art: An Anthology of European and American Writings: 1750–1940*, ed. Isabelle Frank (New Haven, CT: Yale University Press, 2000), 83. [Das Endziel aller bildnerischen Tätigkeit ist der Bau! Ihn zu schmücken war einst die vornehmste Aufgabe der bildenden Künste, sie waren unablösliche Bestandteile der grossen Baukunst. Heute stehen sie in selbstgenügsamer Eigenheit, aus der sie erst wieder erlöst werden können durch Bewusstes Mit- und Ineinanderwirken aller Werkleute untereinander. Architekten, Maler und Bildhauer müssen die vielgliedrige Gestalt des Baues in seiner Gesamtheit und in seinen Teilen wieder kennen und begreifen lernen, dann werden sich von selbst ihre Werke wieder mit architektonischem Geiste füllen, den sie in der Salonkunst verloren.] Gropius, "Bauhaus-Manifest [1919]."

disciplines into one. It also leveled social classes. All were artists contributing to the cathedral of the future.

As Joshua Barone has noted, if music was not a central subject at the Bauhaus, it was central to Bauhaus thought. Some artists translated musical characteristics into their artistic creations. Other artists were close friends and collaborators with composers:

> The school never had a proper music department. But musical thinking permeated the lives of its students and faculty. Some took a synesthetic approach to color and tone or used the language of symphonies to transcribe their work; many were amateur instrumentalists who came together in an exuberant, ad hoc band; and some also cultivated relationships with groundbreaking composers, including Schoenberg and Stravinsky.[178]

Several members of the Bauhaus were amateur musicians, such as Lyonel Feininger, who played the music of J. S. Bach, and Paul Klee, who was a Mozart aficionado. In some cases, music affected their visual art; Wassily Kandinsky, for instance, appreciated the music of Arnold Schoenberg.[179] Both Kandinsky and Klee were visual artists who explored the relationship between space (visual) and time (aural) in their work.[180] Kandinsky specifically saw parallels between dissonance in music and contemporary abstract painting. Klee also contributed to the creation of syncretic spaces believing that sound and appearance could now come together through polyphony. There were also ad hoc performances by students and student-led ensembles. Moreover, the ideas of movement and synesthesia were also central to

[178] Joshua Barone, "At the Bauhaus, Music Was More Than a Hobby," *New York Times* (August 23, 2019). See also Stephanie Probst, "Pen, Paper, Steel"; Fontaine, "Ausdruck und Konstruktion"; Christopher Metzger, "Die Künstlerische Bach-Rezeption bei Paul Klee und Lyonel Feininger," in *Musikwissenschaft zwischen Kunst, Ästhetik und Experiment: Festschrift Helga de la Motte-Haber zum 60. Geburtstag*, ed. Reinhard Kopiez (Würzburg: Königshausen und Neumann, 1998), 371–85; Christoph Vitali, ed., *Paul Klee und die Musik: Schirn-Kusthalle Frankfurt, 14 Juni bis 17 August 1986* (Berlin: Nicolaische Verlagsbuchhandlung, 1986).

[179] Architecture was not part of the regular curriculum at the Bauhaus until around 1927. Prior to that time, Gropius worked independently with some students. One reason for this dearth is that architecture was considered the greatest art form and could not be taught until students had first mastered other crafts. For more on music and the Bauhaus, see Alexander K. Rothe, "Dramaturgy of Sound: Bauhaus, Music, Technology," https://alexanderkrothemusicology.wordpress.com/2019/01/01/dramaturgy-of-sound-bauhaus-music-technology/, posted January 1, 2019 (accessed August 19, 2019).

[180] For more information about the bringing together of spatial and temporal art forms in the modernist period, see Albright, *Untwisting the Serpent*.

Bauhaus teachings and impacted the way the visual arts were taught and created.

Although Gropius intentionally overlooked music in the Bauhaus in terms of instruction, music was brought into the mix of arts during the grand exhibition of 1923, in which artists displayed their crafts, drawings, architectural designs, and more. The first week of the exhibition, known as the Bauhaus week, featured performances by some of Europe's leading modernist composers, such as Igor Stravinsky (*L'histoire du soldat*, conducted by Hermann Scherchen/narrated by Carl Ebert), Paul Hindemith (*Das Marienleben*, Op. 27, performed by Beatrice Lauer-Kottler), Ernst Krenek (Concerto Grosso), and Busoni (Six Short Pieces for Piano, performed by Egon Petri).[181] Gropius opened the 1923 exhibition on August 15, 1923, with a lecture on art and technology, and Kandinsky spoke on synthetic art. There was also an impressive architecture exhibit (see table 1.1).[182]

Unlike Hindemith's *Marienleben* and Stravinsky's *L'histoire du soldat*, Busoni's piano pieces do not explicitly bring together the arts—they do not combine poetry or text and music in obvious ways. They are not connected to a literary or descriptive program. However, they represent the architectural music Busoni envisioned when he described his ideals of *Young Classicality*. They bring together spatial and temporal art forms in unique ways. In a very distinctive manner, they bring together the chromatic colors of neo-Gothic polyphony and the youthfulness, simplicity, and solid geometric structures of the neo-Hellenic, with an expanded tonal language. They are abstract and concise. They explore relationships between form and content in an idiosyncratic manner.

Busoni's pieces explore the new polyphony that he was interested in at the time and reflect ideals of the building of a new Gothic art. As Beaumont

[181] Howard Dearstyne, *Inside the Bauhaus*, ed. David Spaeth (London: Rizzoli International Publications, 1986). See also Magdalena Droste, *Bauhaus-Archiv: 1919–1933* (London: Taschen, 2002). In Weimar, van de Velde headed one of the most successful modern art colleges of the day. Notably absent was Schoenberg, along with his school of disciples, and it is unclear why they were not part of the exhibition.

[182] Herbert Bayer, ed., *Bauhaus, 1919–1928* (New York: The Museum of Modern Art, 1938), 85, https://www.moma.org/documents/moma_catalogue_2735_300190238.pdf (accessed May 8, 2018). For more information about the exhibition and Busoni's role, see Austin Clarkson, "The Would-Be Master Student: Stefan Wolpe and Ferruccio Busoni," in *On the Music of Stefan Wolpe: Essays and Recollections*, ed. Austin Clarkson, Dimension and Diversity Series 6, ed. Mark DeVoto (Hillsdale, NY: Pendragon Press, 2003), 1–31. For more information about music at the Bauhaus, see Clement Jewitt, "Music at the Bauhaus," *Tempo* 213 (July 2000): 5–11. See also Alexander K. Rothe, "Dramaturgy of Sound: Bauhaus, Music, Technology," https://alexanderkrothemusicology.wordpress.com/tag/ferruccio-busoni (accessed September 3, 2019).

Table 1.1. Weimar Bauhaus Week Program, 1923[a]

Aug. 15 (Wed.)
11 a.m.: Opening in the Vestibule of the Bauhaus
8 p.m.: Walter Gropius, "Kunst und Technik eine neue Einheit," lecture with pictures
Aug. 16 (Thurs.)
4 p.m.: Wassily Kandinsky, "Über synthetische Kunst," lecture
8 p.m.: Oskar Schlemmer, "Das triadische Ballett mit der Weimarischen Staatskapelle," performance
Aug. 17 (Fri.)
11:30 a.m.: Jacobus Johannes Pieter Oud, "Die Entwicklung der modernen Baukunst in Holland," lecture with pictures
8 p.m.: Stage Workshop of the State Bauhaus, "Mechanisches Kabarett" (Friedrich Wilhelm Bogler, Marcel Breuer, Oskar Schlemmer, Jurt Schmidt, Joost Schmidt, Kurt Schwerdtfeger, Georg Teltscher, Andor Weininger, music by Hans Heinz Stuckenschmidt), performance
Aug. 18 (Sat.)
10:30 a.m.: Film presentation compiled by the Staatlichen Bauhaus. Comenius Film Company. Educational film and films by the Ufa Culture Department. Microscopic, slow-motion, and time-lapse recordings.
8 p.m.: Paul Hindemith, *Marienlieder* (first performance), with soprano Beatrice Lauer-Kottlar and pianist Emma Lübbeke-Job; and Ferruccio Busoni, *Sechs Klavierstücke* (four premieres), with pianist Egon Petri, performances
Aug. 19 (Sun.)
11 a.m.: Ernst Krenek, Concerto Grosso, directed by Hermann Scherchen, six solo instruments and string orchestra of the Weimarischen Staatskapelle, and Igor Stravinsky, *Die Geschichte vom Soldaten* with narrator K. Ebert, soldier F. Odemar, and devil H. Schramm, performances

[a] Information for this table is derived from the "Bauhaus Woche Programme, August 1923," reproduced in *Das Staatliche Bauhaus in Weimar: Dokumente zur Geschichte des Instituts 1919–1926*, ed. Volker Wahl, Historische Kommission für Thüringen, vol. 15 (Cologne: Böhlau, 2009), 300.

notes, the original title emphasized the polyphony that threads throughout each of the pieces: "Three Pieces for the Cultivation of Polyphonic Part-Playing."[183] The first is like an invention, but very chromatic. The second piece is a two-part canon based on a three-note motive that weaves in and out of a flowing and decorative accompaniment that forms intervals of thirds and sixths. The canon, by contrast, features only seconds, fifths, and inversions. The third piece features a chorale melody as cantus firmus in three-part canonic imitation. The fourth piece is a prelude and fugue, and the fifth is an arrangement of music from Mozart's *Die Zauberflöte* ("Zwei geharnischte Männer," act II, Finale). Mozart's music features the chorale melody, "Ach

[183] Beaumont, *Busoni the Composer*, 301.

Gott vom Himmel sich darein," which was previously set by J. S. Bach and several other composers, including Jan Pieterszoon Sweelinck, Johann Pachelbel, and Heinrich Schütz. Although the first fifty-six measures of Busoni's setting largely transcribe Mozart's piece, his added ending changes the material, making it more complicated by adding in paired sixteenth-note accompanimental figures from the act II terzett sung by the angelic trio of boys. At the same time, he made it more Bachian by adding ornamentation (trills) and a four-voice polyphonic texture beginning in measure 63.

In addition to exploring different contrapuntal approaches in individual pieces, the compositions combine to form a complete architectural whole. The key areas suggest a large-scale structure that is supported as well by balanced tempi and styles. Together, the short pieces form a "strong and beautiful form," as Busoni described it, that has symmetry, and yet that represents continuous variation. Unlike in a Baroque suite, the pieces are all in different keys. As finally combined into a group of seven, they follow a cycle of keys of ascending fourths, except for the first two, which are in parallel major and minor keys. Each key change lends subtle color variations to the whole, yet still contributes to an overall sense of proportion and symmetry. The keys and tempo indications are as follows (see table 1.2):

In addition, individual movements blend a spinning out inherent to polyphony with an overall aural sense of Classical proportion, conciseness, and continuous variation. For instance, the piece in E minor contains a ten-bar chordal introduction that returns at the end; yet on the return it is only nine bars in length, and it has added figural polyphony. In the middle of the piece, passagework continuously spins out even as a cantus firmus melody that

Table 1.2. Overall Structure of Busoni's *Sieben kurze Stücke zur Pflege des polyphonen Spiels*

Piece Number	Key	Tempo Marking
1.	E Major	*Preludietto—Allegro*
2.	E Minor	*Sostenuto*
3.	A Minor	*Andante molto tranquillo e legato*
4.	D Minor/D Major	*Allegro*
5.	G Major	*Preludio—Andante tranquillo*
6.	C Minor	*Adagio—nach Mozart*
7.	F Major	*Andante tranquillo*

Example 1.4. Busoni, Piece no. 1 from the *Fünf kurze Stücke zur Pflege des polyphonen Spiels*, mm. 1–10. (Piece no. 2 from *Sieben kurze Stücke zur Pflege des polyphonen Spiels.*)

weaves through treble and middle voices provides regular punctuation and symmetry (10 bars, 8 bars, 8 bars, 10 bars) (see examples 1.4 and 1.5).

If the piece has a clear frame, thereby contributing to a solid and beautiful form, the opening material is altered when it returns at the end of the piece, thereby evoking a sense of continuous variation and development. The opening and closing sections not only vary in texture, but also affect. While the first ten bars feature sustained chords and creeping chromatic lines, the final nine bars are marked *tranquillo* and sound ethereal as the subtle chromatic sixteenth notes weave a fine polyphonic web of sound.

At the same time, chromaticism aids the expansion of tonality using a variety of approaches that reflect Busoni's desire to combine a multiplicity of possibilities into a new polyharmony: atonality, polytonal polyphony, symmetrical inversion of the harmonic order, and atypical chord formations resulting from brand-new scales.[184] Lines moving in parallel motion suggest different keys. Harmonic progressions in this piece are also nontraditional, as chords and figurations pass through key areas, creating a sense of tonal mutability that at times, suggest atonality. For instance, although the second piece starts with a doubled E (representing two voices) in the bass, and ends with a

[184] Busoni, "The New Harmony [Jan. 1911]," in *The Essence of Music and Other Papers*, 24.

Example 1.5. Busoni, Piece no. 1 from the *Fünf kurze Stücke zur Pflege des polyphonen Spiels*, mm. 47–55. (Piece no. 2 from *Sieben kurze Stücke zur Pflege des polyphonen Spiels.*)

weak E minor cadence, the tonality is not evident throughout. Symmetrical inversion of ascending and descending chromatic lines allow the piece to move freely through remote regions, at times, without a clear center. In the opening measure, the initial E whole note in the tenor voice changes significance as the chords surrounding it move to remote areas and to complex chromatic chords, such as to D♭, F♯ ninth, and G-augmented ninth chords. The tonality is ambiguous and extended throughout. Because the tonality is obscure at the beginning, Busoni omits the key signature, opting instead for marking each accidental individually. The conciseness of the shifts in language and the multiplicity of approaches are what mark Busoni's mature treatment of the musical language.

In addition, Busoni's writing is relatively thin, transparent, and economic—more Mozartian, even despite the slippery chromatic polyphony. It is a blending of ideals into a new musical architecture. It represents his vision of a Young Classical art seamlessly growing out of timeless compositional tools that nevertheless embraced the more austere and concise ideals of Busoni's own age.

Syncretic Art and Building Music of the Future

Busoni's compositions thus evolved as he matured, and in response to the artistic stimuli in his artistic circle; the *Sieben kurze Stücke zur Pflege des polyphonen Spiels* represent a newfound conciseness, abstractness, and variety of the treatment of the musical language that functions within and with structure. They embody his unique theories about the writing of architectural music.

Busoni joined other thinkers, architects, and artists of his generation searching for a holistic art form, and one in which architecture represented greatness. Wolfgang Hildesheimer claims that architectural metaphors encouraged a mindset that composers were builders contributing throughout the centuries to a master cathedral, each adding new and better ideas. History itself becomes a building stone for the future artwork:

> Previously, objectivity had prevailed, concealing the creative impulse (Bach's fugues = mathematics, etc.). Although this objectivity has not been elevated to a preclassical principle or ascribed to a more primitive stage of music's expressive capability, the idea of a greater individual expression

> persists as an implied truth even into this century. It serves to encourage a viewpoint by which we are to see music history as a large building, like a Gothic cathedral, on which different masters have worked at different times, knowing that they would not live to see the crowning climax, and compelled to reconcile themselves to one part in the work.[185]

Many "music builders" of the early twentieth century acknowledged or constructed a lineage in which they participated, such as Schoenberg, who saw himself as connected to earlier German composers, such as Bach and Beethoven, but his emphasis was on freeing himself from traditional tonality to reach toward a new musical language, even if he still embraced past forms. Busoni similarly saw himself as connected to a long lineage of composers, including Bach and Mozart, and attempted to continue building upon the musical "foundation" they had laid in his compositions; he aspired to be part of a musical genealogy, but he hoped to explicitly assimilate previous experiments seamlessly into a new oneness, even while reaching toward an ever-elusive ideal of perfection. In Busoni's words, art was also changing and evolving:

> This art will be old and new at the same time at first. We are steering in that direction, luckily, consciously or unconsciously. But this art, in order to arise intact in its newness, so that it will mean a genuine result to the historian, will be founded upon many hypotheses, which today are not yet fully apprehended.[186]

These not yet fully realized hypotheses are explored in Busoni's mature compositions, which blend historical compositional techniques of counterpoint and a new vision for polyharmony within solid, as well as new and unique, structures characterized by abstractness and economy of expression.

Busoni's continued embrace of tonality and musical traditions even while experimenting with new scales and systems was hardly retrogressive or

[185] Wolfgang Hildesheimer, *Mozart*, trans. Marion Faber (New York: Farrar, Straus & Giroux, 1982), 38.

[186] Busoni, letter of January 1920 to Paul Bekker, in *The Essence and Oneness of Music*, 20–21. [Diese Kunst wird alt und neu zugleich sein—zuerst. Dahin steuern wir—glücklicherweise—bewusst und unbewusst, willig oder mitgerissen. Diese kunst soll aber—um in ihrer Neuheit rein zu erstehen, um dem Historiker wirklich ein Ergebnis zu bedeuten—auf mehreren Vorausetzungen basieren, die heute noch nicht völlig erkannt sind.] Busoni, "Junge Klassizität," in *Von der Einheit*, 277.

anachronistic, even if it was idiosyncratic.[187] It was based on a vision of the future of music that was as varied and open as possible even as it was indelibly connected to history. It was a vision that Busoni implemented, if imperfectly, in his own compositions in the 1920s. If historicist modernism was not unprecedented in Germany around 1900, the way he looked back historically to the music of multiple composers, such as both Bach and Mozart, as a means to discover ways to move beyond the excesses of late romanticism through *Young Classicality* was idiosyncratic. His specific architectural-musical thinking was also idiosyncratic and contributed not only to new ideas about the expansion of the musical language, but also to ideas about how to approach form, timbre, space, and sound, as will be discussed in the following chapters.

Just how important, unique, and influential Busoni's ideas and compositions ultimately were is only beginning to be discovered. It is worth noting that his open approach to the musical language foreshadowed the multiplicity of sounds and procedures in the Postmodern era and directly impacted unorthodox treatments of serialism. It is fitting that even when many of his students and followers adopted serialism, such as Eduard Steuermann, Stefan Wolpe, Wladimir Vogel, and Ernst Krenek, they did it in non-orthodox manners that included tonal treatments of rows.[188] Wolpe, for instance, combined tonal, octatonic, and dodecaphonic procedures, while Krenek's evolution culminated in what he called a general "relaxation of [his] compositional technique."[189] For instance, he employed modal treatments of the row and switched pitches in hexachords. Moreover, many of Busoni's pupils, including Otto Luening, Philipp Jarnach, and Louis Gruenberg, kept an open mind about tonality even when dodecaphony seemed like the only real option for a serious composer in the post–World War I era.[190]

At the same time, this chapter has demonstrated the importance of other influences on the formation of Busoni's ideas about music. In looking to the great architectural edifices of the past, he saw possibilities for the rejuvenation of music composition in the present. The new idealistic approach that Busoni envisioned and implemented in his mature compositions was informed by

[187] For more information about similar approaches in the pieces of Nordic and British composers, consult the introduction.

[188] For more information on this topic, see Knyt, "Intersections, Divergences, and Cross Sections: Eduard Steuermann, the Busoni-Schoenberg Nexus, and a Broadening of Compositional Procedures in the Twentieth Century," *Journal of Musicological Research* 41:1 (2022): 105–32.

[189] Krenek, "A Composer's Influences," *Perspectives of New Music* 3:1 (Autumn–Winter 1964): 40.

[190] See Knyt, *Busoni and His Legacy* (Bloomington: Indiana University Press, 2017).

his vision of ways to take aspects from past historical architectural trends and blend them together with ideas for a new and experimental musical present, even as it was fostered by an intense personal knowledge of architecture. He understood relations between ornamentation and decoration in concrete ways. He knew about proportions, shapes, and the acoustics within structures, and he wanted that for his *Tonkunst* as well. He was not just referring to an ambiguous notion of the dark Gothic or Classical serenity. He understood the nuances of color, shade, variation, expansiveness, optical illusions, and spatial variation that come about from placing stone upon stone or marble slab upon slab, and he attempted to bring the same level of nuance to his compositions, even as he realized that perfection was continually elusive.

In the process of bringing these two art forms together in idealistic ways, he was simultaneously forging his own notions of music as autonomous, but also informed by other arts. In looking outside of music, he was participating in his own modernist age, a *Zeitgeist*, in which a there was a call for a general unification of the arts that extended well beyond the Wagnerian concept of the *Gesamtkunstwerk* toward a unification of temporal and spatial art forms, including architecture. This new oneness considered not only the external structure, but internal content as well. Yet while many contemporaries, such as van de Velde, were interested in learning how music could be a model for the visual arts, Busoni envisioned how architecture could serve as a model for music. He thought not only in metaphorical terms of greatness and vague stylistic categories of architecture, although that too played a role, but also of concrete applications of architectural models to music. In Busoni's idiosyncratic approach, this applied not only to his approach toward the musical language. Another connection he made was with form, when he sought to create forms as unique and varied as buildings, an aspect that will be explored in chapter 2, even as he aspired to create music that was as inclusive and as innovative as long-lasting; he sought after a new classic art that would endure just like the edifices he most admired:

> Now there is an absolute, demonstrable beauty and perfection and there are things that please certain people at certain times and will be look upon as beautiful by them. Whichever direction the work of art adopts it falls ultimately to one of two destinies, it either remains lost or becomes a classic.[191]

[191] Busoni, "What Is Happening at the Present Time," in *The Essence of Music*, 42. The original manuscript was discovered posthumously and without date or title.

2
Busoni's Architectural Structures

> In the face of all you must have heard—more or less directly—about my concerto, I feel the need to assure you that I have created a work for every note of which I can answer, and which will endure, inasmuch as human achievements are at all durable.
>
> —Busoni, 1904[1]

> The façade of a monumental building means nothing more to the architect than the binding of a book does to a bibliophile.
>
> —Busoni, unknown date[2]

Busoni thought architecturally about form. In his quest for solid and unique forms, he sought coherence between the material and overall design. Architectural models, in conjunction with forms found in nature, provided him with idiosyncratic ideas about how to move beyond traditional formal molds to create the new musical structures that he described in his theories of *Young Classicality.* In at least two pieces, the Piano Concerto, BV 247 (1906), and the two-piano version of the *Fantasia contrappuntistica*, BV 256b (1922), Busoni illustrated his conception of the compositional structures visually with architectural drawings.[3] In these instances,

[1] Busoni, letter of November 16, 1904, to Robert Freund, in Busoni, *Selected Letters*, ed. and trans. Antony Beaumont (New York: Columbia University Press, 1987), 72. Thanks are due Erika Babatz (Bauhaus-Archiv Berlin), Christiana Herrgott (Klassik Stiftung, Weimar), Evelyn Liepsch (Goethe-und Schiller-Archiv in Weimar), Jean-Christophe Gero (Staatsbibliothek zu Berlin), Marina Gordienko (Staatsbibliothek zu Berlin), and Annette Otterbach (Bildarchiv Foto Marburg) for their assistance locating archival materials for this chapter.

[2] [Die Façade eines Monumentalen Gebäudes bedeutet dem Architekten nicht mehr als dem Bibliophilen der Buchen eines Einbandes.] Busoni, "Aphorismen," Staatsbibliothek zu Berlin–Preußischer Kulturbesitz, Musikabteilung mit Mendelssohn-Archiv, Nachl. F. Busoni CI, 103.

[3] Busoni's *Fantasia contrappuntistica* exists in three versions (1910, 1912, 1922). The 1912 version is a shortened adaptation of the 1910 version. The 1922 version is scored for two pianos and more closely resembles the 1910 version.

Ferruccio Busoni as Architect of Sound. Erinn E. Knyt, Oxford University Press. © Oxford University Press 2023.
DOI: 10.1093/oso/9780197625491.003.0003

specific buildings or styles of buildings inspired his idiosyncratic formal approaches. However, he was not attempting to mimic their shapes. Instead, he borrowed concepts from architecture to expand structural possibilities in music.

Through close readings of letters, drawings, programs, memoirs, and sketches, in conjunction with analyses of Busoni's compositions, this chapter reveals how architecture provided Busoni with ideas about how to move beyond traditional formal models to create unique structures. Busoni sought inspiration in natural and architectural forms in the early 1900s. In the 1910s he created multi-dimensional architectural montage structures. In the 1920s, his structures also included the fragmentation and combination of smaller discrete forms in a cubist manner.[4]

While revealing Busoni's indebtedness to architecture for his musical structures, this chapter also shows parallels between Busoni's ideas and those in his *Zeitgeist*. For instance, it brings to light parallels between Oskar Schlemmer's "ambulant architecture" in the *Triadisches Ballet* and Busoni's textural layering in *Arlecchino*, BV 270.[5] At the same time, the chapter reveals how ideas from different art forms contributed to Busoni's structural ideas that departed from what other contemporaneous composers were doing. In the process, it simultaneously contributes new knowledge about ways shared early twentieth-century artistic ideals spanned across the arts.[6]

[4] Although Busoni does not seem to have used the term cubist in reference to his own work, he was friends with cubist artists, such as Umberto Boccioni, whose famous painting of Busoni uses cubist techniques.

[5] Philipp Jarnach completed *Doktor Faust* in 1925 (Busoni, *Doktor Faust*, completed by Philipp Jarnach, piano reduction by Egon Petri and Michael van Zadora [Leipzig: Breitkopf & Härtel, 1925]). Beaumont has also created his own version (Busoni, *Doktor Faust*, edited and completed by Antony Beaumont [Wiesbaden: Breitkopf & Härtel, 1984]), and Larry Sitsky has created his own ending as well. For details about Sitsky's ending, see Judith Crispin, "Introducing Larry Sitsky's New Ending for Ferruccio Busoni's *Doktor Faust*," in *Ereignis und Exegese: Musikalische Interpretation, Interpretation der Musik*, Festschrift für Hermann Danuser zum 65. Geburtstag, ed. Camilla Bork et al. (Schliengen: Edition Argus, 2011), 539–51. For information about Beaumont's ending, see Beaumont, "Busoni's *Doktor Faust:* A Reconstruction and Its Problems," *Musical Times* 126:1718 (1986): 196–99.

[6] See, for instance, Daniel Albright, *Untwisting the Serpent: Modernism in Music, Literature, and Other Arts* (Chicago: University of Chicago Press, 2000); Albright, *Putting Modernism Together: Literature, Music, and Painting: 1872–1927*, Hopkins Studies in Modernism, ed. Douglas Mao (Baltimore: Johns Hopkins University Press, 2015); Walter Frisch, *German Modernism: Music and the Arts*, California Studies in 20th Century Music (Berkeley: University of California Press, 2005); David Roberts, *The Total Work of Art in European Modernism*, Signale: Modern German Letters, Cultures, and Thought (Ithaca, NY: Cornell University Press, 2011).

Busoni's Forms: A Melding of Architecture and Nature

Busoni's ideas about form in the early 1900s brought together two seemingly opposing impulses: imitation of nature and architecture. He thereby distanced himself from what he believed to be artificially imposed traditional musical formal molds.[7] Moreover, he did not limit himself to the major and minor scales that were foundational to those forms.[8] At the same time, he criticized music that was organized either according to established musical forms or extra-musical programs. For instance, the following paragraph from 1907 expresses some of his concerns about musical structures shaped around programs:

> The motive in a composition with a program bears within itself the same natural necessity; but it must, even in its earliest phase of development, renounce its own proper mode of growth to mold or, rather, twist itself to fit the needs of the program. Thus, turned aside, at the outset, from the path traced by nature, it finally arrives at a wholly unexpected climax, whither it has been led, not by its own organization, but by the way laid down in the program, or the action, or the philosophical idea.[9]

Instead, in the early 1900s, he sought to emulate structures from nature. Like several German authors and theorists before him, such as Johann Wolfgang von Goethe and A. B. Marx, Busoni found his model for artistic forms in plant life.[10] He maintained that compositions should achieve a synthesis between form and content. To illustrate this, he cited a metaphor from

[7] Busoni, *Sketch of a New Esthetic of Music*, trans. Th. Baker (New York: G. Schirmer, 1911), 3.

[8] Busoni, *Sketch*, 6. Busoni, *Entwurf einer neuen Ästhetik der Tonkunst*, ed. Martina Weindel (Wilhelmshaven: Florian Noetzel, 2001), 15. The universality of musical material, deriving from a common primordial source, philosophically speaking, made all musical styles similar and perceptible as "one," as forming a unity. This primordial source, as Busoni envisioned it, consisted of inaudible tones and rhythms emanating from the vibrating universe and contained all musical possibilities; it encompassed all thematic, stylistic, scalar, harmonic, registral, or timbral possibilities imaginable for all compositions of all times. The composer's job, according to Busoni, was to perceive these multiple possibilities and use them as fully as possible within individual compositions. For more about Busoni's views of absolute music, see Knyt, "Ferruccio Busoni and the Absolute in Music: Nature, Form, and *Idee*," *Journal of the Royal Musical Association* 137:1 (May 2012): 35–69.

[9] Busoni, *Sketch of a New Esthetic of Music*, 10. [Das Klangmotiv des programmusikalischen Werkes birgt die nämlichen Bedingungen in sich; es muss aber—schon bei seiner nächsten Entwicklungsphase—sich nicht nach dem eigenen Gesetz, sondern nach dem des "Programmes" formen, vielmehr "krümmen." Dergestalt, gleich in der ersten Bildung aus dem naturgesetzlichen Wege gebracht, gelangt es schliesßlich zu einem ganz unerwarteten Gipfel, wohin nicht seine Organisation, sondern das Programm, die Handlung, die philosophische Idee vorsätzlich es geführt.] Busoni, *Entwurf*, 20.

[10] See Scott Burnham, *Musical Form in the Age of Beethoven: Selected Writings on Theory and Method by Adolf Bernhard Marx*, ed. and trans. Scott Burnham, Cambridge Studies in Theory and

nature: germinal material in plants unfolds into unique structures with idiosyncratic shapes that differ in color, shape, and structure, just as motives in music unfold into compositions with individualized forms:

> Every motive—so it seems to me—contains, like a seed, its life-germ within itself. From the different plant-seeds grow different families of plants, dissimilar in form, foliage, blossom, fruit, growth and color. Even each individual plant belonging to one and the same species assumes, in size, form and strength, a growth peculiar to itself. And so, in each motive, there lies the embryo of its fully developed form; each one must unfold itself differently, yet each obediently follows the law of eternal harmony. This form is imperishable, though each be unlike every other.[11]

Busoni's distinction between the motive and the "life-germ" [*Trieb*] contained within the motive is one of the most original aspects of the passage. The *Trieb* probably refers here to the human spark, the *Idee*. Busoni considered each musical work to begin with an *Idee* drawn from human experience that became an abstract musical conception, an *Einfall*. This *Idee* emanated from the mind of the creator and was not a strictly musical *Idee* as it was for others, such as Arnold Schoenberg, for instance.[12] The musical motive, for Busoni, was a concrete translation of the *Einfall* that would then grow into a complete work.

He also maintained that each musical artwork should have a unique "grammar" based on the infinite variety of scalar and harmonic possibilities found in nature. This, in turn, facilitated the creation of unique structures that were not bound to conventional harmonic progressions. Busoni believed in an all-encompassing source of music that contained all possible scales and harmonies, and that echoes Platonic theories of the Harmony of

Analysis, ed. Ian Bent (Cambridge: Cambridge University Press, 1997); Johann Wolfgang von Goethe, *Scientific Studies*, ed. and trans. Douglas Miller (New York: Suhrkamp Publishers, 1988).

[11] Busoni, *Sketch of a New Esthetic of Music*, 11. [Jedes Motiv—so will es mir scheinen—enthält wie ein Samen seinen Trieb in sich. Verschiedene Pflanzensamen treiben verschiedene Pflanzenarten, an Form, Blättern, Blüten, Früchten, Wuchs und Farben voneinander abweichend. Selbst eine und dieselbe Pflanzengattung wächst an Ausdehnung, Gestalt und Kraft, in jedem Exemplar selbständig geartet. So liegt in jedem Motiv schon seine vollgereifte Form vorbestimmt; jedes einzelne muss sich anders entfalten, doch jedes folgt darin der Notwendigkeit der ewigen Harmonie. Diese form bleibt unzerstörbar, doch niemals sich gleich.] Busoni, *Entwurf*, 19.

[12] For more information about Busoni's use of these terms, see Knyt, "How I Compose: Ferruccio Busoni's Views about Invention, Quotation, and the Compositional Process," *Journal of Musicology* 27:2 (Spring 2010): 224–64.

the Spheres.[13] He contended that the musical materials emanated from an inaudible heavenly source of music that had to be divined by the composers. In this, Busoni did not simply revise ancient theories about the harmony of the spheres, but drew specific links between the art of composition and this inaudible source: "Just as everything undiscovered was in being from the beginning, and is therefore also now in being; so, too, the cosmic atmosphere teems with all forms, motives, and combinations of past and future music."[14] Based on this concept of a vast natural source of music, he argued for an expansion of scalar possibilities, claiming that major and minor scales were just two of over 100 possibilities:[15] "What we now call our Tonal System is nothing more than a set of 'signs,' an ingenious device to grasp somewhat of that eternal harmony; a meager pocket-edition of that encyclopedic work; artificial light instead of the sun."[16]

At the same time, Busoni looked to architecture for models of solid forms for his musical works. He claimed that structure elevated the musical material to *Tonkunst*: "It is the form which first raises conception, intention, and direction to the rank of a work of art."[17] Architectural models provided him with examples of ways to reconcile natural forms and structure, even if, as he acknowledged, music is inherently different in its temporal liquidity.[18]

Busoni distinguished between what he perceived as effective and ineffective approaches to architectural structure using the term "architectonic" [*architektonisch*] in 1907, as opposed to "architecture" [*Architektur*].[19] As Carl

[13] For more about some of Busoni's aesthetic ideas, see Martina Weindel, *Ferruccio Busonis Ästhetik in seinen Briefen und Schriften*, Veröffentlichungen zur Musikforschung 18 (Wilhelmshaven: Florian Noetzel, 1996).

[14] Busoni, "The Essence of Music: A Paving of the Way to an Understanding of the Everlasting Calendar [1924]," in *The Essence of Music and Other Papers*, trans. Rosamund Ley (New York: Philosophical Library, 1957), 197.

[15] Although Busoni himself failed to use many of these possibilities, his students were captivated by the possibilities and his ideas aided the reception of the experimental music of other composers. One example is Gunnar Johansen's embrace of Busoni's philosophies and the music of Harry Partch. Bob Gilmore, *Harry Partch: A Biography* (New Haven, CT: Yale University Press, 1998), 159.

[16] Busoni, *Sketch of a New Esthetic of Music*, 23. [Zeichen sind es auch, und nichts anderes, was wir heute unser "Tonsystem" nennen. Ein ingeniöser Behalf, etwas von jener ewigen Harmonie festzuhalten; eine kümmerliche Taschenausgabe jenes enzyklopädischen Werkes; künstliches Licht anstatt Sonne.] Busoni, *Entwurf*, 43–44.

[17] Busoni, "Proportion [1913]," in *The Essence of Music and Other Papers*, trans. Rosamond Ley (London: Rockliff, 1957), 34. [Erst die Form erhebt Einfall, Gesinnung und Richtung zum Range des Kunstwerkes.] Busoni, "Von der Proportionen," in *Von der Einheit der Musik* (Berlin: Max Hesses Verlag, 1922). For more information about architecture and form in the twentieth century, see Talbot Hamlin, *Forms and Functions of Twentieth Century Architecture* (New York: Columbia University Press, 1952).

[18] Busoni, *Sketch*, 2–3.

[19] Busoni, *Sketch*, 6.

Dahlhaus explains, the term *architektonisch* was commonly used in the twentieth century with regard to music to describe pieces with balanced phrases and periods as well as clear chord progressions and tonal areas.[20] Busoni equated symmetry at that time with a dehumanized approach that fell short of his ideal for musical structure. He stated: "This sort of music ought rather to be called 'architectonic,' 'symmetric,' or 'sectional'; and derives from the circumstance that certain composers poured their spirit and their emotion into just this mould as lying nearest them or their time."[21] Busoni likened this type of music to a shell with no spirit, claiming: "The composers sought and found this form as the aptest vehicle for communicating their ideas; their souls took flight and the lawgivers discover and cherish the garments Euphorion left behind on earth."[22] He likewise criticized those placing value on pieces based primarily on their use of traditional forms, stating that they "have retained the Form as a symbol, and made it into a fetish, a religion."[23]

Busoni urged composers, instead, to break away from "architectonic" rigidity to compose new and original "architectural" structures. He challenged composers to find congruence between the materials of music (sounding tones in limitless combinations) and the shapes in which composers placed those tones: "Is it not singular, to demand of a composer originality in all things, and to forbid it as regards form? No wonder that, once he becomes original, he is accused of 'formlessness.'"[24] Busoni contended that pieces should be shaped according to human ideas that are translated into music rather than according to notions of symmetry or harmonic progressions. He wanted each structure to be unique: "I am a worshipper of form! I have remained sufficiently Latin for that. But I demand—no! the organism of art demands—that every idea fashions its own form for itself; the organism—not I—revolts against having one single form for itself."[25]

20 Carl Dahlhaus, *Nineteenth-Century Music* (1980), trans. Bradford Robinson (Berkeley: University of California Press, 1989), 255.

21 Busoni, *Sketch*, 6–7.

22 Busoni, *Sketch*, 7. [Die Tondichter suchten und fanden diese Form als das geeignetste Mittel, ihre Gedanken mitzuteilen; sie entschwebten—und die Gesetzgeber entdeckten und verwahren Euphorions auf der Erde zurückgebliebene Gewänder.] Busoni, *Entwurf*, 15.

23 Busoni, *Sketch*, 7. [die Form als Symbol behalten und sie zum Schild, zur Glaubenslehre erhoben.] Busoni, *Entwurf*, 15.

24 Busoni, *Sketch*, 7. [Ists nicht eigentümlich, dass man vom Komponisten in allem Originalität fordert und dass man sie ihm in der Form verbietet?] Busoni, *Entwurf*, 16.

25 Busoni, "Open Letter to Hans Pfitzner," in *The Essence and Oneness of Music*, 18. [Ich bin ein Anbeter der Form! Dazu bin ich reichlich genug Romane geblieben. Aber ich vorlange—nein, das Organische der Kunst verlangt,—dass jede Idee ihre eigene Form sich selbst bilde.] Busoni, "Offener Brief an Hans Pfitzner," in *Von der Einheit*, 249.

It is not surprising that Busoni considered architecture to be an important structural model in the 1900s, because of its reconciliation of natural forms and unique structures. In the late 1800s and early 1900s, architects involved with the Arts and Crafts and *Jugendstil* movements found inspiration in natural forms when planning their buildings. This resulted in several different approaches, including the integration of ornament and structure, integration of the environment and the structure, and the search for unique structures that mimicked the shapes and asymmetry of natural forms. Given the widespread influence of the movements, Busoni would have observed numerous examples on his many concert tours and in everyday life in Berlin.

Frank Lloyd Wright, for instance, whose work Busoni would have encountered at the 1923 Bauhaus exhibition, if not earlier, believed that great artists must be in touch with nature and translate it into solid forms. He likened his art to the growth of a plant from the soil upward. Moreover, he argued that a building should appear to grow from its environment even as he sought to use colors found in nature. His rooms are rarely predictable shapes but are complicated horizontally and vertically by the addition of alcoves, L-shapes, lowered ceilings, and decks, for instance.[26] Images of the Robie House of 1910 (Chicago, Illinois) at the 1923 Bauhaus exhibition would have displayed many of the ideals Wright discussed in his writings. It was a complete work of art in terms of the furnishings, textiles, and furniture. Constructed in a Prairie style, it reflected the landscape and plant life of the Midwest. The many horizontal lines in the cantilevered eaves to the Roman brick veneer also reflected the prairie as much as human movement. The veneer highlighted horizontal lines, in that while vertical seams are filled with brick-colored mortar, the horizontal ones contain vivid cream-colored mortar. The form of the house revolved around the rectangle, in that the overall design consisted of two large rectangles adjacent to one another. In addition, the bricks are also rectangular.

However, Busoni had more extensive exposure to the work and ideas of van de Velde, who similarly sought to discover a relationship between the building and its environment as well as between the building, its inhabitant(s), and its creator.[27] An example is his private residence in Weimar, the Hohe Pappeln Haus, built in 1907. It is possible that Busoni saw it under construction while

[26] Frank Lloyd Wright, "The Architect [1900]," in *Essential Texts*, ed. Robert Twombly (New York: W. W. Norton, 2009).

[27] See chapter 1 for a description of the friendship between Busoni and van de Velde.

he was in Weimar in August 1907.[28] The house itself was situated within gardens and poplar trees and seemed to grow out of its natural surroundings—hence its name. The steeply sloped and asymmetrical, but broad, roof that peers out over straight stone walls covered in ivy and placed in a long and narrow asymmetrical shape bears some resemblance to the shape of white poplar trees. The asymmetrical exterior structure also relates to the interior content of the rooms, which were meant to be as artistic and expressive as functional. Eschewing traditional rectangular shapes, each room displays unusual angles and takes full advantage of natural light. Central to the house is the main living area and hallway. Growing out from this is the salon with a nearby study, the dining room, and the unusually shaped stairway to the upper floor. Built-in closets and cabinetry reflect the shapes of the rooms, as do the furniture and other adornments (see figure 2.1).

However, Busoni did not have to know architects personally, nor to look far to be aware of the newest *Jugendstil* buildings that sought to unite architectural and natural designs; edifices in that style were being built all over Berlin in the late nineteenth and early twentieth centuries. In 1894, Busoni and his family settled into an apartment in Charlottenburg on Kantstrasse 153, and shortly thereafter, the Theater des Westens was erected farther down the street (Kantstrasse 12);[29] the theater was an imposing building that mixed elements from the Renaissance and Empire styles together with emerging *Jugendstil*. The Busonis subsequently moved to several other locations in Charlottenburg, including Tauentzienstrasse 10 in 1895 and Augsburger Strasse 55 in 1902; both were near the zoological gardens.[30] Not far from these residences several prominent public *Jugendstil* style buildings were erected, including the historic Charlottenburg Stadtbad, the oldest public bath in Berlin, built from 1896 to 1898 under the direction of Paul Bratring. Erected with a steel frame covered in bricks, the impressive old building also contained numerous decorative structural elements patterned after nature, including rounded decorative moldings that surrounded square windows and latticework. Another prominent public *Jugendstil* style building in Charlottenburg was the Rathaus, built from 1899 to 1905 under the direction of architects Heinrich Reinhardt and Georg Süßenguth. Interior

[28] Busoni traveled to Weimar, arriving on August 4, 1907, in order to consult sources for the collective Liszt edition. For more about Busoni's connections to that city, consult the following source: Knyt, "Franz Liszt's Heir: Ferruccio Busoni and Weimar," *Nineteenth Century Music Review* 17:1 (April 2020): 35–67.

[29] Della Couling, *Ferruccio Busoni: A Musical Ishmael* (Lanham, MD: Scarecrow Press, 2005), 148.

[30] Couling, *Ferruccio Busoni*, 148.

Figure 2.1. Van de Velde's Weimar-Haus Hohe Pappeln. View from the south. Bildarchiv Foto Marburg. Photographer unknown. Photograph from c. 1915 to 1917.

stairwells and balconies were covered in plant-like filigree that resembled vines, and pillars extending from the floor to the ceilings resembled tree trunks. Curved asymmetrical stairways follow the lines of nature even as the impressive stone exterior contains structural ornamentation around the many windows.

In 1908, the Busonis moved to an apartment in Viktoria-Luise-Platz 11 in Schoenberg, an apartment that Busoni kept until the end of his life. Viktoria-Luise-Platz is a hexagonally shaped design by E. Deneke that is surrounded

Figure 2.2. Image of the Victoria-Luis-Platz on a postcard from 1908.

by residences, some of which were destroyed during World War II (see figure 2.2). The garden, which was created in 1900, contains a fountain in the middle that is adorned by a Neoclassical arch structure. Originally designed by Fritz Encke, the gardens were eventually restored in 1980 to include twenty-four benches, numerous linden trees, and many flowerbeds. Surrounding the plaza are apartment buildings in a range of styles from Wilhelminian to *Jugendstil* and were built by such luminous Berlin architects as Alfred Messel and Richard Göhrmann.[31] Building number seven is still standing today and is in a *Jugendstil* style. It features structural decorations above windows and graceful but asymmetrical rooflines, as well as a dramatically ornamented large front entrance door.

Like these architectural trends of his own age, many of Busoni's compositions of the early 1900s bring together references to architectural and natural forms into original structures. Yet Busoni's approach was idiosyncratic in relation to music. One piece that represents Busoni's early twentieth-century approach to form is his Piano Concerto in C Major. It brings together different architectural styles and natural forms. However, as

[31] For information about Viktoria-Luise-Platz, see http://www.viktorialuiseplatz.de/ (accessed October 12, 2020).

an admirer of architecture, but not an architect himself, Busoni did not restrict himself to mimicking specific architectural styles in music. Instead, he was more eclectic, and brought together architectural concepts as varied as the scope of massive skyscrapers, as well as the serenity and simplicity of the Hellenic temple, coupled with the unpredictable and varied lines of nature.

A central *Idee* for the piece was architectural. Busoni made specific references to architecture in relation to the piece, which he called his "skyscraper concerto" in 1913, ostensibly to describe the tremendous scope of the piece.[32] This is an especially notable nickname given the relative rarity of skyscrapers in the early 1900s. Due to new building materials, such as iron, steel, glass, and concrete, taller buildings became possible, and greatly impressed Busoni during his visits to Chicago and New York. The first ten-story building with steel frame was built in Chicago in 1885, in New York in 1889, and in Europe in 1908.[33] Many skyscrapers featured external features of the Gothic, such as arched windows and the use of stone, yet layered on top of steel and with less decoration. Busoni first visited the United States for the first time in 1891 and stayed until 1894. Upon his multiple returns to the country, he was impressed by the height of the buildings.[34] By 1893, Chicago already had twelve skyscrapers. The Fisher Building (1895), one of the tallest skyscrapers of its time, was neo-Gothic in style. At eighteen stories tall, it was impressive, and even more so with its intricate terracotta decorative carvings and a mix of arched and rectangular windows. Busoni must have also seen the Masonic Temple, built in 1892. With twenty-one stories, it remained the tallest in the city until the 1920s.[35] Built from a mix of steel, terracotta, granite, and marble, the building also features some curved arches at the base.[36] When he was living in New York, New York in 1894, the Manhattan

[32] Busoni called the concerto the "skyscraper concerto" in a letter to Egon Petri: "I was ill when I arrived here [St. Petersburg], had to miss a rehearsal and was obliged to get out of bed for the concert, at which I played my Skyscraper Concerto. A frightful strain, with influenza and a single rehearsal on the same day." Busoni, letter of November 28, 1913, to Egon Petri, in *Ferruccio Busoni: Selected Letters*, 174.

[33] A ten-story building ("Witte Huis") was completed in Rotterdam in 1908 and the eleven-story PAST building was built in Warsaw in 1911. The first skyscraper in the world is arguably the Home Insurance Building in Chicago (1885). It had a steel frame and a brick facade. The first skyscraper in New York was the Tower Building in 1889, which was eleven stories high.

[34] He visited the United States during the following years: 1891–1894, 1904, 1910, 1911, 1915. Marc-André Roberge, "Ferruccio Busoni in the United States," *American Music* 13:3 (Autumn, 1995): 295–332.

[35] Busoni noted in 1911 that he had seen a building in Chicago over twenty stories tall. Busoni, "Die Gothiker von Chicago, Illinois [1910]," in *Von der Einheit der Musik*, 134–35.

[36] For more about the skyscrapers in Chicago, see Thomas Leslie, *Chicago Skyscrapers 1871–1934* (Urbana: University of Illinois Press, 2017).

Life Insurance Building was erected. The architect, Francis Hatch Kimball, studied Gothic architecture in London in 1875 and then devoted himself to Gothic revival designs in New York before building his skyscrapers.[37] This particular building featured a turret and some arched windows as well as an arched doorway before it was demolished in 1955.[38]

Whether or not Busoni had a skyscraper in mind when he began composing the piece in 1901 is difficult to determine. That said, the *Idee* of lofty architecture pervades the piece in several concrete ways. Busoni drew the direct analogy between the impressiveness of Gothic cathedrals of the past and the neo-Gothic skyscrapers of his era, stating that the skyscrapers represented a similar grandiosity and pioneering of architectural ingenuity.[39] He hoped his vast concerto, similarly, would represent a new future direction for the genre, and he seems to have made this connection between the skyscraper and the cathedral in his conception of the piece.[40] Antony Beaumont has documented Busoni's borrowing of some of the thematic material for the men's chorus in the final movement from religious music Busoni overheard emanating from the Strasbourg Cathedral, as unseen men are answered by boys in song.[41] In addition, there is a "cathedral" theme initially appearing in the third movement of the concerto. It is transplanted from Busoni's planned (but incomplete) opera, *Sigune*, BV 231 (1885–1889). Based on a fairy tale by Rudolf Baumbach and adapted by Ludwig Soyaux and Frida Schanz, the plot focuses on Diethart, a young stonemason, who is working on building a new cathedral. Busoni originally composed the theme to depict the majestic emerging cathedral in act I, scene I of *Sigune* to accompany the following text: "Behold the Cathedral in the evening glow, the narrow form through haze and mist."[42] Although the opera was

37 For more about Kimball, see "Obituary: Francis Hatch Kimball," *American Art News* 18:11 (January 3, 1920), 4.

38 By 1910, Busoni had seen skyscrapers over twenty stories high in Chicago. In a letter to his wife from Chicago in 1904, Busoni had already drawn an image of a tall skyscraper with more than sixteen stories, and he stated that he was depicting the tallest building in the world. Busoni, letter of March 10, 1904, to Gerda Busoni, Staatsbibliothek zu Berlin–Preußischer Kulturbesitz, Musikabteilung mit Mendelssohn-Archiv, N. Mus. Nachl. 4, 465.

39 Busoni, "Die 'Gothiker' von Chicago, Illinois," in *Von der Einheit der Musik*, 132.

40 Busoni, letter of February 1902 to Gerda Busoni, in *Letters to His Wife* (London: Edward Arnold, 1938), 54. Busoni first mentioned writing a piano concerto in 1902, and his vision was born out of an original plan to write a work with drama, music, dancing, and magic based on Adam Oehlenschläger's *Aladdin* and inspired by Mozart's *Magic Flute*.

41 Beaumont, *Busoni the Composer* (Bloomington: Indiana University Press, 1985), 62–63.

42 [Da, geht den Dom im Abend scheine, den schlanken Bau im Duft und Dunst!] Busoni, *Sigune*, quoted in Beaumont, *Busoni the Composer*, 69.

never completed, the rising cathedral theme took on new life in the piano concerto.[43]

Busoni initially introduced the simple and largely stepwise *Sigune* cathedral theme in the central movement of the concerto as the main melody in the piano part that is gently accented with grace notes and enriched with octave doublings (see example 2.1).

It serves as a fundamental motivic building block for the movement that is subsequently used in augmentation, diminution, and fragmentation, even as it is varied and developed throughout. Busoni also incorporated the cathedral theme from *Sigune* into the fourth movement of the concerto, a tarantella movement, where it is played on the glockenspiel and subsumed by the wild dance music. Busoni's sketchbook shows some of the planning that went into the composition process (see figure 2.3).

This architectural *Idee* also influenced the overall structure of the composition in terms of scope. As the world's tallest building from 1647 to 1874, and now the sixth tallest church in the world, the Strasbourg Cathedral could very well have been an important inspiration for the length of the concerto—over one hour long. Just like the cathedral's towering presence, characterized by Romanesque and Gothic architectural styles, Busoni's piano concerto still towers over most other concerti in terms of length and diversity of scope.[44]

At the same time, the structure of the concerto is explicitly based on the connections between nature and architecture that Busoni was seeking to emulate in the early 1900s. Busoni's initial plan was to compose seven movements (*Prologo*, *Pezzo giocoso*, *Recitativo strumentale*, *Pezzo serioso in tre parti*, *Finale all'Italiana e stretta*, *Passeggio solenne*, *Cantico e Conclusione*). He eventually settled on five movements, and he described them as three buildings connected by two natural landscapes:

> The three buildings are the first, third, and fifth movements, between which come the two "living" ones: scherzo and tarantella; the first as the nature-play of a magic flower and magic bird—the second represented by Vesuvius

[43] Busoni could not possibly have expected that people would have recognized the theme, given that it was unpublished and not performed. It is more of a hidden message that complements the Strasbourg Cathedral music and documents the hidden conceptual connections in Busoni's composition to architecture.

[44] For perspective, John Ogdon performs the piece in about sixty-eight minutes (John Ogdon, piano, *Busoni: Piano Concerto*, Op. 39, CD, 2007 [remastered], EMI 72467), while Garrick Ohlsson takes seventy-two minutes (Garrick Ohlsson, piano, CD, 2006, Telarc 80207). Kirill Gerstein's recent recording with the Boston Symphony Orchestra takes about seventy-one minutes. Kirill Gerstein, piano, *Busoni Piano Concerto*, CD, 2019, MYR024.

Example 2.1. Busoni, Piano Concerto in C Major, BV 247, mvmt. 3, mm. 46–53.

and cypress trees.—Over the *entrance* the sun rises; a seal is fastened to the door of the end building; the winged being at the close is the nature-mysticism of Oehlenschlaeger's chorus.[45]

[45] [Die drei Gebäude sind der 1. 3. und 5. Satz, dazwischen die beiden "lebendigen": Scherzo und Tarantelle; das erste als Naturspiel einer Wunderblume und eines Wandervogels—das zweite durch Vesuv, Cypressen dargestellt—Über dem *Eingang* geht die Sonne auf; an der Türe des Schlussgebäudes klebt ein Siegel; das geflügelte Wesen am Ende ist die Naturmystik von Oehlenschlägers Chor.]

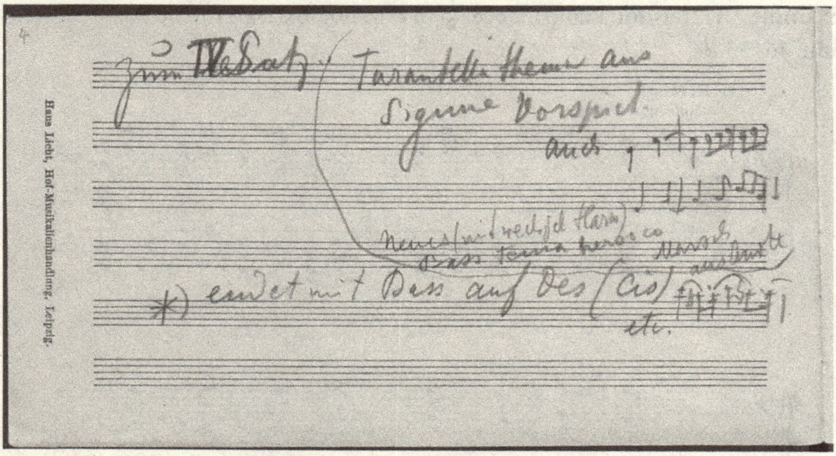

Figure 2.3. Busoni, sketchbook, plans for the Piano Concerto in C Major, BV 247, indicating borrowings from *Sigune*, BV 231. Preussischer Kulturbesitz, Staatsbibliothek zu Berlin, Music Abteilung mit Mendelssohn Archiv, Mus. Nachl. F. Busoni H, 18, 9, 8.

He sent a drawing (now believed to be lost) depicting his structural ideas to his wife in July 1902, which he described as raw and awkward ("roh und ungeschickte"), but that nevertheless represented his architectural-scenic-symbolic ("architektonisch-landschaftlich-symbolischen") idea for the piece.[46] It is fitting that he chose a *Jugendstil* artist to realize his vision; Heinrich Vogeler made the drawing more professional for inclusion in the published score (see figure 2.4). Vogeler was a painter and architect who was best known for his work at the Worpswede colony and for his *Jugendstil* book illustrations. In Vogeler's realization of Busoni's drawing, Greek, Egyptian, and Assyrian style buildings in a *Jugendstil* drawing style symbolize the odd-numbered movements, with mythical flower, bird, cypress and Vesuvius images illustrating the second and fourth. The drawing for the first movement resembles a formidable Greek temple with Doric columns that appears in front of brilliant sunlight. The Egyptian pyramid for the third movement features a mysterious sphynx. It also bears similarity to the Biddulph Grange Egypt Garden, which is guarded by two sphynxes in Staffordshire, UK. The

Busoni, letter of July 21–22, 1902 to his wife, *Briefe an seine Frau, 1889–1923*, ed. Martina Weindel (Wilhelmshaven: Florian Noetzel, 2015), 240.

46 Busoni, letter of July 21–22, 1902, to his wife, in *Briefe an seine Frau*, 240.

Figure 2.4. Busoni's drawing depicting the structure of the Piano Concerto, enhanced by Heinrich Vogeler.

onion-shaped domes in the final building suggest a religious mosque, appropriate for the religious tenor of Oehlenschläger's *Aladdin* text, which Busoni set for male chorus. Each building merges into the natural landscapes that connect them; the Greek temple dissolves into a brilliant sun with radiating rays pointing upward, just like the peak of the temple roof, while being obscured by vegetation on the right and clouds on the left. At the same time, the roof of the mosque mimics the shape of the volcano, and the building is obscured by trees on the left.

Each of the concerto movements is as stylistically and formally different as the drawing suggests, with the first, third, and fifth as the weightiest. Interspersed between these "architectural" movements are two fleeting sections—the second, a lively scherzo featuring Turkish percussion, and the fourth, a virtuosic Italianate tarantella. There is no clear musical precedent for this formal approach.

The Brahmsian first movement features majestic chords, rolling arpeggios, and a lyrical horn solo. It also starts with a massive tutti orchestral section. The piano enters with a new theme that is echoed by woodwinds as they introduce a development, rather than a second exposition; this all contributes to a structure that bears only remote resemblance to Classical concerto form. As Larry Sitsky points out, the multiple themes are composed of recombinations of motives, making the material a constant variation of itself.[47] There are parallels to the Vogeler image, with Doric columns that are similar, but never identical.

The third movement, which is the weightiest and is foregrounded in the image, starts with fugal writing and features much chromaticism. At the same time, the entire musical structure is a mirror, just like the symmetrical image in Busoni's drawing, which features ascending sides that are punctuated by a central door. The short introduction and *prima pars* set the key and introduce the cathedral theme, along with three other themes. The *altera pars* (middle section) moves through diverse keys (i.e., C major and minor, B major and minor, G major and minor, and E♭ major), and transforms the first and second themes from the opening. The final part, the *Come da principio* coupled with the coda-like *Ultima Pars*, re-establishes D♭ major as the tonal area and recombine the cathedral theme with the second theme from the opening, bringing it to a quiet and subtle conclusion.

The final movement, by contrast, is solemn, religious, and reverential with hymn-like block chords. It is a choral adaptation of an intended theater piece based on Oehlenschläger's *Aladdin*. Reverential men's voices rise from the block chords, the "rocks" or solid architecture of which the text speaks, sounding from off stage, as the pianist listens to the mysterious text by Oehlenschläger and then supplements with wide ranging arpeggios, exploring the expanse of the keyboard. The idea of the skyscraper that Busoni mentioned is easily conjured up by the pianistic exploration of vast height and depth. The final chorus from Oehlenschläger's Aladdin brings the connection between music and architecture into full display as unsung text speak of pillars of rocks that magically begin to resound through mystical connections between music as sounding art and liquid stone ("Deep and quiet, the pillars of rock begin to sound").[48]

Individual movements have idiosyncratic structures that are based on a combination of architectural and natural models. As Larry Sitsky has argued, it might be possible to superimpose a sonata form on the first movement because of its arch form and the long orchestral introduction, but "it sits most uneasily on this movement's shoulders. We can always work the

[47] Larry Sitsky, *Busoni and the Piano: The Works the Writings, and the Recordings*, 2nd ed., Distinguished Reprints 3 (Hillsdale, NY: Pendragon Press, 2009), 98.

[48] [Die Felsensäulen fangen an tief und leise zu ertönen.] Busoni, Piano Concerto, BV 247, movement V (Leipzig: Breitkopf & Härtel, 1906), 294.

sonata principle in, but it is not convincing."[49] In this movement, the form seems to transform itself as it unfolds. It could be seen as coinciding with the Greek architecture illustrated in the drawing, in that continuous variation is a guiding principle; no two pillars are alike in a Hellenic Temple, and each stone is cut slightly differently. Yet builders create optical illusions of symmetry based on slight variations in circumference and height that consider the perspective of an observer. In the same way, the three long themes in the orchestral introduction are nevertheless motivically interrelated. Harmonic instability before the piano even enters unsettles the piano entry, suggesting a development, rather than a second exposition. Although a harmonic return to C and a simultaneous return to tempo I could suggest a recapitulation, there is never a sense of return or resolution. Instead, a free piano cadenza opens the piece further and leads to a dramatic climax in which massive chords on piano and orchestra together allow the movement to reach a new level of grandiosity. In retrospect, the opening seems more like an introduction that gradually unfolds and develops. The lack of exact symmetry is reflective of natural forms, even as the thematic variations serve structural functions.

The middle movement, likewise, contains few allusions to traditional musical forms. It contains three basic parts (*prima pars*, *altera pars*, *come da principio*) that are framed on either side by an *introduction* and an *ultima pars*. This is reminiscent of the Egyptian structure, which contains two parts framing a doorway. Harmonic movement centered on D♭ major in the *prima pars* and *come da principio* coupled with harmonic instability in the *altera pars* invokes a sense of symmetry. However, the movement also contains many (six) themes and stylistic diversity that unfold asymmetrically throughout the movement, like decorative lines mimicking nature, and over constantly changing stylistic material. The introduction and *prima pars* in D♭ share four themes between them, By contrast, the Lisztian *altera pars* fluctuates through many keys and introduces two themes before returning to D♭ for the *come da principio*, while the *ultima pars* features F♯ minor over a D♭ pedal. Stylistically, the piece starts regally with a combination of French overture style dotted rhythms and runs over late Romantic tremolos, while the *prima pars* features mystical chromaticism and wispy Lisztian runs. The *altera pars* is more expansive and majestic, while the final two sections hint

[49] Sitsky, *Busoni and the Piano*, 97.

Table 2.1. Diagram of Busoni's Piano Concerto BV 247, mvmt. 3

Section	Key Areas	Number of Themes	Style
Introduction/ Prima pars	D♭ major (briefly in A♭ major, E major, and F major)	Four (a, b, c, d)	*Introduction:* French Overture style dotted rhythms and scalar runs over tremolandos are followed by chromatic passages and lyrical melodies in the piano before regal and majestic block chords appear. *Prima pars:* An overall mystical affect is created by serene grace notes adorning the Cathedral melody followed by Lisztian arpeggiations spanning wide registers through which a melody appears. The section concludes with Brahmsian thick-textured piano writing.
Altera pars	Harmonic instability (C major, B major, G major, C minor, B minor, E♭ major, G minor, and E♭ major)	Three themes from the first sections (a, b, d), plus two additional themes (e, f)	The *altera pars* starts with a dark rhythmic march in $\frac{6}{4}$ with low strings and chordal piano writing. In the $\frac{12}{8}$ section, the orchestra assumes the melody while the piano plays expansive arpeggios. The section increases in texture and intensity with thicker chords/ chromatic octaves in both hands in the piano part and increased dynamic levels in the orchestra.
Come da principio/ Ultima pars	D♭ major, F♯ minor/D♭ major	Two themes from the first sections (b, d), plus one from the *altera pars* (e)	*Come da principio*: The tranquil and mystical arpeggiated writing and low strings/brass return. *Ultima pars* hints at the material in the Introduction with dramatic and regal runs and dotted rhythms, this time reinforced by numerous doublings before movement to a pastoral $\frac{12}{8}$ with horns and lyrical strings and then Lisztian arpeggios.

at the regal opening and mystical *prima pars*, yet transformed, with only two themes (see table 2.1).

Although possessing movements divergent in style and unique in form, the structure of the concerto simultaneously displays Busoni's concern for

Example 2.2. Busoni, Piano Concerto, BV 247, mvmt. 1, mm. 1–2, viola part.

morphological unity, thereby creating a melding of the natural and the architectural on a large scale as well. A rising and falling semitone, characteristic also of the cathedral theme, appears in each movement in varied manners, lending unity to the complete work. For instance, the initial motive appears in the viola line beginning in measure one of the first movement (E-F-E-E♭-D-E) (see example 2.2).

Minor seconds again appear as important thematic material in the *più moderato* section in the first violin, but rhythmically altered (G-A♭-G-G♭). Chromatic seconds likewise pervade the second movement from the virtuosic scalar passages in the piano to the trills in the strings. In the *giovanescamente* section, the first violin ascends chromatically (E to F), while the second descends (C♯ to C). Another reference to the opening motive begins in the piano part in the *più trattendo e fantasticamente* section in the bass octaves (F♯-G-G-F♯-F♯-E♯-E♯-E). The third movement also features plenty of allusions to this motive throughout the movement, including four bars before rehearsal 41 in the winds (E♭-D-C-D♭-C-B♭-C♭), not to mention the connections with the semitonal *Sigune* theme. The fourth movement, the tarantella, is filled with lively passages, some very chromatic, such as around rehearsal 79, that alludes to the opening motive. Four bars after rehearsal 79, the second flute plays the following, for instance: (A-B♭-B-C-C♯-D-E♭-D). In the final movement, it appears in the flute part as well four bars after rehearsal 88 (B-C-D♭-C-C-D♭-C♯-B♯-B).[50]

Busoni's Piano Concerto is thus based on an architectural *Idee*, and it also represents one of Busoni's attempts to blend ideals of nature and architecture. Although not all of his compositions from the period made explicit references to specific architectural buildings or styles, many displayed a similar combination of natural forms and architectural structure. By 1907, he had also made more progress toward his vision of developing a distinctive grammar for each piece, such as in his mysterious Elegy no. 1 "Nach der Wendung," which explores the tritone axis between C and F♯.

50 Busoni, *Piano Concerto in C Major, BV 247* (Leipzig: Breitkopf und Härtel, 1906).

Busoni's Montage Structures

In the 1910s and 1920s, Busoni moved away from a blending of natural lines and architectural forms toward more modernist notions of the juxtaposition of contrasting sections to evoke multi-dimensional structures in music. This montage approach represented a shift from linear notions of the progression of themes and harmonies. In particular, he started organizing the music in sections, some of which are foregrounded, like different parts of a building. As such, he helped pioneer montage approaches to musical structure in a time when they were less common.

Busoni found models for his new structural approach in architecture, especially Gothic and neo-Gothic architecture with its many angles, shapes, and sections. His knowledge of the Gothic and neo-Gothic style of architecture was extensive. In addition, it is worth pointing out his interest in the work of architect Viollet-le-Duc, who was noted for restoring many Gothic cathedrals, and his admiration for Alfred Messel's neo-Gothic Wertheimer department store in Berlin.[51]

One piece displaying Busoni's evolving approach to form in which he explicitly noted the architectural connection is his *Fantasia contrappuntistica*, BV 256 (1910–1922), which is structured like a segmented Gothic building but is updated with new treatments of the musical language and less ornamentation. This non-linear structural approach was inspired by the wealth of architecture to which Busoni was exposed, including the neo-Gothic architecture that was on his mind in 1910 in Chicago; it was also informed by contemporary approaches to architecture with which he was actively engaged throughout the 1910s.

Busoni started working on a critical edition of J. S. Bach's *The Art of Fugue*, BWV 1080, at the end of 1909, while sailing to the United States. This editing activity in conjunction with discussions in 1910 with friends in Chicago

[51] He owned a copy of Eugene Viollet-le-Duc's ten-volume *Dictionnaire raisonné de l'architecture française du XI. au XVI. siècle* (Paris: B. Bance, 1858–1864). This is noted in the auction records of his personal library after his death. Max Perl, *Bibliothek Ferruccio Busoni: Werke der Weltliteratur in schönen Gesamtausgaben und Erstdrucken, illustrierte Bücher aller Jahrhunderte, eine hervorragende Cervantes- und E. T. A Hoffmann-Sammlung, Bücher mit handschriftlichen Dedikationen, ältere und neuere Literatur aus allen Wissensgebieten, Musik; Versteigerung Montag, den 30. und Dienstag, den 31. März 1925* (Berlin: Max Perl Antiquariat, 1925), https://digi.ub.uni-heidelberg.de/diglit/perl1925_03_30/0017/text_ocr (accessed October 17, 2020). Viollet-le-Duc lived from 1814 to 1879, and he famously restored such landmarks as the Notre-Dame de Paris. For Busoni's views on Messel, see Busoni, "Gedanken über den Ausdruck in der Architektur" [(fragment), spring 1916], in *Von der Einheit der Musik*, 234.

("The Gothics of Chicago"), Bernhard Ziehn and Wilhelm Middelschulte, led to the composition of the *Fantasia contrappuntistica. Preludio al corale "Gloria al Signore nei Cieli" e fuga a quattro soggetti obbligati sopra un frammento di Bach*. He wrote this piece shortly after writing about the neo-Gothic skyscrapers in Chicago.[52] To create his composition, he combined two contrasting pieces: his third piano Elegy (1908) based on the chorale *Meine Seele bangt und hofft zu Dir*, BV 249, and a fantasia-like arrangement of Bach's *Art of Fugue*, the *Grosse Fuge kontrapunktische Fantasie*, BV 255 (1910).[53]

Busoni created three different versions of the *Fantasia contrappuntistica* (1910, 1912, 1922). The third represents his most developed approach to structure. It features two main sections and twelve smaller ones. The opening elegy is based on a chorale melody, but Busoni's treatment of the melody is entirely his own.[54] The first part develops fragmented portions of the chorale melody over unconventional scales and arpeggios based on unrelated triads. It expands the tonal system through chromaticism and through excursions into bitonality when an A major chorale melody appears over an E♭ pedal point in the bass.

The second part is Busoni's adaptation of Bach's *The Art of Fugue*. In 1910, Busoni published the *Grosse Fuge kontrapunktische Fantasie über Joh. Sebastian Bachs letztes unvollendetes Werk für Klavier*, in which he incorporated fantasia elements into Bach's fugue and added a vastness of scale patterned after Ludwig van Beethoven's *Grosse Fuge*, op. 133. Although the piece begins with a fairly literal translation of the first three fugues from Bach's unfinished composition, Busoni also adds an intermezzo on the BACH motive, three chromatic variations, a cadenza, and a coda. Variation II introduces a fifth theme that Busoni later incorporates into the final fugue, a theme characterized

52 Busoni, "Die Gothiker von Chicago," 134–135.

53 A few of the alterations include the addition of an extra voice in fugue I to introduce the BACH theme. He also made a cut in the fourth fugue while adding a chorale recapitulation at the end. In 1912, Busoni revised the work extensively, eliminating the opening elegy as well as the fantasia elements from the fugue. Known as the "edizione minore," Busoni gave this version the title *Choral-Vorspiel und Fuge über ein Bachsches Fragment (der "Fantasia Contrappuntistica" kleine Ausgabe)*. Although based on the same chorale melody as the elegy, he rewrote the opening, which consists of the theme and three variations. Moreover, Busoni supplied an optional ending, should anyone want to perform the work without the final fugue. For the final fugue Busoni eliminated all of the fantasy elements and provided a simple and nearly exact transcription of Bach's original *Art of Fugue* with little effort to make it distinctively pianistic. The publication date of the two-piano version is 1922, even if Busoni completed it on July 3, 1921.

54 For more about Busoni's treatment of harmony, see Colin Davis, "'The New Harmony' of the *Fantasia Contrappuntistica*," *Journal of Musicological Research* 37:3 (2018): 239–73.

by a highly chromatic and tonally unstable accompanimental line. Busoni introduced his version of the incomplete fourth fugue in the transposed key of B♭ minor over a syncopated and chromatic accompanimental line. The piece ends with a virtuosic stretto in the tonic.

In the two-piano version (entitled *Fantasia contrappuntistica: Choral-Variationen über "Ehre sei Gott in der Höhe" gefolgt von einer Quadrupel-Fuge über ein Bachsches Fragment für zwei Klaviere*),[55] structural montage elements come into full display. Busoni expanded the elegy section, incorporating into it a set of variations on the chorale melody composed for the 1912 version. Busoni also modified the fugal section by inserting cuts in the first and fourth fugues, by adding chromaticism in the second, and by inserting a fughetta in the third.[56]

The use of two pianos contributes to a sense of multi-dimensionality as sound comes from different instruments, and there is possibility for greater textural variety. In that way, this new scoring can be seen as representing a maturation of Busoni's ideas about sound and space. While the 1910 version starts with a chorale melody in octaves in tremolandos in the bass, for instance, the two-piano version from 1922 features the melody in dramatic octaves in piano I, which are echoed by piano II in a lower register, thereby creating the impression of call-and-response. An ensuing cascade of octaves evokes an orchestral sound. Busoni also plays with the register, at times placing the melody in block chords in the first piano one octave higher, while the second piano plays in the low bass one octave lower, thereby allowing textural and registral diversity. One example of this occurs in the passage beginning in measure 24 (see example 2.3).

However, Busoni was thinking in terms not just of sonorous dimensions, but also of formal ones. He was not planning the structure in a traditional linear sense, but in a sectional montage where parts of the music assume different roles, focal points, and levels of importance.

Busoni's inspiration for the unusual structure of the *Fantasia contrappuntistica* was architectural from the beginning. He drew a rough

[55] In 1920, Frida Kwast-Hodapp requested a two-piano version of the piece to play with her husband, James Kwast. Busoni was happy to comply, especially since he was anxious to experiment with the possibilities offered by two pianos. Beaumont, *Busoni the Composer*, 172.

[56] Busoni wanted to score the piece for orchestra. He unfortunately never completed this task, but Helmut Bornefeld later realized his vision. For a more detailed analysis of the 1910 version of the composition see Julie Ra, *Rückblick und Erneuerung: Bachs Fuge in Klaviermusik von Reger, Busoni, und Hindemith*, Quellen und Studien zur Musikgeschichte von der Antike bis in die Gegenwart 40, ed. Michael von Albrecht (Frankfurt am Main: Peter Lang, 2002).

Example 2.3. Busoni, *Fantasia contrappuntistica*, BV 256b, mm. 24–33.

sketch illustrating his conception of the form of the *Grosse Fuge* of 1910 (that eventually formed the basis for the conclusion of the *Fantasia contrappuntistica*). The drawing features a circular base, perhaps for a tower and suggestions of two arched entryways. In his notes, Busoni explained that there were three themes, four voices, and Gothic thematic material (see figure 2.5). The drawing itself is crude and undeveloped, without dimension and detail.[57]

[57] Busoni also drew a picture on the score of a ship with five sails that represented the fugue; each sail corresponded to a subject (Bach's four subjects and his own fifth subject). The surrounding dodecahedron corresponded to the ten structural parts of the work. Although not architecture, the ship is nevertheless a construction based on human design. For more on the topic, see Beaumont, *Busoni the Composer*, 169.

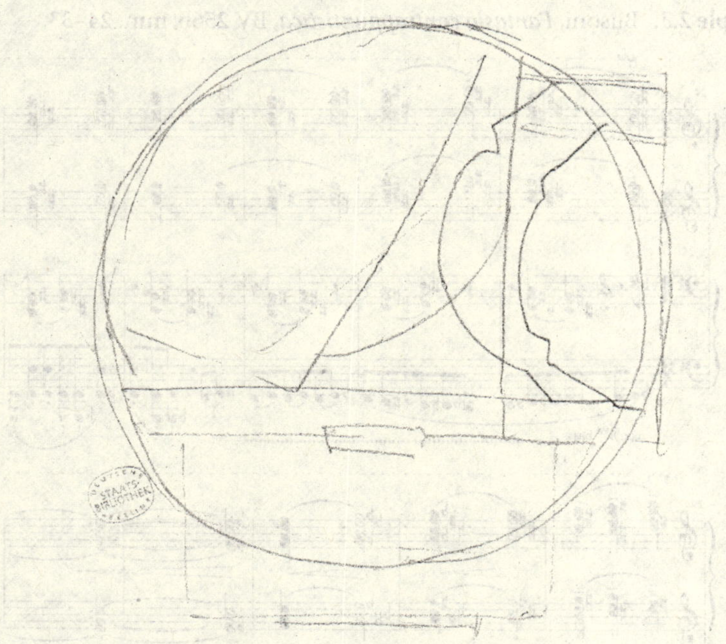

Figure 2.5. Busoni, diagram of the formal structure of Busoni's *Grosse Fuge: Kontrapunktische Fantasie über Joh. Seb. Bach's letztes unvollendetes Werk für Klavier ausgeführt*. Staatsbibliothek zu Berlin–Preußischer Kulturbesitz, Musikabteilung mit Mendelssohn-Archiv, Mus. Nachlass F. Busoni, C1-59.

When working on the two-piano version, Busoni illustrated his multi-dimensional conception of the structure of the entire piece with greater clarity. An image—published together with the score in 1922—demonstrates his architectural conception of the structure (see figure 2.6), which contains two main sections and twelve subsidiary ones.

Busoni reportedly stated to Hugo Leichtentritt that the west entrance of the Papal Palace at Avignon provided inspiration for the musical structure of the piece.[58] Indeed, there is a close correlation between the drawing and the Papal

[58] Beaumont, *Busoni the Composer*, 174. It is unclear exactly where Busoni made this statement to Leichtentritt (it is not in his 1916 biography of the composer, nor in his text on musical form), but the connection between Busoni's drawing and the Papal Palace supports the statement. In his biography of Busoni, Leichtentritt stated that Busoni was not trying to restore Bach in the composition, but to build a new edifice: "Die Fantasie als Ganzes tritt nicht mit dem Anspruch auf, eine Vollendung des bachschen Fragments zu sein; es handelt sich nicht um Restaurierung sozusagen einer Ruine,

Plan des Werkes

A. Analytischer:

1. Choral - Variationen (Einleitung — Choral und Variationen — Übergang)
2. Fuga I. 3. Fuga II. 4. Fuga III. 5. Intermezzo. 6. Variatio I. 7. Variatio II.
8. Variatio III. 9. Cadenza. 10. Fuga IV. 11. Corale. 12. Stretta.

B. Architektonischer:

Figure 2.6. Busoni, drawing illustrating the form of the two-piano version of the *Fantasia contrappuntistica.*

Palace. The west side of the Papal Palace, like Busoni's drawing, features twelve arches, even if they are distributed differently (groups of one, seven, two, and two). In the Papal Palace, the group of seven arches is farthest back, with an entrance in the third arch from the left that is ornamented with two small turrets. The first arch is the widest and projects forward. The ninth and tenth are taller and also project forward. Some of these arches can be seen in figure 2.7.

In his drawing, Busoni, however, foregrounds four arches that represent the four fugues, and these tower over the other sections of the piece

sondern die Ruine wird in ein ganz neues Bauwerk eingebaut, dessen künstlerische Reise teils in dem Kontrast zwischen alt und neu liegen, teils in der berschmelzung dieser verschieden Elemente" [The fantasy as a whole does not aim to be a completion of the Bach fragment; it is not the completion of a ruin so to speak, but rather, the ruin is being built into an entirely new building, the artistic realm of which lies partly in the contrast between the old and new, and partly in the fusion of these elements.] Hugo Leichtentritt, *Ferruccio Busoni* (Leipzig: Breitkopf & Härtel, 1916), 43.

Figure 2.7. Image of the Papal Palace at Avignon.

(2, 3, 4, 10). The most impressive and massive archway in the drawing, number 10, depicts the final fugue (fugue IV). The first three fugues are counterbalanced by the three variations, which nevertheless are less important, as indicated by their lower height in the diagram (numbers 6, 7, 8). These foregrounded sections are balanced by the freer sections (chorale, intermezzo, cadenza, and stretto), which are represented by recessed sections in the building. Busoni's drawing thus adapts the many dimensions (height, width, and depth) of the Papal Palace to illustrate the formal dimensions of his composition.[59]

Gradually expanding registers, such as in the concluding chorale section, correspond to the vertical scope of buildings. Themes from Bach's *Art of Fugue*, contrapuntal textures, vastness of scope, improvisatory passages, and ornamental figures reference Busoni's notion of Gothic architectural style encapsulated in sound. Added to that are aspects of Beethoven's *Grosse Fuge*—especially in terms of the use of trills and octave doublings

59 The visual proportions in the drawing are not representative of actual performance time. Instead, they indicate the formal role. The opening chorale takes up about a third of the length of the piece. Fugues I–III also comprise just over one-third of the total length, while everything else comprises about the final third of the piece. Toomas Siitan points maintains that in order to appreciate the architectural structure of the work as illustrated by Busoni, a listener has to comprehend the piece in its entirety. See Siitan, "Muusika: Elustunud arhitektuur?," in *Tekste modernismist. II: Muusika ja arhitektuur*, ed. Gerhard Lock, Maris Valk-Falk, and Saale Kareda (Tallinn: Scripta Musicalia, 2008), 16.

and nearly atonal passages representative of Busoni's era. Busoni exclaimed that although he had used Bach's subjects, he had turned them into something new.[60]

If Busoni began developing a non-linear segmented formal approach in the 1910s that he continued into the 1920s, his structures increasingly resembled montages in the latter part of the decade (during and after World War I), a formal approach that became important in the twentieth century. Busoni's architectural structures of the period bear similarity to the montage-like ambulant architecture at the Weimar Bauhaus through contrasting musical textures.[61]

Ideas connecting architectural forms and movement in time were discussed by several theorists in the late nineteenth and early twentieth centuries.[62] For instance, in 1886, Wölfflin, a professor at Berlin University from 1901 to 1912, described architecture as lived experience, and space as movement.[63] Architectural forms should reflect how humans move. Theodor Lipps, a German philosopher famous for his theory of *Einfühlung*, or empathy, similarly argued in 1903 that visual forms emulate bodily forms: "One has to say, man is not beautiful because of his forms but rather that forms are beautiful because they are human forms and thus, they are for us the bearer of human life."[64] In this way, architectural forms can reflect human vitality. Friedrich Theodor Vischer, an art philosopher, similarly describes architectural forms not as merely rigid objects, but as spaces that can be occupied by the human mind.[65]

[60] Busoni, "Self Criticism [1912]," in *The Essence of Music and Other Papers*, 47–48. By the later 1910s and 1920s, van de Velde similarly began to create less ornate constructions, such as *De Tent*, with sleeker lines and distinct segmented sections. This project, which he was working on in Zurich, would, in turn, influence his successors, such as Walther Gropius and Le Corbusier.

[61] Oskar Schlemmer was associated with the Bauhaus from 1919 to 1925. He was initially in charge of the mural workshop and taught drawing, but in 1922 took over stone and woodworking. At the 1923 exhibition, he displayed drawings and filled his workshop with murals. The works of Kandinsky and Busoni have already been compared. See, for instance, Jed Rasula, *History of a Shiver: The Sublime Impudence of Modernism* (New York: Oxford University Press, 2016), 23.

[62] For an overview, see Vlad Ionescu, "Architectural Symbolism: Body and Space in Heinrich Wölfflin and Wilhelm Worringer," *European Architectural History Network*, https://journal.eahn.org/articles/10.5334/ah.213 (accessed October 8, 2020).

[63] "Die ästhetische Anschauung überträgt diese intimste Erfahrung unseres Körpers auch auf die leblose Natur." Wölfflin, *Prolegomena zu einer Psychologie der Architektur* [1886], in *Kleine Schriften*, ed. J. Gantner (Basel: Benno Schwabe & Co., 1946), 22.

[64] [Der Mensch, so müssen wir sagen, ist nicht schön wegen seiner Form, sondern die Formen sind schön, weil sie Formen des Menschen und dennoch für uns Träger menschlichen Lebens sind.] Theodor Lipps, *Ästhetik: Psychologie des Schönen und der Kunst* (Hamburg: Voss, 1903), 105.

[65] Friderich Theodor Vischer, *Das Symbol* [1887], in *Kritische Gänge*, 4th ed. (Munich: Meyer und Jesser, 1922).

Philosophical connections between form and movement, or architecture and the body, were part of Busoni's *Zeitgeist* and became increasingly important for artworks during and after World War I. These ideas blending spatial and temporal art forms influenced Busoni's own works and the works of others during his lifetime, including at the Bauhaus, where theater became the means for the practical working out of these ideals.

The economic situation in the Weimar Republic, with its extreme hyperinflation, prevented the production of many architectural projects at the Weimar Bauhaus in the early 1920s. As a result, theater, which was seen as second in importance only to architecture because of its similar ability to bring together the arts in space, became an important place for experimentation at the Bauhaus.[66] It became a catalyst for multi-dimensional forms that moved in time—an alternative kind of liquid architecture in which the forms reflected how people moved while occupying space.

Oskar Schlemmer was at the forefront of this type of experimentation with "ambulant architecture." Schlemmer, who was in charge of some of the first important theatrical pieces at the Bauhaus, including one at the 1923 exhibition, taught his students to indicate movement and gesture with lines/stick figures before surrounding the lines with shapes (i.e., circles, rectangles, etc.) to provide the structure. In this way he linked together the organic world and movement with multi-dimensional shapes. As explained in the essay "Man and Theater" [Mensch und Kunstfigur], Schlemmer believed that form possessed not only geometrical aspects ("form is manifest as extensions of height breadth, and depth; as line, as plane, and as solid or volume"), but also movement and color: "Non-rigid, intangible form occurs as light, whose linear effect appears in the geometry of the light beam and of pyrotechnical display, and whose solid- and space-creating effect comes through illumination."[67] Theater, according to Schlemmer, was unusual in that it offered "form and color in motion . . . and furthermore as transformable architectonic

[66] Schlemmer, letter of June 14, 1921, in *Oskar Schlemmer: The Triadic Ballet* (Berlin: Druckhaus Heinrich, 1985), 8.

[67] Schlemmer, "Man and Art Figure," in *The Theater of the Bauhaus*, ed. Walter Gropius and Arthur S. Wensinger, trans. Arthur S. Wensinger (Middletown, CT: Wesleyan University Press, 1961), 21. [Die Form tritt in Erscheinung in der Höhen-, Breiten-, und Tiefenausdehnung als Linie, als Fläche, und als Körper. . . . Unstarre nicht als Licht, das in der Geometrie des Lichtstrahls und Feuerwerks linear und als Lichtstein körper- und raumbildend wirkt.] Oskar Schlemmer, "Mensch und Kunstfigur," in *Die Bühne im Bauhaus*, ed. Walter Gropius and László Moholy-Nagy, Bauhausbücher 4 (Munich: Albert Langen, 1924), 11.

structures."[68] In addition, he stated that the future of theater resided in considerations of space and building in relation to human form:

> The history of the theater is the history of the transfiguration of the human form. It is the history of *man* as the actor of physical and spiritual events, ranging from naiveté to reflection, from naturalness to artifice. The materials involved in this transfiguration are form and color, the materials of the painter and sculptor. The arena for this transfiguration is found in the constructive fusion of *space and building*, the realm of the architect.[69]

Schlemmer used the term "ambulant architecture" [wandelnde Architektur] to describe montage-like human shapes encased in cubical forms: "Here the cubical forms are transferred to the human shape: head, torso, arms, legs are transformed into spatial-cubical constructions. Result: ambulant architecture."[70] What he envisioned was moving architecture. In his sketches, the ambulant architecture features a human figure clothed in shapes. The face is encased in a cube, as is the chest, while the arms and legs are rectangular cuboids. The hands and feet are cubes as well (see figure 2.8).

Schlemmer's *Triadisches Ballett*, which Busoni probably witnessed when it was performed during the Bauhaus week in 1923, took these still form drawings to a new level by adding movement in time in the theater.[71] Although Busoni never writes about witnessing Schlemmer's composition, it can be presumed that he was present in Weimar in time for the performance, because his pupil, Wladimir Vogel, whom he invited to the Bauhaus week, mentions the importance of the piece in his memoirs. Vogel also describes how impressed he was by the exhibition. Whether Busoni, who was ill at that time, was well enough to view all of the performances at the exhibition is difficult to determine. At the very least, he would have discussed the music and events with his pupils.[72] Moreover, it is probable that Schlemmer's ideas

68 Schlemmer, "Man and Art Figure," 363. [die Bewegung von Form und Farbe . . . desgleichen veränderlicher beweglicher Raum und verwandelbare arkitechtonische Gebilde.] Gropius and Moholy-Nagy, eds., *Die Bühne im Bauhaus*, 12.

69 Schlemmer, "Man and Art Figure," in *The Theater of the Bauhaus*, 17.

70 Schlemmer, "Man and Art Figure," 363. [Hier werden die kubischen Formen auf die menschlichen Körperformen übertragen: Kopf, Leib, Arme, Beine in räumlich-kubishe Gebilde verwandelt. Ergebnis: Wandelnde Architektur.] Oskar Schlemmer, "Mensch und Kunstfigur," 16.

71 The first performance took place in Stuttgart on September 30, 1922.

72 The performance of Schlemmer's concert took place on August 16. Busoni's pieces were performed on August 18, and Stravinsky's *L'histoire du soldat* was performed on August 19. For Vogel's mention of Schlemmer's ballet, see Vogel, "Eine Begegnung," Wladimir Vogel Nachl.,

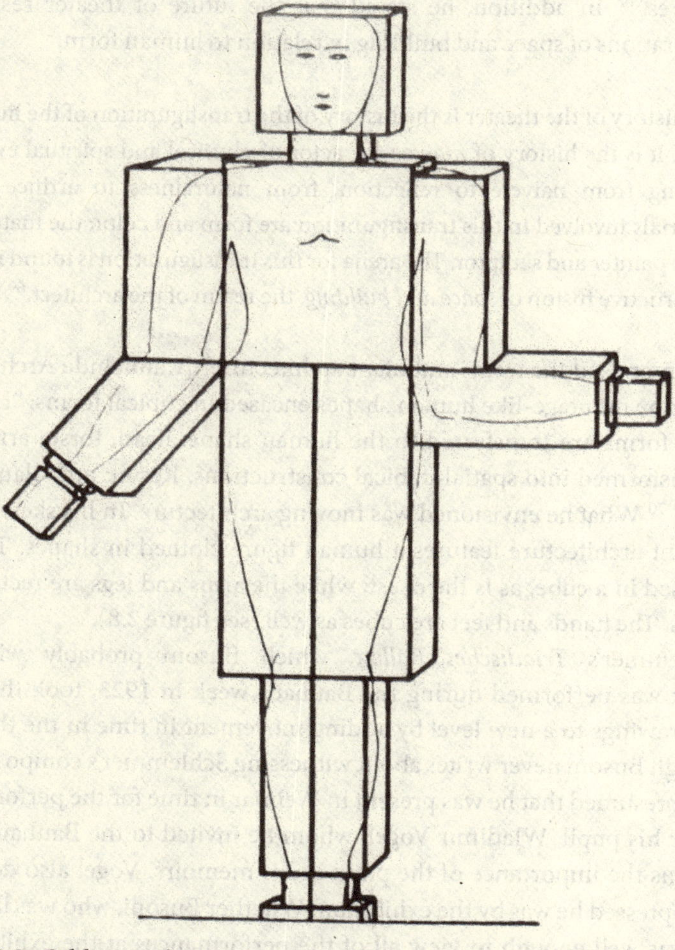

Figure 2.8. Schlemmer's ambulant architecture drawing in "Mensch und Kunstfigur."

were part of discussions in Berlin in the early 1920s in Hermann Scherchen's circle, with which Busoni was closely connected.

Schlemmer, who had been conceptualizing the piece since 1912 in conjunction with Albert Burger's dance troupe in Stuttgart, oversaw the design, production, and creation of the costumes for his ballet that incorporated these

Zentralbibliothek zu Zurich, MUS_NL_116_1_9, p. 2. See also Hans M. Wingler, *The Bauhaus: Weimar, Dessau, Berlin, Chicago* (Cambridge, MA: MIT Press, 1969).

ambulant architectural models. The costumes visually depict intersections between form, the human body, and the human idea, even as they are composed of basic shapes such as circles and squares that encase human bodies and move in time. Yet it was not just the costumes that were geometric; the structure of the ballet was too. It is triadic, with three main sections subdivided into twelve dances. Each section has its own mood and color scheme (in terms of costumes and decorations: yellow, pink, and black, respectively).[73] There were also three performers (one female and two male).[74] Gropius, in particular, was struck with Schlemmer's theatrical innovations, describing it as "moving architecture":

> My own great impression of Schlemmer's stage work was to see and experience his magic of transforming dancers and actors into moving architecture. His deep interest and intuitive understanding of the phenomena of architectural space also developed his rare gift as a muralist. With empathy he would sense the direction and dynamics of a given space and make them integral parts of his mural compositions.[75]

While movement is a natural part of music, as sounds progress through time, the concept of music as moving masses of sounds also developed in the 1910s, especially after World War I. This idea bears similarity to Bauhaus theories about architectural forms moving in time, and became broadly disseminated, in part, because of the music and lectures of one of Busoni's pupils, Edgard Varèse, in the early twentieth century.[76] He famously described "music as masses of sound evolving in space, rather than . . . notes in some prescribed

[73] Schlemmer eschewed any program in his ballet. His exploration of space, form, and color focused on the presentation of the visual rather than the music, which was a pastiche of excerpts of compositions by other composers from diverse time periods (e.g., Handel, Debussy, Mozart, and others). He did commission some music from Stefan Wolpe and from Paul Hindemith, which has been lost. Drafts date back to 1916. He was influenced by Schoenberg's *Pierrot lunaire*, which also inspired Busoni's *Arlecchino.* The performance of *Pierrot lunaire* in Busoni's Berlin home on June 17, 1913, had a lasting impact on Busoni, who initially incorporated *Sprechstimme* into his drafts for *Arlecchino.* See Busoni, letter of June 19, 1913, to Egon Petri, in Busoni, *Selected Letters*, 169.

[74] In the Weimar performance on August 16, 1923, Schlemmer played the role of the second dancer. An orchestra played selections by Mozart and Beethoven. All other music was performed by piano alone. See also Oskar Schlemmer, László Moholy-Nagy, and Farkas Molnár, *The Theater of the Bauhaus*, ed. Walter Gropius, trans. Arthur S. Wensinger (Middleton, CT: Wesleyan University Press, 1961).

[75] Gropius, "Introduction," in *The Theater of the Bauhaus*, 9–10.

[76] For more about the Busoni-Varèse connection, including about Varèse's indebtedness to Busoni for ideas about musical form, see Erinn Knyt, *Ferruccio Busoni and His Legacy* (Bloomington: Indiana University Press, 2017), 89–136.

order," and sought to create musical sound, beginning with *Amériques* (1918–1921), that mimicked the growth of hyperbolic curves.[77] Olivia Mattis has, unsurprisingly, compared his music to sculpture and the plastic arts.[78]

What is less known is that Busoni was also experimenting with moving sound masses in the 1910s, and this is evident in pieces such as *Arlecchino* (1917). It is noteworthy that leaders at the Bauhaus greatly admired *Arlecchino*, which was subsequently performed in Weimar four times (January 26/31 and February 5/20, 1924) under the directorship of Ernst Latzko and staged by Maximilian Moris. Gropius, Klee, and Kandinsky wrote a joint letter, together with their wives, in February 1924, calling *Arlecchino* a captivating gift ["entzückende gabe"].[79]

Although an opera with a plot, and thus unlike Schlemmer's more abstract ballet, Busoni's piece similarly featured pantomime and objectified figures—in his case—masked *commedia dell'arte* figures in the spirit of the marionette, such as Arlecchino and Columbina, a doctor, and a priest. Busoni called it a "Marionetten Tragödie" in the score and called the characters "puppet-like."[80] In his drawing of Arlecchino, Busoni emphasized the marionette-like character of Arlecchino by drawing him sideways with a mask (see figure 2.9).

Like Schlemmer's drawings, Busoni's character depicts life and motion. Intentional or not, the main body forms an overall triangular shape. However, that is probably reading too deeply into the visual aspects, which were not Busoni's main concern.

The greatest parallel is in the musical reconciliation of the temporal and the spatial. Busoni created architectural musical forms as textures in motion that are juxtaposed to create aural multi-dimensionality. Busoni's *Arlecchino* is similar to Schlemmer's ambulant architectural figures in that it is composed of many small multi-dimensional sections (comprising themes, timbres, and densities) that move through time and create the larger structure. *Arlecchino* is not just composed of many small numbers, like early opera, but each scene

[77] Edgard Varèse, "Edgard Varèse on Music and Art: A Conversation between Varèse and Alcopely," *Leonardo* 1 (1968): 194.

[78] Olivia Mattis, "Edgard Varèse and the Visual Arts" (PhD diss., Stanford University, 1992).

[79] Paul and Lily Klee, Wassily and Nina Kandinsky, Walter and Ise Gropius, letter of February 1924 to Busoni, Staatsbibliothek zu Berlin–Preußischer Kulturbesitz, Musikabteilung mit Mendelssohn-Archiv, Mus. Nachl. F. Busoni BII 2574, http://resolver.staatsbibliothek-berlin.de/SBB0001C5150 0000000 (Digitalisat) (accessed December 16, 2018). Programs for the Weimar performance of *Arlecchino* can be found in the Goethe- und Schiller-Archiv in Weimar.

[80] Busoni, letter of May 26, 1921, to Franz Hörth, quoted in Beaumont, *Busoni the Composer*, 236–37.

Figure 2.9. Busoni, sketch of Arlecchino. Preussischer Kulturbesitz, Staatsbibliothek zu Berlin, Musikabteilung mit Mendelssohn Archiv, N. Mus. Nachl. 4, 97.

or number is also composed of smaller textures that mix and overlap to create the larger structures in time.

Overall, *Arlecchino* is divided into four main sections (according to Arlecchino's roles as mischief maker, warrior, husband, and victor); the sections are further subdivided into nine numbers. Busoni was not aiming for perfect symmetry. Many of these sections are additionally composed of short segments that are differentiated by style, instrumentation, and character. The opening *Introduzione*, for instance, bears little resemblance to a traditional opera overture or sinfonia. Instead, it contains two main textures that alternate, layer, and mix, thereby unfolding like a multi-dimensional form in space and time. Texture 1 (see example 2.4) is characterized by broken triads, trills, and swirling scales as well as trumpet solo plus winds and strings. An opening triadic trumpet fanfare of four bars that suggests a tonal center of A (even despite chromatic saturation) is then fragmented and developed by winds and strings for another twenty bars while accompanied by swirling trills and scales.[81]

By contrast, texture 2 is characterized by march rhythms, block triads, and the timbres of winds, brass, and percussion. Brief march material with repetitive block triadic material in winds accompanied by tambourine aurally signals a new texture beginning in measure 25, along with a tonicization of F.

After the presentation of the two main textures, Busoni layers and mixes the textures. Opening material reappears in the winds beginning in measure 31, and it appears on top of the march material and tambourine, thus representing a layering of two textures. Although the triads drop out, the tambourine continues through measure 42 as the fragmented opening material takes over again. In measure 41, the chordal opening thematic material returns in the brass, but with additional percussion, such as timpani, triangle, and snare drums, plus steady march rhythms in the brass underneath swirling triplets in the winds and strings, leading to a grand and climactic cadence in measure 58. An ensuing codetta is also a mixture of the two textures. It is characterized by a jaunty trumpet solo over triplets in the timpani, followed by descending triads reminiscent of material from texture

[81] The opening fanfare contains all twelve notes of the chromatic scale, but outlines several triads (A major, B♭ major, B major, C major, A♭ major) and ends on A. Any strong sense of A as a tonal center is obscured in the introduction due to phrasal elisions and a metatonal treatment of the material. At the same time, the opening trumpet fanfare, with its arpeggiated triads, became important thematic material threaded throughout the entire opera.

Example 2.4. Busoni, *Arlecchino*, Introduzione, mm. 1–13.

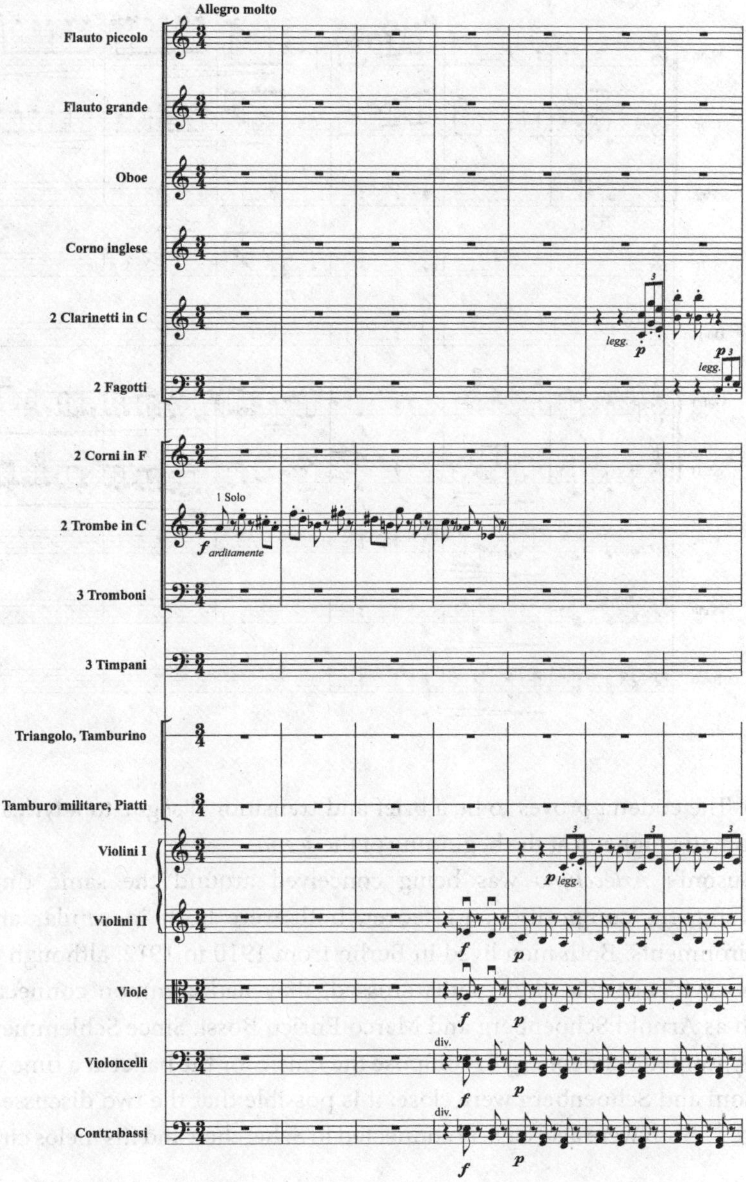

Example 2.4. Continued

two. The codetta proves to be a brief and transitional segue to a lyrical and chromatic fughetta at the beginning of the *scena*.

Busoni's *Arlecchino* was being conceived around the same time as Schlemmer's composition. Moreover, both were born in similar artistic environments. Both men lived in Berlin from 1910 to 1912; although there is no evidence that their paths crossed, they had common connections, such as Arnold Schoenberg and Marco Enrico Bossi. Since Schlemmer initially wanted Schoenberg to compose the music for the ballet at a time when Busoni and Schoenberg were close, it is possible that the two discussed the work.[82] Both were also closely connected to Scherchen and his melos circle.[83]

82 Schlemmer described his indebtedness to Schoenberg's *Pierrot lunaire* and his request for music from him for his own ballet in a letter to Otto Meyer. Schlemmer, letter of January 5, 1913, to Otto Meyer, in Oskar Schlemmer, *The Letters and Diaries of Oskar Schlemmer*, ed. Tut Schlemmer, trans. Krischna Winston (Middletown, CT: Wesleyan University Press, 1972), 10–11.

83 For more about the melos circle, see Ole Hass, "*Melos*," *Retrospective to Music Periodicals*, https://www.ripm.org/?page=JournalInfo&ABB=MEL (accessed April 14, 2021).

Moreover, it is interesting that both works were inspired by Schoenberg's *Pierrot lunaire* (1912).[84]

Even if the two were unaware of each other's works during the creative process, the comparison shows similar ideas were part of the *Zeitgeist*. It is striking that both men arrived at their ideas about moving forms by applying architectural principles to their respective fields. Additionally, both were considering ways their particular arts could take on multi-dimensional aspects. In Schlemmer's case, he considered how cubist visual art could take on multi-dimensional aspects in relation to movement and the human body. This became possible in the 1920s due to his study of sculpture and subsequent consideration of ways architecture and the arts were related. In Busoni's case, a long engagement with architecture became a catalyst for his textural music and multi-dimensional forms moving through time. In both cases, the architectural art forms were liquid, or "ambulant."

Busoni's views about form continuously evolved in relation to his developing observations about architecture and changing ideals of the age. In the early 1900s he sought to blend architectural and natural forms into new structures. In subsequent decades, he embraced a montage approach in which he combined and layered contrasting sections. By the 1920s, he also imagined that larger montage structures could be constructed from the combining of traditional forms and shapes. Busoni's hope was that historical musical forms could be considered, but that they would also be distilled, fragmented, and combined to create new structures.[85] Practically speaking, in his maturity, he created structures that were united by common musical material, but that had audible stylistic, harmonic, and coloristic textures or blocks of sound resulting from a colliding of traditional formal structures.

84 Schlemmer might have been present at the Berlin premiere on October 16, 1912, as he mentions having seen it some time ago in a letter dated January 5, 1913. Schlemmer, letter of January 5, 1913, to Otto Meyer, in Schlemmer, *The Letters and Diaries of Oskar Schlemmer*, 10–11. Busoni sponsored a private performance of the piece in his own home at Viktoria-Luise-Platz 11 on June 17, 1913. Busoni, letter of June 19, 1913, to Egon Petri, in Busoni, *Selected Letters*, 169. For more about the background of *Arlecchino*, see Knyt, "From Nationalism to Transnationalism: Ferruccio Busoni, The Liceo Musicale di Bologna, and *Arlecchino*," *Music and Letters* 99:4 (November 2018): 604–34. After Schoenberg, Schlemmer turned to Bossi to write music for a preview performance of the ballet that took place in 1915.

85 For more about Busoni's use of a diversity of styles that contribute to this fragmentation, see Knyt, "Approaching the Essence of Music: Ferruccio Busoni and Stylistic Heterogeneity in *Doktor Faust*," *Journal of Musicological Research* 35:3 (August 2016): 176–99. See also Busoni, "The Essence and Oneness of Music [1922]," in *The Essence of Music and Other Papers*, trans. Rosamond Ley (London, Salisbury Square, 1957), 1.

In a letter to Paul Bekker in 1920, Busoni stated that although he was against following traditional musical formal molds, he still envisioned the possibilities of combining forms in new ways to create new structures.[86] The composer explained his approach in his description of his compositional process in *Doktor Faust*. He thought first of the larger structure in relation to the *Idee* and related that to perceptions of time and movement. He then sought to write unique structures built from a combination of smaller forms:

> Before anything else it was necessary to sketch out the complete plan, the larger outlines of which were previously indicated by the words, to think over the choice, distribution, and employment of means (forms in time and in movement). The principal thing for me to do was to mould musically independent forms which at the same time suited the words and the scenic events and which also had a separate and sensible existence detached from the words and the situation.[87]

One example of this creation of a larger structure out of the recombination of small basic forms is the Wittenberg tavern scene from *Doktor Faust*, BV 303, a scene that he started in 1921, and considered one of his very best, but that he left incomplete at the time of his death (1924). The effect is one of assemblage as the construction of the music becomes its own structure. The lengthy scene, over 1,200 bars, features multiple textural and melodic changes ranging from double choral writing, to an instrumental polonaise, a ballata, a minuet, mystical instrumental writing, and lyrical and dance-like solo material.

It is a long scene built from many small forms that are not treated conventionally. This distillation of basic forms that Busoni sought after in his maturity is evident, for instance in the opening jaunty triple-meter instrumental minuet in C minor (mm. 1–260). Busoni replicated the character of the minuet. Moreover, the structure initially bears some resemblance to a traditional ternary minuet and trio structure. There are three main sections of very different lengths, that could be thought of as resembling the typical minuet, trio, minuet structure.

[86] Busoni, "Young Classicism," in *The Essence of Music and Other Papers*, 20. [Unter einer "jungen Klassizität" verstehe ich die Meisterung, die Sichtung und Ausbeutung aller Errungenschaften vorausgegangener Experimente: ihre Hineintragung in feste und schöne Formen. Diese Kunst wird alt und neu zugleich sein—zuerst. Dahin steuern wir—glücklicherweise—bewusst und unbewusst, willig oder mitgerissen.] Busoni, "Junge Klassizität," in *Von der Einheit*, 277.

[87] Busoni, "The Score of *Doktor Faust*," in *The Essence of Music and Other Papers*, 73.

Table 2.2. Diagram of the Wittenberg Tavern Scene from *Doktor Faust*

Section	Measures	Subsections (Measures)	Keys	Time Signature(s)	Style
Section A	1–43	a) 1–21 b) 22–43	C minor/ major (with tonicizations of A major, G major, F major, and E♭ major)	$\frac{3}{4}$	Jaunty minuet
Section B	44–141	c) 44–60 d) 61–91 d′) 92–141	First part: Tonally unstable 2nd Part: Mainly F minor 3rd part: Tonally unstable ends on G major	$\frac{3}{4}$, $\frac{2}{4}$	First part: Chromatic counterpoint with irregular phrasing Second and third parts: Lively duple-meter dance
Section A′	142–260	a′ and b′) 142–61 a′, b′, c′, and d′) 162–240 c″) 240–60	Begins and cadences in C minor	$\frac{3}{4}$	Jaunty minuet, Meyerbeerian march, Chromatic counterpoint

However, the proportions are unusual, with each section significantly longer than the previous one. Moreover, the middle section is not like a trio in character, and the final section is largely developmental, while also featuring the return of material from the B section at the conclusion (see table 2.2).

The opening section of the minuet contains two main parts and ends with a dramatic cadence on C major (albeit with the third at the bottom of the chord). Yet it is hardly a conventional rounded binary opening. It starts in the tonic but quickly emphasizes several other keys due to chromatic inflection, plurisignificance, and sequences (i.e., A major, G major, F major, and E♭ major). The overall style is jaunty and characterized by broken triads and a rhythmic motive of four repeated chords in different time values (e.g., three eighths followed by a quarter note or three eighths plus eighth rests followed by a dotted half note). The first part contains a half cadence in measure 21 that is elided by a choral entrance, and the opening section does not immediately repeat as expected.

By contrast, the second part of the opening A section, beginning in measure 21, centers on the parallel major, and features the addition of the chorus.

Despite the return of the main rhythmic motive, and some broken triadic writing, the material contrasts overall with more homorhythmic writing, leading to a dramatic and rousing cadence in C major (see example 2.5).

The B section contrasts with the A section in tempo, meter, texture, and motivic material, but it is not in the character of a trio. It also contains three main sections that contrast in terms of meter, texture, key center, instrumentation, register, and style (mm. 44–60, 61–91, 92–141). The beginning of the B section hardly resembles a trio, with irregular phrasing and

Example 2.5. Busoni, *Doktor Faust*, Wittenberg tavern scene, mm. 1–73.

Example 2.5. Continued

Example 2.5. Continued

Example 2.5. Continued

Example 2.5. Continued

Example 2.5. Continued

the juxtaposition of two contrasting solos followed by a chorus of tenors and basses. Lugubrious chromatic sequential canonic writing in stepwise motion, coupled with the timbre of the bassoon, viola, and flute, introduces the tranquillo B section in measure 43, but the ensuing music features material reminiscent of the choral melody from the opening minuet bars 21–24. Although highly chromatic, the section ends with a slight tonicization on F for a fleeting cadence in measure 60.

The second part of the middle section, which initially suggests F minor, features a lively duple meter dance with offbeat accents and staccato attacks with imitation in the instruments, which feature much brass and wind instruments. Clearly a parody, Busoni switches to four-bar phrasing. The third section, although still featuring similar sequential scalar patterns, is initially more tonally stable and hints at the dominant, in which the section finally ends, with a perfunctory half cadence in measure 141.

A return to triple-meter minuet rhythms and the key of C minor in measure 142 initially seems to complete the strange minuet form, this time with voices added, but the repetition is overlaid with choral imitation at measure 149 when Busoni combines material from sections A and B. Choral polyphony is layered on top of the minuet material. Through hemiolas, a brief duple-meter march interrupts the minuet in measure 161. A swirling fantasia of motives from the duple dance, the chromatic dialogue, and the minuet are interwoven into a complex medley before a return of the conclusion of section A in measure 240 that is followed by a tranquil chromatic transition (mm. 250–59) based on material from the opening of the B section.[88]

The final A section is thus the most unexpected in that it not only returns to the original A material, but also conflates it with B section material, and develops and fragments material. It represents a culmination of the preceding materials (vocally and instrumentally). Although the first six bars of material closely resemble the opening instrumental minuet, it returns overlaid with choral and solo singing before spinning out into new material that modulates. The second part of the A section also returns, but this time in D major, up a major second. Moreover, the ensuing choral writing is imitative and conflates several texts simultaneously (i.e., "Prosit," "So lang man Jugend hat . . .," and "Juvenes dum . . ."). This is followed by reference to the

[88] Busoni looked to historical models as well, such as J. S. Bach, whose music did not simply follow archaic forms, but also blended forms together—a classic example being the Brandenburg Concerto no. 5 in D Major, BWV 1050, which blends concerto, fantasia, and dance forms.

opening ascending chromatic three-note motive from the trio section and other material from the previous A and B sections that is fragmented and developed. The cadential material from the A section finally returns after this lengthy development section from measures 236–45, leading to a cadence in C, and is followed by tranquillo transitional material reminiscent of the B section, before leading to the end of the section at measure 259.

Busoni thus continued developing montage forms in the 1920s but added to his approach a distillation of small basic forms. To this minuet, Busoni added parts of a waltz, a polonaise, and a Te Deum, all within the same scene.

At the same time that Busoni was creating the larger structure of *Doktor Faust* out of distillations of smaller forms, Bauhaus architects and advocates of *Neues Bauen* also created structures out of many small basic forms that were combined and recombined in many creative ways beginning in 1919.[89] The movement grew out of the neo-Gothic Chicago school that had so impressed Busoni in 1910. The same basic materials used to create skyscrapers in Chicago, such as iron and steel frames with brick veneers and plenty of glass, now became useful for residences and office buildings. If Busoni was not interested in the settlement buildings and mass-produced homes that drove some *Neues Bauen* architects, the play with form would have been of greater interest, and especially the synthesis of internal and external structure. This modern style of architecture featured simpler and sleeker lines derived from the juxtaposition of basic geometric shapes, even if they simultaneously featured a formal montage resulting from jutting balconies, passageways, and areas of egress. The structure shines clearly, and devoid of ornamentation or curved natural lines even if exact symmetry is often avoided, and artistry is displayed through the clever and tasteful juxtaposition of shapes. The new simplicity and objectivity of this style was in line with Busoni's vision of *Young Classicality*, along with its drive for an integration of inner content and outer shape, as inseparable organic wholes, even if he never relinquished a stylistic pluralism that was fundamental to his output.

As Bradley Brookshire explains, discussions of *Neues Bauen* were common in certain Berlin circles in the 1920s, where one of Busoni's mentees, Edwin

[89] Erwin Anton Gutkind invented the term in 1919. Gutkind, *New Building: Basics of Practical Settlement Activity* (Berlin: Verlag der Bauwelt, 1919). For more information, see Norbert Huse, *New Building 1918–1933* (Munich: Heinz Moos, 1975); Tanja Poppelreuter, *The New Building for the New Person: On the Change and Effect of the Image of Man in the Architecture of the 1920s in Germany* (New York: Olms, 2007).

Fischer, visited, such as in the salons of hostesses Jenny Mautner and Marie von Bülow.[90] Fischer met Busoni at his masterclass in Basel, Switzerland, in 1910, and remained friends with him until his death in 1924.[91] While there is no indication that Busoni attended the salon gatherings of Mautner and von Bülow, there would have been cross influence for Busoni through Fischer, as well as through Gropius and Scherchen's melos circles.

Moreover, Berlin underwent a transformation during and after World War I, as new buildings were erected that were devoid of Wilhelmine and *Jugendstil* decoration. What they featured instead was multi-dimensional shape and a notion of the integration of the part and whole into a new organism characterized by simplicity.[92] An early example of *Neues Bauen* in Berlin is the Siedlung Schillerpark, a group of residences designed in 1914 by Bruno Taut in the Wedding district and completed by 1921. Flat roofs and sleek lines on the red brick facades are accented by jutting balconies and entryways that add dimension and angles to the cubist buildings.

Busoni's political views were widely divergent from socialism that was behind the philosophical mindset of some of the urban developments associated with *Neues Bauen*. Moreover, he was not an advocate of mass-produced houses. However, the idea of a new simplicity and the combination of simple basic forms was one of his priorities in the 1920s and articulated in his theories of *Young Classicality*.

Busoni's *Doktor Faust* similarly displays a play with shapes, basic forms, and textures in space to produce unique structures. Antony Beaumont has documented that Busoni drafted the first part of the Wittenberg tavern scene for *Doktor Faust* quickly in 1921, just when *Neues Bauen* was developing, and he continued working on the movement until his death in 1924, ultimately leaving it incomplete.[93] It would be accurate to state that there was a *Zeitgeist* common to both in which structure was created out of small pieces and discontinuities.

This cubist, or geometric, approach extended from music, to visual art, to architecture at the time. It is worth noting that Busoni was also exposed

[90] Bradley Brookshire, "Edwin Fischer and Bach Performance Practice of the Weimar Republic" (PhD diss., CUNY, 2016), 120.

[91] For more about this connection, see Brookshire, "Edwin Fischer," 45–47.

[92] See, for instance, the following for an explanation of new architectural ideals of the 1920s: Le Corbusier, "Towards a New Architecture: Guiding Principles," in *Programs and Manifestoes on 20th-Century Architecture*, ed. Ulrich Conrads (Cambridge, MA: MIT Press, 1975), 59–62.

[93] Antony Beaumont, *Busoni the Composer*, 345.

to cubist Dadaist art during World War I in Switzerland, and that doubtless played a role as well. For instance, he attended a Dadaist show at the Waag Guild House in 1916 along with Othmar Schoeck. One of his pupils, Otto Luening, was performing the "Wet Dream Gavotte."[94] He also attended performances at the Cabaret Voltaire that included recitations of poetry by Ivan Goll, Hugo Ball, Hans Arp, Tristan Tzara, Emmy Hennings, and others.[95] Busoni also had direct insight into the movement from his pupil, Gabrielle Buffet-Picabia, who had married Francis Picabia in 1909; Buffet-Picabia studied with Busoni in Berlin prior to World War I. She and her husband moved to Switzerland in 1918.[96] Busoni also knew Max ("Mopp") Oppenheimer, who combined techniques of expressionism and cubism in his famous portrait of Busoni from 1916. During his lifetime, some of Busoni's compositions, such as his Sonatina seconda, BV 259, were referred to as cubist.[97]

In addition, Busoni would have most likely observed this cubist *Neues Bauen* style in the Haus am Horn, the lone Bauhaus model in the 1923 architectural exhibition. The house is composed almost entirely of two basic shapes, squares and rectangles that are juxtaposed and reconfigured in numerous ways (see figure 2.10). The combinatorial process of taking small recognizable shapes in varied combinations to create a new whole is similar to Busoni's mature process of fragmenting and combining small musical forms.

The exterior building is a square with a nearly flat roof that contains many small square and rectangular windows of differing heights and widths. The top of the building is outlined by a long rectangular accent and a small square that juts out of the center of rooftop as the second story. The outer shell frames an internal square living area that is in turn surrounded by unusually shaped rooms (i.e., L-shaped, long and narrow, boxy, etc.) and built out of small squares or rectangles. The kitchen features rectangular tiles and square

94 Chris Walton, *Othmar Schoeck: Life and Works* (Rochester, NY: University of Rochester Press, 2009), 67. For more about the music of Dada, see Peter Dayan, *The Music of Dada: A Lesson in Intermediality for Our Times* (New York: Routledge, 2019).

95 Stuckenschmidt, *Ferruccio Busoni: Chronicle of a European*, trans. Sandra Morris (New York: St. Martin's Press, 1967), 58.

96 For more about Busoni's exile in Switzerland, see Laureto Rodoni, "Die Gerade Linie ist unterbrochen: L'esilio di Busoni a Zurigo, 1915–1920," in *La Svizzera: Terra d'Asilo*, Atti-Kongressbericht-Ascona, 1998 (Bern: P. Lang, 2000), 27–106.

97 "Busoni's cubist creation, the second sonatina, which was first performed in America three years ago, will also be played." "Rudolph Reuter's Chicago Recital," *Music Magazine-Musical Courier* 75 (November 1, 1917), 33. Busoni was also acquainted with Ferdinand Hardekopf, Hans Richter, and Ludwig Rubiner.

Figure 2.10. Georg Muche, architect, Haus am Horn, from the 1923 Bauhaus Exhibition. Bauhaus-Archiv, Berlin.

and rectangular cabinets of all sizes. An all-white bathroom features four large white tiles behind a large white built-in bathtub. Accessories include a carpet of colorful squares under a table, and colorful square and rectangular blocks in the children's room.

Although the architectural exhibit of 1923 at the Bauhaus that Busoni attended included a display of 170 illustrations and photos and eight models of architectural creations from architects throughout Europe and the United States diverse in style, certain characteristics, such as experimentation with new materials (such as concrete), emphasis on spatial forms, and montage structures or those built from variations on simple geometric shapes, were emphasized; these would later help establish what became known as the "International Style."[98] Some of the images in the exhibition displaying

[98] Barry Bergdoll and Leah Dickerman, *Bauhaus 1919–1933: Workshops for Modernity* (New York: D. A. P., 2009), 50–52. The exhibit (Ausstellung Internationaler Architektur) was on display from August 8 through September 30, 1923, including throughout the famed "Bauhaus Week." Some of the contributors included Walter Gropius, Adolf Meyer, Mies van der Rohe, Frank Lloyd Wright, Le Corbusier, Bruno Taut, and Erich Mendelsohn. Taut, Mendelssohn, and Mies were at the exhibition in person.

these approaches included Gropius's Auerbach House and the municipal theater in Jena, as well as his skyscraper entry to the Chicago Tribune Tower Competition, and Ludwig Mies van der Rohe's proposal for an office building with reinforced concrete. Wright provided photographs of the Larken Administration Building in Buffalo, New York (1904) and the Robie House (1908), and Le Corbusier offered photos of the Citrohan model house from 1921 and the designs for "A City for Three Million Residents" (1922).

In his book on international architecture in 1925, an outgrowth of the exhibition, Gropius specifically advocated for an architectural palette built from basic forms. The *Internationale Architekten* section of the 1923 display publication about the exhibition included an array of international contemporary architecture. Axonometric projections appeared repeatedly, placing emphasis on spatial formal conceptions as well that Busoni had already discussed with van de Velde.[99]

Le Corbusier, whose work was featured at the 1923 exhibition, claimed that humans are trained to recognize and see simple primary geometric structures (such as cubes, cones, spheres, cylinders, or pyramids): "Our eyes are constructed to enable us to see forms in light. Primary forms are beautiful forms because they can be clearly appreciated."[100] Like Busoni, he aimed for congruity between form and content, claiming that the interior should determine and be congruent with the exterior: "The plan proceeds from within to without; the exterior is the result of the interior. The elements of architecture are light and shade, walls and space."[101]

[99] Very little research has been done on the 1923 architectural exhibition. However, it was re created in 2009 thanks to the work of Norbert Korrek: https://www.uni-weimar.de/de/universitaet/partner-und-alumni/alumni/alumni-treffen/events/jubilaeum-2010/zum-programm/begleitausstellungen/architektur-ausstellungen-am-fruehen-bauhaus-weimar-1919-1922-1923/ (accessed August 26, 2019).

[100] Le Corbusier, "Three Reminders to Architects: Mass," in *Towards a New Architecture*, trans. Frederick Etchells (New York: Dover, 1986), 24–29. [Nos yeux sont faits voir les forms sous la lumière. Les forms primaires sont les belles forms parce qu'elles se lisent clairement.] Le Corbusier, *Vers une Architecture* (Paris: G. Crèss, 1929), 13.

[101] Le Corbusier, "Architecture: The Illusion of Plans," in *Towards a New Architecture*, trans. Frederick Etchells (New York: Dover, 1986), 178. [Le plan procède du dedans au dehors; l'extérieur est le résultat d'un intérieur. Les elements architecturaux sont la lumière et l'ombre, le mur et l'espace.] Le Corbusier, *Vers une Architecture* (Paris: G. Crèss, 1929), 169. For more information about his views, see Isabelle Frank, ed., *The Theory of Decorative Art: An Anthology of European and American Writings: 1750–1940* (New Haven, CT: Yale University Press, 2000); Winfried Nerdinger, *The Walter Gropius Archive: An Illustrated Catalogue of the Drawings, Prints, and Photographs in the Walter Gropius Archive at the Busch-Reisinger Museum, Harvard University*, Vol. 1 (New York: Garland Publishing and Harvard University Art Museums, 1990). Many of Corbusier's ideals are reflected in his Citrohan house. Busoni would most likely have seen images of it at the exhibition; the rectrolinear form is both functional and artistic. The many windows ensure that it is filled with light. The living

Coda

Busoni knew traditional musical forms well, but he was participating in an early modernist exploration of ways to break free from those forms and the traditional scalar and harmonic relationships upon which they were based. In moving away from more traditional formal molds in the early 1900s, he sought to create structures that were solid, original, and artistic. During his evolution, Busoni went from idealizing imitations of natural and architectural forms, to idealizing montage forms in which textures emerge and combine in multiple dimensions, or short basic forms are dissected, fragmented, and recombined. In the process, he participated in a modernist quest to combine temporal and spatial art forms in new ways, even if his specific solutions were idiosyncratic.

As this chapter shows, Busoni's journey to discover new musical structures was not made in isolation and was inspired by elements outside his discipline; it reflects Germanic philosophical thought and parallels developments in visual art and architecture. Busoni's allusions to architecture in his compositions ranged from explicit reference to architectural styles or shapes of buildings to its spatial properties and multi-dimensionality. In many ways, Busoni was more indebted to the models of architects for his musical experiments than to contemporary composers.

That said, these connections in no way negate obvious parallels in music, with plenty of other theorists, such as Busoni's colleague and friend Heinrich Schenker, who was also exploring what it meant to write organically coherent music. Arnold Schoenberg, a mentee of Busoni in the early 1910s, similarly sought to write unique forms with musical materials. French and Russian composers, with whom Busoni was familiar, such as Claude Debussy and Igor Stravinsky, also composed disjointed music comprising short segments. Yet some of this music is more like a two-dimensional collage of styles, rather than a multi-dimensional montage.[102] The closest parallels are perhaps with the music of Charles Ives, who composed textural collages as early as 1906,

room is open with a tall ceiling leading to a balcony on the second floor. Although free from most types of ornamentation, there is a spiral staircase and a roof garden on the flat roof. There is an emphasis on light and air, with a large display window in the living room and space for a garden on the roof.

[102] For more about the development of transnationalism in Busoni's music, see Knyt, "From Nationalism to Transnationalism."

but there is no indication that Busoni was aware of his compositions.[103] Indeed, both Ives and Busoni seemed to be arriving at music organized by textures quite independently, and by looking outside of music for inspiration.[104] Lawrence Starr, similarly, has found more parallels between Ives's music and contemporary literature than with other music examples. Busoni, in turn, was inspired by architecture and visual art.

It is also probable that some of Busoni's ideas came from Hugo Leichtentritt and his *Musikalische Formenlehre* (1920). In the second edition, which Busoni read, Leichtentritt explained how the motives and tones relate to one another in a coherent manner based upon the human perception of motivic connections, as opposed to the cellular unfolding of motives. Leichtentritt maintained that unity could be found between contrasting themes, motives, or styles as the mind drew connections between them.[105] What concerned Leichtentritt most of all was not the continuous growth of a single motive throughout a piece, but rather how disparate elements were connected:

> What matters now is not so much the continuation of an idea, but the connection of two different ideas. Aesthetic effects and logical connections are derived not from the similarities, but from the differences.[106]

Yet, this chapter shows that Busoni was simultaneously influenced by the other arts, with which he was so fascinated, even as he participated in a general *Zeitgeist* interested in seeing and hearing shapes moving in time. It was in the work of architects that Busoni found many models for what he was trying to do in music. He wanted to compose music that was as durable as Classical architectural masterpieces, yet as fluid as the rays of the sun. When Busoni thought about form, he often thought about it in an architectural sense—in terms of space, texture, and dimension—yet at the same time as fluidly moving in and through time.

[103] For more information about Ives's approach, see Lawrence Starr, *A Union of Diversities: Style in the Music of Charles Ives* (New York: Schirmer Books, 1992); J. Peter Burkholder, "Stylistic Heterogeneity and Topics in the Music of Charles Ives," *Journal of Musicological Research* 31 (2012): 166–99; Lawrence Starr, "Charles Ives: The Next Hundred Years—Towards a Method of Analyzing the Music," *Music Review* 38 (May 1977): 101–11.

[104] Starr, "Charles Ives," 101–2.

[105] Busoni, letter of September 21, 1918, to Hugo Leichtentritt, in *Selected Letters*, 274. The copy Busoni received must have been of the second edition, which appeared in 1920. For an English translation, see Hugo Leichtentritt, *Musical Form* (Cambridge, MA: Harvard University Press, 1951), 219.

[106] Leichtentritt, *Musical Form*, 234.

In thinking of musical structure in this way, Busoni was both of his time and anticipating the textural and process music of the latter part of the twentieth century. For Busoni, good structures build upon ideas such that they seem to unfold in a state of becoming until they are eminently revealed and suggestive of what can yet come. Yet, montage structures were just part of Busoni's vision of ideal music, which, as he noted, should also fill the air and reflect the spatial areas that sound waves occupy, as will be discussed in chapter 3. If he sought to model his formal structures after architectural designs, he also sought to create, metaphorically speaking, *Tonkunst* that offered "frozen" glimpses of the essence of music, that is, "rays of the original light through immeasurable space."[107]

[107] [Strahlen des Urlichts durch unermesslichen Raum.] Busoni, "The Essence of Music: A Paving of the Way to an Understanding of the Everlasting Calendar [1924]," in *The Essence of Music and Other Papers*, trans. Rosamond Ley (London: Rockliff), 200; Busoni, "Vom Wesen der Musik: Anbahnung einer Verständigung für den immerwärenden Kalender," *Melos: Jahrbuch für zeitgenossische Musik* 4:1 (August 1, 1924): 13. For more information about historical notions of music and architecture, see Siitan, "Muusika: Elustunud arhitektuur?"

3
The Circle of Sound

> Music is not, as the poet says, an "ambassador" of heaven, but the ambassadors of heaven are those chosen ones on whom the high charge is laid to bring us single rays of the original light through immeasurable space.
>
> —Busoni, 1924[1]

Ferruccio Busoni's compositions feature not only montage forms and expansive treatments of the tonal language, but also sounds radiating from different directions, textural layering, and evocations of depth and height through experimentation with register, timbre, acoustics, and time. In this he participated in an enthusiasm for experimentation with sound that was characteristic of composers in the early twentieth century. Yet many of Busoni's ideas were informed by his study of architecture as well as by metaphysical notions of inaudible sound in the universe. He conceived of music itself as possessing spatial properties. Moreover, he posited more radical theories about how music could encircle the stage and envelope listeners in a circle of sound (*Klang-horizont*) in the theater as it emanated from different locations simultaneously (e.g., below the stage, behind the stage, above the stage, in front of the stage, and on the sides of the stage). At the same time, he used his knowledge of physical and architectural space to invoke senses of distance in traditionally placed ensembles through his play with time.

[1] Thanks are due Jerry McBride (Stanford University), Erin Jerome (University of Massachusetts, Amherst), Jean-Christophe Gero (Staatsbibliothek zu Berlin), and Marina Gordienko (Staatsbibliothek zu Berlin) for their assistance locating archival materials for this chapter. [Nicht die Musik ist ein "Abgesandter des Himmels," wie der Dichter meint, sondern des Himmels Abgesandte sind gerade jene Erwählten, denen das hohe Amtaufgebürdet ist, einzelne Strahlen des Urlichts durch unermesslichen Raum uns zuzubringen.] Busoni, "The Essence of Music: A Paving of the Way to an Understanding of the Everlasting Calendar [1924]," in *The Essence of Music and Other Papers*, trans. Rosamond Ley (London: Rockliff), 200; Busoni, "Vom Wesen der Musik: Anbahnung einer Verständigung für den immerwärenden Kalender," *Melos: Jahrbuch für zeitgenossische Musik* 4:1 (August 1, 1924): 13.

Ferruccio Busoni as Architect of Sound. Erinn E. Knyt, Oxford University Press. © Oxford University Press 2023.
DOI: 10.1093/oso/9780197625491.003.0004

While the spatialization of music in the twentieth century has received considerable attention, Busoni's role has largely escaped consideration.[2] Through analyses of letters, essays, unpublished documents, and the composer's own scores, especially some of his operas (*Doktor Faust*, BV 303, and *Die Brautwahl*, BV 258) and symphonic works (*Berceuse élégiaque*, BV 252a), this chapter documents Busoni's ideas about spatialized sound. It delineates his views about space and dimensionality, documenting how they influenced his decisions about timbre, placement of instruments, and dramaturgy in his compositions from the 1910s and 1920s.

In the process, it shows that many of Busoni's idiosyncratic aesthetic ideas were based on metaphysical notions of inaudible sound in the universe that he translated into audible sounds using models of known physical spaces in specific architectural styles and buildings. For instance, the composer re created the sounds he imagined in the inaudible vibrating universe based on his understanding of reverberation, morphology of sound, and the resonance associated with the vast space in cathedrals. Architectural drawings for novel theatrical spaces, such as a triple stage opening inspired by Henry van de Velde, or a multilevel stage area, although never realized, also informed his ideas about instrument placement and inspired simultaneity of musical textures in *Doktor Faust*, BV 303. This chapter thus documents a little-understood aspect of Busoni's aesthetics and compositional style. In addition, it calls for a reconsideration of the composer's importance in the development of spatialized music, thereby also enriching understanding about the development of early twentieth-century music in general.

Contemporaneous Ideas about Spatial Music

Busoni's aesthetic theories are based upon notions of dimension and space, aspects that became increasingly important for music in the twentieth century.[3] That said, specific perceptions of relationships between space and

[2] A few relevant sources include the following: Jens Blauert, *Spatial Hearing: The Psychophysics of Human Sound Localization*, trans. John S. Allen (Cambridge, MA: MIT Press, 1983); Kurt Blaukopf, "Space in Electronic Music," in *Music and Technology* 2:1 (1971), 157–72; John Cage, *Silence: Lectures and Writings* (Middletown, CT: Wesleyan University Press, 1961); Edward T. Cone, "Berlioz's Divine Comedy: The Grande messe des morts," *19th-Century Music* 4:1 (1980): 3–16.

[3] One of the major discrepancies between the two art forms is "time"—sounds and pitches unfold in time, whereas the materials of architecture are "frozen" in place. Yet, architecture can also be experienced similarly, with the eye slowly taking in details of architecture over a span of time, just as

music vary widely from one composer or theorist to the next.[4] And while music has always been spatial, it was only in the last century that it was more regularly spatialized. Busoni was thus participating in a general fascination with music as a spatial art form in his era, even if his ideas were idiosyncratic.

The spatialization of sound in compositions from prior centuries frequently served as a model for Busoni. It sometimes involved antiphonal or split choral singing, such as in the choral music of Andrea and Giovanni Gabrieli at St. Mark's Basilica in the sixteenth century or the double chorus in J. S. Bach's *St. Matthew Passion* in the eighteenth century. On other occasions, composers placed instruments or solo voices in offstage locations. For instance, brass and percussion instruments were frequently positioned offstage to imitate outdoor military, hunting, or funeral music, and offstage voices indicated action beyond the stage. In Mozart's *Don Giovanni*, Don Giovanni's voice appears offstage in Mozart's opera while he tries to seduce Zerlina in act I, scene 4. The use of offstage brass and percussion was especially common in the early nineteenth century in operas and program music to depict military and hunting scenes, as regal attention-getting devices, or to aid the ambiance, especially the pastoral, where offstage instruments suggest the vastness of the outdoors. For instance, Beethoven used an offstage trumpet fanfare in *Fidelio* to herald the impending death of Florestan. Offstage choirs were particularly effective in creating religious and ceremonial ambiance and for crowd scenes. In Italian opera, the choir sometimes voiced the thoughts of God. Berlioz's Requiem, which premiered in Les Invalides, a large domed cathedral in a military hospital, took advantage of the cavernous acoustical space by placing four brass ensembles in different locations to evoke a very dramatic effect, especially in the "Tuba Mirum" section, which is associated with God's judgment.

Yet if offstage diegetic music for dramatic effect was not uncommon in program music or opera in the nineteenth century, the uses of spatialized sound increased dramatically in the late nineteenth and early twentieth centuries and became essential to the structure of the pieces. Composers experimented with new placements for instruments and new types of offstage instrument groups, the use of spatialized sound in a structural sense,

musical notes unfold in the listener's ears over a span of time. Additionally, musical notes are usually fixed in notation even before they are experienced aurally.

[4] For an overview about spatialized music in the twentieth century, see Maria Anna Harley, "Space and Spatialization in Contemporary Music" (PhD diss., McGill University, 1994), 7. Harley's birth name was Maria Anna Trochimczyk. She is also known as Maja Trochimczyk.

the use of spatialized sound without programmatic connections, and the use of spatialized sound placement to portray multiple actions simultaneously in dramatic pieces. In some cases, a separation of textural layers was designed to aid comprehensibility in complex music.

Notions of how music is spatialized in the twentieth century vary depending on whether the focus is on the music itself, the way music is presented, or the way sound is received by the listener. Busoni considered all three possibilities. Spatial music can be thought of as possessing different musical layers, as being organized by diverse textures, as relating to actual interaction with physical space, or as adhering to more speculative or conceptual theories of spatialization. A common topic in writings by composers and scholars is that of the spatial nature of pitches themselves.[5] Some also consider dynamics, time, and physical space as contributing to the multidimensional aspects of music. Hans Mersmann, for instance, described music in 1926 as two-dimensional, with melody and harmony forming horizontal and vertical dimensions.[6] Arnold Schoenberg, similarly, was also primarily interested in successive musical sounds and how they combine into simultaneous vertical ones.[7]

Authors with phenomenological or dynamic orientations during Busoni's lifetime, such as Ernst Kurth, for instance, also considered pitch motion in time to be important.[8] Form also plays a role, insofar as it organizes the progression of pitches.[9] It is possible that Busoni read Kurth's *Grundlagen des linearen Kontrapunkts* (1917) and was familiar with some of the concepts, or that Kurth had read some of Busoni's essays.[10] At the very least, some of Busoni's circle, such as Ernst Krenek, admired the text, and Philipp Jarnach, one of Busoni's closest composition students, referred to it in lessons.[11] Kurth

[5] Thomas Clifton, *Music as Heard: A Study in Applied Phenomenology* (New Haven, CT: Yale University Press, 1983); Gisèle Brelet, *Le temps musical: Essai d'une esthétique nouvelle de la musique* (Paris: Presses universitaires de France), 1949; Ernst Kurth, *Musikpsychologie* (New York: Georg Olms Verlag, 1969); Viktor Zuckerkandl, *Sound and Symbol: Music and the External World*, trans. W. R. Trask (New York: Pantheon Books, 1956).

[6] Hans Mersmann, *Angewandte Musikästhetik* (Berlin: M. Hesse, 1926), ii.

[7] Arnold Schoenberg, "Composition with Twelve Tones, [1941]," in *Style and Idea: Selected Writings of Arnold Schoenberg*, ed. Leonard Stein, trans. Leo Black (London: Faber and Faber, 1975), 220.

[8] Kurth, *Musikpsychologie*; Roman Ingarden, *The Work of Music and the Problem of Its Identity* [1958], trans. Adam Czerniawski (Berkeley: University of California Press, 1986).

[9] Theodor W. Adorno, *Philosophie der Neuen Musik* (Tübingen: J. C. B. Mohr, 1948), 186.

[10] Ernst Kurth, *Grundlagen des linearen Kontrapunkts Einführung in Stil und Technik von Bach's melodischer Polyphonie* (Bern: Drechsel, 1917). For an English translation, see Lee Rothfarb, ed. and trans., *Ernst Kurth Selected Writings* (Cambridge: Cambridge University Press, 1991).

[11] Ernst Kurth stated his support in a letter to his publisher dated April 13, 1921, in Nora Schmid and Lea Hinden, eds., "Volltextbriefe zum Inventar Nachlass Ernst Kurth," Vers. 4.0 (Bern: University,

mentions several dimensions, including melody, harmony, energy/movement, sonority, time, and texture, in his writings. Harmony results from multiple lines; yet harmony is not a stack of inert chords, but rather, potential energy that helps propel the lines forward. The linear aspects of music also take on additional dimensions as Kurth sees them manifesting the creative will of the composers. Form, similarly, represents a struggle in motion to solidify flowing lines.[12] Kurth describes some of these dimensions thus: "The interaction between dynamic tensions and a harmonic equilibrium, between energy and tone, as manifest in the [single] melodic line, determines analogously the relationship in polyphonic music."[13]

Busoni and his near contemporaries thus thought deeply about relationships between space and music. At the same time, they envisioned ways to expand offstage and spatialized sound in compositions (see table 3.1). In so doing, they built upon past traditions, but also applied spatial techniques to purely instrumental music and explored new techniques for placing instruments within physical space. In addition, they examined ways multiple layers of sound could be separated in space even if occurring simultaneously; they did this using techniques such as stylistic heterogeneity or a play with metrics, timing, or dynamics.

Busoni's Piano Concerto in C Major (1904) is one of the first non-programmatic instrumental compositions to feature an offstage chorus. His addition of vocal sounds, the chanting of a mystical text syllabically from Adam Oehlenschläger's *Aladdin*, adds an additional textual dimension on top of the piano's widespread arpeggios, the orchestra's plaintive melodies, and sustained harmonies as three sonorous bodies sound simultaneously, each with their own characteristic textures and sonorities. Similarly, he added an offstage vocal part to *Rondò arlecchinesco*, BV 266 (1915), an orchestral suite. The tenor's lighthearted text-less vocalizations ("la-la-las" and laughing) at the end of the composition add an unexpected texture to the already stylistically diverse composition. Just one year later, Gustav Holst added textless choral writing to the Neptune movement of *The Planets* (1916).

Institut für Musikwissenschaft, September 2007), http://www.musik.unibe.ch/dienstleistungen/nachlass_kurth/index_ger.html (accessed October 22, 2020). See also Knyt, *Ferruccio Busoni and His Legacy* (Bloomington: Indiana University Press, 2017), 264.

[12] See also Stephanie Probst, "Sounding Lines: New Approaches to Melody in 1920s Musical Thought" (PhD diss., Harvard University, 2018).

[13] Kurth, *Grundlagen des linearen Kontrapunkts*, 37–38.

Table 3.1. Pieces with Offstage Instruments during Busoni's Lifetime (1866–1924)[a]

Composer	Composition	Offstage Instrument (s)/ Sound(s)	Date	Annotations
Franz Liszt	*Christus*, S. 3	Chorus	1866	The invisible chorus announces the resurrection.
Arrigo Boito	*Mefistofele*	Chorus and bells	1867	God speaks through the unseen chorus. The bells resound offstage on the right and the left.
Giuseppe Verdi	*Messa da Requiem*	4 trumpets	1874	The four trumpets surround the stage during the "Tuba Mirum" to evoke the sound of judgment.
Edvard Grieg	*Peer Gynt*, op. 23	1 viola	1875	The viola plays from backstage during the prelude and evokes the sound of a rustic country dance for the wedding.
Richard Wagner	*Götterdämmerung*, WWV 86D	1 French horn, 1 C horn, Ox horns	1876	In act II, the ox horns are positioned both on and off stage to evoke the sounds of hunting horns from coming from different locations.
Pyotr Ilyich Tchaikovsky	*Orleanskaja deva*	3 trumpets, 4 trombones, military drum	1879	In act II, the sound of distant trumpets is heard during a battle. The offstage instruments suggest military action.
Pyotr Ilyich Tchaikovsky	*1812 Overture*	Brass instruments and cannon	1880	Offstage ensembles suggest military sounds and action. The cannon adds additional drama.
Jules Massenet	Orchestral Suite no. 7: *Scènes alsaciennes*	Bugles and drums	1882	The offstage bugles and drums evoke the sound of the French military retreat in this piece of program music.
Richard Wagner	*Parsifal*	6 trumpets, 6 trombones, tenor drum, bells, and voices	1882	The brass, drums, and bells played from the wings suggest a religious ceremony. Two choruses also sing from above the stage, and Titurel sings from behind the stage. These different placements not only coincide with the sacred nature of the topic (the Holy Grail), but also the phenomenon of music making in real life (i.e., choirs from church balconies and brass in nature).

Charles-Camille Saint-Saëns	*Henry VIII*	Military orchestra and chorus	1883	The Chorus follows an entr'acte in act II that heralds the arrival of Don Gomez and comments on the action. It also appears in act IV when Catherine hears her ex-husband praised. In act IV there is an instrumental offstage funeral march as Buckingham is taken away to a torture chamber.
Vincent d'Indy	*Le chant de la cloche*, op. 18	3 natural trumpets and three trumpets offstage, snare drum, E♭ bell	1885	The offstage bell is featured prominently in the final movement, where it resounds at the conclusion of the work.
Pyotr Ilyich Tchaikovsky	*Cherevichki*	Military wind band	1885	The offstage military wind band appears in act III (nos. 19 [Polonaise] and 23 [Scene]).
Charles-Camille Saint-Saëns	*Proserpine*	Orchestra (flute, harp, bell, organ, viola, cello)	1887	In act II, there is an offstage Pavane.
Giuseppe Verdi	*Otello*	6 trumpets, 4 trombones, bagpipes, mandolins, guitars, strings, and voices	1887	There are numerous offstage crowd scenes; there are also offstage trumpet fanfares, as pages (bearing gifts) enter the Castle. The chorus "Dove guardi splendono raggi" is a descriptive pastoral tableau that is complemented by the coloration of a bagpipe, mandolins, and guitars.
Gustav Mahler	Symphony no. 1 in D Major	3 trumpets	1888	Offstage trumpet fanfares appear at the beginning of the symphony.
Pyotr Ilyich Tchaikovsky	*Nutcracker*, op. 71	Children's choir	1892	This offstage chorus takes place during the "Waltz of the Snowflakes." The delicate children's voices add to the ethereal affect as snowflakes fall.
Giacomo Puccini	*La bohème*	*Banda* (military)	1893	The *banda* appears at the end of act II as Musetta and friends leave a café.

(*continued*)

Table 3.1. Continued

Composer	Composition	Offstage Instrument (s)/ Sound(s)	Date	Annotations
Jules Massenet	*Thaïs: Meditation*	Oboe, English horn, and wordless chorus	1893	The meditative violin melody is backed by a (backstage) wordless chorus that is sometimes omitted from performances.
Giuseppe Verdi	*Falstaff*	Guitar	1893	The offstage guitar is used during a solo by Alice in place of a lute.
Gustav Mahler	Symphony no. 2	4 trumpets/4–6 horns/bass drum with cymbals/ triangle/timpani	1895	During the finale, offstage horn calls are answered by onstage trumpets.
Antonín Dvořák	*The Wild Dove* (Holoubek), op. 110	2 trumpets for part of piece, 3rd trumpet always offstage	1896	Offstage trumpets herald the beginning of the wedding.
Gustav Mahler	Symphony no. 3	Snare drum and post horn (flugelhorn)	1896	The striking post horn solo appears in the trio section of the Scherzo movement (III), and the instrument was traditionally used to announce the arrival of mail.
Edward MacDowell	Suite no. 2 ("Indian"), op. 48	1 horn and 1 trumpet	1897	The offstage (behind-the-stage) instruments resound in movement 4 ("Dirge"). The horns open the movement, one off and one on stage, to imitate horn calls in nature. The offstage trumpet plays mournfully at the end of the movement.
Richard Strauss	*Ein Heldenleben*, op. 40	3 trumpets	1898	The fourth movement ("The Hero at Battle") begins with offstage trumpet fanfares.
George Enescu	*Poème roumain*, op. 1	1 flute	1898	The flautist leaves the stage temporarily to play a poignant and chromatic melody over sustained strings.

Giacomo Puccini	*Tosca*	Flute, 4 horns, 3 trombones, rifle, cannon, viola, harp, drums, voices	1900	Tosca sings a cantata with an offstage chorus celebrating Napoleon's defeat offstage in act II. A shepherd boy sings "Io de sospiri" offstage in act III. The act II gavotte is performed by offstage flute, viola, and harp (indicative of court music). The rifle and cannon resound from the distance during a choral "Te Deum" accompanied by organ. Offstage drums announce the gallows.
Charles-Camille Saint-Saëns	*Les barbares*	*Banda*	1901	In act I, Floria is in prayer as a battle rages beyond the walls (offstage). The offstage *banda* contributes to the aural complexity.
Anton Arensky	Suite pour grand orchestre: *tirée du ballet Nuit d'Egypte*, op. 50a	*Banda*	1902	The offstage *banda* appears in act VII, during Antony's entrance.
Edward Elgar	*The Apostles*, op. 49	3 oboes and English horn	1903	The distant winds evoke a sultry night in Palestine in part 1 ("The Calling of the Apostles").
Giacomo Puccini	*Madama Butterfly*	1 viola d'amore, voices, and chorus	1903	In act I, there is an offstage chorus coming to celebrate the wedding. Sailors also sing in the distance (usually offstage) in Act II. The viola d'amore doubles a vocal part during the "Humming Chorus," and is marked "interno ma vicino."
Ferruccio Busoni	Piano Concerto, BV 247	Male chorus	1904	The male chorus (invisible) sings in the final movement of the piano concerto and conjures up a mystical affect.
Engelbert Humperdinck	*Die Heirat wider Willen*	Trumpet, snare drum, and tam-tam	1905	The offstage music occurs in the introduction and interlude (*Eine Trauung in der Bastille*).
Richard Strauss	*Salome*, op. 54	Harmonium and organ	1905	The harmonium appears near the beginning of the orchestra from the side that Salome appears (like a ghostly aural apparition of Salome), while the offstage organ appears at the end.

(*continued*)

Table 3.1. Continued

Composer	Composition	Offstage Instrument (s)/ Sound(s)	Date	Annotations
Gustav Mahler	Symphony no. 6 in A Minor	Cowbells and tubular bells	1906	The offstage cowbells occur in the first and fourth movements, and the tubular bells also appear in the fourth movement. The cowbells offer sounds of pastoral tranquility.
Charles Ives	*The Unanswered Question*, S. 30	Strings (and sometimes the trumpet as well)	1906	The three instrument groups (trumpet, woodwind quartet, and strings) play in different locations, and in different tempi to create a sense of musical independence. The strings play offstage and the woodwinds are dispersed around the stage. The trumpet is sometimes placed offstage.
Gustav Mahler	Symphony no. 7 in E Minor	Cowbells	1906	The cowbells appear toward the end of the second movement during a restatement of the march. The cowbells add a pastoral ambiance.
Gustav Mahler	Symphony no. 8	4 trumpets and 3 trombones	1906	During part I ("Veni creator spiritus"), an offstage brass ensemble adds to the grandiosity of the ending by playing the "Accende" theme while the main orchestra and choir perform a scalar passage.
Engelbert Humperdinck	*Musik zu Shakespeares Komodie "Was ihr wollt,"* op. 11	Snare drum, strings	1908	The offstage music occurs during the instrumental intermezzo.
Richard Strauss	*Elektra*, op. 58	Chorus	1909	There are offstage cries of "Orest" near the end of *Elektra*.
Igor Stravinsky	*Firebird* (ballet version)	Tubas	1910	The tubas appear in the wings.

Ferruccio Busoni	*Die Brautwahl*, BV 258	Chorus, organ, and cornet, chimes	1912	There is a lengthy offstage ("hinter dem geschlossenen Vorhang") cornet solo at the beginning of act III, part I. During the Cathedral scene (act III, part II: during Albertine's vision), an offstage choir and organ resound, providing the music with a religious affect. The piece ends with an Epilogue that also contains an offstage chorus (6 parts). This piece also contains onstage music, including the onstage march in act I, part I, played by winds and brass (based on music from Rossini's *Moses*, and the *Tempo die menuetto vivo* based on Mozart's *German Dances*, K. 600). Albertine also accompanies herself onstage at the harpsichord in act II, part II.
Charles Ives	*A Symphony: New England Holidays*	Trumpet	1912	The offstage trumpet solo appears in movement II: *Decoration Day.* The offstage muted trumpet plays a military funeral tune.
Maurice Ravel	*Daphnis et Chloé*	Trumpet	1912	Offstage trumpets play fanfares and muted melodies.
Jules Massenet	*Suite parnassienne*	Trumpet, harp, and 6 violins	1913	The instruments, marked "invisibles pour le public" in the score, appear in the first movement, "Rêverie." The offstage sounds contribute to the celestial and contemplative nature of the music.
Jean Sibelius	*Scaramouche*, op. 71	1 small orchestra	1913	There is a large pit orchestra and two smaller orchestras, one onstage and one offstage. The offstage orchestra includes cornet fanfares in act II.
Richard Strauss	*Festliches Präludium*, op. 61	6–12 trumpets	1913	The six to twelve trumpets act as heralds and are stationed on both sides of the stage.
Richard Strauss	*Eine Alpensinfonie*, op. 64	12 horns, 2 trumpets, and 2 trombones	1915	The offstage brass represents a hunting party in the *Sehr lebhaft und energisch* section.
Ferruccio Busoni	*Rondò arlecchinesco*, BV 266	Tenor voice	1915	The voice sings "la-la-la" in harlequin's Round Dance from offstage ("dietro la Scena, al di fuori") near the end of the composition. Busoni originally considered adding the solo using a phonograph recording, but ultimately deemed that impractical.[b]

(*continued*)

Table 3.1. Continued

Composer	Composition	Offstage Instrument (s)/ Sound(s)	Date	Annotations
Gustav Holst	*The Planets*	Female voices	1916	Holst adds wordless choral writing midway through the Neptune movement to add to the mystical ambiance.
Ferruccio Busoni	*Arlecchino, oder die Fenster*, BV 270	Tenor voice	1917	In act I, Arlecchino begins speaking onstage, but displaced (usually from above Matteo and through a window). This allows two conversations to happen simultaneously and from different locations on stage. Arlecchino also sings a solo from offstage ("hinter der Szene") and later ("entfernter"), singing "la-la-la" in act I after escaping from Matteo's house (after dallying with his wife, Annunziata). There is also an onstage ("Vor dem Vorhang") trumpet fanfare at the beginning of the piece.
Frederick Delius	*Eventyr (Once Upon a Time)*	20 male voices	1917	The voices only have two notes to sing. They are supposed to imitate wild shouts.
Ferruccio Busoni	*Turandot*, BV 273	Timpani, tam-tam, female chorus	1917	Busoni used the offstage timpani as a regal attention getting device; in act I, a female chorus represents sylvan deities ("hinter der Bühne"). The queen-mother also sings from behind the stage. An offstage tam-tam accompanies a pantomime. In act II, a choir is positioned behind the curtain ("hinter dem geschlossenen Vorhange") in the opening number and behind the stage ("hinter der Bühne") in the *Letztes Bild*.
Charles Ives	Symphony no. 4	1 harp, violins, and chorus	1918	In the first movement, an offstage harp and violins play a fragment of "Nearer My God to Thee" before an unseen chorus resounds. These are the "Vox angelica." The orchestra is divided in half, each in a different tempo in movement II. A second conductor is generally required for the second movement, which features much contrasting material.
Darius Milhaud	*L'homme et son désir*	Multiple ensembles	1918	The ensembles are spatially distributed and play independently of each other.

Giacomo Puccini	*Suor Angelica*	Chorus and voices	1918	Offstage chimes play an opening theme, representing the convent's bells. Angelica's voice is heard before she is seen. There is also an offstage chorus.
Charles Ives	Orchestral Set no. 2	Horn, 2 harps, piano, chimes, strings, and optional chorus	1919	The offstage music occurs in the third movement.
Richard Strauss	*Die Frau ohne Schatten*	Voices	1919	In act I, scene 2, there are offstage voices of unborn children. In act III, scene 3, Dyer and the wife dialogue offstage.
Ferruccio Busoni	*Doktor Faust*, BV 303	Voices, choir, organ, brass, bells, viola, chimes, and percussion	1924 (incomplete)	An offstage ("hinter dem Vorhang")[c] choir sings during the opening number. During Vorspiel II, the choir and instruments (trombones and horns [muted]) are under the stage ("unter der Bühne, unsichtbar"), while the timpani appears *on* the stage ("auf der Bühne"). The choir later moves farther away ("entfernter als zu Anfang"). The six spirit voices appear as flames, to be enunciated and doubled or amplified as needed, for clarity ("nötigenfalls verdoppelt, oder durch schallrohr verstärkt"). At Mephistopheles's appearance, horns herald his arrival from behind the stage ("hinter der Szene"). Later, trumpets resound from on stage ("auf der Bühne"). By the time Mephistopheles announces his name from offstage, the choir is at the back of the stage and below it ("hinten und tief"). It also sings during the Pact scene from behind the stage ("hinter der Bühne"), but to be heard from afar and above ("von weiter, und vom oben her vernehmbar"). Later, the choir is supposed to sound closer ("weniger entfernt"). Bells from behind the stage complement the voices and then trumpets and horns on the stage before the timpani appear behind the stage. In the Intermezzo, the organ is to be heard throughout the main theater (no exact placement is provided). Two trombones and a military tambourine join from behind the stage ("hinter der Bühne").

(*continued*)

Table 3.1. Continued

Composer	Composition	Offstage Instrument (s)/ Sound(s)	Date	Annotations
				Later, Busoni instructs the tambourine to sound farther away ("entfernt sich"). In Hauptspiel I (*vivace assai*), with an onstage choir, a horn plays from offstage to add to the pastoral ambiance. The section ends with on stage drums. Three trumpets appear on stage during the *Tempo di Minuetto*. In the *doppio movimento* section, there is a long lyrical viola solo from behind the stage. In the *Zweites Bild*, the choir begins behind the curtain ("noch hinter dem Vorhange"), which opens to reveal groups of students. In *Zweites Bild*, two choirs, the Catholic students and the Protestant students, add to the spatialized effects—especially when Busoni further subdivides the Catholic student choir into two groups. In *Letztes Bild*, the horn of the night watchman is played from behind the stage and the voice of the night watchman is to sound distant ("entfernt"). During the tempo della Serenata, the night watchman cries in the background over the stage ("im hintergrunde über die Bühne"). A choir joins from the distance ("aus der Entfernung").
Ottorino Respighi	*Pines of Rome*	6 buccine and 1 trumpet	1924	There is a notable (and lyrical) offstage trumpet solo in the second movement. The buccine appear in the final movement. The buccine add to the pastoral atmosphere of the movement.

[a] Some of this information is derived from the following sources: Clinton F. Nieweg, "Compositions Including Offstage Instruments" (August 2017) www.orchestralibrary.com (accessed May 26, 2020), and David Daniels, *Orchestral Music: A Handbook*, 4th ed. (Lanham, MD: Scarecrow Press, 2005). This table does not include pieces with optional offstage instruments, and it only includes published compositions. The table ends in 1924, the year of Busoni's death. It starts in 1866 to provide some historical context.

[b] Beaumont, *Busoni the Composer*, 214.

[c] Busoni required two curtains on the stage. He wanted a main curtain, and then a second black veil.

An expansion of possibilities in relation to instrument placement also proliferated in the last decades of the nineteenth and beginning of the twentieth centuries. Richard Wagner was particularly thoughtful in his use of space in *Parsifal* (1882), where he positioned brass, drums, and bells in the wings to suggest a religious ceremony. Two choruses also sing from above the stage, and Titurel sings from behind the stage. These different placements, however, mainly add ambiance, by coinciding with and supporting the sacred nature of the topic (the holy Grail); they also imitate the phenomenon of music making in real life (i.e., choirs from church balconies and brass in nature).

Composers in the late nineteenth and early twentieth century also used textural layers in a structural sense in conjunction with new spatial placements within physical space. In Mahler's Symphony no. 2 (1888–1895), for instance, offstage instruments (4 trumpets, 4 horns, triangle, cymbal, and bass drum) alternate with onstage instruments. Moreover, the trumpets resound from different directions before alternating and then forming unisons. In addition, the music itself is texturally layered, with military fanfares juxtaposed to more lyrical string music.

Although it is unlikely that Busoni would have been aware of his compositions, it is noteworthy that Busoni's contemporary Charles Ives added the dimension of time to create the impression of spatial distance. For instance, in his *Unanswered Question* (1906), he placed three types of instruments in different locations, each with their own musical materials.[14] The three instrument groups (trumpet, woodwind quartet, and strings) play in different locations, and in different tempi to create a sense of musical independence. The strings play offstage, and the woodwinds are dispersed around the stage. The trumpet is sometimes placed offstage. The strings play slow, sustained tones, while the trumpet interjects with short phrases, and the flutes answer in dissonant and irregular phrases. In addition, in Symphony no. 4, S. 4 (1910–1924), Ives divided the orchestra in two in the second movement, each half at a different tempo, thereby creating a sense of musical distance and diversity of texture.

As will be described in more detail below, Busoni's *Doktor Faust* (1924) participated in these trends and farther expanded the possibilities of the spatialization of sound based on models of space in architecture. He added new

[14] For more information about spatial music, see Robert P. Morgan, "Ives and Mahler: Mutual Responses at the End of an Era," *19th-Century Music* 2:1 (July 1978): 72–81. See also Siegfried F. Nadel, "Zum Begriff des musikalischen Raumes," *Zeitschrift für Musikwissenschaft* (1931): 329–31.

types of offstage sounds, explored a greater diversity of offstage placements of instruments to create what he called a circle of sound ("Klang-horizont"), and channeled the effects of resonance, decay, and textural layering even while experimenting with metric simultaneity.

These composers helped pioneer new ways of spatializing sound and were directly succeeded by composers like Edgard Varèse, a Busoni pupil, who used textual layers in a structural sense to create multi-dimensional "sound objects." He saw music as spatial, like cubist art, in which blocks of sounding forms are composed of diverse textures, timbres, and densities. He upheld a notion of sound masses and described a type of music in which nonlinear textures of sound re create the aural depiction of different densities and colors. For Varèse, there were four dimensions, the fourth being the projection of sound:

> We have actually three dimensions in music: horizontal, vertical, and dynamic swelling or decreasing. I shall add a fourth, sound projection—that feeling that sound is leaving us with no hope of being reflected back, a feeling akin to that aroused by a beam of light sent forth by a powerful searchlight—for the ear as for the eye, that sense of projection, of a journey into space.[15]

In *Ionisation* (1928), for instance, Varèse evoked a sense of space in music through the use of structural sections characterized by a combination of rhythmic motives, instrumental color, and textures that appear, combine, and develop.[16] For Iannis Xenakis, Varèse's musical heir, as it were, pitches no longer needed to represent width and height, but could be curved to create new musical shapes and structures, much like geometric shapes on graphs.[17] For John Cage, as for many spectral composers and electronic or electro-acoustic composers, many of them also in the Varèse circle, music has multiple dimensions, including pitch, dynamics, timbre, duration, and morphology.[18] A textural approach was subsequently adopted by

[15] Edgard Varèse, "New Instruments and New Music [1936]," in *Contemporary Composers on Contemporary Music*, ed. Elliott Schwartz and Barney Childs (New York: Holt, Rinehart, and Winston, 1967), 197.

[16] Varèse, "Music as an Art-Science [1939]," in *Contemporary Composers on Contemporary Music*, ed. Elliott Schwartz and Barney Childs (New York: Rinehart and Winston, 1967), 199.

[17] See, for instance, Xanakis's *Metastasis*.

[18] Cage, *Silence*. See also Branden W. Joseph, *John Cage in Music, Art, and Architecture* (New York: Bloomsbury, 2016).

numerous composers in New York in the 1950s, many of them friends or pupils of Varèse; they similarly produced electronic music that involved unsynchronized tapes (i.e., Cage's *William Mix*, 1952, and Morton Feldman's *Intersection*, 1953), in which the lack of synchronization aided perception of the different parts.

By the mid-1950s, sound and timbre were viewed as important musical material as composers distorted, manipulated, and reconstructed it. Karlheinz Stockhausen, born four years after Busoni's death, and also influenced by Varèse, among others, famously organized timbre and pitches according to a series of proportions in *Gesang der Jünglinge* (1956), in which he created a continuum ranging from pure tones to noise based on timbre, vowel tone, and consonants. He serialized many parameters, including textual intelligibility and the use of space itself, which became part of the structural fiber of the composition, which was stereophonically projected through five loudspeakers. This kind of spatialized projection took on new dimensions in the later 1950s, with music directly connected to the space in which it was performed and using multi-track projection systems, such as Varèse's *Poème électronique* (1958) and Xenakis's polytopes, such as *Terretektorh* (1965–1966). Moreover, composers experimented with separate spatial layers of music in electro-acoustic compositions, such as Milton Babbitt's *Philomel* (1964) for live soprano and pre-recorded soprano and orchestra.[19]

Busoni's Ideas about Spatial Music

Busoni's ideas, which describe music in theoretical, conceptual, and perceptual senses, expressed new approaches toward spatialized music in the early twentieth century. His writings reveal a fascination with space and dimensionality, and his thoughts about the subject range from the

[19] Since World War II, composers have also experimented with additional types of ensemble dispersion throughout (and beyond) halls, dynamic gradations, and the overlapping of independent sounds. Luciano Berio (1925–2003), for instance, requires the solo singer to move from one music stand to another in his *Circles for Female Voice, Harp, and Two Percussionists* (1960). One more recent development is the virtual choir or orchestra—separated by geography, time, and physical space, but united musically using electronic means. In Eric Whitacre's virtual choirs, for instance, singers from around the world have been uploading videos, which Whitacre then combines into single virtual performances of pieces, such as *Lux aurumque* (2000). His choir began with around 185 people and now numbers around 8,000 singers. Several composers have also proposed new types of physical space in which they envisioned their new music could take place. Karlheinz Stockhausen (1928–2007), similarly, wrote much spatialized music, such as his "Helikopter Streichquartet," first performed in Amsterdam in 1995 by four musicians on separate helicopters.

speculative to the concrete.[20] Although they share characteristics with those of his contemporaries, they are also idiosyncratic in their multifaceted conceptual, aesthetic, phenomenological, and musical emphases. In addition, many of his ideas are based on an understanding of the physical and architectural space in which audible sound moves. In particular, the composer considers the specific ways physical locales have and should influence music composition and reception and connects them to more abstract notions of idealized metaphysical heavenly music.

From a theoretical standpoint, Busoni considered several tangible ways pitches could be considered multi-dimensional. His writings describe unique scales (horizontal) that combine in different polyphonic textures (vertical and volume), as melodies coexist simultaneously. Differences in musical depth arise from the independent voices as they interweave into varied textures. Busoni stressed that this interweaving of melodies through linear counterpoint would also be the catalyst for new harmonies as the coincidence of intervals generate new chords. He describes these textures in several essays, including one entitled "The New Harmony":

> Keeping the voices independent of each other in polyphonic compositions produces the third road (I have, as an experiment, constructed a five-part fugue in which every voice is in a different key so that the harmony flows in quite new chord successions.) . . . The New Harmony could only arise naturally from the foundation of an extremely cultivated polyphony and establish a right for its appearance; this requires strict tuition and a considerable mastery of melody.[21]

If a notion of verticality and horizontal movement in music was not unique to Busoni,[22] he was one of the first to consider the vertical space between pitches. The composer was preoccupied with understanding the space

[20] See, for instance, Busoni, *Sketch of a New Esthetic of Music* trans. Th. Baker (New York: Schirmer, 1911), and Busoni, *The Essence of Music and Other Papers*.

[21] Busoni, "The New Harmony, [1911]," in *The Essence of Music and Other Papers*, trans. Rosamond Ley (London: Rockliff, 1957), 24. [Ein dritter Weg ergibt sich durch die von einander unabhängige Führung der Stimmen in polyphonischen Sätzen. (Ich habe, als Experiment, eine fünfstimmige Fugen-durchführung konstruiert, in welcher jede Stimme in einer anderen Tonart steht, so dass der Zusammenklang neue Akkordfolgen bildet).] Busoni, "Die neue Harmonik," in *Von der Einheit der Musik* (Berlin: Max Hesses Verlag, 1922), 60. It is possible that Busoni is referring to the following sketch: "Beispiel eines poly-harmonischen freien Contrapunktes," Staatsbibliothek zu Berlin–Preußischer Kulturbesitz, Musikabteilung mit Mendelssohn-Archiv, Mus. Nachl. F. Busoni, 294.

[22] Ernst Kurth expressed similar ideals in 1917.

between notes, because he thought of pitch as a continuum. He specifically advocated for expanding the possibilities of pitch space by advocating for microtones, including third tones and a whole spectrum of new scales and resultant harmonies:

> In order not to renounce the semitones, and consequently, the minor third and perfect fifth, I had a second row of tripartite tones added to the first row at a distance of a semitone. Through this, every third tripartite tone preserves its semitone. The blending of other rows produces, of course, sixths of tones.[23]

Although his attempts to commission microtonal keyboard instruments were largely unsatisfactory, he never stopped dreaming about a future in which electronic or acoustic instruments could play an uninterrupted spectrum of pitches.[24]

Yet he also considered other dimensions of music beyond melody and harmony, including time, timbre, and dynamics. He created a new term, "absolute orchestration," to describe the process of thinking in instrumental color when composing (as opposed to adding the instrumentation after composing the work):

> There are two kinds of instrumentation: that which is demanded and directed by musical thought—absolute orchestration—and the instrumentation of what was originally only an abstract musical composition, or one conceived for another instrument. The first is the only genuine one, the second belongs to "arrangements."[25]

[23] Busoni, "Report on the Division of the Whole Tone into Three Parts [1922]," in *The Essence of Music and Other Papers*, 30. [Um nicht auf die Halbtöne—und somit auf die kleine Terz und die reine Quinte—zu versichten liess ich der ersten Dritteltonreihe eine zweite, in der Entfernung eines halben Tones hinzufügen wodurch jeder Drittelton seinen halbton erhält. Die Vermengung der beiden Reihen ergibt natürlichweise Sechsteltöne.] Busoni, "Bericht über Dritteltöne," in *Von der Einheit*, 355.

[24] Busoni commissioned a harmonium with three manuals and tripartite tone divisions from a keyboard manufacturer in New York in 1910. He also commissioned a harmonium from Schiedmayer in Stuttgart in the 1920s. Busoni described the 1910 instrument, which he ultimately deemed impractical as containing "two rows of tripartite tones at a distance of a semitone from one another." Busoni, "Report on the Division of the Whole Tone into Three Parts [1922]," in *The Essence of Music*, 29–30. [mit zwei Dritteltonreihen, in Entfernung eines halben Tones voneinander umbauen.] Busoni, "Bericht über Dritteltöne," in *Von der Einheit*, 354. For an image of the 1920 instrument, which contains alternating white and black keys and two manuals, each playing third tones (but with the second tuned a sixth higher than the first), see Christian Schaper, "'Man zerstöre darum nicht, man baue auf!'—Ferruccio Busoni's *Entwurf einer neuen Ästhetik der Tonkunst*," in *Busoni: Freiheit für die Tonkunst!* (Kassel: Bärenreiter, 2016), 208.

[25] Busoni, "The Theory of Orchestration [1905]," in *The Essence of Music and Other Papers*, 35. [Es zwei Arten der Instrumentation gibt: die vom musikalischen Gedanken geforderte und

Busoni advocated for employing the whole range of each instrument, and considered the timbre of each instrument in relation to the collective sound of all instruments. He also dreamed of ways to expand timbral colors by using less conventional instruments, such as the saxophone, gypsy cymbals, chromatic harps, complete families of instruments, pedal drums, and instruments yet to be conceived, including electronic ones.[26]

Busoni additionally considered dynamics to be a dimension of *Tonkunst* that is fundamental to its construction. He suggested that sound gradations should be inherent to the scoring, and should be used to draw attention to specific inner voices, thereby contributing the ever-shifting textures and colors:

> A good score should be created in such a way that the sound gradations are included in it and allowed to be heard without special assistance from the executants. The prominent middle voice must be orchestrated, not sounded more loudly or more fully. The crescendo must take place through the arrangement of the instruments, the theme must shine forth of itself.[27]

Busoni's vision of multi-dimensional aspects of music was based on conceptual notions of sound in space. He believed in a realm beyond earth, a realm in which music resounds inaudibly in the universe. If his ideas resemble the archaic vision of *musica mundana*, they are also influenced by the acoustic theories of Hermann von Helmholtz, with whose famous text on acoustics he was familiar.[28]

Notions of space, distance, and dimension permeate Busoni's more abstract descriptions of ideal music, which, he claims, earthly music should imitate.

vorgeschriebene, absolute Orchestration; und die "Instrumentierung" eines ursprünglich nur abstract musikalischen oder für ein anderes Instrument gesachten Satzes. Die erste ist allein die echte, die zweite gehört in das "Arrangement."] Busoni, "Etwas über Instrumentationslehre," in *Von der Einheit*, 73–74.

[26] The potential with this mindset for new and expansive textures was realized more fully by Iannis Xenakis, György Ligeti, Kzrysztof Penderecki, and others, who wrote individual parts for each instrument within instrument families—such as for each violin and viola and cello and bass.

[27] Busoni, "The Theory of Orchestration," 37. [Eine gute Partitur soll so beschaffen sein, dass sie die Klanggradationen, ohne besonderes zu tun der Ausführenden, schon in sich begreift und erklingen lassen. Die "hervorzuhebende" Mittelstimme soll "instrumentiert," nicht stärker geblasen oder gestrichen sein. Das "Crescendo" muss sich aus der Anordnung der Instrumente ergeben, das "Thema" von selbst herausleuchten.] Busoni, "Etwas über Instrumentationslehre," in *Von der Einheit*, 76–77.

[28] Helmholtz's *Die Lehre von den Tonempfindungen als physiologische Grundlage für die Theorie der Musik* was first published in 1863 and was a volume in Busoni's Berlin library.

Each body (star, planet, etc.), sounding from a different location in the universe, vibrates with sound waves. Pitch decay and the perception of tones from the distance therefore become themes in Busoni's consideration of the possibilities of spatialized music. In a gloss on writings by E. T. A. Hoffmann, he stated: "This makes me think of an essay on old and new church music which gives the impression of dying away wondrously in an unearthly distance and height at the end."[29] He also uses his notion of music in the universe to describe tones that radiate from different directions. Music surrounds and envelops listeners in sounds that emanate from the heights and depths, and all around. The phenomenological experience is one of sensory overload, where nothing is immediately perceptible. However, listeners can train themselves to focus in on some of the individual sounds before eventually learning to perceive the totality. In addition, Busoni stresses the physical and spatial aspects of this sound, describing it as vibrating air. His description of tones as the "centre of immeasurable circles" suggests overtones, although he does not use that term.[30] Busoni also broaches the aspect of time in this passage, noting that simultaneity of rhythms add a dimension as pitches resound concurrently, yet independently, in time. In addition, he addresses the notion of the liquidity of the sounds that are always vibrating:

> You still hear nothing because everything *sounds*. Now already you begin to differentiate. Listen, every star has its rhythm and every world its measure. And on each of the stars and each of the worlds, the heart of every separate living being is beating in its own individual way. And all the beats agree and are separate and yet are a whole. Your inner ear becomes sharper. Do you hear the depths and the heights? They are as immeasurable as space and endless as numbers. Unthought of scales extend like bands from one world to another, *stationary* and yet *eternally in motion*. Every tone is the centre of immeasurable circles. And now *Sound* is revealed to you! Innumerable are

[29] Busoni, "Introduction to E. T. A. Hoffmann's *Phantastischen Geschichten* [1914]," in *The Essence of Music and Other Papers*, 188. [Ich denke hierbei an einen Aufsatz über alte und neue Kirchenmusik, der am Schlüsse wundersam, in unirdliche Fernen und Höhen ausklingt.] Busoni, "Zum Geleit von E. T. A. Hoffmanns Geschichten," in *Von der Einheit*, 196. This is a reference to Hoffmann's essay "Old and New Church Music." See David Charlton, *E. T. A. Hoffmann's Musical Writings*: *"Kreisleriana," "The Poet and the Composer," Music Criticism*, trans. Martyn Clarke (Cambridge: Cambridge University Press, 1989), 351–76.

[30] Busoni, "The Realm of Music," 189. Severine Neff has stated that Busoni discussed overtones with his pupil Otto Luening while in Zurich. Severine Neff, phone interview with the author, May 22, 2014. Given that Busoni often spoke metaphorically to illustrate his points, is not an improbable reading of the text.

its voices; compared with them the murmuring of the harp is a din; the blare of a thousand trombones a chirrup. All, all melodies heard before or never heard, resound completely and simultaneously, carry you, hang over you, or skim lightly past you—of love and passion, of spring and of winter, of melancholy and of hilarity, they are themselves the souls of millions of beings in millions of epochs. If you focus your attention on one of them you perceive how it is connected with all the others, how it is combined with all the rhythms, coloured by all kinds of sounds, accompanied by all harmonies, down to unfathomable depths and up to the vaulted roof of heaven.[31]

At the same time, Busoni described acoustic music in very physical terms, as entities that occupy space, as sound waves floating in the air:

Let Music be naught else than Nature mirrored by and reflected from the human breast; for it is sounding air and floats above and beyond the air; within Man himself as universally and absolutely as in Creation entire; for it can gather together and disperse without losing in intensity.[32]

Busoni thus articulated some very practical and original ideas about ways music is multi-dimensional, and these included the interaction of melody, harmony, instrumental color, dynamics, pitch level, and time. At the same

[31] Busoni, "The Realm of Music: An Epilogue to the New Aesthetic [1910]," in *The Essence of Music and Other Papers*, 188–89. [Noch hört ihr nichts, weil *Alles tönt.* Nun beginnt ihr schon zu unterscheiden. Lauscht, jeder Stern hat seinen Rhythmus und jede Welt ihren Takt. Und auf jedem der Sterne und jeder der Welten, schlägt das Herz jedes einzelnen Lebendigen anders, und nach seinem [eigenen] Müssen. Und alle Schläge Stimmen überein und sind ein Einziges und ein Ganzes. Euer inneres Ohr wird schärfer. Hört ihr Tiefen und die Höhen? Sie sind unmessbar wie der Raum und unendlich wie die Zahl. Wie Bänder ziehe sich ungeahnte Skalen von einer Welt zur anderen, *festehend* und ewig *bewegt*. Jeder Laut ist ein Centrum unermesslicher Kreise. Und jetzt offenbart sich euch der *Klang!* Ungezälte sind seine Stimmen, ihnen verglichen ist das Säuseln der Harfe ein Gepolter, das Schmettern von tausend Posaunen ein Gezirp. Alles, alle Melodien, gehörte und ungehörte vorher, erklingen vollzählig und zugleich[,] tragen euch, überhängen euch, streifen euch der liebe und der Leidenschaft, des Frühlings und des Winters, der Schwermuth und der Ausgelassenheit, sind selbst die Gemüther von Millionen von Wesen in Millionen von Epochen.—Fasst ihr Eine davon näher ins Auge so merkt ihr wie sie mit allen übrigen zusammenhängt, mit allen Rhythmen kombinirt, von allen Klangarten gefärbt ist, Harmonien begleitet, bis in den Grund der Gründe, und die Wölbung aller Wölbungen in den Höhen.] Busoni, letter of March 3, 1910, to his wife, in Busoni, *Briefe an seine Frau, 1889–1923*, ed. Martina Weindel (Wilhelmshaven: Florian Noetzel, 2015), 473.

[32] Busoni, *Sketch of a New Esthetic of Music*, 34. [Sie sei nichts anderes als die Natur in der menschlichen Seele abgespielt und von ihr wieder zurückgestrahlt; ist sie doch tönende Luft und über die Luft hinausreichend; im Menschen selbst ebenso universell und volldständig wie im Weltenraum; den sie kann sich zusammenballen und auseinanderfliessen, ohne an Intensität nachzulassen.] Busoni, *Entwurf*, 53.

time, he penned more abstract and metaphysical notions of sound in space that evoke issues of pitch placement, decay, and overtones. Although he did not implement all these ideas in his own work, many of his pieces put into practice some of his ideas, and thereby contribute to his spatialized approach to composition.

Busoni's Spatial Music and Architecture

While some of Busoni's aesthetic theories remained unrealized speculations, they did inform his musical practice in several ways, including in the spatial placement of instruments, the exploration of new timbres, the use of reverberation and decay to evoke certain types of spaces, and the use of multiple textures at once. Yet while his aesthetic theories often described abstract spaces, his mature compositions that experimented with spatial aspects were frequently connected to known types of physical spaces, such as specific buildings or architectural styles. Busoni used these concrete associations to evoke distinctive acoustics, resonances, morphologies of sound, textures, and colors.

Cathedrals seem to have been particularly inspirational for Busoni, who regularly composed spatialized music in relation to that type of architecture. For instance, in the opening section of his posthumously completed *Doktor Faust* (1925), the Symphonia, Busoni re created the aural sensation of different sized bells tolling in a cathedral tower. The process required re creating characteristic dimensions of height, distance, timbre, resonance, decay, and the varying speeds of different sized church bells with acoustic instruments.

Busoni confessed that he "devoted special study to the peal of bells" to recreate the aural qualities of bells.[33] In sketches to *Doktor Faust* dated May 29, 1916, the composer noted that he was interested in both imitating bells with acoustic orchestral instruments and in using real ones (offstage) in the opening movement in the following order:

1. Imitation in the orchestra
2. Choir-bells (glockenspiel?)

[33] Busoni, "The Score of *Doktor Faust* [1922]," in *The Essence of Music and Other Papers*, 76. [Ein apartes Studium widme ich Glockengelaüte das ich in drei "Zusänden" Wiedergabe.] Busoni, "Über die Partitur des 'Doktor Faust,'" Staatsbibliothek zu Berlin–Preußischer Kulturbesitz, Musikabteilung mit Mendelssohn-Archiv, Mus. Nachl. F. Busoni C I, 8.

3. Real bells (live)
4. Christmas bells at the end[34]

Busoni wanted the sound of the bells, which symbolized the spiritual to him, to be realistic. This required not only a replication of their unique timbre, resonance, and overtones, but also of their timing and physical placement. To create the proper spatial effects, Busoni had to learn about the science of bells. Although he considered alternatives, such as the Chinese gong, other gongs, and the four-octave Glass-Glocken, none of these was able to produce the same spatial and timbral effects.[35] He therefore corresponded with a famous bell maker in Aarau, Switzerland, Rüetschi Erben, to learn about real church bells.[36] Busoni first wrote on April 28, 1919, to inquire about the possibility of using four to five real church bells on the stage, including the difficulties this could pose with regard to weight, transportation, and cost.[37] In a follow-up letter of May 2, the composer inquired about differences in speed and register given the potential scenario of four bells—two higher and two lower.[38] By May 21, he had selected three different pitches for the bells (C, F, G).[39] By July 3 he was considering aspects of placement, should he use real bells, to achieve the most realistic spatial effect. He considered the placement of the bells on a scaffold or having them hang behind the stage out of sight.[40] Shortly thereafter, he provided a drawing of the bells that he envisioned in a letter to Otto Amsler, who had apparently demonstrated the bells for him in Arrau (see figure 3.1).[41]

Busoni eventually abandoned the idea of using real church bells in the opening movement, opting instead for the evocation of bells using traditional acoustic instruments. However, he used them during the Pact scene just as

[34] Busoni, "Sketches for *Doktor Faust*," Staatsbibliothek zu Berlin–Preußischer Kulturbesitz, Musikabteilung mit Mendelssohn-Archiv, Mus. Nachl. F. Busoni, 345, 1, p. 7. The sketches about the order of the bells are dated May 29, 1916.

[35] Busoni, letter of May 30, 1919, to H. Rüetschi Erben, Staatsbibliothek zu Berlin–Preußischer Kulturbesitz, Musikabteilung mit Mendelssohn-Archiv, Mus. Nachl. F. Busoni BI, 1021.

[36] For more information about the bell makers, see the following website: "Glockengiesserei Rüetschi AG," https://www.aarauinfo.ch/entdecken/glockengiesserei (accessed August 9, 2018).

[37] Busoni, letter of April 28, 1919, to H. Rüetschi Erben, Staatsbibliothek zu Berlin–Preußischer Kulturbesitz, Musikabteilung mit Mendelssohn-Archiv, Mus. Nachl. F. Busoni BI, 1018.

[38] Busoni, letter of May 2, 1919, to H. Rüetschi Erben, Staatsbibliothek zu Berlin–Preußischer Kulturbesitz, Musikabteilung mit Mendelssohn-Archiv, Mus. Nachl. F. Busoni BI, 1019.

[39] Busoni, letter of May 21, 1919, to H. Rüetschi Erben, Staatsbibliothek zu Berlin–Preußischer Kulturbesitz, Musikabteilung mit Mendelssohn-Archiv, Mus. Nachl. F. Busoni BI, 1020.

[40] Busoni, letter of July 3, 1919, to H. Rüetschi Erben, Staatsbibliothek zu Berlin–Preußischer Kulturbesitz, Musikabteilung mit Mendelssohn-Archiv, Mus. Nachl. F. Busoni BI, 1027.

[41] Busoni, letter of unknown date to H. Rüetschi Erben, Staatsbibliothek zu Berlin–Preußischer Kulturbesitz, Musikabteilung mit Mendelssohn-Archiv, Mus. Nachl. F. Busoni BI, 1031.

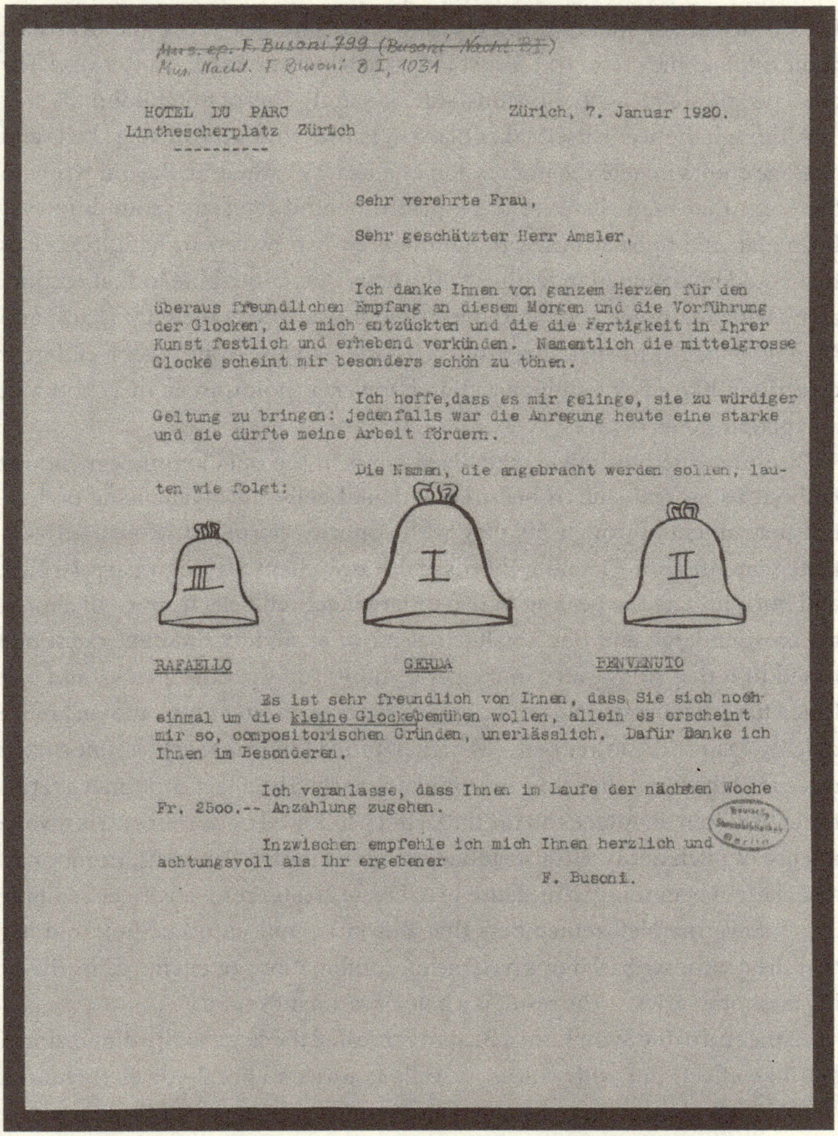

~~Mus. ep. F. Busoni 799 (Busoni' Nachl. BI)~~
Mus. Nachl. F. Busoni B I, 1031

HOTEL DU PARC
Linthescherplatz Zürich

Zürich, 7. Januar 1920.

Sehr verehrte Frau,

Sehr geschätzter Herr Amsler,

Ich danke Ihnen von ganzem Herzen für den überaus freundlichen Empfang an diesem Morgen und die Vorführung der Glocken, die mich entzückten und die die Fertigkeit in Ihrer Kunst festlich und erhebend verkünden. Namentlich die mittelgrosse Glocke scheint mir besonders schön zu tönen.

Ich hoffe,dass es mir gelinge, sie zu würdiger Geltung zu bringen: jedenfalls war die Anregung heute eine starke und sie dürfte meine Arbeit fördern.

Die Namen, die angebracht werden sollen, lauten wie folgt:

<u>RAFAELLO</u> <u>GERDA</u> <u>BENVENUTO</u>

Es ist sehr freundlich von Ihnen, dass Sie sich noch einmal um die <u>kleine Glocke</u> bemühen wollen, allein es erscheint mir so, compositorischen Gründen, unerlässlich. Dafür Danke ich Ihnen im Besonderen.

Ich veranlasse, dass Ihnen im Laufe der nächsten Woche Fr. 25oo.-- Anzahlung zugehen.

Inzwischen empfehle ich mich Ihnen herzlich und achtungsvoll als Ihr ergebener

F. Busoni.

Figure 3.1. Busoni, letter of January 7, 1920, to Gerda Busoni and Otto Amsler. Preussischer Kulturbesitz, Staatsbibliothek zu Berlin, Musikabteilung mit Mendelssohn Archiv, Mus. Nachl. F. Busoni B I, 1031.

Faust proclaimed, "there is no mercy" and then signed the pact while an unseen choir intoned the credo text. Faust immediately responded: "Easter day! The good people are going to the Münster [Cathedral]. Day of my childhood!"[42]

Although the scene itself takes place in Faust's study, the offstage bells and offstage choirs invoke the impression of a nearby cathedral. Busoni wrote in the score that the bells were to be placed behind the stage, sounding as if from afar, and to be struck with hammers by two players or handheld laces that could be wrapped in leather.[43] The bells thus contribute in that section, along with an unseen choir and the visible characters on the stage (Faust and Mephistopheles) to spatialized music that emanates from several different directions, like a bell tolling in a church tower, a choir unseen in a choir loft, and people down below.

Busoni created a similar spatialized effect in the opening movement, yet without using real church bells. He imitated bells effectively using orchestral instruments through his play with sonority, harmony, acoustics, resonance, and rhythm. Opening chords of the movement played by harp, strings, and horn imitate the pealing of two different church bells from a tall church tower—one large and one small—that move at slightly different rates: one tuned to F that rings every four quarter notes (on the downbeats), and one tuned to G that begins later and rings every three quarter notes, moving more quickly against the lower bell—as higher-tuned (and smaller) bells normally do—until the two bells are heard simultaneously. The effect continues as still-faster bells join in. Attacks on the initial pitch followed by decrescendos invoke a sense of pitch decay. He also added sustained muted trumpets, trombones, and clarinet beginning in measure 14 to create greater resonance (see example 3.1).[44] Severine Neff remembers that Busoni's pupil Otto Luening told her that the composer based this passage on combinations of pitches reflective of the overtone series.[45] The result is a halo of resonant sound.

At the end of the Symphonia, Busoni re created the same multi-dimensional bell-like effect, but with voices as well, as unseen choral voices (behind a

[42] [Ostertag! Da ziehen die Guten zum Münster. Tag meiner Kindheit!] Busoni, *Doktor Faust*, Klavierauszug mit Text, ed. Philipp Jarnach, arr. Egon Petri and Michael von Zadora (Wiesbaden: Breitkopf & Härtel, n.d.), 89–91.

[43] [Hinter der Bühne, entsprechend entfernt mit Hämmern anzuschlagen; (zwei Spieler) oder der hand geführten Klöppeln; letztere sind je nach bedürfnis, mit Leder zu umwickeln.] Busoni, *Doktor Faust*, 97.

[44] This was first noted in my earlier article about *Doktor Faust*. See Knyt, "Approaching the Essence of Music: Ferruccio Busoni and Stylistic Heterogeneity in *Doktor Faust*," *Journal of Musicological Research* 35:3 (August 2016): 176–99.

[45] Severine Neff, phone interview with the author, May 22, 2014.

Example 3.1. Busoni, *Doktor Faust*, Sinfonia, mm. 1–26.

curtain)[46] imitate the bell sounds from the beginning by chiming "Pax" on diverse pitches in close imitation and in increasing speed. The sound seems to envelope the stage as it comes from several directions. Sopranos I and II start by sustaining B♭ for one measure in imitation before Soprano I begins

[46] It could be presumed that the "unseen" choir is on the stage and behind a curtain. Whether the choir is positioned at the back of the stage or on the sides is difficult to determine from Busoni's stage directions.

Example 3.2. Busoni, *Doktor Faust*, Sinfonia, mm. 128–32.

intoning a C in imitation (see example 3.2), like bells on those two pitches. By the fifth measure after the choral entrance, Soprano II sings B♭ on beat one, Soprano I sings D on beat two, alto sings F (above middle C) on beat three, and tenors sing F (below middle C) on beat four. Basses I and II enter five measures later. Together, the voices move in parallel motion in fifths (G–D to A–E), minor triads (G–D–B♭ to A–E–C), or, including the glockenspiel, seventh chords—echoing one another reverentially from behind the curtain.[47]

[47] Busoni wrote to Vittorio Podrecca (1883–1959), Italian impresario and director of a marionette company, to see if he could supply a glockenspiel: "Would it be possible to acquire in Berlin chimes (glockenspiel) and bells for the theater in good condition?" [Sarebbe possibile acquisitare a Berlino carillon (glockenspiel) e campane per teatrino a buone condizioni?] Busoni, letter of February 28, 1922, to Vittorio Podrecca, in Silvano Salvadori, *Arlecchino ovvero si riapra il sipario!: Il rogetto di Ferruccio Busoni e l'opera grafica del figlio Rafaello* (Empoli: Ibiskos, 2016), 133.

The sound seems to come from all around (above, below, behind, in front) as a circle of sound introduces the opera that is to unfold.[48]

While Busoni was not the first to use church bells in an opera, he might have been the first to imitate them so realistically with acoustic instruments. What was different about other attempts and Busoni's was the spatial component. He was trying to imitate not just the timbre, but also the tolling in time and the sense of distance and resonance one might expect from distant bells in wide-open space. Giuseppe Verdi used lighter tubular bells in *Il trovatore* (1853) and *Un ballo in maschera* (1859), while Giacomo Puccini used tubular bells in *Tosca* (1900) as well. However, the emphasis was on imitating the timbre, and not the spacing or timing. Wagner desired to use four bells in transition sections in *Parsifal*.[49] However, since he was aiming for low registers, the bells would have had to be extremely heavy (some more than 20 tons) and large (up to eight meters in diameter). After rejecting the idea of tam-tams, he finally settled on a specially commissioned keyboard instrument by Eduard Steingraber to be played alongside tam-tams, gongs, and the tuba. The sound was hardly realistic, and these instruments were soon replaced by four very large barrels, which were thought to have had better sound. Modest Mussorgsky used gongs, woodwinds, and plucked basses in the original *Boris Godunov* Coronation scene. It was not until 1940 in Shostakovich's arrangement that a real church bell was used, long after Busoni's *Doktor Faust*.

Busoni's approach in *Doktor Faust* was one that he arrived at gradually. Even so, his earlier attempts to evoke the sound of tolling bells took into consideration more than timbre. As early as *Sigune* (1885–1889), an incomplete opera in two acts based on a tale by Rudolf Baumbach, he invoked the cathedral symbolically, with tolling bells. Diethart, a stonemason, assists Ulrich, a master builder, in erecting a cathedral in the center of a town.[50] As Diethart entered the town, Busoni instructed that church bells should ring, ("feierglocken vom Turme" [celebration bells from the tower]), but instead of imitating the sonority of cathedral bells, he suggests them by imitating the resonance of vibrating pitches in a large space. At the beginning of act I, repeated and accented G octaves resonate once per measure while the

[48] Judith Crispin has also discussed the formal ramifications of the circle, as well as its connections to esoteric traditions. Crispin, "Evoking the Mystical: The Esoteric Legacy of Ferruccio Busoni," in *Music and Esotericism*, ed. Laurence Wuidar (Leiden: Brill, 2010), 265–93.

[49] For more information about Wagner's use of bells in *Parsifal*, see William Kinderman, *Wagner's Parsifal* (New York: Oxford University Press, 2013).

[50] Busoni, *Sigune*, Staatsbibliothek zu Berlin–Preußischer Kulturbesitz, Musikabteilung mit Mendelssohn-Archiv, Mus. Nachl. F. Busoni, CI, 18b.

bass resounds with open octaves in several harmonies—initially outlining C minor and then G major, before moving to A diminished. The increasing dissonance suggests residual sounds from tolling bells that decay slowly, and the registral distance between high and low pitches creates a sense of aural separation, but the timing is not realistic.

Before *Doktor Faust*, Busoni was thus interested in evocations of space in music, even if the results were not as realistic. He largely evoked a sense of distance and vastness of space through a combination of sustained pitches and arpeggios coupled with offstage choral and instrumental placements. This is evident in *Die Brautwahl*, act III. Although Busoni followed E. T. A. Hoffmann's text closely in the libretto, the cathedral scene featuring a vision of Edmund Lehsen's great future masterpiece was his own idea. Stage instructions describe an Italian church with an impressive altar painting. In the distance, the sound of an organ and religious song resounds. The vision requires several dramatic elements, as increasingly clear and bright light appears, to complement the music.[51] Instead of the marches and dances that characterize much of the music of the opera, the cathedral section is characterized by long and sinuous melodies reminiscent of plainchant, parallel organum-like octaves in the choir, accompanied by rich arpeggiated harmonies that emanate out in all directions (upward, downward, widthwise)—suggesting rising and echoing sounds in a resonant cathedral, some of which are based on the overtone series—resulting in a halo of sound.[52] As the light increases, the unseen choir voices, which sing in Latin praising a trinity of God, art, and nature, move up in register from baritones and basses, to baritones and tenors, to sopranos and altos, in parallel fifths and octaves at the moment of greatest light. An organ doubles the low octaves of the voices, and the harp joins with trills, adding to the depth in a swirl of timbral virtuosity that conjures up flavors of the religious, while suggesting the height, depth, and resonance of a cathedral. To this is added Leonhard's voice in simple repeated chant-like tones. "All my youthful recollections of the Catholic atmosphere are in it," wrote Busoni (see example 3.3).[53]

[51] Busoni, *Die Brautwahl: Musikalisch-phantastische Komödie nach E. T. A. Hoffmanns Erzählung*, arr. Egon Petri (Berlin: Harmonie-Verlag, 1914), 321.

[52] See Antony Beaumont, *Busoni the Composer* (Bloomington: Indiana University Press, 1985), 132–33.

[53] Busoni, letter of April 2, 1912, to Gerda Busoni, in Ferruccio Busoni, *Letters to His Wife*, trans. Rosamond Ley, Da Capo Music Reprint Series, ed. Roland Jackson (New York: Da Capo Press, 1975), 202. [Darin ist allgemeine Jugenderinnerung von katholischer Stimmung wiederzufinden.] Busoni, *Busonis Briefe an Seine Frau*, ed. F. Schnapp (Zurich: Rotapel, 1935), 249, https://archive.org/details/BusonisBriefeAnSeineFrau/page/n296/mode/1up (accessed June 12, 2020).

Example 3.3. Busoni, *Die Brautwahl*, Cathedral scene, excerpt.

Example 3.3. Continued

Example 3.3. Continued

*) gegen die dominierende Stimme des Leonhard soll alles andere, and Hintergrund, zurücktreten

A similar sense of distance and space can also be observed in the middle chorale-like section of the *Sonatina in diem nativitatis Christi MCMXVII*, which was composed in December 1917, and that Beaumont believes to be the "music originally visualized for the end of *Doktor Faust*."[54] Whether or not that is the case, Busoni's bell music, marked in sketches as "Campane di Natale," displays the same kind of attention to spatial ambiance as his orchestral works. In measure 118 (bar 6 of the *sostenuto alla breve* section), the composer begins evoking a sense of resonance by stating that two pedals should be held down continuously (*con 2 Pedali continuamente*).[55] At the same time, Busoni creates vast registral differences; the bass begins with a repeated descending pattern, sometimes doubled in octaves, that spans a seventh (D, B♭,

[54] Busoni, *Busonis Briefe an Seine Frau*, 255.
[55] Busoni, *Sonatina in diem nativitatis Christi MCMXCVII* (Wiesbaden: Breitkopf & Härtel, 1918), 6.

Example 3.4. Busoni, *Sonatina in diem nativitatis Christi MCMXVII*, mm. 118–23.

F♯, C) and eventually transitions to an upward-moving pattern in measure 10. Even as the bass extends to the low registers, to the C four octaves below middle C in measure 123, the treble expands upward, to the D♭ two octaves above middle C in measure 124. Moreover, the subtly shaded harmonies contribute to a haze of sound and indistinct harmonic colors; the chords in the treble constantly change ever so slightly in varied registers due to harmonic plurisignificance, moving from B♭ major and B♭ minor to F♯ half-diminished seventh, through other chords, to end with a bitonal haze in measure 124 (D♭ major and D minor), thereby creating a halo of reverberant sound suggestive of tolling bells (see example 3.4).

Busoni plays with the possibilities of the dimensions of music to evoke specific physical spaces. He creates interplay between vertical and horizontal dimensions of music coupled with timbre, dynamics, and timing. In *Doktor Faust*, for instance, Busoni used the spacing of chords and arpeggios coupled with the massive and powerful timbre of the organ at a forte dynamic to evoke the dimensions of an age-old romanische chapel in Münster on the stage. The composer was no doubt thinking specifically of the Münster Cathedral, built between 1225 and 1264. Although there is a Gothic transept and ring of chapels, the Westwerk is Romanesque, a medieval style characterized by semi-circular arches, massive walls, weighty stone, strong pillars, and large towers (see figure 3.2).

Figure 3.2. Image of the Münster Cathedral Westwerk with Late Gothic portal from c. 1900.

Busoni evoked this type of architecture musically by featuring the thick timbre of the organ in a fantasia that starts with simple, but massive, block intervals and chords before breaking out into free rhapsodic arpeggiations that cycle through various keys.[56] The opening notes expanding to massive block

[56] For more information about the organ part from the perspective of an organist, see "The Organ in Opera: James Welch Performs with the San Francisco Opera," *The Diapason* (December 30, 2004), https://www.thediapason.com/organ-opera-james-welch-performs-san-francisco-opera (accessed September 8, 2019).

intervals and chords, coupled with the powerful tone of the organ, resemble the vertical expansiveness of the Westwerk with its massive stone walls. The sound expands and envelops. The pitches also spread out horizontally with sustained pitches at the same time, creating a sense of resonance such as one would experience in an expansive nave. Ascending and descending pitches in outer voices are added as the register expands outward, suggesting vertical growth and expansiveness. Subsequent arpeggiated and scalar figurations resounding over low pedal tones and imitative lines visually and aurally resemble the semi-circular windows and arches so characteristic of Romanesque architecture. A softer dynamic level suggests distance (see example 3.5).

In addition to combining distinctive horizontal and vertical dimensions coupled with timbre, dynamics, and timing to depict spatial dimensions, Busoni also composed textural layers to evoke multiple spaces simultaneously. The organ fantasia is but one layer in the previously mentioned intermezzo texture, and it returns as a refrain throughout the movement. He also called for an offstage (from the back of the stage) military ensemble consisting of a snare drum and two trumpets, low brass, and winds in quasi-canonic octaves suggestive of judgment or doom. These instruments contrast spatially and texturally with the religious organ music that can be heard in the nave (the placement of the instrument in relation to the stage is not specified), and diabolical string figurations emanating from the main orchestral ensemble that is frequently positioned in front of the stage in a pit area.

The three different orchestral forces contribute to a counterpoint of timbre and texture that conveys dramatic meaning and suggests what is happening aurally even when it cannot be viewed with the eyes. A soldier, the brother of Gretchen, who has been violated by Faust, appears in the Romanesque chapel to pray for Faust's death. His prayer, beginning in measure 71, is accompanied by the religious organ music, which emanates from diverse directions depending upon the theater and the placement of the pipes of the organ. However, his prayer is overlaid with a second texture—foreboding canonic and imitative writing in the low brass, woodwinds, and timpani (beginning in m. 75), suggestive of judgment or death. These sounds occurring simultaneously present diverse dramatic cues. Soon thereafter, Mephistopheles, dressed as a monk, appears, and is accompanied by pit orchestra strings in front of the stage (beginning in m. 153)—first pizzicato, and then bowed, and with plenty of chromaticism, as the diabolical Mephistopheles convinces Faust to order the soldier's death. An offstage (behind the stage) military ensemble (beginning in m. 221) eventually heralds the arrival of a group

Example 3.5. Busoni, *Doktor Faust*, Intermezzo, piano score, mm. 1–30. Published 1925.

Example 3.5. Continued

of soldiers with march rhythms in the percussion and low brass, and this contrasts with the sinuous strings, as the soldier and Mephistopheles dialogue, ultimately leading to the brother's unjust execution. After a funeral march followed by string tremolos coupled with an offstage tambourine and low brass and winds (beginning in m. 283), the piece settles down to a two-textured organ solo together with the ominous low brass and winds (beginning in m. 304). The different layers of music, each heard distinctly, and the different placement of the instruments thus invoke spatialized listening, as the ears take in the dramatic layers simultaneously.

Like Ives and Mahler, Busoni thus divided orchestral forces in his compositions to create spatial and textural layers, and this is true not only of his dramatic works, but also his orchestral ones. What is unique about his approach is his subtle use of instrumental color in relation to interval and instrument spacing. The *Berceuse élégiaque* illustrates the constantly changing textures and timbral colors of Busoni's approach. The composer evokes a sense of distance and space using registral distance, timbre, and metric simultaneity. He does this by grouping instruments into small subsets, but distinguishing them based on key area, register, or rhythm, so that there is very little overlap in role or function.

In the initial measures, for instance, he features harmonics on the harp and viola (on beats 1 and 3) in the treble, which contrast with muted low tones in the cello (with emphasis on beats 2 and 4) and contrabass (on the pickup to beat 1 of each measure). A second texture begins in measure 4 when Busoni layers winds (clarinets and horns) on top. Clarinet 1 and the bass clarinet in A alternate pitches C and E♭ in registers separated by an octave and on alternating beats of the measure—an emphasis on beat 1 for the bass clarinet and an emphasis on beat 3 for clarinet 1. Bitonality enhances the sense of spatial, timbral, and textural divisions, with the strings centering on F major and the winds centering on A♭ minor. Subsequent unisons in the winds contrast with the previous expansive octaves and emerge into a lyrical melody over chromatic and registrally displaced strings—first in the clarinets in measure 8, and then followed by divisi flutes in measure 12 in a quasi-canonic texture. Underneath, the strings play undulating eighth notes with entrances on separate beats of the measure while the harp continues to play on beats 1 and 3, with harmonics on beat 3.

At bar 20, there is a major shift, created mainly by a change in color—a reversal of roles. The rocking movement transfers to the clarinets while the strings play sustained tones (or pizzicato in the contrabass). A languid melody emerges in the oboe, later joined by flutes, and then viola, adding distinctive colors to the melody, while the harp continues haunting harmonics on beat 3. At measure 81, celesta and harp overlap in bitonal contrast in A major (celesta)/C minor (harp) or E major (celesta)/G minor (harp), to which a violin melody joins sweetly.

The material beginning in bar 58 reveals an even more complex interplay of instruments as the violas play triplets over other sustained strings while the flutes assume the melody and take to increasing heights for greater registral contrast. The upper strings gradually begin to rock back and forth again in eighth notes while the bass ascends slowly and intervalically, from semitones, to whole tones, to thirds, fourths, fifths, etc., until an octave is reached. The undulating and expanding strings are complemented by the winds that pass around fragments of the melody from instrument to instruments until the piece gently seems to evaporate. Overall, the thin textures allow Busoni to give instruments individual parts with contrasting rhythms, pulses, characters, and harmonies, thereby creating an orchestra chiaroscuro of color that could be seen as metaphorically reminiscent of the way light falls in architecture to cast shade, thereby accentuating formal sections.[57]

Theatrical Space and Architecture

Busoni's evocation of space, distance, and depth were not only informed by his study of certain types of architecture, such as cathedrals, but also reflected his interactions with contemporary architects, such as van de Velde, who were actively rethinking architectural space. He discussed ways physical spaces—especially theatrical ones—could be redesigned architecturally to invoke and invite spatialized music. He considered multiple ways tones could come from different directions to create a "horizon" or "circle" of sound.

In his aesthetic writings, Busoni stated that he wanted sound to surround the stage and envelope listeners, rather than to come from only one location and direction, and this reflects some the spatial elements heard in *Doktor Faust*. The composer aimed to write music that would encircle the action and represent the unseeable and unknowable thoughts of the characters. It would convey truths, actions, and ideas beyond the visible stage (see figure 3.3):[58]

[57] It is fitting that Gustav Mahler conducted the first public performance of this piece in New York City on February 21, 1911.

[58] Although Busoni disagreed with many of Richard Wagner's ideas about the music drama, there are definite similarities that can be observed in this regard.

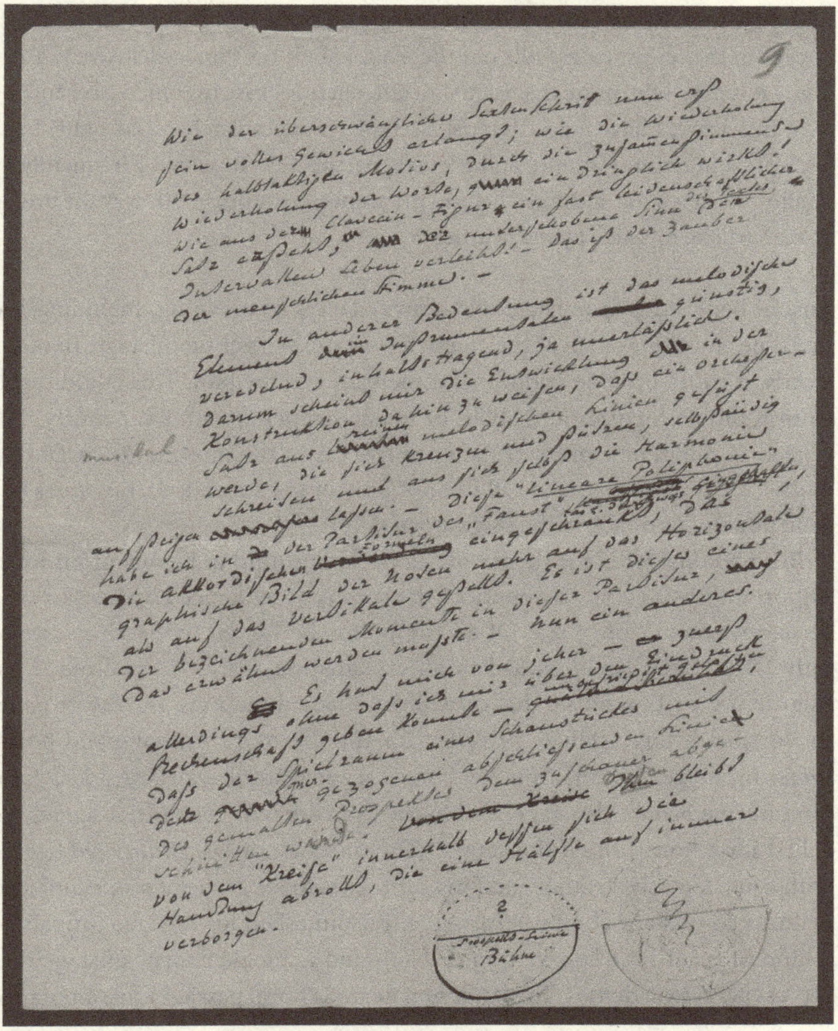

9

Wie der überschwängliche Seligkeit nun erst
sein volles Gewicht erlangt; wie die Wiederholung
des halbtaktigen Motivs, durch die zusammenstimmende
Wiederholung der Worte, ein dringlich wirkt!
Wie aus der Clavecin-Figur ein fast leidenschaftlicher
Satz entsteht, der unterschobene Sinn den
Intervallen Leben verleiht! – Das ist der Zauber
der menschlichen Stimme. –

In anderer Bedeutung ist das melodische
Element dem Instrumentalen günstig,
veredelnd, inhaltstragend, ja unerläßlich.
Darum scheint mir die Entwicklung in der
Konstruktion dahin zu weisen, daß ein orchester-
Satz aus reinen melodischen Linien gefügt
werde, die sich kreuzen und stützen, selbständig
schreiten und aus sich selbst die Harmonie
aufsteigen lassen. – Diese "lineare Polyphonie" [illegible],
habe ich in der Partitur des „Faust" [illegible] eingeschränkt, das
die akkordischen Formeln nicht mehr auf das Horizontale
graphische Bild der Noten [illegible] gestellt. Es ist diese Partitur,
als auf das Vertikale gestellt [illegible]
der bezeichnenden Momente in dieser Partitur nun ein anderes.
Das erwähnt werden mußte. –

Es hat mich von jeher – zuerst
allerdings ohne daß ich mir über den Eindruck
Rechenschaft geben konnte – [illegible] mit
daß der Spielraum eines Schaustückes mit einer
der [illegible] gezogenen abschließenden Linie
des gemalten Prospektes dem Zuschauer abge-
schnitten wurde. [illegible] bleibt
von dem "Kreise" innerhalb dessen sich die
Handlung abrollt, die eine Hälfte auf immer
verborgen.

musikal-

Figure 3.3. Busoni's diagram of the visible and invisible stage (in the unpublished version) that he hoped music would encompass (Prospektus-Linie Bühne). Preussischer Kulturbesitz, Staatsbibliothek zu Berlin, Musikabteilung mit Mendelssohn Archiv, Mus. Nachl. F. Busoni, CI, 8.

The onlooker's imagination is asked to work at the completion. If a figure goes out of a door, the departure gives the onlooker a vivid picture of the person going out into the street. At times too, he knows where the person is going (imagined) and thus he fathoms the invisible half of the circle with

> the eye of imagination. It is different with music in the theater which (except in the fewest cases) fills out the front half of the circle exclusively. To me it is precisely music that is qualified to encircle this circumference, and, in this score, I have made the first attempt (not completely carried out) to create a horizon of sound, and acoustic perspective, in which I frequently allow what is sung and acted behind the scenes to sound; in this way the unseen will be revealed by the hearing.[59]

Busoni believed that music could convey layers of meaning, including the invisible emotional state of the characters or unseen action offstage. In other words, it could provide additional dimensions to the plot. This could result from multiple textures and styles of music happening simultaneously that related to different aspects of the narrative (as in the intermezzo in *Doktor Faust*). He desired to make full use not only of the stage itself, but areas behind and under or above the stage as well.

Busoni considered his theory of the circle of sound to be one of his most important ideas about the opera of the future, as evidenced by his sketches for a new theory of opera. Of all the points he hoped to elaborate upon, only "Der Klang-Kreis" ended in an exclamation mark. He realized these theories by writing music that came from many directions. In *Doktor Faust* in Vorspiel I, for instance, he called for the use of a trombone and horns *under* the stage.[60] In the Münster chapel scene (intermezzo), he asked for a tambourine *behind* the stage, and in the Watchman's scene (final scene), he called for a horn *behind* the stage.[61] The third act of *Die Brautwahl* begins with a particularly striking and long offstage solo for *cornet à piston* and also features an offstage choir. In *Turandot*, Busoni asked for offstage timpani—a kind of regal attention-getting device—and a female chorus offstage that represents sylvan deities. The latter non-texted choral passage adds ambiance

[59] Busoni, "The Score of *Doktor Faust*," 75. [Die Fantasie des Zuschauers wird aufgefordert auf der Ergänzung zu arbeiten. Geht eine Figur durch eine Thüre ab, so gells er sich das Hinaustreten der Person auf die Strasse ihr Sich Entfernen, lebhaft vor. Zuweilen, weiss er auch *wohin* diese Person sich (fingiert) begiebt, und er dringt so und dem Blicke der Imagination in die unsichtbare Hälfte des gedachten Kreises. Anders verhält es dies mit der Musik auf dem Theater, die—wenige Fälle ausgenommen, wo die "hinter der Szene" erklingt—aufschliesses den vorderen Halbkreis ausfüllt. Es schwebt mir vor, dass gerade die Musik dazu berufen sei diese Peripherie vollständig zu umgürten nur ich habe in dieser Partitur dem ersten (nicht völlig durchgeführten) versuch unternommen, einen *Klang-Horizont!* eine *prophetische Perspetive* zu schaffen, indem ich haüfig gesungenug und gespieltes und hinter der Bühne erdacht!, wodurch das Augenschaute dur es das gehörte enthüllt werden voll.] Busoni, "Über die Partitur des 'Doktor Faust,'" Staatsbibliothek zu Berlin–Preußischer Kulturbesitz, Musikabteilung mit Mendelssohn-Archiv, Mus. Nachl. F. Busoni C I, 8.

[60] Busoni, *Doktor Faust*, 42.

[61] Busoni, *Doktor Faust*, 121 and 281.

Example 3.6. Busoni, *Turandot*, Act I, "Lament," mm. 1–14.

(Die *Königin-Mutter von Samarkand*, eine Mohrin, phantastisch mit bunten Straußfedern geschmückt, erscheinet in einem Tragsessel geschwenkt, von rasenden Klageweibern gefolgt. Sie halten vor dem Tore. Bei diesem Auftritt treten Kalaf und Barak seitwärts, um erst, nachdem der Zug sich entfernt hat, wieder hervorzukommen.)

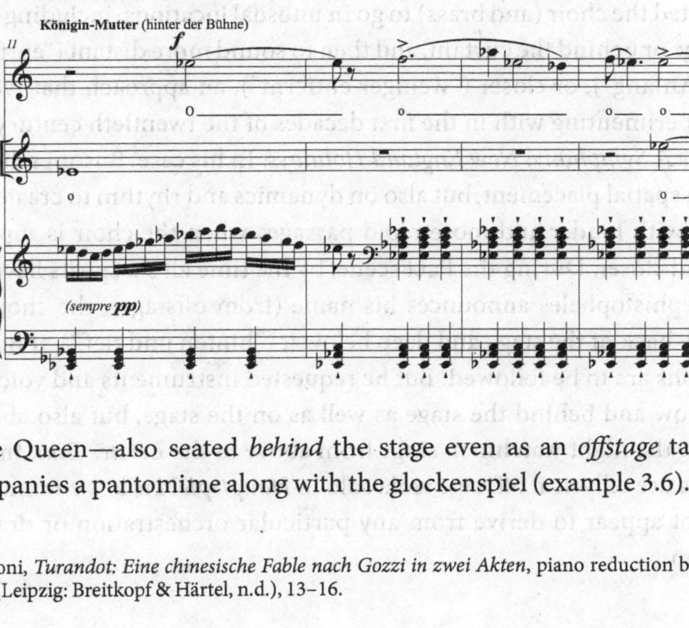

for the Queen—also seated *behind* the stage even as an *offstage* tam-tam accompanies a pantomime along with the glockenspiel (example 3.6).[62]

62 Busoni, *Turandot: Eine chinesische Fable nach Gozzi in zwei Akten*, piano reduction by Philipp Jarnach (Leipzig: Breitkopf & Härtel, n.d.), 13–16.

Busoni was not alone in placing instruments in different locations, and he was by no means the first to do so, but the diversity in spatialized approaches he took in his opera was unprecedented; he was unusual in his attempts to create a circle of sound by placing instruments and voices under, behind, above, and in front of the stage simultaneously, while suggesting their movement closer and farther away in *Doktor Faust*. The opera is also unusual in the frequency with which he used groups of instruments in different locations. In some ways, Busoni was continuing nineteenth-century traditions. It is particularly noteworthy that several previous Faust settings also used offstage choirs, such as those by Berlioz, Charles Gounod, and Arrigo Boito. For instance, in Gounod's *Faust* (1859), the invisible chorus, a choir of angels, appears in act IV in the church as Marguerite prays. God speaks through the unseen chorus. In Boito's *Mefistofele* (1867), the voice of God speaks through the chorus mysticus as bells also resound. In Berlioz's *La damnation de Faust*, op. 24 (1846), an offstage women's chorus also resounds when Faust and Mephistopheles set off to rescue Marguerite. Moreover, the composer also chose to place a military ensemble offstage in the Intermezzo and primarily set brass, percussion, and voices offstage. He also used brass as regal attention-getting devices.

However, his directions also suggest movement of the offstage ensembles, and this was uncommon, such as noting that the tambourine in the Intermezzo should sound farther away ("entfernt sich"). Likewise, he instructed the choir (and brass) to go in unusual locations, including under the stage or behind the curtain, and then to sound more distant ("entfernter als zu Anfang"), or closer ("weniger entfernt"), an approach that Ives was also experimenting with in the first decades of the twentieth century, such as in his *A Symphony: New England Holidays*. In his case, Busoni relied not only on spatial placement, but also on dynamics and rhythm to create these effects, with louder and more rapid passages when the choir is supposed to sound closer. During the Pact scene, by the time all six spirits have sung and Mephistopheles announces his name (from offstage), the choir is at the very back of the stage and deep below it ("hinten und tief"), if Busoni's directions are to be followed. But he requested instruments and voices not just below and behind the stage as well as on the stage, but also above it, as when the night watchman sings from above in the *Letztes Bild*. In addition, his use of lyrical offstage viola solo in *Hauptspiel I* is less common and does not appear to derive from any particular orchestration or dramatic tradition.

Busoni took the idea of the circle of sound one step farther, thinking about placing performers not only in front, underneath, and behind the stage, but also above it. Although it was never staged, he planned to use theatrical space unconventionally to evoke special sonic effects and invoke this circle of sound he imagined in a staging of Bach's *St. Matthew Passion*, BWV 244, as well. This is one of the first known plans (1921) to stage the piece operatically.[63] In this case, the composer's ideas were inspired by the dimensions of a Gothic architecture. In a brief essay, Busoni suggested re creating the vertical and horizontal dimensions found in Gothic cathedrals on the stage as well as the chiastic shape, with the two choirs placed on the far right and left, respectively. The two choirs would surround the sounds of the narrator and other characters on the stages not only horizontally, but also vertically, as they would be placed above the main stage area. Busoni described the intended effect as sound radiating in all directions, including from *above* the stage. He envisioned hearing Bach's music in the theater in a spatialized manner as it could have been heard in a cathedral, yet with added visual aspects of costumes, acting, and sets:

> To lend rhythm and clearness to the intricate tempo, the two stages placed one over the other, which are to be seen in the primitive sketch, should be of service. Through it we acquire space and simultaneousness. Between these stages, half a storey high, the chorus sits right and left; in the middle pulpit stands the narrator, dominating all, and at the same time acting as the centre from which the threads of the action and score extend, radiating in all directions. The fixed position of the chorus affords the convenience of the beginning or after effect of a dramatic chapter being enacted in dumb show while they sing. Care should be taken to be sure that the space displayed brings a concentrated intimate (and at the same time uniform and unchangeable) character to the whole with the harmony of a Gothic cathedral.[64]

[63] See Bettina Varwig, "Beware the Lamb: Staging Bach's Passions," *Twentieth-Century Music* 11:2 (September 2014): 245–74. Varwig has documented only one earlier planned staged performance, by Edward Gordon Craig.

[64] Busoni, "Sketch for a Dramatic Performance of St. Matthew Passion, [1921]," in *The Essence of Music and Other Papers*, 102–3. [Diesem verwirrenden Tempo Rhythmik und Übersichtlichheit zu verleihen, sollen die beiden übereinander gestellten Bühnen dienen, die auf der primitive Skizze erkennbar sind. Durch sie gewinnen wir an Raum und an Gleichzeitigkeit.—Zwischen diesen beiden Bühnen, in der Höhe eines Halbstocktes, sitzt rechts und links die Gemeinde; auf der mittleren Kanzel steht der Erzähler, dominierend und zugleich als Zentrum, von dem aus

Figure 3.4. Busoni, pencil sketch to illustrate his plan for the staging of Bach's *St. Matthew Passion*. Preussischer Kulturbesitz, Staatsbibliothek zu Berlin, Musikabteilung mit Mendelssohn Archiv, N. Mus. Nachl. 4, 1181.

Busoni illustrated his vision in a drawing that was later published in slightly altered form (see figure 3.4). The drawing suggests that action happens simultaneously on both stages and that the choirs are positioned in between the two stages, as if in choir lofts. Although not visible in the initial drawing, the choirs appear in the published drawing on the right and left sides, respectively.

Busoni's vision of the circle of sound and the multi-dimensional theater was linked to very practical ideas about making the theatrical space itself

die Fäden der handlung und der Partitur nach allen Richtungen strahlenförmig sich ziehen. Die unbewegliche Aufstellung der Gemeinde ergibt die Annehmlichkeit, dass während ihres Gesanges der Beginn oder der Nachklang eines szenischen Kapitels sich Stumm abspielen kann. Während einerseits Sorge getragen wurde, dass der dargestellte Raum einen gesammelten, innerlichen (zugleich einheitlichen und unwandelbaren). Charakter zum Ausdruck bringe (mit Anklang an die gotische Kathedrale), ist dem Ausschnitt (durch den die obere Bühne entsteht) ein Horizont als Hintergrund und dadurch die Andeutung der öffentlichen Strasse gegeben, wo ein Vorgang "im Freien" abgespielt zu denken ist.] Busoni, "Zur szenischen Aufführung der Matthäuspassion," in *Von der Einheit*, 342–43.

multi-dimensional through architectural adaptations.[65] He proposed his own ideas about theater construction that explain how his vision for a circle of sound could be facilitated by a multi-dimensional architectural approach. He stated that ideal stages require height and depth—like a cathedral. In 1915, he thus proposed a plan for having two stages—one overhead and one underneath—and provided a diagram to illustrate his ideas. The added height would allow for special effects with vertical dimensions (see figure 3.5).

He considered it important to have two floors so that the theatrical experience could overwhelm the viewer, with a movable floor and high roof. In an initial drawing, which Busoni later crossed out, the floor divisions are solid lines. In the second, they are dotted, suggesting the fluidity of the boundaries of the stage in which added height or depth would be possible: "Today's stage demands such an increased depth that the whole stage appears raised a full level from the ground up. At the same time, its height (of the protective floor) has grown so much that the roof overhangs the auditorium."[66] Busoni likened his proposed theater to a staircase, making possible ascent and descent.[67] He also suggested that the stage should converge in vision like a half circle to allow the sound to encircle audience members.

In envisioning a multi-dimensional stage space, Busoni was participating in a growing interest in reconsidering the shape and possibility of theater architecture. However, while many contemporaries were primarily concerned with visual aspects, the composer was approaching the space primarily in terms of musical considerations. While older stages are primarily two-dimensional, most of the visionary stages of the twentieth century (frequently never built) were multi-dimensional—often circular or annular. Even so, Busoni's proposal in 1915 predated most. Guillaume Apollinaire, a French poet and playwright, provocatively suggested a new type of theater in the prologue to the *Les mamelles de Tirésias* (1916); his vision for new theater

[65] See Busoni, "Aufzeichnungen z. Operntheorie," Staatsbibliothek zu Berlin–Preußischer Kulturbesitz, Musikabteilung mit Mendelssohn-Archiv, Mus. Nachl. F. Busoni CI, 163.

[66] "Die heutige Bühne heischt eine derart gesteigerte Tiefe, dass die ganze Bühne un ein volles Stockwerk vom Grund aus erhoht erscheint. Zugleichst auch ihre Hohe (der Schutzboden), so sehr gewachsen, dass ihr dach jenes des Zuschauerraums ausprechene überragt." Busoni, "Über theaterbau," Staatsbibliothek zu Berlin–Preußischer Kulturbesitz, Musikabteilung mit Mendelssohn-Archiv, Mus. Nachl. F. Busoni CI 55A.

[67] Busoni, "Über theaterbau."

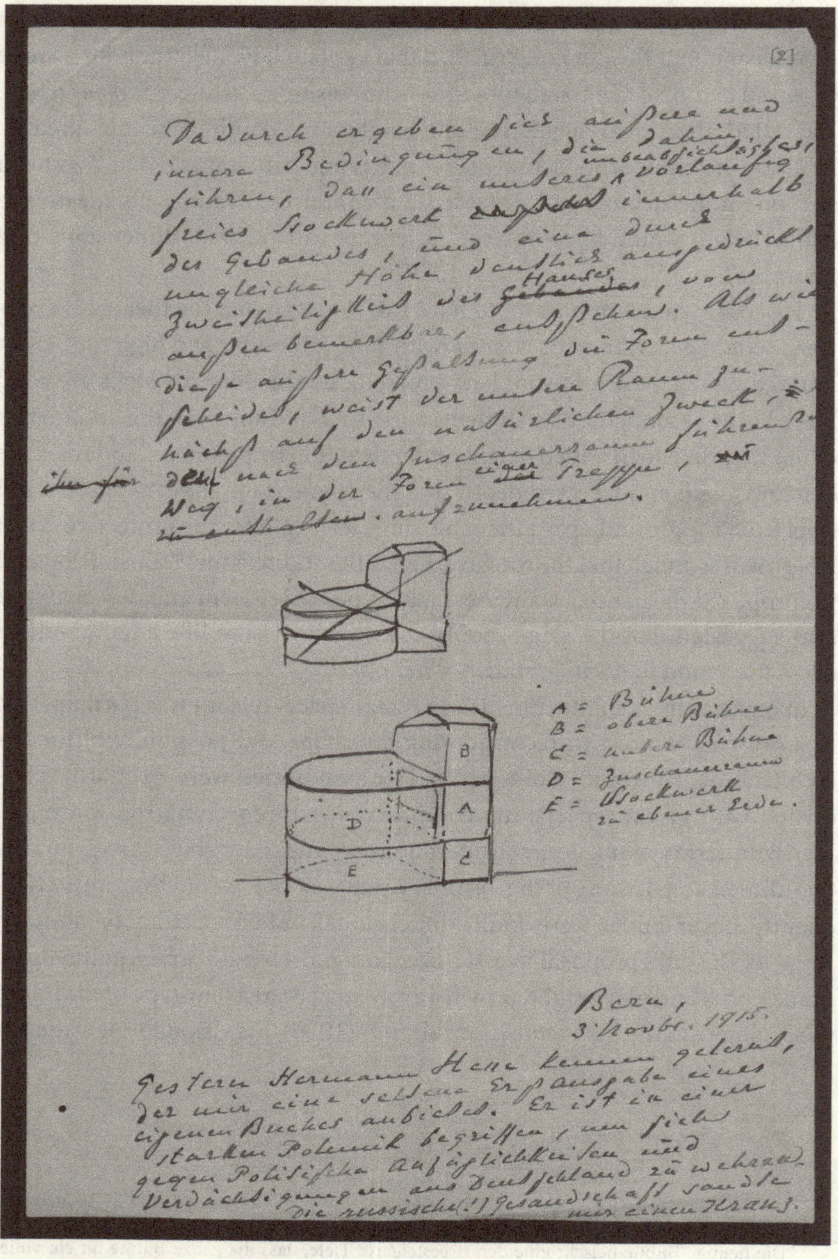

[2]

Dadurch ergeben sich äußere und innere Bedingungen, die dahin führen, daß ein unteres, vorläufig freies Stockwerk innerhalb des Gebäudes, und eine durch ungleiche Höhe deutlich ausgedrückte Zweitheiligkeit des Hauses, von außen bemerkbar, entstehen. Als wie diese äußere Gestaltung die Form entscheidet, weist der untere Raum zunächst auf den natürlichen Zweck, den nach dem Zuschauerraum führenden Weg, in der Form einer Treppe, aufzunehmen.

Bern, 3 Novbr. 1915.

Gestern Hermann Hesse kennen gelernt, der mir eine seltene Erstausgabe eines eigenen Buches anbietet. Er ist in einer starken Polemik begriffen, um sich gegen Politische Anzüglichkeiten und Verdächtigungen aus Deutschland zu wehren. Die russische(!) Gesandtschaft sandte mir einen Kranz.

Figure 3.5. Busoni's proposed and rejected visions for the spatial theater of the future. Busoni, "Über Theaterbau," Staatsbibliothek zu Berlin-Preußischer Kulturbesitz, Musikabteilung mit Mendelssohn-Archiv, Mus. Nachl., CI, 163, 2.

also called for two stages—one encircling the other and the spectators—allowing for multiple events simultaneously:

> A circular theatre with two stages
> One in the middle and the other like a ring
> Around the spectators permitting
> The full unfolding of our modern art
> Often connecting in mysterious ways
> As in life sounds, gestures, colors, cries, tumults,
> Music, dancing, acrobatics, poetry, painting,
> Choruses, actions, and multiple sets.[68]

Pierre Albert-Birot, a French poet and dramatist, also proposed a new theatrical design in 1916 characterized by a rotating stage revolving around spectators, with minimal sets, in which a play with light served a most important role, the Théâtre Nunique. The impetus, like that at the Bauhaus, was a concept for a total work of theater that brought all elements (including pantomime, film, acrobatics, and light play) together into a new whole.[69] Walter Gropius, similarly, designed a "total theater" in 1927 that had a stationary annular stage and could be used in arena fashion or proscenium fashion by lowering and raising the stages (similar to Busoni's suggestion).[70] He wanted to reduce the distance between actors and spectators using all possible spatial means. One of the most famous spherical theaters is the Kugel Theater by Andor Weininger, also of the Bauhaus, and proposed in 1927. These new

[68] [Un théâtre rond à deux scenes
Une au centre l'autre formant comme un anneau
Autour des spectateurs et qui permettra
Le grand deployment de notre art modern
Mariant souvent sans lien apparent comme dans la vie
Les sons les gestes les couleurs les cris les bruits
La musique la danse l'acrobatie la poésie la peinture
Las choeurs les actions et les décors multiples.]

Apollinaire, *Les mamelles de Tirésias: drame surréaliste en deux actes et un prologue* [1917], ed. Didier Alexandre (Paris: Labix Obvil, 2014).

[69] Pierre Albert-Birot, "A Propos d'un Théâtre Nunique," *Sic* 8, 9, 10 (August–October 1916): n.p.. For more about his views on the theater, see Debra Kelly, *Pierre Albert-Birot: A Poetics in Movement, a Poetics of Movement* (London: Associated University Presses, 1997), 100–2. See also Arnold Aronson, "Theatres of the Future," *Theatre Journal* 33:4 (December 1981): 489–503.

[70] See *The Theatre of the Bauhaus*, ed. Walter Gropius (Middleton, CT: Wesleyan University Press, 1961).

Figure 3.6. Busoni, sketch for a theatrical space with a triple opening. From "Projekt für eine Dreifache Bühnenöffnung" (Zurich, 1918). Reproduced in *Von der Einheit der Musik* (1922), 378–79. The original drawing seems to have been lost.

theaters have influenced drama, with special spaces often inspiring new dramatic and possibilities.

Busoni was especially influenced in his vision of a multi-dimensional theater by studying the work of van de Velde. The composer drafted his ideas about a triple stage opening after discussions with the architect. He drew the picture in 1918 and sketched an accompanying explanatory text in 1922 (see figure 3.6).

Busoni's drawing was likely inspired by discussions about van de Velde's Werkbund Theater (1914), an impressive concrete modernist theater designed to accommodate different types of productions. It featured a stage divided by three movable pillars that could slide on rails. Van de Velde was intent upon moving away from the French and Italian horseshoe shaped theater models with a single stage opening and galleries with box seating, and was not interested in replicating the Wagnerian Bayreuth double proscenium and orchestra pit that reinforced the distance between the audience and the performers. He hoped to create a space that allowed for intimate plays, like those of Max Reinhardt and Gordon Craig, and to break down the divide between the viewer and the stage.[71] Van de Velde's ideas were already directed toward this new theater with a proposed Weimar theater (Dumont

[71] Van de Velde, *Geschichte*, 256–58.

Theater, 1903) that unfortunately never came to fruition, and a smaller one for Reinhardt in 1906 (the plans of which disappeared during World War I).[72]

In his plan for a new theatrical space, Busoni, like van de Velde, paid great attention to the viewer, and hoped to erase the artificiality created by a single stage with curtains that acted like a frame, thereby separating the audience from the action. He proposed adding two invisible side wings that could open and add width when needed for extra action and more complicated plots.[73] The ramifications of such a stage extend well beyond the visual to aural and formal possibilities, including having sound coming from multiple (horizontal) directions or having textural layering in the music to suggest multiple dramatic happenings at the same time.

These new thoughts about theatrical space coincided with a period in Busoni's output when he was deeply interested in composing operas or stage works and in seeking new ways to make theatrical space more multidimensional. While this imagined architectural space invites new spatial and sonorous possibilities, it also opened up the possibility of multiple musical forms happening simultaneously in theatrical works. In addition, multiple actions and musical events can take place simultaneously horizontally (and not just vertically, as he previously imagined), resulting in diverse textures and layers of sound.

In re-envisioning the theatrical space, Busoni was not as interested in dissolution of boundaries between art and life, as were later authors like Cage, but rather—in highlighting the disparity between the fantastical on the stage and real life—to create distance, much like Reinhardt, whom he greatly admired. Like Busoni, Reinhardt rejected the realistic stage and searched for new ways to mix the arts with the lighting and sets, leaving much of the drama unseen and unspoken. He and Busoni, like Bertolt Brecht, desired to inspire critical reflection through drama. Unlike Brecht's plays, Busoni's operas usually contain hidden messages about art and life, as opposed to social ills. At the same time, he too used defamiliarizing techniques, such as having the poet directly address the audience.[74] However, it was primarily in the music that Busoni hoped to convey drama.

72 Ibid., 273.

73 Busoni, "Projekt für eine dreifache Bühnenöffnung," in *Von der Einheit der Musik*, 268.

74 See Joachim Lucchesi, "Brecht und Busoni: Entwürfe zu einem Theater der Gegenwart," in *Man muss versuchen, sich einzurichten in Deutschland: Brecht in den Zwanzigern*, Der Neue Brecht, vol. 14, ed. Jan Knopf and Jürgen Hillesheim (Würzburg: Königshausen & Neumann, 2015), 203–11.

Conclusions

Busoni sought to be an architect of sound. In that regard, his approaches were not limited to metaphorical connections or to notions of architectural structure. He also considered multifaceted notions of dimension and space that influenced his decisions about texture, timbre, and instrument placement. It was a vision of music that encompassed music coming from different directions in physical space, music that was polyphonic and multilayered, music that was timbrally diverse, and music that teemed with diverse textures. Although his writings contain many references to mysterious metaphysical ideas, his compositions realize his spatial theories largely through tangible connections to specific architectural spaces.

Busoni hoped to create a new spatialized sound world that transformed the listening experience as audiences were surrounded by sound coming from up high, down low, behind, and in front in a wide breadth of space. This, in turn, helped create layers of sound that could have different symbolic and timbral significance during dramatic works. While part of what Busoni was doing was not necessarily novel (i.e., using offstage instruments for dramatic purposes), his re-envisioning of theatrical space and his use of simultaneous textural and timbral layers pioneered newer twentieth-century concepts of spatialized music. Moreover, what marks his music as different is not just that offstage instruments are used, but in how they are used for dramatic purposes, for commentary, and to help create diverse layers simultaneously. Busoni composed music in layers of sonority and sound to create texture, and he re-envisioned opera and symphonic music based on ways sound could be projected into space. In the process, he created new sounds and approaches to composition in an era when they were just emerging. It is these aspects of sound in space that also influenced how he performed and adapted the music of others, as will be discussed in chapter 4. Busoni thus helped forge new directions in music through his metatonal approach, his unique montage and multi-dimensional forms, and through his new uses and evocations of space, aspects that had a lasting impact on his mentees and subsequent generations of composers.

4
Busoni's Liquid Architecture

> These combined impulses of architecture and visual arts are considered to be the central features of Busoni's artistic thinking.
>
> —Grigory Kogan[1]

Busoni not only shaped his own compositions based on his knowledge of and veneration for architecture, thereby expanding the musical language, creating unique montage forms, and pioneering the spatialization of sound, but also molded the music of others in an architectural manner in his notated arrangements, in his editions, and during his performances in response to the physical spaces in which he performed pieces.[2] He reworked other composers' pieces into monumental and multi-dimensional structures, reshaping them through his idiosyncratic use of sound, color, terraced dynamics, and formal restructuring.[3]

[1] Grigory Kogan, *Busoni as Pianist*, trans. Svetlana Belsky, Eastman Studies in Musicology (Rochester, NY: University of Rochester Press, 2010), 45. Thanks are due Erin Jerome (University of Massachusetts Amherst), Jean-Christophe Gero (Staatsbibliothek zu Berlin), and Marina Gordienko (Staatsbibliothek zu Berlin) for their assistance locating archival materials for this chapter.

[2] The term "liquid architecture" has assumed different meanings in diverse eras and in different disciplines. Markos Novak, for instance, used it to describe his work on changeable three-dimensional computer-generated architectural designs in the 1990s. Markos Novak, "Liquid Architectures in Cyberspace," *Cyberspace: First Steps* (October 1991), 225–54, https://www.evl.uic.edu/datsoupi/coding/readings/1991_Novak_Liquid.pdf (accessed October 7, 2021). "Liquid Architecture" is also currently the name for an Australian organization of artists working with sound. Historical and metaphorical equations of architecture and frozen music or music and liquid architecture have also been attributed to Goethe, Friedrich Schlegel, and Friedrich Wilhelm Joseph von Schelling in the nineteenth century. For an explanation of the use of the term in the nineteenth century, see Thomas Grey, "Metaphorical Modes in Music Criticism," in *Music and Text: Critical Inquiries*, ed. Steven Paul Scher (Cambridge: Cambridge University Press, 2004), 96. It is possible that Busoni might have encountered the term ("flüssige Architektur") in the writings of Schopenhauer (*Die Welt als Wille und Vorstellung II* (Leipzig: F. A. Brockhaus, 1844), whose writings he admired. See also the following source for additional discussion of the topic: Khaled Saleh Pascha, "Gefrorene Musik: Das Verhältnis von Architektur und Musik in der ästhetischen Theorie" (PhD diss., Technische Universität Berlin, 2004). In this chapter, I am using the term "liquid architecture" to refer to sounds moving through space in time.

[3] By "terraced," I am referring to abrupt changes, such as in dynamics, tone colors, or texture. Busoni, who used the term "terraced" in his own writings, likened these abrupt shifts to changes in

Ferruccio Busoni as Architect of Sound. Erinn E. Knyt, Oxford University Press. © Oxford University Press 2023.
DOI: 10.1093/oso/9780197625491.003.0005

In annotated comments for his editions and to his students, he mentioned how architecture inspired his alterations, especially regarding how he modified formal structures. During his recitals and in his notated arrangements, Busoni became known as a sound sculptor, creating monumental-sized pieces to better fit the architectural spaces in which he performed them. Although he did not employ a metatonal approach in his reworking of the music of other composers, he modified the pieces to exhibit his compositional ideals of montage forms and sound projecting out in space. It is in these reworked sound structures, some created in real time, or else tied to Busoni's responses to physical buildings and acoustics, that music, space, and time converged to create liquid architecture.

Focusing primarily on his piano arrangements, this chapter documents the role Busoni's architectural conceptions played in his reworking of the music of other composers. Scholars have already shown how his authoritative interpretive style, in which he altered the music of others, reflects his blurring of boundaries between the roles of composer, interpreter, and arranger.[4] For Busoni, arrangements and interpretations were part of his creative activity; he aimed for similar ideals when working with the materials of others as he did with his own compositions.[5] His arrangements also reflected his innovative creative ideals.

Architectural Spaces

Busoni responded to the resonant and large concert halls of his era when he added to the registral height and depth of pieces by enriching chords and adding octave doublings so that tones would resonate throughout the

registration on an organ. Busoni, notes to *The First Twenty-Four Preludes and Fugues of The Well-Tempered Clavichord* (New York: G. Schirmer, n.d.), 49; 167.

[4] For Busoni's ideas about the fluidity between the roles of arranger and composer, see Erinn Knyt, "'How I Compose': Ferruccio Busoni's Views about Invention, Quotation, and the Compositional Process," *Journal of Musicology* 27:2 (Spring 2010): 224–63. For Busoni's views in his own words, see Ferruccio Busoni, "Wert der Bearbeitung," in Busoni, *Von der Einheit der Musik: Von Dritteltönen und Junger Klassizität, von Bühnen und Bauten, und anschliessenden Bezirken, Verstreute Aufzeichnungen*, ed. Martina Weindel, Quellenkataloge zur Musikgeschichte 36, ed. Richard Schaal (Wilhelmshaven: Florian Noetzel Verlag, 2006), 55–56. This essay originally appeared in a concert program in Berlin, in November 1910.

[5] Although we can no longer listen to Busoni perform, we can rely on concert programs, reviews, eyewitness accounts, recordings, piano rolls, published editions, and unpublished manuscripts.

spacious buildings.[6] In his authoritative reworkings of pieces, he avoided the popular practice of nuanced and progressive changes in dynamics, tone, or register, for instance, in favor of a terraced approach, characterized by abrupt changes in tempo, color, and touch. This created the aural impression of structural blocks. In addition, he sought to meld tones into the architectural music that he idealized as he aimed for a melding of spatial and temporal art forms in new ways.

That Busoni's creative activity was connected to acoustics and architecture is unsurprising. It has been well documented that the sounds composers and musicians sought after are often linked to the architectural spaces in which the pieces would have been performed. John Mauvan, for instance, has stated that "from the early seventeenth century the best composers have had a strong understanding of the way their music was affected by space. Thus, the buildings of the period and the acoustic ambience were stylistically akin."[7] Christopher R. Herr and Gary W. Sieben have similarly traced connections between musical spaces, compositional style, and instrumentation back to medieval times.[8] At the same time, Leo Baranek has documented specific

[6] Busoni's architectural interpretive approach can be inferred, in part, from his surviving acoustic recordings, which, unfortunately were recorded late in Busoni's life and under less-than-ideal circumstances. Busoni, who excelled in longer works, had to fit music onto short-playing records. In addition, Busoni complained about the bench and the piano. Busoni, letter of February 1, 1922, to Mr. Tillet, quoted in Jonathan Summers, liner notes to Busoni and His Legacy: Piano Recordings by Busoni, Ley, Petri, http://arbiterrecords.org/catalog/busoni-and-his-legacy (accessed November 27, 2016). He considered his first attempt at making an acoustic recording in 1919 so unsatisfactory, that none of the recordings were released, and the originals were later destroyed in a fire. For more about the 1919 recordings, see Christopher Dyment, "Ferruccio Busoni: His Phonograph Recordings," *Journal of the Association for Recorded Sound* 10 (1979): 185–87. Surviving acoustically recorded pieces from 1922 include the following:

J. S. Bach, Prelude and Fugue in C Major (*Well-Tempered Clavier*, book I)
Bach, "Nun freut euch lieben Christen gmein," BWV 734, transcription for piano by Busoni
Ludwig van Beethoven, Ecossaisen, WoO 83, arranged by Busoni
Frederic Chopin, Prelude in A Major, op. 28, no. 7
Chopin, Etude in G♭ Major, op. 10, no. 5 (recorded twice)
Chopin, Nocturne in F♯ Major, op. 15, no. 2
Chopin, Etude in E Minor, op. 25, no. 5
Franz Liszt, Hungarian Rhapsody no. 13 in A Minor, S. 244, no. 13

For a list of the roll recordings, see: Marc-André Roberge, *Ferruccio Busoni: A Bio-bibliography* (New York: Greenwood Press, 1991). Busoni's essays, letters, and editions, in conjunction with reviews and concert programs, also provide glimpses into how he played.

[7] John Mauvan, "Shoe Box: An Analysis of the Concert-Hall and Its Adaptation to Small-Scale Music Performance Space" (MA thesis, University of Wellington, 2011), 9. https://core.ac.uk/download/pdf/41337425.pdf (accessed May 12, 2021).

[8] Christopher R. Herr and Gary W. Siebein, "An Acoustical History of Theaters and Concert Halls: An Investigation of Parallel Developments in Music, Performance Spaces, and the Orchestra," in "Souped-Up and Unplugged: Proceedings of the 86th ACSA Annual Meeting and Technology

ways that architecture, acoustics, and compositions or performances were linked. For instance, he argued that in the Baroque period, compositions were often created with one of two types of spaces in mind: large and reverberant churches or dry acoustic rectangular rooms.[9] The latter were most appropriate for intimate polyphonic pieces for chamber groups or solo instruments. Classical composers, by contrast, placed greater emphasis on fullness and depth than on contrapuntal clarity even as they still prized acoustic intimacy and saw the emergence of many public concert halls. One key example is the Altes Gewandhaus in Leipzig (1781–1885), which seated about 400 people. Mauvan asserts that much Classical era music was best suited to smaller and crowded halls with dryer acoustics and little sound distortion.[10] Classical era halls were often still rectangular in shape with relatively dry acoustics. By contrast, during the second part of the nineteenth century, numerous large concert halls were built that could seat thousands of people and that featured very reverberant acoustics; these larger and resonant halls were ideal for showcasing larger sounds and the varied colors characteristic of much Romantic era music.

Many of these concert halls were erected around the time Busoni was born or during the first three decades of his life. Baranek notes that "in the romantic era, a relatively long reverberation time, about 1.9–2.1 sec. is preferred."[11] Many of these halls were still rectangular in shape, but were much larger, and some had balconies, thereby enabling greater sound reflection and reverberance. These halls also emphasized color and richness of sound as opposed to intricate clarity or line. For instance, the old Boston Music Hall, erected in 1863, in which Busoni performed concerti when he was a professor at the New England Conservatory of Music in 1892, reportedly had a resonance time of over 1.8 seconds with a full audience (see figure 4.1). Resonance times were longer if fewer people were in attendance.[12] He

Conference" (n.p.: Association of Collegiate Schools of Architecture, 1998), 146 https://www.acsa-arch.org/proceedings/Annual%20Meeting%20Proceedings/ACSA.AM.86/ACSA.AM.86.29.pdf (accessed May 12, 2021).

[9] Leo Baranek, *Concert Halls and Opera Houses: Music, Acoustics, and Architecture*, 2nd ed. (Cambridge, MA: Springer, 1996), 8–11.

[10] Mauvan, "Shoe Box," 9.

[11] Mauvan, "Shoe Box," 11.

[12] For a list of some of Busoni's performances in the Boston Music Hall, the Boston Symphony Hall, and other venues in the United States, see Knyt, "Ferruccio Busoni and the New England Conservatory: Piano Pedagogue in the Making," *American Music* 31:3 (Fall 2013): 289–99. See Baranek, *Concert Halls and Opera Houses*, 11, for more information about the resonance in the hall.

Figure 4.1. Photograph of the Boston Music Hall from c. 1900. Photo by A. H. Rickards.

similarly performed several times at Boston Symphony Hall, built in 1900 for an audience of 2,600 people, and with reverberation times of about 2 seconds in the middle frequencies. He also performed at Carnegie Hall in New York, with a seating capacity of 2,760 people and a reverberation time of at least 1.7 seconds at full capacity.[13] The Concertgebouw of Amsterdam, erected in 1887, had a reverberation time of 2 seconds, and Busoni was also familiar with this hall, having conducted his own piano concerto there in 1905, with pupil Egon Petri at the piano. It would not be until the mid-to-late 1920s that dryer acoustic fan-shaped designs would again be commonly featured in the architectural design of concert hall spaces.

While resonant sounds, thick chords, emphasis on tone color, and bold dramatic contrasts sounded well within the walls of the large concert halls of the late nineteenth century, it was harder to effectively project the thin

[13] Mauvan, "Shoe Box," 23–24. For more information about concert hall acoustics, consult the following sources: M. David Egan, *Architectural Acoustics* (New York: McGraw-Hill, 1988), and Michael Forsyth, *Buildings for Music* (Cambridge, MA: MIT Press, 1985).

contrapuntal lines of a Baroque fugue or the more intimate strains of a Mozart sonata.

Yet at the same time larger resonant concert halls were being erected, numerous performers also began to feature historical concerts of pieces that were not designed for those halls. It is thus not surprising, especially before the advent of amplification devices or variable architectural acoustic techniques, such as artificial shells, ceiling panels, or adjustable walls to change the acoustics for different purposes or types of pieces, that many performers, conductors, and composers felt it necessary to modify the pieces they were performing to better suit the architectural spaces. If Busoni idealized the highly reverberant acoustics in Gothic cathedrals, he also responded to the highly reverberant sounds in the concert halls. Many aspects of his own compositions and the modifications he made to the music of others were well suited to the larger reverberant concert halls erected during his lifetime. And while Busoni was not alone in responding to these new spaces through octave doublings and other enrichments, he also went beyond them in his structural alterations and in the way that he approached dynamics and pedaling to maximize the sound as it projected up and out in the concert halls.[14] In the process of adapting and composing pieces for the new architectural spaces, Busoni not only responded to the buildings around him, but also applied his own compositional ideals to historical music of previous eras.

Copious numbers of recital programs, now housed in his Nachlass at the Staatsbibliothek, document the breadth of venues that Busoni performed in or had his compositions performed in. Some that he repeatedly returned to include the Beethovensaal (1898–1945) and Berlin Philharmonie (1876–1952) in Berlin, Wigmore Hall (formerly Bechstein Hall, 1901–1941) and Queen's Hall (1893–1941) in London, the Tonhalle in Zurich (1895–present; see figure 4.2), the large Konzertsaal (1876–present) in Basel, the Salle Érard

[14] Given the high reverberation time in these concert halls, it is easy to understand the purported connections between the nineteenth-century resonant concert halls and a notion of *Kunstreligion*; some of the Gothic cathedrals in Europe have a reverberation time of 5.6 seconds. Denise Gail Prince, "Kleinhans Music Hall: A Study in Modern Sound" (MA thesis, University of Buffalo, State University of New York, 2011), 13, https://buffaloah.com/a/sym/klein/prince.pdf (accessed May 12, 2021). If Franz Liszt was the first to place the piano sideways, which had obvious acoustic advantages for his performances to thousands of people at a time, he was also an important pioneer of recitals containing pieces spanning the historical common practice period. Liszt and Busoni were not alone in modifying historical scores; they adapted them not only for the modern instrument, but also so that they would sound forth to the last seat in a resonant hall. For more about Liszt's influence on Busoni, see Knyt, "Franz Liszt's Heir: Ferruccio Busoni and Weimar," *Nineteenth-Century Music Review* 17:1 (April 2020): 35–67.

Figure 4.2. Image of the Zurich Tonhalle from c. 1905. Print no. 8013 in the Views of Switzerland Photochrome Print Collection. Detroit Publishing Co. Catalog J-Foreign Section (Detroit: Detroit Publishing Co., 1905).

in Paris (early nineteenth century–present), and Symphony Hall in Boston (1900–present.)[15]

Due to their destruction during World War II, or else due to general aging, some of these venues are no longer standing, or else are reconstructed; thus,

[15] Busoni, concert programs of various dates, Preussischer Kulturbesitz, Staatsbibliothek zu Berlin, Music Abteilung mit Mendelssohn Archiv, Mus. Nachl. F. Busoni, E. For instance, he performed a series of three concerts in February 1918 at the Konzertsaal in Basel, and the programming ranged from Bach (i.e., the "Goldberg Variations," arr. Busoni) to Beethoven (Sonatas, op. 53, op. 106, and op. 111), to Chopin (all four ballads), to Liszt ("Italie"/Don-Juan Fantasy), to César Franck (Prélude, Choral, et Fugue), to Busoni (three Elegies, Sonatina ad usam infantis, and three Tanzstücke). Busoni, Concert Program of February 13/15, and March 18, 1918, Preussischer Kulturbesitz, Staatsbibliothek zu Berlin, Music Abteilung mit Mendelssohn Archiv, Mus. Nachl. F. Busoni, E, 1918, 3. He also performed a program of Bach (an arrangement of the Organ Prelude and Fugue in D Major), Beethoven (Sonata op. 53), and Liszt ("Italie"/"Venezie e Napoli") in the large Tonhalle in Zurich on April 19, 1917. Busoni, concert program of April 19, 1917, Preussischer Kulturbesitz, Staatsbibliothek zu Berlin, Music Abteilung mit Mendelssohn Archiv, Mus. Nachl. F. Busoni, E, 1917, 6. He also gave a series of concerts at the Salle Érard in Paris in January 1914 playing pieces ranging from Bach-Busoni, Mozart-Busoni, Beethoven-Busoni, and Liszt, to Chopin. Busoni, concert program of January 16, 20, and 26, 1914, Preussischer Kulturbesitz, Staatsbibliothek zu Berlin, Music Abteilung mit Mendelssohn Archiv, Mus. Nachl. F. Busoni, E, 1914, 2.

it is difficult to know with certainty the exact acoustical properties of some of the halls at the time Busoni would have frequented them. While Wigmore Hall and the Salle Érard are more intimate venues, holding only several hundred spectators, Busoni also performed in larger venues. Wigmore Hall, with a capacity of 552, was built between 1899 and 1901 by the Bechstein Piano Company for performances of chamber music and solo piano recitals; it has a mid-range reverberation time of 1.5 seconds (occupied) after the 2004 refurbishment.[16] Its sound quality is a blending of clarity and reverberance that is well suited to solo performances. Busoni performed at the opening concert for the hall on May 31, 1901, together with violinist Eugène Ysaÿe and returned there repeatedly for solo recitals throughout his career. Busoni also performed frequently in resonant larger halls, such as in the mid-sized Berlin Beethovensaal, which had a capacity of 1,066, the larger Berlin Philharmonie hall with around 2,500 seats, and Queen's Hall, which also seated around 2,500.[17] The Tonhalle in Zurich, seating around 1,455 people, has an average

[16] It is unclear what the reverberation time was before the refurbishment, although the plan was to preserve the acoustics of the hall during the refurbishment. T. Wulfrank and R. J. Orlowski, "Acoustic Analysis of Wigmore Hall, London, in the Context of the 2004 Refurbishment," Proceedings of the Institute of Acoustics, https://www.researchgate.net/publication/257361623_Acoustic_Analysis_of_Wigmore_Hall_London_in_the_Context_of_the_2004_Refurbishment (accessed May 12, 2021). Busoni performed a recital there on October 16, 1909, playing only his own arrangements of pieces by Bach, Mozart, Paganini, Liszt, and Beethoven. Busoni, concert program of October 16, 1909, Preussischer Kulturbesitz, Staatsbibliothek zu Berlin, Music Abteilung mit Mendelssohn Archiv, Mus. Nachl. F. Busoni, E, 1909, 12. Toward the end of his performing career, he performed a recital of Bach (Prelude and Fugue no. 1 from the *Well-Tempered Clavier I* and his arrangement of the "Goldberg Variations") and Beethoven (Sonata op. 106), along with a few pieces by Liszt. Busoni, concert program of an unspecified date in 1919. Preussischer Kulturbesitz, Staatsbibliothek zu Berlin, Music Abteilung mit Mendelssohn Archiv, Mus. Nachl. F. Busoni, E, 1919, 7.

[17] For instance, Busoni performed three recitals at the Beethovensaal on January 23, January 31, and February 7, 1900, featuring music by Schumann, Brahms, Liszt, and Chopin. Busoni, concert program of January 23/31 and February 7, 1900, Preussischer Kulturbesitz, Staatsbibliothek zu Berlin, Music Abteilung mit Mendelssohn Archiv, Mus. Nachl. F. Busoni, E, 1900, 2. Another concert on January 24, 1907, in the Beethovensaal featured music by Brahms, Chopin, Schumann, and Liszt, including all twenty-four Preludes, op. 28, by Chopin, the *Abegg-Variationen* by Schumann, and the *Paganini-Variationen* by Brahms. Busoni, concert program of January 24, 1907, Preussischer Kulturbesitz, Staatsbibliothek zu Berlin, Music Abteilung mit Mendelssohn Archiv, Mus. Nachl. F. Busoni, E, 1907, 2. He subsequently performed works by Bach, Mozart, Brahms, Beethoven, Schumann, and Chopin at the larger Philharmonie on April 5, 1907. The Bach Praeludium and Fuge in D major was his own arrangement. Busoni, concert program of April 5, 1907, Preussischer Kulturbesitz, Staatsbibliothek zu Berlin, Music Abteilung mit Mendelssohn Archiv, Mus. Nachl. F. Busoni, E, 1907, 5. He performed at the Philharmonie closer to the end of his life, featuring a program of Bach ("Goldberg Variations"), Weber (Sonata, op. 39), Busoni (*Kammerfantasie über Carmen* and a yet unpublished Toccata [Preludio, Fantasia, Ciaccona]), and Liszt (*Don-Juan Fantasie*). Busoni, concert program of November 18, 1920, Preussischer Kulturbesitz, Staatsbibliothek zu Berlin, Music Abteilung mit Mendelssohn Archiv, Mus. Nachl. F. Busoni, E, 1920, 17. It was also at the Berlin Philharmonie in 1921 that he performed six of his arrangements/enrichments of Mozart Piano Concertos. Busoni, concert program of December 14/16, 1921, Preussischer Kulturbesitz, Staatsbibliothek zu Berlin, Music Abteilung mit Mendelssohn Archiv, Mus. Nachl. F. Busoni, E, 1921, 19. In 1908 at the Beethovensaal, he performed his own piano elegies along with pieces by

reverberation time of 2.5 seconds when 1,000 viewers are present.[18] At the same time, the Konzertsaal in Basel holds around 1,397 people. Although Queen's Hall was a common venue for orchestral performances, Busoni also gave a solo piano recital there at the height of his concertizing career on March 14, 1912.[19] He also performed numerous times at the large Tonhalle in Zurich, including an all-Chopin evening on April 13, 1916.[20]

Enlargement and Verticalization of Sound

Busoni's arrangements of the music of others and his own original compositions were often described as architectural, in part because of the ways he enlarged the scope of the sound to fit into the large concert hall spaces constructed during his lifetime. Using the term "architectural" as a descriptor for piano interpretations was not unheard of in Busoni's time, but it was used primarily to refer to the bold and assertive style of the Russian School, which differed from the contemporary French *jeu perlé* or Viennese approaches that were characterized by constantly fluctuating nuances of expression and fine detail. *Jeu perlé* performers favored quick, light, delicate, and clear playing, while the Viennese school favored arm and finger movement that contributed to drama and color, but without great power.[21] Neither of the French or Viennese approaches were particularly well suited to filling the larger concert hall spaces being erected throughout Europe and the

Franck, Charles-Valentin Alkan, and Liszt. Busoni, concert program of March 12, 1908, Preussischer Kulturbesitz, Staatsbibliothek zu Berlin, Music Abteilung mit Mendelssohn Archiv, Mus. Nachl. F. Busoni, E, 1908, 12.

[18] K. H. Lorenz-Kierakiewitz and M. Vercammen, "Acoustical Survey of 25 European Concert Halls" (Rotterdam: NAG, 2009), 2, https://pub.dega-akustik.de/NAG_DAGA_2009/data/articles/000314.pdf (accessed May 12, 2021).

[19] Busoni, concert program of March 14, 1912, Preussischer Kulturbesitz, Staatsbibliothek zu Berlin, Music Abteilung mit Mendelssohn Archiv, Mus. Nachl. F. Busoni, E, 1912, 5b.

[20] He also reached out to Volkmar Andreae to see if he could perform a Mozart piano concerto in the hall. Busoni, letter of October 7, 1917, to Volkmar Andreae, in Antony Beaumont, ed., *Ferruccio Busoni: Selected Letters* (New York: Columbia University Press, 1987), 267.

[21] See E. E. Kellett and E. W. Naylor, *A History of Pianoforte and Pianoforte Players*, trans. Oscar Bie (New York: Da Capo Press, 1966), 301–2; Christina Kobb, "Viennese Piano Technique of the 1820s and Implications for Today's Pianists," *Music and Practice* 4 (2019), https://www.musicandpractice.org/volume-4/viennese-piano-technique-of-the-1820s-and-implications-for-todays-pianists/ (accessed July 28, 2019); Malwine Brée, *The Groundwork of the Leschetizky Method: Issued with His Approval*, trans. Dr. Th. Baker (Mainz: Mayence, 1903); Brée: *The Leschetitzky Method: A Guide to Fine and Correct Piano Playing*, trans. Arthur Elson (Mineola, NY: Dover Publications, 1997).

United States at the end of the nineteenth and beginning of the twentieth century with sound.

By contrast, "colossal," "monumental," and "architectural" are common descriptors for Busoni's performances and pieces, which featured use of arm weight, the back, and the whole body.[22] This powerful style, which he applied to pieces across a wide historical spectrum, was often associated with the Russian school of piano playing, even if Busoni was largely a self-taught pianist. This technical approach helped fill up the reverberant acoustic space in the large concert halls. Anton Rubinstein, who had a reputation of performing lengthy concert programs with powerful tone, first modeled this style of playing for Busoni. As Edward Dent notes, even though Busoni did not officially study with Rubinstein, Busoni did encounter him frequently in Vienna during his youth and was present at some of Rubinstein's lessons to others.[23] He also heard five of his monumental recitals in Vienna in 1884. In return, Busoni dedicated his Sonata in F minor, BV 204 (1883–1884), to Rubinstein.

Busoni not only played powerfully, however, he also creatively recomposed pieces. If Busoni used his whole body to create strength of sound, he also reinforced vertical aspects of sound by modifying the pieces to add depth and massiveness, a sound quality he sought after in his original compositions as well. In some cases, especially in his Bach transcriptions, he sought to re create the powerful sound of pipe organs in reverberant cathedrals on the piano. For instance, he specifically insisted that chords should not be arpeggiated, such as in his transcription of the Prelude and Fugue in E♭ major ("St. Anne"), BWV 552. He argued that the notes should not be displaced, but that everything should be played together for a more solid sound: "In order to obtain the approximate effect of an organ sound on the piano, it is essential for the chords, no-matter how widely spaced, to be played with all voices sounding simultaneously, that is, without arpeggiation."[24]

He also sought to reinforce vertical harmonic pillars in compositions by inserting note doublings. Although octave doublings were common in the

[22] Egon Petri, for instance, reportedly described his playing as "intellectual (!) and architectural." Egon Petri, quoted in Alfred Kanwischer, *Egon Petri: Musician to the World* (Göttingen: Cuvillier, 2019), 69.

[23] Edward Dent, "Ferruccio Busoni," *The Listener* (October 16, 1935), 685.

[24] [Um die Wirkung des Orgelklanges auf dem Pianoforte annähernd zu erzielen, ist es unerlässlich, dass die Accorde, selbst in weitester Spannung, in allen Tönen zugleich, ohne arpeggieren, angeschlagen warden.] Busoni, notes, in J. S. Bach, Prelude and Fugue in E♭ Major ("St. Anne") (BWV 552, freely arranged for concert use on the piano by Ferruccio Busoni [1890] (Mineola, NY: Dover, 1996), 15.

late nineteenth and early twentieth centuries, Busoni was much more liberal than his contemporaries in adding them. His transcriptions, arrangements, and even performances feature many enrichments of vertical textures through octave doublings, such as in his transcription of J. S. Bach's Violin Chaconne or his arrangement of the Organ Prelude and Fugue in D Major, BWV 532 (see example 4.1). In the opening measure alone, for instance, Busoni tripled the single pedal line. In addition, he doubled chord pitches throughout.

This contrasts with Franz Liszt, who, as Busoni asserted, was a master of arpeggiation. Although he also included octave doublings and registral enrichments in his arrangements of Bach's music, especially toward climaxes, he also excelled in the arpeggios and single-note figurations that moved the music forward: "Liszt gathers all the attainments of his predecessors together, in a finished pianistic style, and exalts the 'arpeggio,' by accentuating its characteristic and tonally picturesque points, into a higher sphere of ornamentation."[25] This same richness of texture that Busoni sought after in his arrangements was also common in his original piano compositions. For instance, although the *Fantasia nach Bach*, a piece based on Bachian subjects, began with a simple melody interwoven into undulating arpeggios, Busoni began doubling the melody notes in octaves by measure 7. Inner sections feature rich block chords as well, including one section marked *con Sonorità*.[26] He sought to fill the space when creating his own pieces or re creating the music of others.

Busoni did not just limit doublings to piano transcriptions of organ writing to mimic the instrument. Egon Petri remembers that Busoni also doubled notes frequently in Chopin's piano music for the spatial expansion and character the sound provided: "He would sometimes take a good part of the *Etude in F major*, Op. 10, by Chopin, in octaves; and although the notes were not true, the veracity of its spirit under his fingers could not be denied."[27] In addition, in his 1915 Duo-Art recording of the second prelude of Chopin, he

[25] Busoni, Notes to Prelude 15 in G Major, in Bach-Busoni, *The First Twenty-Four Preludes and Fugues of The Well-Tempered Clavichord* (New York: G. Schirmer, n.d.), 86. [Liszt alle Resultate seiner Vorgänger in pianistisch-vollendeter Setzung zu vereinen und die "Arpeggien" durch Betonung des charakteristischen und des tonmalerischen Momentes in eine höhere Rangordnung der Ornamentik zu Rücken.] Bach, *Das wohltemperierte Klavier*, vol. 1, ed. Busoni, Joh. Seb. Bach Klavierwerke, ed. Busoni, Egon Petri, and Bruno Mugellini (Leipzig: Breitkopf & Härtel, 1894), 86.

[26] For an analysis of this piece, see Knyt, "How I Compose," 256–61.

[27] Egon Petri and Friede F. Rohe, "How Ferruccio Busoni Taught," 710.

Example 4.1. Busoni's arrangement of J. S. Bach's Organ Prelude and Fugue in D Major, BWV 532, mm. 1–9.

chose not to arpeggiate the final chord as notated, thereby bringing the piece to a fuller conclusion.[28]

Expansion of Colors and a Multi-Dimensional Approach

Busoni's alterations to the music of others went beyond mere enlargement of tone, to added color. If he followed Rubinstein's lead in his commanding tone and in the broad scope of his programming, he was idiosyncratic in his attention to tonal and timbral color, which was especially audible in the new concert halls. Although one could limit the definition of an arrangement to a piece in which pitches are altered, Busoni considered color to be an essential element of music. Therefore, in changing the colors, he was consciously reworking and re creating the piece.

Although he sought after unique instrumental colors in his original orchestral compositions, he was also able to achieve similar effects through his unique touch at the piano as well when he played his own pieces or altered the music of others to create architectural sounds. Much of what he did to the sound quality was so distinctive that it shocked and enthralled listeners, even if there was no clear way to notate the alterations. In the process of altering pieces through unexpected colors, he simultaneously made the pieces sound multi-dimensional, or like moving architectural forms, as he foregrounded lines or phrases through his distinctive play with timbre.

Distilling main points from Hugo Leichtentritt's 1916 Busoni biography, H. H. Stuckenschmidt notes the convergence of color and power in Busoni's playing.[29] Leichtentritt stated that he noticed monumentality, scope, and treatment of the individual lines and ornaments in Busoni's playing, and this made him think of large architectural spaces. He praised Busoni's performances for: "the feeling for the monumental power of Gothic architecture, [and] for the subtle structure of linear rhythms showing their vitality in the various segments of structure, from the massive pilasters to the delicate fantastic ornamental tracery."[30] At the same time, Leichtentritt claims that Busoni was

[28] Many of the preludes from the piano rolls have been reissued on the following CD: Ferruccio Busoni, *Liszt, Bach-Busoni, & Chopin*, Nimbus Records (NI 8810). His recordings of the preludes are also available on YouTube: https://www.youtube.com/watch?v=d9sB65-rS5I (accessed July 30, 2019).

[29] H. H. Stuckenschmidt, *Ferruccio Busoni: Chronicle of a European*, trans. Sandra Morris (New York: Saint Martin's Press, 1967), 74.

[30] Stuckenschmidt, *Ferruccio Busoni*, 74.

able to bring out the most unusual colors, thereby creating a wealth of timbral and dynamic shades.[31] Grigory Kogan, similarly, likened Busoni's playing to that of a fresco painter or sculptor of sound, bringing different textures into relief through his varied and colorful playing: "Busoni's 'picturesque' architectural performing style, on the other hand, is compared with the art of various painters, within the grandeur of cathedrals; it evokes 'colorful canvases,' 'frescoes,' 'sound sculptures,' it is as though carved in marble."[32]

Edward Dent describes some of the tones that Busoni was able to achieve at the piano in orchestral terms—and these colors did not always have much to do with the originally intended timbre or strength levels of pieces. Busoni's arrangement of Bach's "Goldberg Variations," which sounded so different from piano or harpsichord tone, is but one example. Dent asserts that Busoni's firm and clear/crisp tone was closer to that of brass instruments than a harpsichord, an effect he created through touch and the use of the pedal.[33] This firmer and louder tone contributed to the overall conception of monumentality he sought to convey. Egon Petri likewise noted: "When Busoni played, the most surprising sounds emerged from the piano. They resembled sounds one would expect from a wind instrument rather than from a percussion instrument."[34]

This varied tone strength and color contributed to unexpected structural articulations and dimensions. In relation to the Prelude and Fugue in D major, from *The Well-Tempered Clavier*, book I, by Bach, for instance, he contended that the ascending scale was to be played with weighty and jagged, non-legato sound, rising in intensity and strength, leading to a climax at the topic, like a pyramid:

> Bars 1, 2, 4: The rising scale must tower up like a pyramid. Heavy and weighty, each tone—not legato. In the right hand I play the notes of the scale with the second finger: the "pad" of the second finger, however pressing against the tip (nail) of the pad.[35]

[31] Hugo Leichtentritt, "Ferruccio Busoni," *Music Review* 6:4 (November 1945): 209. See also Leichtentritt, *Ferruccio Busoni* (Leipzig: Breitkopf & Härtel, 1916), 18–19.
[32] Kogan, *Busoni as Pianist*, 44–45.
[33] Edward Dent, *Ferruccio Busoni: A Biography* [1933] (London: Clarendon Press, 1966), 33.
[34] Egon Petri and Friede F. Rohe, "How Ferruccio Busoni Taught," 657.
[35] [Takt 1, 2, 4: Die aufsteigende Skala muss sich auftürmen wie eine Pyramide. Schwer und gewichtig, jeden Ton—non legato. In der rechten Hand spiele ich die Noten der Skala mit dem zweiten Finger: der "Polster" des zweiten Fingers aber drückt gegen die Spitze (Nagel) des Daumens.] Busoni, quoted in Galston, *Studienbuch* (1910), 32.

Guido Guerrini has described the wealth of colors in Busoni's playing as ranging from soft string tones to the crisper, harder sounds of woodwinds. These act as antitheses in his interpretations to demarcate formal and structural divisions, in addition to adding to the emotional and expressive possibilities of the music.[36] As for his performances of Chopin, Guerrini asserted that Busoni's "trumpet-like" tone at the piano created a sense of multi-dimensionality through his play with voices and space, evoking a sense of mass with recesses and foregrounded material. His approach of foregrounding lines by using different colors differentiated those lines even in large reverberant spaces:

> In performances of Bach's music, his [Busoni's] polyphony was miraculous, sometimes almost frightening. The parts had, under his fingers, the relief that, not lines, but only voices can give. The polyphonic play emerged clear and obvious; more than audible, it was visible as every new voice was thrown open a door and a new character entered and with such authority as to obscure all the others. The architecture of the composition thus assumed such clarity, that it could be heard through the auditory senses, almost the weight of the mass, with its volumes, spaces, shadows, and projections.[37]

When Esther Fischer heard Busoni's 1920 recitals in Paris, she also described how Busoni foregrounded certain passages.[38] He created this differentiation through subtle changes in tone quality—thereby allowing certain passages to shine forth with great clarity:

> It was a revelation: many of the so-called brilliant passages were sunk into the background, and the melody stood out clearly with beautiful singing

[36] [E nel contempo una dolcezza di tocco, una morbidezza, un velluto, una fluidità, una leggerezza, che transformavano il pianoforte volta a volta in clavicembalo, in voce angelica, in arpa, in flauti. Queste due possibilità contrastanti, la potenza e la dolcezza, avevano fatto di Busoni il più famoso interprete di due autori in assoluta antitesi tra loro: Liszt e Mozart.] Guido Guerrini, *Ferruccio Busoni: La vita, la figura, l'opera* (Florence: Monsalvato, 1944), 199.

[37] [Di Bach egli fu il più profondo conoscitore; lo dimostrano la sua edizione del Clavicembalo e le infinite revisioni e trascrizioni fatte su questo autore. Nelle esecuzioni di musica bachiana, la sua polifonia era miracolosa, a volte quasi paurosa. Le parti avevano, sotto la sua dita, il rilievo che, non corde, ma voci soltanto possono dare. Il gioco polivocale ne usciva tutto chiaro, evidente; ogni entrata più che udibile, era "visibile," come se ad ogni voce nuova si spalancasse una porta e un nuovo personaggio entrasse e con tale autorità da offuscare tutti gli altri. L'architettura della composizione assumeva così chiara evidenza, che se ne sentiva, attraverso l'audizione, quasi il peso della mole, coi suoi volumi, spazi, ombre ed aggetti.] Guerrini, *Ferruccio Busoni*, 202.

[38] Esther Fischer studied with Isidore Philipp, but she also took at least one lesson with Busoni.

> tone. He understood Liszt's nobility and grandeur. I remember particularly his playing of the variations by Liszt on a theme of Bach—"Weinen, Klagen"—unforgettable grand and dramatic.[39]

Busoni transformed pieces through his blending of structure, strength of tone, and color, a combination that resounded especially clearly in the recently built concert halls.[40]

Busoni transformed pieces not only because of his bold tone, note doublings, and evocation of diverse orchestral colors, but also because of his terraced approach, in which he made abrupt changes, often every few measures, or at large structural divisions. While other contemporary pianists, such as members of the Leschetizky school, featured rubato and constant tempo fluctuations as well as endless gradations of tone, Busoni introduced changes suddenly and abruptly, like new stops on an organ, regardless of whether that was the original intention of the composer. The rounded and supple wrists of Leschetizky and his followers were well suited to such nuanced sound. Yet while Rubinstein might have used the whole-body approach, like Busoni, even he did not aim for this same type of terraced approach, instead building to climaxes more gradually.

Busoni's terraced approach was much more audible in the reverberant concert hall spaces built during his lifetime, while more-nuanced approaches were more effective in smaller, more intimate halls. Although Busoni's letters rarely criticize specific technical approaches of other performers, he was decidedly critical of a nuanced approach. On one occasion, he pontificated against what he considered to be an old-fashioned Viennese approach characterized by scooping, swooping, and rhythmic irregularity. For instance, while teaching at the Helsinki Music Institute, he criticized his violinist colleague Hermann Csillag for such nuanced mannerisms that included sliding into notes and playing with a great deal of rubato.[41]

Busoni avoided such nuanced interpretations, playing notes together rather than dislocating them and keeping a steady tempo overall to create sudden changes in dynamics that he believed better highlighted structural moments in the pieces he was playing. In this way, he created the impression

[39] Guerrini, *Ferruccio Busoni*, 245–246.

[40] Dent, "Ferruccio Busoni," 685.

[41] Hermann Csillag (1852–1922) was an Austro-Hungarian violinist that studied in Budapest and Vienna. He then worked in Baden-Baden, Dusseldorf, Hamburg, and Rotterdam, before teaching at the Helsinki Music Institute. Busoni, letter of October 14, 1888, to Henri and Kathi Petri, in *Ferruccio Busoni: Selected Letters*, ed. Beaumont (New York: Columbia University Press, 1987), 38.

of musical montages. He brought time and space together in his re creations of the music of others. Kogan notes, "he [Busoni] used terraced phrasing not just in Bach's music, but with the music of other composers as well, including with Liszt's compositions, so that it opened the door to a torrent of sound colors."[42] Busoni's terraced approach, as opposed to a gradual approach, with discrete sections, set in relief key moments in pieces in large architectural spaces due to sudden changes of dynamics, tempo, and color that were so vivid and audible. It was "terraced construction of the whole from 'layers,' separated from one another by clear boundaries [that was] the basic creative principle of Busoni's playing."[43]

This terraced approach is evident in his acoustic recording of J. S. Bach's Prelude in C Major from the *Well-Tempered Clavier*, vol. 1, in which he alternates groups of two measures with and without pedal to create a terraced effect; the added moments of pedal are luminous and shine, thereby contrasting with dryer, leaner passages.[44] The contrasts create blocks of color and sound that resonated even in the largest halls. Similarly, in the Chopin Etude, op. 10, no. 5, in G♭ major, Busoni played the opening measure material forte and the subsequent measure piano upon each repetition. The stark contrast of dynamic levels similarly creates contrasting colors of material.[45]

Busoni's terraced approach was also enhanced by steady rhythm, thereby making the contrast in colors even more sudden, striking, and vivid. Kogan maintains, "Busoni was a big advocate of steady rhythm (no frequent rubatos and slowing at cadences)."[46] Petri notes, however, that Busoni's approach varied slightly depending on the composer. Surprisingly, he reportedly applied more rubato in arrangements of Mozart's compositions than in Chopin's.[47]

Architectural Musical Structures

If Busoni reworked the music of others aurally by creating terraced blocks of sound and by adding to the vertical dimensions through octave doublings and registral expansion, he also restructured the form according to his own

42 Kogan, *Busoni as Pianist*, 44.
43 Kogan, *Busoni as Pianist*, 44.
44 Busoni, pianist, *Busoni and His Legacy: Piano Recordings by Busoni, Ley, Petri*, CD, Arbiter 134.
45 Busoni, pianist, *Busoni and His Legacy.*
46 Kogan, *Busoni as Pianist*, 44.
47 Egon Petri and Friede F. Rohe, "How Ferruccio Busoni Taught: An Interview with the Distinguished Dutch Pianist," *Etude* 58 (October 1940): 710.

ideals of unique architectural structures. He delineated formal sections, climaxes, and created larger montages out of smaller movements. In some cases, he made direct connections between his choices about structures and specific types of buildings.

Busoni sometimes changed the music to emphasize structural aspects or specifically connected forms to architectural shapes in his notes in published editions and essays. For instance, he reportedly mentioned similarities between tripartite structures and the structure of Greek temples to his pupil Augusta Cottlow:

> Form in music may often be found similar to forms of architecture. For example, the usual three-part form may be analogous to one of the styles of the Greek Temple with all parts balancing in perfect harmony and all subservient to and centralized in the façade with its portico and its columns supporting the symmetrical pediment, which in turn is ornamented with groups of figures, usually in high relief. These figures, in their turn, range from a prominent group in the middle or highest part, of the pediment, to the low, reclining figures at each end under the cornices.[48]

In his edition of the Sinfonias by J. S. Bach, he indicated formal sections in the copious notes and with double bar lines (non-bold), often connecting the structure to architectural principles. In one note, for instance, for Sinfonia no. 7 in E minor, he compared a tripartite formal structure to a building with a central section and two side buildings: "The second section, consisting of two nearly equal parts, is as long as the combined first and third sections. If one imagines, the architectural relations of a central structure to wings on either side, he will perceive the logical basis for the analogous musical form found here."[49] Busoni also contributed to the overall shape of the piece himself by adding a three-measure coda and doubling the bass to add vertical dimension. In the preface to his edition of J. S. Bach's *Well-Tempered Clavier*, Busoni likened the entire work to an imposing edifice built out of blocks of sound:

> To the foundations of the edifice ["Gebäude"] of Music, Johann Sebastian Bach contributed huge blocks, firmly and unshakably laid one upon the

[48] Augusta Cottlow, "My Years with Busoni," *Musical Observer* 24:6 (June 1925): 11.

[49] Busoni, Notes for Sinfonia no. 7 in E Minor, in Johann Sebastian Bach, *Fifteen Three-Voice Inventions for Piano*, ed. Ferruccio Busoni, trans. Lois Maier and Guy Maier (Philadelphia: Theodor Presser, 1914) 19.

> other. And in this same foundation of our present style of composition is to be sought the inception of modern pianoforte-playing. Outsoaring his time by generations, his thoughts and feelings reached proportions for whose expression the means then at command were inadequate. This alone can explain the fact, that the broader arrangement, the "modernizing," of certain of his works (by Liszt, Tausig, and others) does not violate the "Bach style"—indeed, rather seems to bring it to full perfection.[50]

Busoni also likened individual numbers to parts of the great edifice. For instance, he likened the Fugue in C♯ Minor to architecture, emerging vertically from the crypt to the nave, to the dome:

> In this fugue we seem to be borne upward out of the crypt of a mighty cathedral, though the broad nave and onward to the extreme height of the vaulted dome. Midway in our flight, the unadorned gloom of the beginning is supplanted by cheerful ornamentation; mounting to the close, the structure grows in austere sublimity; yet the presence of the unifying idea is felt everywhere,—the single fundamental motive leaves its impress on every part.[51]

By contrast, he likened J. S. Bach's Prelude and Fugue in B♭ Major from *The Well-Tempered Clavier*, book I, to two side chapels that functioned as vaults in which precious things are kept.[52]

In specific fugues, such as the Fugue in F♯ Major, from *The Well-Tempered Clavier*, book I, he also challenged traditionally held conceptions about

[50] Busoni, "Introduction," in Bach-Busoni, *The First Twenty-Four Preludes and Fugues of The Well-Tempered Clavichord*, i. [Zum Gebäude der Tonkunst wältzte Johann Sebastian Bach Riesenquadern herbei und fügte sie unerschütterlich fest, zu einem Fundament zusammen. Wo er den Grund zu unserer heutigen Kompositionsrichtung legte, da ist auch der Ausgangspunkt des modernen Klavierspiels zu suchen. Seiner Zeit um Generationen vorausgeteilt, fühlte und dachte er in solchen Grössen verhältnissen, dass die damaligen Ausdrucksmittel diesen nicht genügten. Diese allein erklärt, dass die Erweiterung, die "Modernisierung" einiger seiner Werke (durch Liszt, Rausig, u.a.) nicht gegen den "Bachschen Stil" verstösst,—ja, diesen erst zu vervollständigen scheint,—es erklärt.] Bach, *Das wohltemperierte Klavier*, vol. 1, i.

[51] Busoni, notes to Fugue no. 4 in C-sharp Minor, in Bach-Busoni, *The First Twenty-Four Preludes and Fugues of The Well-Tempered Clavichord*, 29. [Es ist bei diesem Stücke, als stiege man vom Grabgewölbe eines mächtigen Domes, durch die geräumigen Schiff, bis in die höchste Wöhlbung der Kuppel hinauf. In der Mitte unserer Wanderung treten heiterere Ornamente an der früheren, düsteren Schmucklosigkeit; gegen die Höhe zu wird der Bau erhebener und strenger: das überall kommt die einheitliche Idee zur Erscheinung, aus jedem Theile leuchtet das eine, durchgeführte Grundmotiv hervor.] Bach, *Das wohltemperierte Klavier*, vol. 1, 29.

[52] Busoni, notes to Prelude and Fugue no. 21 in B♭ Major, in Bach-Busoni, *The First Twenty-Four Preludes and Fugues of The Well-Tempered Clavichord*, 132.

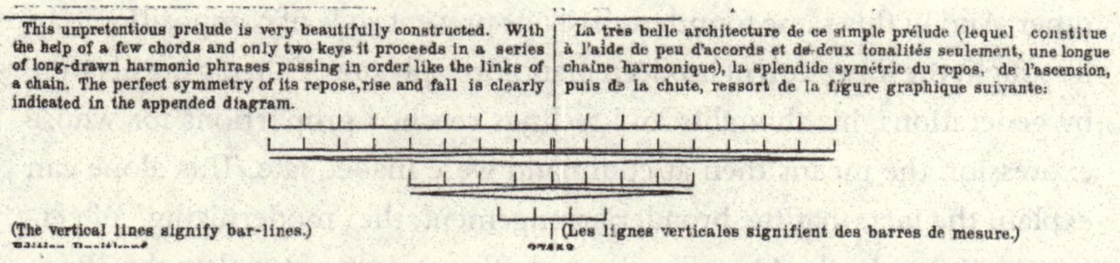
This unpretentious prelude is very beautifully constructed. With the help of a few chords and only two keys it proceeds in a series of long-drawn harmonic phrases passing in order like the links of a chain. The perfect symmetry of its repose, rise and fall is clearly indicated in the appended diagram.
La très belle architecture de ce simple prélude (lequel constitue à l'aide de peu d'accords et de deux tonalités seulement, une longue chaine harmonique), la splendide symétrie du repos, de l'ascension, puis de la chute, ressort de la figure graphique suivante:
(The vertical lines signify bar-lines.)
(Les lignes verticales signifient des barres de mesure.)

Figure 4.3. Busoni's diagram illustrating the form of J. S. Bach's Little Prelude in C Minor, BWV 999.

structure, claiming that conceived in certain ways, it assumes multi-dimensionality based on the musical contour. For instance, he argued for a bipartite, rather than a tripartite formal conception, and then claimed: "the outline of the Fugue then stands out plastically, like a relief map of a mountain-region."[53] Busoni also often created terraced sections within these larger structural groupings. When writing about the form of the little Prelude in C Minor, BWV 999, for instance, he stated, "this unpretentious prelude is very beautifully constructed. With the help of a few chords and only two keys it proceeds in a series of long-drawn harmonic phrases passing in order like the links of a chain. The perfect symmetry of its repose, rise, and fall is clearly indicated in the appended diagram"[54] (see figure 4.3).

Form was not just predetermined, in Busoni's mind, but could be shaped or reshaped in real time using dynamics, tempo, and color. Cottlow specifically remembers Busoni's use of tone color and rhythm as aiding his innate ability to build up to climaxes in music:

> We are apt to think of form as something inactive and fixed, but Busoni brought to his hearers the activity of form, its definite announcements, leadings, and developments, etc. The great variety of his tone-coloring and fine sense of rhythmical values were probably his greatest aids in expressing

[53] Busoni, notes to Fugue no. 13 in F-Sharp Major, in Bach-Busoni, *The First Twenty-Four Preludes and Fugues of The Well-Tempered Clavichord*, 84. [allsogleich tritt auch der Grundriss der Fuge plastisch, wie eine Gebirtskarte, hervor.] Bach, *Das wohltemperierte Klavier*, vol. I, 84.

[54] [Die sehr schöne Architektur dieses unscheinbaren Vorspiels (welches mit wenigen Akkorden und mit hilfe nur zweier Tonarten einen langatmigen harmonischen Kettenrung bildet) die prächtige Symmetrie des Ruhens, Steigens und Fallens—sie sind aus der folgenden graphischen Figur erkenntlich]. Busoni, notes, J. S. Bach, Little Prelude in C Minor, arr. Busoni (Leipzig: Breitkopf & Härtel, 1916), 5.

> a well-defined direction. Especially in building up climaxes one felt a rare discretion in the use of these means.[55]

Busoni sometimes took more authoritative means to reshape form, including cutting out portions of a piece, or else melding pieces together that were never intended to be performed that way. In Bach's Aria mit 30 Veränderungen ("Goldberg Variations"), for instance, he eliminated nine variations, and created a tripartite structure by grouping the variations into three main sections with a climax at the end of the second section: Variations 1–13 (discarding nos. 3, 9, and 12); Variations 14–25 (discarding nos. 16, 17, 18, 21, and 24); and Variations 26–30 (discarding no. 27). In addition, he suggested linking certain of the variations together to create a larger structural feel, such as launching into Variation 10 without a pause (*attacca*). These changes represent a major shift from the piece as Bach envisioned it.[56]

With the Prelude and Fugue in E♭ major, BWV 998, he suggested repeating the entire first part of the fugue and playing the allegro just after the end of the second part of the fugue, and before finishing the last section of the fugue. He described his conception for the piece thus:

> The entire Allegro then follows, without repetitions, whereupon the fugue is dovetailed to it in such a manner, that the two last bars of the Allegro take the place of the first two of the fugue, now taken up again. The fugue itself, intensified in tone and character, appears then in the following form.[57]

It was not just Bach that Busoni altered, but pieces from other eras as well. For instance, rather than treat Chopin's preludes as fragmentary miniatures, as was typical in his day, he turned them into larger structural wholes by adding additional repetitions of measures, repeating pieces in their entirety (e.g., Prelude 7), or repeating main sections without the codas (e.g., Preludes 1, 3, and 22). In his recordings of the Prelude in A Major, op. 28, no. 7, for instance, Busoni's repetition of the entire prelude adds gravity to the piece, especially in conjunction with a substantial concluding ritard. In the Prelude

[55] Cottlow, "My Years with Busoni," 11.

[56] For more about Busoni's version of the "Goldberg Variations," see Knyt, "The Bach-Busoni 'Goldberg Variations,'" *Bach Perspectives* 13 (December 2020): 74–100. This paragraph is largely adapted from that chapter.

[57] Busoni, Notes, J. S. Bach, Prelude and Fugue in E♭ Major, BWV 998, Busoni Ausgabe (Joh. Seb. Bach, Klavierwerke), vol. 16 (Leipzig: Breitkopf & Härtel, 1915), 77–78.

in G Major, op. 28, no. 3, he extended the coda by two measures and the introduction by one.[58]

Busoni's touch that was bold and sometimes resembled wind and brass instruments at the piano, his modifications to pitches to verticalize the sound, and his terraced approach were well suited to performing even historical music in large concert halls. At the same time, he not only reworked the form of individual pieces, but also created montages of small pieces. Large concert halls with resonant sounds called for longer pieces and longer programs. Harold Schonberg described his programs as "titanic," "gigantic," and "colossal," and as he notes, included "giving fourteen concertos in four programs."[59] Arthur Abell was amazed that Busoni played Liszt's complete *Années de pèlerinage* from memory along with the Chopin Preludes, op. 28, in one sitting. He concluded "there is something gigantic and inspiring about the man and that his playing makes their pulses beat faster."[60] But he did not just play gigantic programs, he linked the pieces together, turning them into architectural wholes.

Busoni's long programs often involved a reworking of the formal structures of the pieces to create new montage-like assemblages out of short pieces. It is possible that he sometimes improvised interludes between the pieces to connect them, as he did between the Prelude in A Major, op. 28, no. 7, and the Prelude in G♭ Major, op. 10, no. 5, by Chopin on his 1922 Columbia acoustic recordings. During a March 19, 1906, recital, at the Salle Érard in Paris, for instance, Busoni played four different sets. The first featured a grouping of six different pieces by Chopin, the second featured six etudes by Chopin, the third featured a grouping of three different pieces by Liszt, and the fourth was a Mendelssohn arrangement by Liszt. In the Liszt grouping, for instance, *Harmonies du soir* and *Mazeppa*, both dramatic, lengthy, and monumental etudes, frame the more whimsical *Feux follets*. While *Harmonies du soir* opens horizons with its exploration of colors on the piano and quiet ending, *Mazeppa* brings the set to a rousing and dramatic conclusion. The contrasts between the pieces create textures in an otherwise newly constructed and longer structure.

[58] This paragraph is largely based on material from Knyt, "Ferruccio Busoni and the 'Halfness' of Frédéric Chopin," *Journal of Musicology* 34:2 (Spring 2017): 264.

[59] Harold Schonberg, "Doktor Faustus of the Keyboard," in *The Great Pianists: From Mozart to the Present* (New York: Simon & Schuster, 1963), 351.

[60] Arthur Abell, "Ferruccio Busoni's Great Art," *Musical Courier: A Weekly Journal Devoted to Music and the Music Trades* 59:13 (1909): 6. Kenneth Hamilton notes that that Busoni started giving massive programs from an early age, some of which also featured free improvisations and some of which displayed pieces from diverse historical eras. Kenneth Hamilton, *After the Golden Age: Romantic Pianism and Modern Performance* (New York: Oxford University Press, 2008), 65.

Programma

1. Beethoven. Grande Sonata Op. 106 (Sib. Magg.)
   Allegro—Scherzo—Adagio sostenuto.
2. Chopin. A) Fantasie-Polonaise
   B) Nocturne Mib. Magg.
   C) Polonaise Lab. Magg.
3. Brahms-Paganini. Variazioni.
4. Liszt. A) Marcia di Nozze e Danza della Silfidi. (Mendelssohn)
   B) Adelaide (Beethoven).
   C) Les Ruines d' Athènes (Beethoven)[61]

In yet another example from a recital that took place on January 24, 1907, in the Berlin Beethovensaal, he created a set of pieces by Schumann and Liszt that included Schumann's *Abegg Variations*, op. 1; Schumann's *Papillons*, op. 2; and Liszt's *Grand galop chromatique* (see figure 4.4). Although adding Liszt's *Grand galop chromatique* at the end of two sets of variations could be seen as a move to merely garner applause, it also helped provide a certain symmetry to the groupings.[62]

Busoni also created a suite of Bach Preludes from the *Well-Tempered Clavier*, book I: B Major as the prelude, A Minor as the fughetta, B Minor as an andante, and B♭ Major as the toccata finale. Busoni noted that all numbers would have been transposed to the same key, probably B♭ Major.[63] In practice, Busoni sometimes grouped preludes in varying configurations, and not always transposed. A concert program from January 12, 1917, at the Neuer Konzertsaal at the Stadtkasino in Basel, for instance, featured a grouping of preludes from Bach's *Well-Tempered Clavier* in the following order (untransposed): A♭ Major (book II), C♯ Major (book I), B Minor (book I), F♯ Major (book II), D Major (book II).[64] Busoni seems to have grouped the preludes together based on contrasting styles and affects, with the second

[61] Busoni, recital program, March 19, 1906, Preussischer Kulturbesitz, Staatsbibliothek zu Berlin, Music Abteilung mit Mendelssohn Archiv, Mus. Nachl. F. Busoni E, 1906, 7.

[62] Busoni's livelihood depended, in part, on the success of his recitals, and influenced his decisions too. As much as he would have vigorously denied this, practical necessities sometimes superseded his lofty ideals (such as in the unexplainably virtuosic ending to his otherwise esoteric final movement of his piano concerto).

[63] Bach-Busoni, *The First Twenty-Four Preludes and Fugues of The Well-Tempered Clavichord*, 143.

[64] Busoni, concert program, January 12, 1917. Preussischer Kulturbesitz, Staatsbibliothek zu Berlin, Music Abteilung mit Mendelssohn Archiv, Mus. Nachl. F. Busoni, E 1917, 1.

CONCERT-DIRECTION HERMANN WOLFF, BERLIN W.

Donnerstag, den 24. Januar 1907

Abends 8 Uhr

IM BEETHOVEN-SAAL

Klavier-Abend

von

Ferruccio Busoni

PROGRAMM.

1.	Variationen und Fuge über ein Thema von Händel	J. Brahms.
2.	24 Préludes, op. 28	F. Chopin.
3.	a) Abegg-Variationen, op. 1	R. Schumann.
	b) Papillons op. 2	
	b) Grand Galop chromatique	F. Liszt.
4.	Paganini-Variationen	J. Brahms.

Concertflügel: **BECHSTEIN**

Während der Vorträge bleiben die Saalthüren geschlossen.

Eintrittskarten zu 5, 3, 2 u. 1 MK.

Figure 4.4. Busoni, concert program, January 24, 1907. Preussischer Kulturbesitz, Staatsbibliothek zu Berlin, Musikabteilung mit Mendelssohn Archiv, Mus. Nachl. F. Busoni, E 1907, 2.

and fourth in the grouping being slower and more contemplative. Busoni indicated the second prelude (C♯ Minor) was to be played *Andante serioso, non troppo sostenuto ed expressive* in his edition.[65] It is written in a vocal recitative or parlante lyrical style. If the B Minor Prelude from book I is in a trio sonata texture, Busoni marked in his edition that it should be played in a religious manner and described it as "a classic specimen of double counterpoint over a *basso continuo*."[66] The fourth one is in French overture style with dotted rhythms. The final prelude selected is in a vigorous and virtuosic style with allusions to hunting *topoi*.

Busoni often assembled larger structures by combining pieces of the same genre and composer, such as his series of six all-Liszt repertoire recitals in Berlin on the 100th birthday year of Liszt (1911) and his all-Mozart concerti cycles. The 1921 Mozart concerto cycle at the 2,500 seat Berlin Philharmonie, featuring two nights with three concerti each night, took place in Berlin in December 1921 with the Berlin Philharmonic. The six concerti were as follows, and were part of his project to edit/arrange the works for modern piano and contemporary concert hall and piano:

December 14, 1921
- I. Mozart, Concerto in C Minor, K. 491
- II. Mozart, Concerto in G Major, K. 453
- III. Mozart, Concerto in E♭ Major, K. 482

December 16, 1921
- I. Mozart, Concerto in D Minor, K. 466
- II. Mozart, Concerto in A Major, K. 488
- III. Mozart, Concerto in C Major, K. 467[67]

The groupings of the concerti represent careful thought about overall aural structure. In the first grouping, the keys are related by thirds. The C Minor concerto, one of only two concerti by Mozart in a minor key and the one with the longest first movement, is one of Mozart's most esoteric concerti. The E♭ Major concerto, K. 482, one of his more triumphant and heroic, provides a natural counterbalance to the weight and seriousness of the C minor

[65] Bach-Busoni, *The First Twenty-Four Preludes and Fugues of The Well-Tempered Clavichord*, 23.
[66] Bach-Busoni, *The First Twenty-Four Preludes and Fugues of The Well-Tempered Clavichord*, 143.
[67] Busoni, concert program of December 14 and 16, 1921, Staatsbibliothek zu Berlin–Preußischer Kulturbesitz, Musikabteilung mit Mendelssohn-Archiv, Mus. Nachl. F. Busoni E, 1921, 19.

Concerto, K. 491. The concerto Busoni selected for the center of these two weighty pieces, the Concerto in G Major, K. 453, contains many moments in buffo style, and much stylistic and topical variety, thus offering comic and aural relief to an otherwise serious evening.

Busoni not only made the pieces weightier by grouping them together, but he also altered the writing to make it thicker and bolder for the modern piano and contemporary concert hall. Although few records of his modifications exist beyond performance reviews, a partially completed score for the Concerto no. 17 in G Major, K. 453, still exists in Busoni's Nachlass. The manuscript shows that Busoni's modifications included adding additional ornamentation, thickening textures, and rewriting some of the left hand. He placed his own version under Mozart's (see figure 4.5).

His 1911 Berlin Liszt recitals in the Beethovensaal, likewise, featured an array of pieces ranging from Liszt's Sonata in B Minor, S. 178; all three books of *Années de pèlerinage*, S. 160, S. 161, S. 163; the transcendental etudes, S. 139; various Liszt-Schubert arrangements; and Busoni's own arrangements of Liszt's music, all grouped to create new aural structures.[68]

When performing complete cycles, Busoni sometimes played them without a break, as was noted by a reviewer in Zurich in 1916 after he performed the complete cycle of Chopin's set of twelve etudes, op. 10: "The 12 Etudes of Chopin, op. 10, are, played in succession without pause and interruption, as only a Busoni can manage."[69] In that way, Busoni constructed new musical structures out of individual pieces.

Busoni's creative approach thus considered structure, line, ornamentation, and color. As this chapter shows, his playing integrally interconnected the large-scale aspects and the nuanced details, just as the materials in a building constructed from natural materials contain color inherently. He molded the music of others through voicing, form, register, and color; how he uses color and phrasing structurally brings sections of music into relief and contributes to a sense of climax and repose.

Busoni's architectural arrangements were markedly different from any provided by his contemporaries. At the same time, they were well suited to the acoustics in many contemporary concert halls built during Busoni's

[68] For the complete six-program set see Staatsbibliothek zu Berlin–Preußischer Kulturbesitz, Musikabteilung mit Mendelssohn-Archiv, Mus. Nachl. F. Busoni E 1911, 9.

[69] [Die 12 Etuden von Chopin, op. 10, sind, so hintereinander gespielt ohne Pause und Unterbruch, eine Leistung, wie sie nur rein Busoni fertig bringt.] "Zürcher Konzerte," *Zürcher Post* (May 26, 1916).

Figure 4.5. Busoni's modification of the solo piano part of Mozart's Piano Concerto in G Major K. 453. Preussischer Kulturbesitz, Staatsbibliothek zu Berlin, Musikabteilung mit Mendelssohn Archiv, Mus. Nachl. F. Busoni, 341.

lifetime. Moreover, they represent an application of personal compositional ideals to the music of other composers. Large-scale architectural-structural planning that emphasizes blocks and segments of sound as well as the expansion and scope of sonority and registral height and depth were all aspects he worked through in his own pieces as well. When he performed, edited, and arranged the music of others, he did it his way, which was informed by his architectural ideals.

Coda

Busoni was an architect of sound; he created liquid architecture with his arrangements and compositions as space, sound, and time converge. In moments of performance, and when notating changes to the music of others, he examined ways to create multi-dimensional structures. Although some of these characteristics were shared by contemporaries, Busoni also left his own indelible marks that were informed by his compositional ideals, including a terraced approach, registral expansions, and the reworking of form. In many cases, he was directly influenced in his decisions by models of architectural structure and style.

He thought of audible musical materials as "liquid" because of their connectedness to time, but he also solidified them through his verticalization of sound through bold doublings. Some of these alterations have been written down in editions, arrangements, and transcriptions, or even his own notes. Some are preserved in concert programs or noted by concert reviewers. A very few are captured on recordings. Similarly to his own compositions, Busoni's re creations of the music of others bring together temporal and spatial art forms in new ways. As such, he was constructing a new and idiosyncratic architectural vision of *Tonkunst* that was adopted by his pupils and passed down to the next generation.

5
Beyond Busoni
Building Music in the Twentieth Century

Antony Beaumont concluded his seminal text, *Busoni the Composer*, with the idea that many of Ferruccio Busoni's thoughts reflected a "dream-journey" beyond the everyday "into [his] own soul."[1] Beaumont thereby emphasized the esoteric and transcendental nature of some of his ideas, as well as their connectedness to late Romantic ideology. Moreover, his concluding sentence described both the capaciousness of Busoni's ideas and the boundlessness of them: "And many have come to share Busoni's love of dreaming, have found dreams more convincing than reality, have found freedom in dreaming that is not granted to us in reality."[2] As Beaumont has noted, in dreaming about musical possibilities, Busoni, like others of his generation, envisioned a future of music that was unfettered by the conventions of his own age. He was not constrained in his thoughts by the known and the possible.

Yet in focusing on disparities between the reality of Busoni's compositions and his visions and dreams, it is easy to lose sight of the ways his compositions and arrangements realized some of his unconventional ideas by exploring new sounds, new structures, and new harmonic systems.[3] Although he never lived to experience the wealth of electronic sounds and new instruments that

[1] Beaumont, *Busoni the Composer* (Bloomington: Indiana University Press, 1985), 354. I am grateful to the following for their assistance locating archival materials: Heinrich Aerni (Wladimir Vogel Nachlass: Zentralbibliothek, Zurich), Erika Babatz (Bauhaus-Archiv Berlin), Jake Fewx and Jonathan Manton (Papers of Kurt Weill and Lotte Lenya—Archives at Yale University), Jean-Christophe Gero (Staatsbibliothek zu Berlin), Felix Meyer, Michèle Noirjean, and Heidy Zimmermann (Paul Sacher Foundation, Basel), Anne Moore (University of Massachusetts, Amherst, Howard Lebow Collection), Lisa Schoblasky (The Rudolph Ganz Papers), Larry Scott and Leif Anderson (Special Collections, Stanford University), Paul Sommerfeld (Library of Congress, Edward and Clara Steuermann Collection), and Dave Stein (Kurt Weill Foundation). I am also grateful to Lois Brandwynne (University of California at Davis), Ken Bruckmeier, Daniell Revenaugh (d. 2021), Janice Braun (Mills College), Jeong Lee (San Francisco Conservatory of Music), and Dean Smith (University of California at Berkeley) for sharing memories about Egon Petri.

[2] Beaumont, *Busoni the Composer*, 354.

[3] See the following text for a discussion of the coming together of the art forms: Daniel Albright, *Untwisting the Serpent: Modernism in Music, Literature, and Other Arts* (Chicago: University of Chicago Press, 2000).

Ferruccio Busoni as Architect of Sound. Erinn E. Knyt, Oxford University Press. © Oxford University Press 2023.
DOI: 10.1093/oso/9780197625491.003.0006

could fill in the musical space between diatonic pitches in an unbroken spectrum, he nevertheless wrote music that expanded tonal, timbral, and textural possibilities, and in that way, was both experimental and reflective of a newfound interest in breaking down divisions between art forms, even as it simultaneously drew on historical styles without a sense of rupture from the past.

In comparing Busoni's compositions with atonal expressionists of his era who made a more definite break with certain musical traditions, such as tonality, it is also easy to lose sight of the novel aspects of some of his compositions. Just because he never relinquished tonality does not necessarily make his music anachronistic or retrogressive. His innovations had less to do with finding a completely new path than in forging a future of music that was capacious enough to encompass past, present, and future sounds, scales, forms, and textures at the same time. Busoni foresaw a future teeming with possibilities, and his own compositions reflected that vision in featuring all twelve tones of the chromatic scale without rejecting consonances, in fragmenting and juxtaposing different forms, and in creating means by which novel sounds could be heard and combined. In some ways, his ideas and compositions were better suited to the postmodernist age he would never live to experience. Yet they were simultaneously part of a modernist interest in bringing together the temporal and the spatial.

In grasping at the future of music that he dreamed about, Busoni relied on models rooted in reality. As this book has shown, in a very pragmatic and unromantic way, he frequently resorted to the known and the tangible for inspiration. However, there were no clear models in music for Busoni. Architecture, other arts, and Busoni's own experiences hearing simultaneities of sounds in the world around him provided him with tangible models for spatializing and physicalizing sound in concrete ways. While one normally associates this approach with later composers such as Edgard Varèse and John Cage, for instance, it was already surfacing in Busoni's mature compositions. Busoni's compositions and arrangements are very much indebted to personal experiences with sound in space. Resonance and reverberation in the spaces he visited or performed in provided models that helped him realize his dream of imitating vibrating celestial music in compositions with acoustic instruments. Seeing the shapes of buildings, similarly, showed him how he could shape pieces he composed and arranged in unique ways. Hearing the way sounds changed in different acoustic settings influenced the way he approached color, instrumentation, and texture in compositions and arrangements.

Thus, even despite the intangibility and esotericism of many of Busoni's ideas, architectural metaphors and known physical spaces helped him translate many of those ideas in idiosyncratic and tangible ways. Gothic cathedrals and large contemporary concert halls became catalysts for his exploration of vastness of scope, resonance, and sonorous possibilities, qualities he envisioned in an ethereal realm of music, even as he patterned new and unusual formal structures after the varied shapes of diverse architectural styles. At the same time, Hellenic temples became a model for continuous variation and youthful renewal in music. If his ideas are mystical, his music is rooted in human experience. His compositions and arrangements include sounds radiating from different directions, montage-like formal structures, multi-voice polyphony, and diverse timbres and registers that evoke depth and height. His performances consider human perception by emphasizing coloristic changes, terraced phrasing, or dynamics, and by reinforcing a perception of dimensionality through the verticalization of chords.

As a musical architect, he explored some of these ideas about space, form, and tonal expansion that would become increasingly important throughout the twentieth century. Moreover, he communicated these ideas to the next generation of musicians and composers, even if he never developed a systematic method.[4]

Because the working out of Busoni's aesthetic ideals was closely connected to architectural and visual art forms, it is hardly surprising that references to forms outside of music are often keys to understanding how his esoteric ideas apply to compositional processes. For many of his students, friends, and mentees, it took visual models to make sense of them. Such was true for Busoni's closest Berlin composition master class (1921–1924) pupils and other mentees. He invited several to the Bauhaus exhibition of 1923, including Wladimir Vogel, Kurt Weill, Stefan Wolpe, and Egon Petri, and this composition master class "field trip" proved to be a climactic moment.[5]

[4] He transmitted his ideas to his mentees by example and through conversations.

[5] Although Stefan Wolpe was not an official composition master class pupil, he did take a few composition lessons with Busoni. For more information about Busoni's Berlin composition master class, consult the following source: Tamara Levitz, "Teaching New Classicality: Busoni's Master Class in Composition, 1921–1924" (PhD diss., University of Rochester, 1994). Although Levitz published her dissertation in abbreviated form, I choose to refer here to the more comprehensive dissertation version.

As several stated, it helped them understand how to apply his esoteric teachings.[6]

It cannot be a coincidence that soon after the field trip, Vogel started producing compositions that explored textural means of organization as well as spatialized choral writing. He also paid greater attention to register and timbre. Weill's mixed-genre montage forms, similarly, emerged through Busoni's formal teachings and after experiencing the visual models at the Bauhaus. Moreover, Wolpe, who was influenced by both Bauhaus teachings and Busoni's ideas, pioneered spatial approaches to music, including geometric pitch relations. Petri, who performed his compositions at the Bauhaus exhibition, likewise created sound structures at the piano through his concert programming, verticalization of sound, and terraced dynamics.

Some of Busoni's earlier composition mentees that were similarly involved in visual arts and architecture, such as Edgard Varèse, also an amateur painter who shared many ideals with architect Le Corbusier, assimilated Busoni's ideas about spatialized sound, thereby revealing continuity in his teachings. Varèse's most obvious melding of spatialized sound, architectural space, and music was his *Poème électronique*, composed in conjunction with Le Corbusier and Iannis Xenakis for the Brussels World Fair in 1958. However, he wrote spatialized music long before that, and, as this chapter

[6] Busoni also brought along Hans Hirsch, who was a close disciple at the time. However, because Hirsch did not later pursue a serious career in composition, he is not covered in detail in this chapter. After studying with Busoni, he pursued a career as a singer. Levitz has argued that Busoni only attended the exhibition to hear his composition performed, and that he was "very much opposed the ideals of Bauhaus . . . because he rejected art which too greatly blurred reality." Levitz, "Teaching New Classicality," 386. While there are marked differences between Busoni's approach and those at the Bauhaus, especially in terms of the Bauhaus's emphasis on the functionality of art, Busoni's continued connections with members of the Bauhaus and some very close similarities in their approach to form suggest closer connections than previously thought. If Levitz also relies on an entry in the diary of Gottfried Galston noting that Busoni criticized the expressionistic style of Paul Klee and the Russianness of Wassily Kandinsky, that does not necessarily imply a widespread rejection of all their works. The fact that Busoni brought the closest members of his composition master class with him to the Bauhaus exhibition is noteworthy. The accounts provided in this chapter also reveal that Busoni was socializing with the Bauhaus masters and that his students took in much more than only Busoni's performance. More information about the Bauhaus Festival in Weimar in 1923 can be found with the following call numbers at the Bauhaus Archiv (Berlin): Inv. Nos. 5627/12,5, 8453/1,8436/2,8438/1-2,8430/1,8437,8430/2-4,8435/1-3, Mappe Bauhaus Weimar II, Bauhaus Woche 1923. For reviews, see "Bauhaus Konzerte," *Berliner Börsen-Courier* (August 22, 1923); "Die Bauhauswoche," *Deutsche Allgemeine Zeitung* (August 21,1923); "Die Weimarer Bauhauswoche," *Allgemeiner Anzeiger für Stadt und Kreis Erfurt* (August 21, 1923); "Die Konzerte der Bauhaus-Woche," *Das Volk* (August 24, 1923); "Musik in der Bauhaus-Woche," *Berliner Tageblatt* (August 25, 1923); "Das Bauhaus in Weimar," *Allgemeine Zeitung* (September 2, 1923); Otto Reuter, "Bauhaus-Woche: Neue Musik in Weimar," *Deutschland* (August 21, 1923); Gisella Selden-Goth, "Das andere Weimar," *Prager Tagblatt* (August 26,1923).

reveals, Busoni was a primarily catalyst. Together, Busoni's mentees took his ideas in new directions, picking up where he left off with his compositions.

In addition, Busoni's ideas about music became catalysts for some of the creative activities of visual artists and early cubist film creators, such as Hans Richter, who knew Busoni in Switzerland during World War I, and Henrik Neugeboren, who studied piano with Busoni in Berlin in the 1920s.[7]

Based on essays, scores, diaries, images, and interviews, some unpublished, this chapter documents ways that his mentees assimilated his ideas via architectural and visual models. In the process, this chapter not only reassesses Busoni's importance as a composer and arranger including in relation to his ideas about spatialized sound, non-linear formal structures, and tonal expansion, but also reveals ways that those ideas took on new life in the creative works of his mentees, as well as ways that his perspectives became important for developments in music in the twentieth century.

Busoni as Architect of Sound

As this book has shown, Busoni was fascinated by architecture and found inspiration in it for some of his compositional and interpretive decisions. He created compositions that combined Gothic and Hellenic ideals and in which independent voices generated new harmonies and textures while contributing to unique montage forms[8] that resemble cathedrals or skyscrapers with innumerable rooms and vast scope.[9] He created spatialized sound that reflected the shifting densities, colors, and dimensions of the architecture he most admired.

[7] I am grateful to Marianna Ritchey and Andrew Ritchey for drawing my attention to the Busoni-Richter connection.

[8] In visual art, montage typically refers to the joining of diverse materials to create a new multi-dimensional whole. It differs from collage, which is usually more two-dimensional, and more coherent in material. In music, montage often refers to the juxtaposition of audibly stylistically disparate materials to create a larger structure, often with the sensation of aural multi-dimensionality, which is how I am using the term here. This technique was a direct reaction to nineteenth century linearity. See Christine Poggi, *In Defiance of Painting: Cubism, Futurism, and the Invention of Collage* (New Haven, CT: Yale University Press, 1992).

[9] For more information about the Gothic tradition in the twentieth century, see Enrique Alberto Arias, "Wilhelm Middelschulte's 'Kontrapunktische Symphonie' and the Chicago Gothics," *The Diapason* 94:6 (June 2003): 17–22; Marc-André Roberge, "Ferruccio Busoni: His Chicago Friends, and Frederick Stock's Transcription for Large Orchestra and Organ of the Fantasia Contrappuntistica," *Musical Quarterly* 80 (1996): 302–31. For a summary of some of Ziehn's theories, see Severine Neff, "Otto Luening (1900–) and the Theories of Bernhard Ziehn (1845–1912)," *Current Musicology* 39 (1985): 21–41. For more information about Busoni's structural use of stylistic heterogeneity, see Erinn Knyt, "Approaching the Essence of Music: Ferruccio Busoni and Stylistic Heterogeneity in *Doktor Faust*," *Journal of Musicological Research* 35:3 (August 2016): 176–99.

He also thought of idiosyncratic ways to mimic physical spaces to invoke resonance or overtones as well as to project music from different directions. Busoni pioneered a spatialized approach in which sound gave the impression of coming from up high, down low, behind, and in front of audiences, wrapping them in circles of sounds. While part of what the composer was doing was not necessarily novel (i.e., using offstage brass instruments for dramatic purposes), his re-envisioning of theatrical space (like Walter Gropius), his use of simultaneous textural and timbral layers (like Charles Ives), and his use of timing, resonance, and overtones to mimic resonant architectural spaces occurred in an age when these practices were just emerging.

Busoni's compositional style evolved, and his final composition, *Doktor Faust*, exemplifies many of his ideals. It was his last, and arguably greatest, attempt to grasp at the unheard scales and styles of music of which he dreamed. His magnum opus, with its instrumental sarabandes and fantasias, its mysterious instrumental colors, overtones, and resonances, the layers of meaning hidden in plot and music, the sounds surrounding the stage, the choirs and bell sounds from afar, the formal fragments melded together into unique structural wholes, and the simultaneity of diverse textures, remains a little-understood and infrequently performed edifice; it was one that Busoni hoped would reflect the multivariability of the acoustical rays of the musical sun of which he dreamed. At the same time, it brought together Gothic melodiousness and Hellenic youthfulness into a new art form. His mature compositional style as exemplified in his magnum opus can be understood in relation to the syncretic artistic practices of his own age, such as the Bauhaus, for instance, where the music of Bach and the Gothic cathedral also became symbols for artistic perfection and wholeness.

Cross influence between music and architecture or the other arts went both ways. At an inaugural lecture by Paul Klee during the 1921–1922 academic year, Klee included a reinterpretation of the notation of a passage by Bach as a linear graphic. As Stephanie Probst has documented, he devoted two lectures in January 1922 to discussing modes for capturing music graphically and created graphs of Bach's music, including the Adagio from the Sonata for Violin and Harpsichord, BWV 1019.[10] At the same time, Neugeboren (Henri Nouveau), who had, prior to his work at the Bauhaus, studied music in Berlin with Busoni, Egon Petri, and Paul Juon from 1921 to 1925, produced at least

[10] Stephanie Probst, "Pen, Paper, Steel: Visualizing Bach's Polyphony at the Bauhaus," *Music Theory Online: A Journal of the Society for Music Theory* 26:4 (December 2020), https://mtosmt.org/issues/mto.20.26.4/mto.20.26.4.probst.html (accessed April 23, 2021).

two works graphically depicting Bach. There is a 1928 depiction of the four-part Fugue no. 1 from the *Well-Tempered Clavier* by Bach and a 1970 sculptural representation of bars 52–55 of the E♭ Minor Fugue by Bach that can be viewed today in a park in Leverkusen, Germany.[11] While Neugeboren was undoubtedly influenced by ideas at the Bauhaus, which he attended in Dessau in 1928, Heinrich Poos has also suggested that Neugeboren might have decided to work with these two particular Bach pieces because of Busoni's commentary about them, which linked them to architecture.[12] Probst has similarly drawn the connection to Busoni's ideas about constructivism in music, stating: "Featuring that particular fugue, Neugeboren's description of his project echoes Busoni's declaration, when he stated that he aimed for rendering visible the 'construction' of Bach's music in an 'instructive' way."[13] Indeed, Neugeboren's reproduction of four measures of the E♭ Minor Fugue from Busoni's edition in his explanatory comments seems to cement the connection.[14] Neugeboren created both a two-dimensional drawing and plans for a three-dimensional monument. He insisted that "in both cases, it is not a matter of personal reinterpretation, but of a scientifically exact transfer to another system."[15] Probst has described it as a reflection of the "combinatorial" or "mathematical" aspects of Bach's music.[16] Moreover, Neugeboren stated that he was motivated by a desire to depict the temporal ("zeitlichen") and spatial ("räumlichen") aspects of music, aspects that Busoni was actively trying to bring together in his own music in Berlin in the 1920s.[17] At the same

[11] See Oskar Schlemmer, László Moholy-Nagy, and Farkas Molnár, *The Theater of the Bauhaus*, ed. Walter Gropius, trans. Arthur S. Wensinger (Middleton, CT: Wesleyan University Press, 1961). For more on this subject, see Peter Christensen and Marc Aurel Schnabel, "Spatial Polyphony: Virtual Architecture Generated from the Music of J. S. Bach," Advanced Study Report, University of Sydney, 2007, https://www.researchgate.net/profile/Marc_Aurel_Schnabel/publication/30868841_Spatial_polyphony_Virtual_Architecture_Generated_from_the_Music_of_JS_Bach/links/0a85e52d6195cf2301000000.pdf (accessed June 13, 2019). See also Heinrich Poos, "Henrik Neugeborens Entwurf zu einem Bach-Monument (1928): Dokumentation und Kritik," in *Töne, Farben, Formen: Über Musik und die bildenden Künste—Festschrift Elmar Budde zum 60. Geburtstag*, ed. Elisabeth Schmierer et al. (Laaber: Laaber-Verlag, 1995), 45–57.

[12] Poos, "Henrik Neugeborens Entwurf zu einem Bach-Monument," 52. See chapter 1 for more information about Busoni's commentary on this particular fugue.

[13] Probst, "Pen, Paper, Steel."

[14] Neugeboren, "Eine Bach-Fuge im Bild," quoted in Poos, 46–49, quoted from *Bauhaus, Vierteljahr-Zeitschrift für Gestaltung*, ed. Hannes Meyer 3:1 (January 1929): 16–19.

[15] [in beiden fällen handelt es sich nicht um stimmungsgemässe persönliche umdeutungen, sondern um wissenschaftliche exakte übertragungen in ein anderes system.] Neugeboren, "Eine Bach-Fuge im Bild," quoted in Poos, "Henrik Neugeborens Entwurf zu einem Bach-Monument," 46–47.

[16] Probst, "Pen, Paper, Steel."

[17] Neugeboren, "Eine Bach-Fuge im Bild," quoted in Poos, "Henrik Neugeborens Entwurf zu einem Bach-Monument," 47.

time, Probst notes that Neugeboren "chose to represent Bach's polyphony as a 'paralinear' texture."[18] Yet while Probst has no evidence that Neugeboren was familiar with Ernst Kurth's theories, it is clear that he was aware of Busoni's theories on a similar topic, thereby bringing his work in dialogue with Busoni's theories about melody and counterpoint that were discussed in chapter 1. Moreover, as Probst notes, while Klee's more traditional graphic interpretation was rooted in tonality that corresponded better to Kurth's ideology, Neugeboren's graphs are based on the chromatic scale and transcend diatonic tonal bounds, an approach more aligned with Busoni's thinking. In Neugeboren's graphic drawing, "each vertical side of a square corresponds to two semitones, [and] each horizontal side to two eighths."[19] The drawing visually conveys images of the converging of lines without clear visualizations of the vertical harmonies. Yet, the paralinear graphs are supplanted by the three-dimensional sculptural versions by Neugeboren that more closely approach Busoni's visual of architectural music. For his three-dimensional monument, Neugeboren described the three dimensions as the vertical, the horizontal, and space, or distance between pitches. In his case, the vertical dimension was still related to a paralinear reading of the music in that it represents the relationship of pitches to the fundamental tone:

> This type of representation shows the following on three flat planes: 1. Horizontal: the course 2. Vertical, the distance of each tone from one fundamental tone (tonic) for all three voices and 3. From front to back, increasing both on the base and at an angle of 45 degrees: the distance of 45 degrees: the distance of the voices from each other.[20]

In his 1928 three-dimensional model, each shape represents one of the three voices of the fugue, and height is linked to register; the result, as he described it, was architectural ("architektonisch") (see figure 5.1).[21]

[18] Probst, "Pen, Paper, Steel."

[19] [bei dem jeder vertikalen seite eines quadrats zwei halbtöne, jeder horizontalen zwei achtel entsprechen.] Neugeboren, "Eine Bach-Fuge im Bild," quoted in Poos, "Henrik Neugeborens Entwurf zu einem Bach-Monument," 47.

[20] [Diese darstellung lässt auf drei hintereinander gestellten flächen folgendes sehen: 1. horizontal: den konstruktiven verlauf, 2. vertikal: die entfernung jeden tones von einem für alle drei stimmen gleichen grundton (tonika), und 3. von vorne nach rückwarts, sowohl auf der basis als auch im winkel von 45 grad steigend: die entfernung der stimmen voneindander.] Poos, "Henrik Neugeborens Entwurf zu einem Bach-Monument," 48.

[21] For more detailed analyses of the graphic representations of Bach by Klee and Neugeboren, see Probst, "Pen, Paper, Steel."

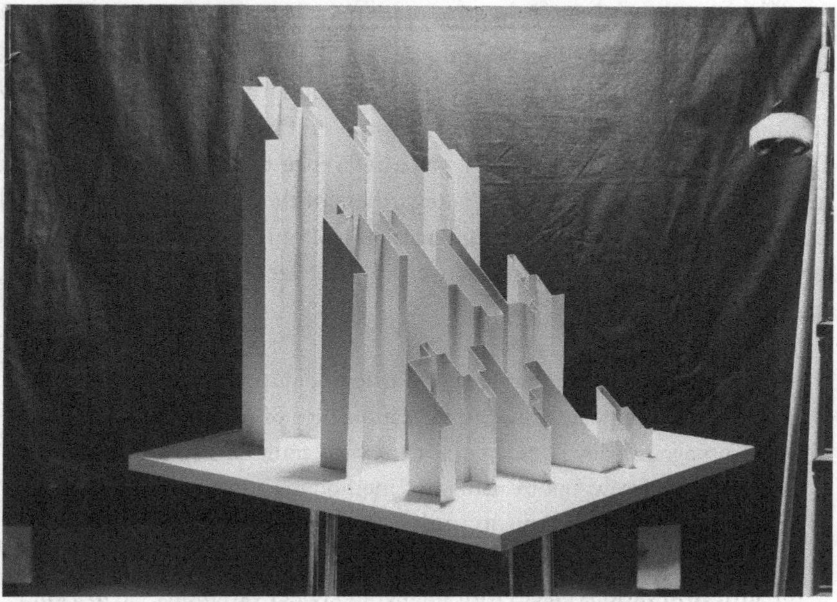

Figure 5.1. Henrik Neugeboren (Henri Nouveau), proposal for a Bach monument based on mm. 52–55 of the E-flat Minor Fugue of J.S. Bach, designed in 1928. Bauhaus-Archive, Berlin, Germany. Photo by Klaus Baum.

The 1970 metal sculpture version in Leverkusen brings these relationships in full view, as it is possible to walk through the sculpture. If bass notes are the shortest and higher registers are taller, thereby creating odd optical illusions, the towering nature of the structure recalls not only the monumentality and power of Bach's music, but also its intricate vertical relationships. At the same time, it erases the temporal aspect of musical architecture, thereby reducing its ephemerality, even while bringing the temporal and spatial aspects of music together in new ways.

During World War I, Hans Richter also transcribed Busoni's ideas about music to abstract film and visual art. In his autobiography, Richter noted that interactions with Busoni in Switzerland had been pivotal for the development of his creative activities. He relates that Busoni encouraged him to study musical counterpoint through the preludes and fugues of Bach and to translate that into visual art.[22] It is unclear which pieces Richter is referring

[22] Hans Richter, *Dada: Art and Anti-Art* (New York: Oxford University Press, 1978), 61.

to here. He mentions "little preludes and fugues" for Bach's wife. Based on Busoni's interests and editorial activities at the time, it could be a reference to Bach's *Well-Tempered Clavier*, part of which derived from the *Notebook for Anna Magdalena Bach.* Busoni finished editing the second volume in 1915. It is also possible that this was a reference to the little preludes and fughetta that he edited in 1916.[23] Regardless of the actual pieces discussed, Busoni's suggestion of consulting Bach's polyphonic works proved to be the key for Richter in his quest to discover how to effectively create abstract and spatialized figures in visual art:

> And trying to translate that idea of music to painting, I began to orchestrate very simple positive-negative relationships of surfaces, black against white, up against down, etc. . . . in that way I found a key which allowed me to operate freely. But by using this method the subject lost its essential importance and allowed me to work with elementary relationships exclusively, with abstract forms. Repetitions of the same element, distributed on the surface in various places with smaller or greater variations, led to a kind of musical relationship between form complexes and a clearer composition of the whole.[24]

These were concepts that he applied in 1920 to time as well when he created his abstract silent film, *Rhythmus 21*; he "made [his] paper rectangles and squares grow and disappear, jump and slide in well-articulated time-spaces and planned rhythms."[25] In his short (c. 3 minute) film, white and gray squares and rectangles emerge, grow, and disappear on a black background, sometimes alone, and sometimes in counterpoint with other shapes. The interest lies in the movement of the shapes and how they interact, pulsating and moving into the foreground or receding into the background, just like contrapuntal musical voices passing through time. The rhythms and textures of the silent film emerge from the movement of the shapes, thereby creating a linear polyphony of shapes in time. Like

[23] Bach, Kleine Präludien, Fughetta, Duette, ed. Busoni (Leipzig: Breitkopf & Härtel, 1916): Bach, *Das Wohltemperierte Klavier*, ed. Busoni, Klavierwerke: Bach-Ausgabe (Leipzig: Breitkopf und Härtel, 1915).

[24] Hans Richter, *Hans Richter: Plastic Arts of the Twentieth Century* (Neuchâtel, Switzerland: Editions du Griffon, 1965), 22.

[25] Richter, *Hans Richter*, 29. The film can be viewed online: Richter, *Rhythmus 21*, https://www.youtube.com/watch?v=FjQ-lpu8kjk (accessed May 30, 2020).

Busoni, he was trying to reconcile spatial and temporal art forms yet using a different medium.

While there were some artists like Klee, Neugeboren, and Richter that were interested in transposing music to visual arts or spatial forms, there were fewer people translating spatialized forms into music in the early twentieth century, as Busoni was. True, Charles Ives was pioneering spatialized music in the United States, but his pieces were largely written as music about music. Many are collages with themes and quotations receding in and out of the texture. Ives also experimented with a spatial placement of performing forces (as in *The Unanswered Question*). While these are tools that Busoni used as well, he also evoked aural distance through volume and rhythm, and experimented with timbre, the overtone series, and register.[26] At the same time, Busoni envisioned novel architectural or ambient forms. In addition, he melded the music of others in performance into architectural shapes through terraced phrasing, nuanced colors, and monumental groupings. In the process, he engaged in new approaches toward melodic lines, the musical language, musical structure, and spatialized sound.

Dissemination: Wladimir Vogel

Busoni's architectural approach, although little remembered today, did not die with him, and it has a direct lineage. His students, mentees, and followers, such as Vogel, Weill, Wolpe, Petri, and Varèse, joined him in translating architecture into music. In this respect, Busoni not only pioneered spatialized music himself, but also contributed to its dissemination. For some of these students, as for Busoni, architectural models and metaphors became seminal for their individualized and concrete explorations of his abstract ideals.

Although Vogel had been trained in Russia in an expressionistic tradition under Alexander Scriabin, he adopted an architectural approach under Busoni's mentorship. In particular, lessons with Busoni led to a multi-textural and multi-formal montage approach patterned primarily after Busoni's *Fantasia Contrappuntistica*, BV 256, and *Doktor Faust*, BV 303.

[26] For a comparison of the music of Charles Ives and Busoni, see Erinn E. Knyt, "Approaching the Essence of Music."

Vogel first approached Busoni for lessons in March 1921, and by summer 1921 he had officially joined Busoni's Berlin composition master class.[27] There, he would have attended biweekly classes.[28] In addition, other more informal gatherings (often described as "black coffee hours") were also held in Busoni's Berlin apartment at Viktoria-Luise-Platz 11; these often led to discussions about diverse topics, such as music, painting, literature, architecture, and aesthetics.

Busoni was proud of his sometimes-headstrong student, whom he considered to be one of the more talented in the class. He wrote a short tribute to Vogel in 1921, in which he documents some of his aspirations for his promising pupil; he also describes the ways his pupil was beginning to adopt some of his teachings, which he described as experimental, as representing the "neuer Wege":

> Besides a feeling, arising from parentage, of rebellion against the existent and accepted things, there dwells in him [Vogel] a vibrating soul and an individual sensibility. When the whole class received as a composition task *Die Bekehrte* by Goethe, Vogel's exposition of it, if not the most masterly, proved to be the most unusual work. In any case, as most suitable of all, it represents a characteristic example of the "new road."[29]

For his part, Vogel was impressed by Busoni's intellect, wit, and cultural expertise, even if he was confronted with a dilemma about how to reconcile Busoni's approach with his own expressionist training. Vogel recorded impressions of Busoni in which he summarized his teachings about form,

[27] Vogel (1896–1984) was born in Moscow and raised in Russia. His mother was Russian, and his father was German. During World War I, he studied instrumentation with Alexander Lamm and then moved to Berlin where he studied first with Hans Tiessen and then with Busoni before earning a teaching position and the Berlin Klindworth-Scharwenka Conservatory. After leaving Germany in 1933, he spent time in Brussels, Paris, and London, before making Switzerland his home (Ascona and Zurich).

[28] For a thorough description of the master class, see Tamara Levitz, "Teaching Young Classicality: Busoni's Master Class in Composition, 1921–1924" (PhD diss., Eastman School of Music, 1993).

[29] Busoni, "*Die Bekehrte* [1921]," in *The Essence of Music and Other Papers*, trans. Rosamond Ley (London: Salisbury Square, 1956), 177. [Neben einem durch Abstammung gegebenen Rebellions-Gefühl gegen Bestehendes und Eigenbürgertes, leben in ihm eine zitternde Seele und ein persöhnliches Empfinden.—Als die gesamte "Klasse" die Komposition von Goethes "Die Bekehrte" zur Aufgabe erhielt, erwies sich Vogels Lösung derselben, wenn auch nicht als die meisterlichere, doch als die aussergewöhnlichere Arbeit. Jedenfalls als die geeignetste von allen, um hier als ein charakteristisches Beispiel "neuer Wege."] Busoni "*Die Bekehrte*," in *Von der Einheit der Musik* (Berlin: Max Hesses Verlag, 1922), 344.

noted his indebtedness to Bach and Mozart, and simultaneously expressed interest in experimental music:

> I encountered a completely different, opposing aesthetic and atmosphere from 1920 [*sic*] to 1924 in the class of Ferruccio Busoni. This great intellect was a Renaissance man; half Italian, half German, he combined Faustian spiritual characteristics with the classical formal perfection of Latin culture. Bach and Mozart were his ideals. My world, which I brought from the Russian tradition and Scriabin, clashed violently with Busoni's world of "New Classicality." Two completely different musical and worldviews confronted each other, especially because my contact with contemporary German music after my arrival in Berlin had led me toward Schoenberg as a continuation of the Scriabin line.[30]

Busoni provided Vogel with a solid foundation in Classical forms and polyphony, which he used as launching points for discussing new directions in music, including in relation to color, form, and spatialized sound. For instance, during the master class, Vogel reworked the fugue from Beethoven's String Quartet op. 133 ("*Grosse Fuge*") for two pianos as an instructional activity that not only required students to immerse themselves in the music, but also to consider doublings, voice leading, and spatial distributions between instruments. Annotations, likely by Busoni, indicate some of his suggestions, including changes to voice leading and doublings (see figure 5.2).

Although Vogel studied several years with Busoni, it was the final class trip to the 1923 Bauhaus exhibition in Weimar that solidified his teachings about structure, color, and space. Vogel left several memories of the trip, suggesting it had a major impact on his development. His memories range from detailed descriptions of interactions with those present during the exhibition, including the Bauhaus instructors, to discussions about structure and music. He used the terms "striking" and "stirring" to describe how the event had aroused latent understandings of Busoni's aesthetics. In one section of his

[30] [Eine ganz andere, entgegengesetzte Ästhetik und Atmospäre traf ich 1920/24 bei Ferruccio Busoni. Dieser grosse Geist war ein Renaissance-Mensch; halb Italiener, halb Deutscher, verband er faustische Züge des Geistes mit der Welt der klassischen Form-Vollendung der lateinischen Kultur. Bach und Mozart war seine Ideale. Der Anprall meiner, von der russischen Tradition und Skrjabin mitgebrachten Welt mit derjenigen der "Jungen Klassizität" Busonis war heftig. Zwei gänzlich verschiedene Musick- und Weltschauungen standen sich gegenüber, besonders da ich nach meiner Ankunft in Berlin, durch die Berührung mit der jungen deutschen Musik, in der Weiterführung der Skrjabin-Linie zu Schönberg tendierte.] Vogel, quoted in Hans Oesch, *Wladimir Vogel: Sein Weg zu einer neuen musikalischen Wirklichkeit* (Munich: Francke Verlag, 1967), 22.

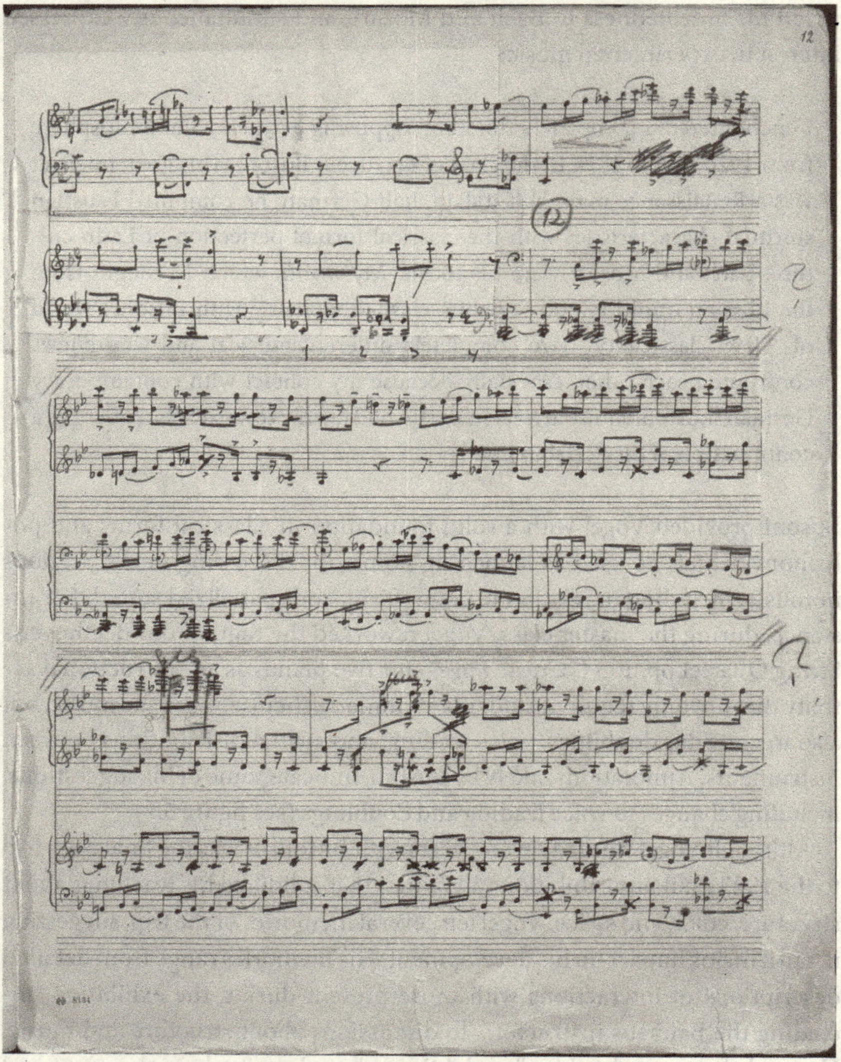

Figure 5.2. Vogel, arrangement of Ludwig van Beethoven's *Grosse Fuge* for Two Pianos. Wladimir Vogel Nachlass, Zentralbibliothek zu Zurich, MUS_NL_116_A_5, p. 12.

memoirs, Vogel stated that he suddenly understood how small shapes in space and in relation to color and rhythm come together to create formal balance and coherence, something that Busoni had already been talking about in relation to music in a more abstract sense:

> In viewing the many works displayed in the Bauhaus exhibition I saw how the most basic elements of the visual arts had been grasped, understood, taught, and applied there. How clearly they had shown the viewer the real meaning of a "circle," a "line," a "square," and a "dot"; and their reciprocal function in a "given" space . . . [as well as] the relative effect of colors, the absolute nature of rhythm, static equilibrium, and balancing, etc. . . . How systematically they forced the most asymmetrical compositions into complete balance, and thus—formed them! All these things determined my own instincts in this direction.[31]

In addition, he remembers a conversation at the Hotel Zum Erbprinzen, over a meal, where Busoni discussed his concept of new counterpoint and its textural ramifications in a very physical way with hands waving in space like independent musical lines; this conversation provided clarity about the potential for multi-dimensional music created by differing textural densities. Vogel stated that he finally understood at that moment that the counterpoint Busoni emphasized was not imitative of older styles and forms, but a means to new dimensions in music. He concluded: "You can understand how I absorbed these words, spoken in the Bauhaus air. They immediately explained what years of class study and all the counterpoint books in existence never had; in a few short moments everything was clairvoyantly clear to me. 'Impressed,' I realized my goals and turned to 'playing with elements.' "[32] In addition, Vogel noted that the importance of what he described as Schlemmer's "movement art" for the exhibition. No doubt, he was referring to Schlemmer's *Triadisches Ballett* and his ambulant architecture:[33]

31 Vogel, quoted in Levitz, "Teaching New Classicality," 387. [Bei der Besichtigung der Arbeiten des Bauhauses sah ich an den zahlreichen Arbeiten wie dort die ursprünglichsten Elemente der bildenden Kunst erfasst, verstanden und gelehrt und angewandt wurden. Mit welch klarer Darstellung man dem Beschauer die eigentliche Bedeutung eines "Kreises" einer "Linie" eines "Vierecks" eines "Punktes," ihre gegenseitige Funktion im "gegebenen" des Statischen Gleichgewichts—der Ausbalancierung etc. . . . mit welcher Systematik man die unsymetrischste Komposition—völlig zum Gleichgewicht zwang—und so—*formte!* Alle diese Dinge verbewussten in mir meine eigene Triebe in dieser Richtung.] Vogel, letter of March 27, 1928, to Max Butting, quoted in Dietrich Brennecke, *Das Lebenswerk Max Buttings* (Leipzig: VEB Deutscher Verlag für Musik, 1973), 68–69.

32 Vogel, in Levitz, "Teaching New Classicality," 388. [Sie können verstehen wie damals diese Worte in der Bauhausluft von mir aufgegangen wurden und mir klarlegten, was einem—Jahrelanges—Klassen—Studium und sämtliche Kontrapunktlehrbücher nie geben könnten—in einem Augenblick hellseherisch öffneten. . . . Ja . . . und so . . . "beeindruckt" . . . erkannte ich meine Ziele und wande mich zum . . . Elementenspiele.] Vogel, letter of March 27, 1928, to Max Butting, quoted in Brennecke, *Das Lebenswerk Max Buttings*, 69.

33 Vogel, "Meisterklasse Busoni," in *Schriften und Aufzeichnungen über Musik: "Innerhalb—Ausserhalb,"* 220. For more about Schlemmer's *Triadisches Ballett*, see chapter 2.

> When the "Bauhaus," then in Weimar, showed the first, Gothic-like exhibition of works by young artists, this most modern art school in Europe, to the astonished and stunned public, and not just pictures and sculptures, the impetus of Kandinsky, Gropius, Klee, Feininger, Schlemmer, and others, who took the first decisive steps in the systematization of new forms of art, but also included the sound and movement art (ballet) in the context of this memorable show.[34]

Vogel finally understood Busoni's abstract teachings about forms and sounds after seeing the Bauhaus exhibition. It was like seeing his ideas in concrete ways. At the same time, hearing the performance of Busoni's piano pieces in that atmosphere solidified an understanding of the ideals realized in music. He heard Busoni's short piano pieces for the first time as examples of moving art forms. He was particularly impressed by Busoni's approach that included contrasting polyphonic and homophonic textures in montage forms that were, nevertheless, simultaneously coherent:

> What distinguishes Busoni's instrumental music is the inner and outer coherence. Meaning, content, and formal elements are well covered, and they bear the imprint of genuineness and uniqueness, despite new melodic and harmonic phrases which, though formed with great art and great ability, never appear artificial or mannered, but are marked by a great personality, even despite featuring many often very contradictory components.[35]

[34] [Aber 1923, als das "Bauhaus," damals in Weimar, die erste, grossartige Ausstellung von Arbeiten jünger Künstler, dieser modernsten Kunstschule Europas der erstaunten und verblüfften Öffentlichkeit zeigte, und nicht nur Bilder und Skulpturen, die unter leitung von Kandinsky, Gropius, Klee, Feininger, Schlemmer und andern, die ersten entscheidenden Schritte in der Systematisierung neuer Kunstformen vollbrachte—sondern ebenfalls die Ton und Bewegungskunst (Ballett) in der Rahmen dieser denkwürdigen Schau ein Herzog.] Vogel, "Eine Begegnung," Wladimir Vogel Nachlass, Zentralbibliothek zu Zurich, MUS_NL_116_1_9, p. 2.

[35] [Was Busonis Instrumentalwerke dieser Art entscheidend kennzeichnet, ist die innere und äussere Stimmigkeit. Sinn, Inhalt und Formelemente decken sich und sie tragen das Zeichen der Einsdruck der Echtheit und der Eindeutigkeit, trotz neuer melodischer und harmonischer Wendungen, die, obwohl mit grosser Kunst und grossem Können geformt, nie künstlich oder maniriert erscheinen allerdings von einer grossen Persönlichkeit gezeichnet, die viele, auch gegensätzlich Komponenten in sich vereinigte. Die Forderung nach dieser Stimmigkeit, die Busoni aufstellte, hebt die neue Klassizität von der Neo-Klassik, welche in der nachfolgenden Jahren popularisiert wurde, deutlich ab. Erstere beruht aufdem Gleichgewicht zwischen dem neuen musikalischen Material, der Formgebung und dem Inhalt.] Vogel, "Eine Begegnung," Wladimir Vogel Nachlass, Zentralbibliothek zu Zurich, MUS_NL_116_1_9, p. 4.

He also finally understood music as a spatial art; he began thinking in musico-spatial terms of mass, that is, as proportion in relation to multi-dimensional ("architectural") formal textures:

> Only the form raises the idea and the direction to the status of the work of art. The appropriation of the correct inner and outer proportions of the mass, of the sound, of the intervals—as the work of art is even more invested, raising it to the rank of classicity, in the original sense of ultimate perfection.[36]

After the Bauhaus exhibition, Vogel thought about ways to concretely realize Busoni's abstract and idealistic teachings. While he spoke of constructing forms based on the idiosyncratic properties of the musical material, the Bauhaus showed him how unique forms could result from the repetition of the smallest basic shapes. Hans Oesch has claimed that Vogel began doing something similar by seeing how movements arise from what he perceived as the combinations of the smallest elements of music:

> He [Vogel] seeks to return to the Ur-elements of music out of which he creates the individual technical formal manifestations. Movements emerge, which carry descriptions, such as, Pizzicato, Glissando, Rhythmica. If Busoni requires the artist to seek a new law of form for each work and to destroy it again after use, so that it does not even become repetitive, Vogel fulfills that demand in the highest measure.[37]

Textural variety and architectural structure were already emerging in Vogel's pieces prior to the Bauhaus field trip, suggesting Busoni had already laid the foundation for this aspect of Vogel's style.[38] On December 7, 1922, during the

[36] [Erst die Form erhebt Einfall, Gesinnung und Richtung ist Merkmal der Zeit; erst die Form erhebt Einfall, Gesinnung und Richtung zum Range des Kunstwerks. *Die Berücksichtigung der richtigen inneren und äusseren Proportionen der Maasse* [*sic*], *des Klangs, der Intervalle*—wie das Kunstwerk auch immer angelegt oder geartet sei—*erhebt es zum Range der Klassizität*, in dem ursprünglichen Sinne endgültiger Vollendung.] Vogel, "Ein Testament," Wladimir Vogel Nachlass, Zentralbibliothek zu Zurich, MUS_NL_116_1_10.

[37] [Darum greift er zurück auf die Urelemente der Musik; aus den einzelnen technischen Erscheinungsformen des tones sucht er ein Gebilde zu schaffen. Sätze entstehen, welche Überschriften wie Pizzicato Glissando Rhythmica tragen. Wenn Busoni vom Künstler verlangt, er sole für jedes Werk ein neues Formgesetz suchen und nach der Anwendung wieder zerstören, auf dass er nicht selbst in Wiederholung verfalle, so ist diese Forderung bei Vogel in hohem Masse erfüllt.] Oesch, *Wladimir Vogel*, 478–79.

[38] Vogel's manuscript is in the Wladimir Vogel Nachlass, Zentralbibliothek, Zurich.

sole public concert by Busoni's pupils and the Berlin Philharmonic Orchestra, Vogel presented his *Symphonischer Vorgang* (now lost, see figure 5.3), which reportedly contained much intricate polyphony, thus representing a major textural departure from his earlier expressionistic compositions, many of which were motoric and more consistent texturally.[39] One example of his earlier approach is his *Nature vivante: Quatre morceaux poètiques pour piano* (1920).

Vogel also experimented with a new architectural manner of composition in his *Komposition fur ein und zwei Klaviere* (1923) that contains a montage form with distinct segments comprised of variations, a fugal section, and a cadenza-coda. Vogel's piece was modeled after Busoni's *Fantasia contrappuntistica*, and he showed it to Busoni for critique during the class. A list of the formal sections can be viewed in figure 5.4.

Even so, it was after the class trip that Vogel began to describe his compositions more regularly in architectural terms. For instance, he called the theme of his *Variètude* (1931), which is a combination of variation and etude forms, "constructive" [konstruktiv], even if the piece was also expressive.[40] Vogel's mixed-genre composition that he likened to a chaconne synthesizes variation and etude techniques as the theme keeps reappearing in ever-varied contexts. Contrasts of texture between polyphony and homophony provide a sense of montage that is also characteristic of forms by Busoni and at the Bauhaus.

The change in Vogel's compositional style after the Bauhaus field trip was apparent, and others described it repeatedly as architectural. Erich Mendelsohn, for instance, whose works were on display at the 1923 Bauhaus exhibition, reportedly described Vogel's Etudes for Orchestra (1930) as architectural in shape. Vogel has left the following memory of his interactions with Mendelsohn:

> I brought the score of the "Two Etudes for Orchestra," which had just been conducted by Hermann Scherchen, and which the publishing house Bote &

[39] The *Symphonischer Vorgang* was, unfortunately, lost. Levitz, "Teaching New Classicality," 327, note 178.

[40] Wladimir Vogel, "Variétude (1932)," Wladimir Vogel Nachlass, Zentralbibliothek zu Zurich, MUS_NL_116_Ca_2. This terminological choice could be partially a reference to constructivism in art, which was an outgrowth of Russian Futurism during and after World War I, and with which Kandinsky was associated. That movement referred to an object's objective material properties and spatial presence. Often, such works featured jagged angles and contrasts resulting in montage-like forms with many diverse textures, but with few overtly expressive qualities.

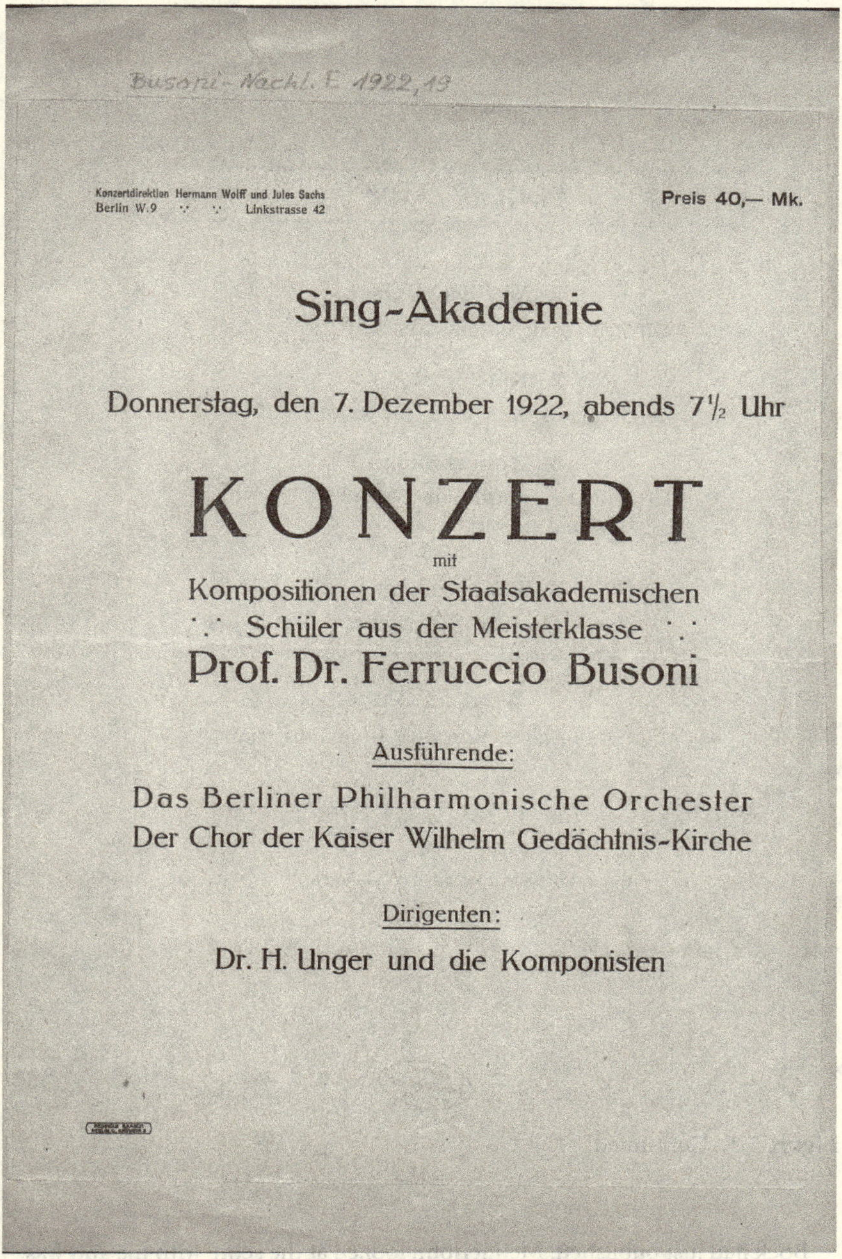

Busoni-Nachl. F 1922,13

Konzertdirektion Hermann Wolff und Jules Sachs
Berlin W.9 ∵ ∵ Linkstrasse 42

Preis 40,— Mk.

Sing-Akademie

Donnerstag, den 7. Dezember 1922, abends 7½ Uhr

KONZERT

mit

Kompositionen der Staatsakademischen
Schüler aus der Meisterklasse

Prof. Dr. Ferruccio Busoni

Ausführende:

Das Berliner Philharmonische Orchester
Der Chor der Kaiser Wilhelm Gedächtnis-Kirche

Dirigenten:

Dr. H. Unger und die Komponisten

Figure 5.3. Program for the composition recital by Busoni's composition master class pupils on December 7, 1922.

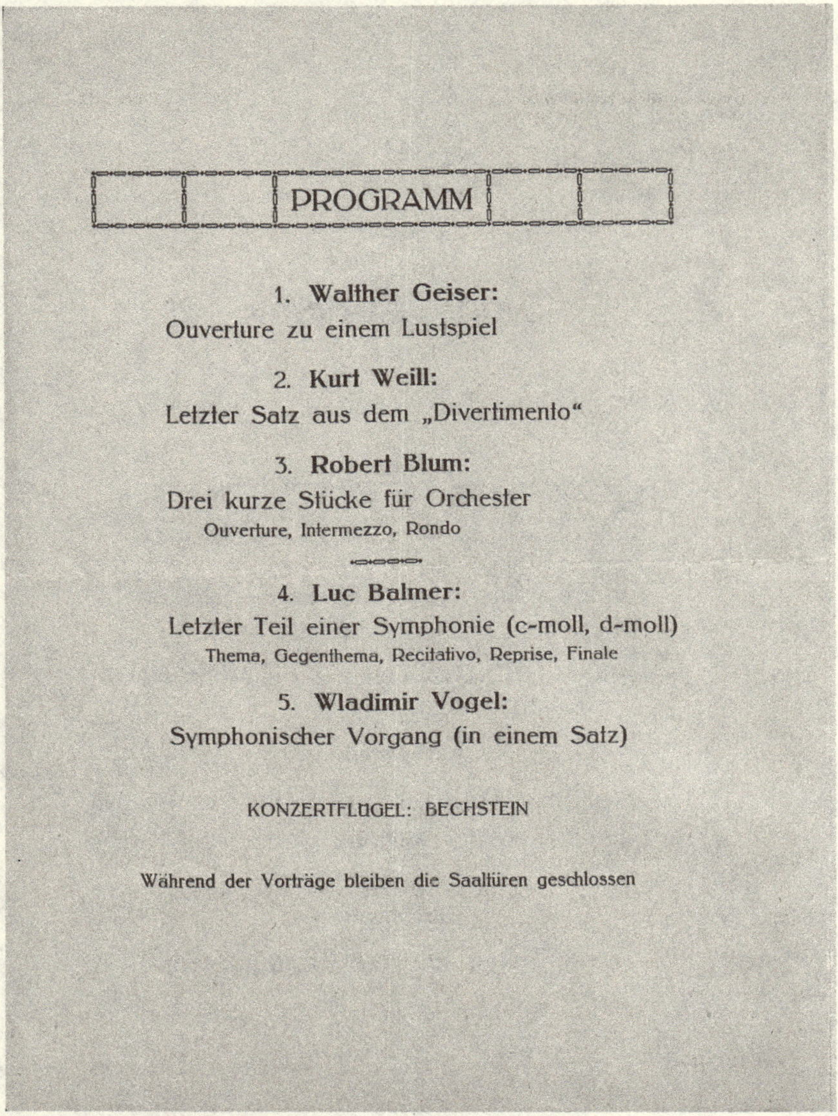

PROGRAMM

1. **Walther Geiser:**
Ouverture zu einem Lustspiel

2. **Kurt Weill:**
Letzter Satz aus dem „Divertimento"

3. **Robert Blum:**
Drei kurze Stücke für Orchester
Ouverture, Intermezzo, Rondo

4. **Luc Balmer:**
Letzter Teil einer Symphonie (c-moll, d-moll)
Thema, Gegenthema, Recitativo, Reprise, Finale

5. **Wladimir Vogel:**
Symphonischer Vorgang (in einem Satz)

KONZERTFLÜGEL: BECHSTEIN

Während der Vorträge bleiben die Saaltüren geschlossen

Figure 5.3. Continued

Bock had just published. Mendelsohn looked at the score with me and was astonished, recognizing in the graphic image "clear architectural forms." I then explained to him—from the musical standpoint—the function of the various instrumental groups in the structure of the whole piece. From then

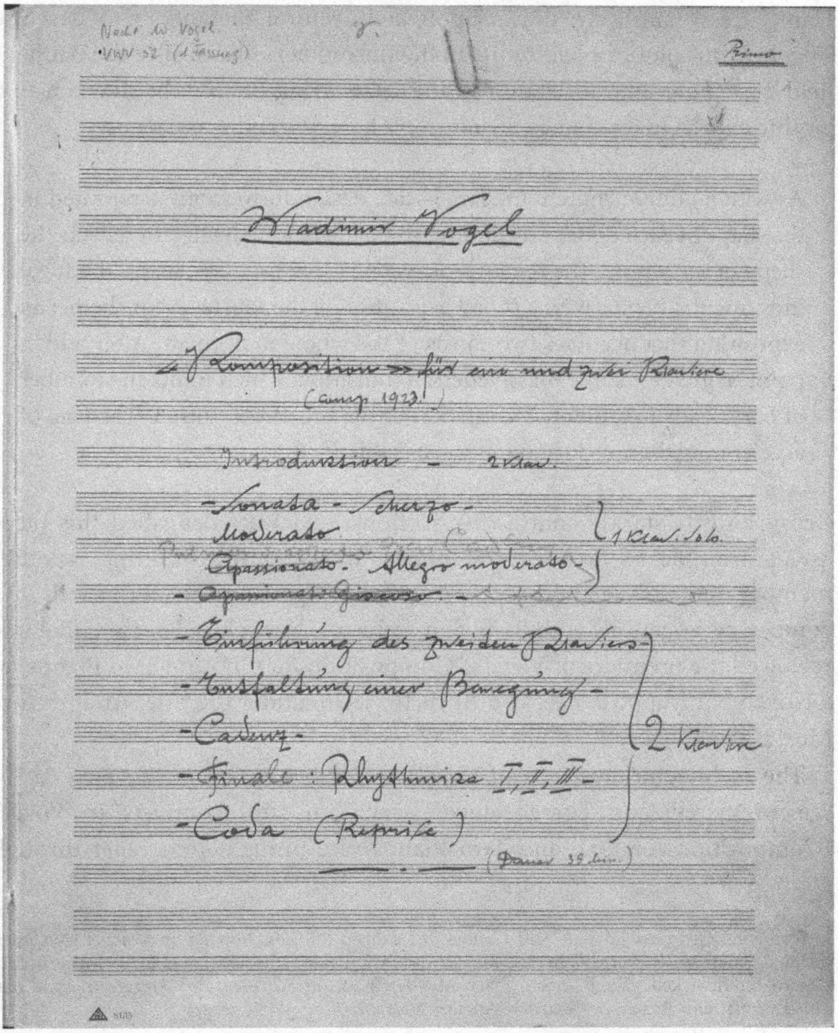

Figure 5.4. Vogel, Komposition für ein und zwei Klaviere. Wladimir Vogel Nachlass, Zentralbibliothek zu Zurich, MUS_NL_116_52_1_1, p. 1.

on, I was dealing with such "common denominators" in music and architecture, which I developed further during my time in Zurich.[41]

[41] [Ich die Partitur der damals gerade von Hermann Scherchen aus der Taufe gehobenen "Zwei Etüden für Orchester" brachte, welche der Verlag Bote & Bock eben herausgegeben hätte. Mendelsohn sah sich die Partitur mit mir und wir verblufft, im graphischen Bild "klare architektonische Formen" zu erkennen. Ich erklärte ihm dann—vom Musikalischen her—die Funktion der verschiedenen

Hans Oesch, similarly, draws upon architectural metaphors to describe Vogel's form solutions beginning in the Busoni period and after the Bauhaus field trip, including in relation to the 1924 string quartet; he likens it to a Gothic church in its themes, structure, coherence, and massiveness:

> As with a Gothic church, the large-scale design form motif is repeated in the shape of each door and window, so that here too, the fugato reflects the shape of the whole. The fugato—or, as one more properly states, the fugal movement—begins with a broad exposition of the fourteen-bar theme; an exposition that occupies two thirds of the whole movement. After a high point of greatest sonic massiveness, a transition, which limits the number of bars, leads to a pointed escalation of the broad exposition. The idea of accelerating the conclusion is unmistakable.[42]

Because of its starkly contrasting sections, reviewers described this piece as an example of architectural music. In 1928, Max Butting, another member of the Novembergruppe, stated that "again and again one falls into comparing Vogel's art with that of an architect."[43] Joachim Lucchesi likewise reviewed the premiere of Vogel's "Composition for One and Two Pianos" at a Novembergruppe concert on April 16, 1926, under the title "Architecture Music."[44]

The architectural aspects of Vogel's music beginning in the early 1920s are amply evident. For instance, stark structural contrasts in Vogel's "Composition for One and Two Pianos" are brought into relief through

Instrumental-Gruppen im Bau und Gefüge des ganzen Stückes. Von da an beschäftigen mich solche "gemeinsame Nenner" in der Musik und Architektur, die ich dann in meiner Zürcher Zeit weiterentwickelt habe.] Vogel, "Erich Mendelssohn," in *Schriften und Aufzeichnungen über Musik: "Innerhalb-Ausserhalb"* (Zurich: Atlantis, 1977), 194.

[42] [Wie bei einer gotischen Kirche ein im Grossen durchgeführtes Formmotiv sich in der Form jeder Tür je des Fensters wiederholt, so spiegelt auch hier das Fugato die Form des Ganzen. Den auch das Fugato—oder wie man besser sage müsste: die fugale Bewegung—hebt in breiter Exposition des 14 taktigen Themas an; einer Exposition die allein zwei Dritten des ganzen Satzes einnimmt. Nach einem Hochpunkt von grösster klanglicher Mässigkeit setzt mit einer Entführung, die das Thema auf die halbe Taktzahl beschränkt, die ebenso plotlziche wie scharfe Zuspitzung der breit anlaufenden Exposition ein. Die Idee, den Schluss beschleunigen herbeizuführen ist unverkennbar.] Oesch, *Wladimir Vogel*, 480.

[43] [Immer wieder verfallt man darauf Vogels Kunst mit der eines Architekten zu vergleichen.] Max Butting, "Vogel," *Sozialistische Monatshefte* 34 (March 1928): 271.

[44] Joachim Lucchesi, "Architektonische Musik," *Berliner Börsen-Courier* (April 21, 1926). See also Friedrich Geiger, *Die Dramma-Oratorien von Wladimir Vogel, 1896–1984*, Musik im "Dritten Reich" und im Exil 5, ed. Hans-Werner Heister and Peter Peterson (Hamburg: von Bockel Verlag, 1998), 37–38.

contrasting musical textures and formal approaches, much like diverse sections of a Gothic cathedral, with some ornamented and highly textured. The opening and closing sections are structurally foregrounded in that they are performed by two pianos with varied rhythms and textures. The middle part, by contrast, played by only one pianist, is more ornamented, featuring decorative fantasia-like improvisatory figurations played by solo piano (see figure 5.5). It resembles the improvisatory sections designated as "recessed passageways" in the drawing of Busoni's *Fantasia contrappuntistica* included in chapter 2 of this book.

Even after the conclusion of the master class and Vogel's subsequent experimentation with dodecaphonic procedures during the 1930s, he continued to compose pieces that were considered "architectural," and these bear the imprint of Busoni's influence. In honor of Busoni, Vogel composed the *Sinfonia fugata* (1925–1928). Written in emulation of Busoni's *Fantasia contrappuntistica*, it contains a fugue with four different subjects, cadenzas, and a concluding chorale. The juxtaposition of contrasting structural sections is a direct reference to Busoni's composition. Vogel's piece starts with a pre-movement marked *deciso* before a fugue with four different subjects. This virtuosic fugue concludes with a cadenza that leads to an adagio (to be played without a break). A virtuosic *allegro furioso* follows, and the piece concludes with a reverential chorale. Vogel's *Preludio-interludio-lirico-postludio für Orchester (zum 30. Todestage von Ferruccio Busoni)* (1954) also paid direct homage to Busoni. The prelude, for instance, is based on musical material from Busoni's Toccata (1921), but Vogel's work is dodecaphonic. Even so, Vogel uses Busoni's theme for five notes of the series, while the additional pitches of the row served harmonic functions, an approach Vogel frequently took. Yet while his use of serial rows is an unorthodox adaptation of the Schoenberg tradition, the varied formal approach resembles Busoni's. This synthesis is summarized best by Vogel himself:

> What I adopted from the aesthetician and theorist Busoni as fruitful for my own work were his views on form, on the inner and outer proportions of music. He suggested—and emphasized repeatedly in the master class—that subjectivity in music and exaggerated Expressionism were coming to an end and would be replaced by a New Classicality. . . . For me the principle that elements of new music had to be integrated in new forms was a guide. Every musical language had to satisfy the criteria of

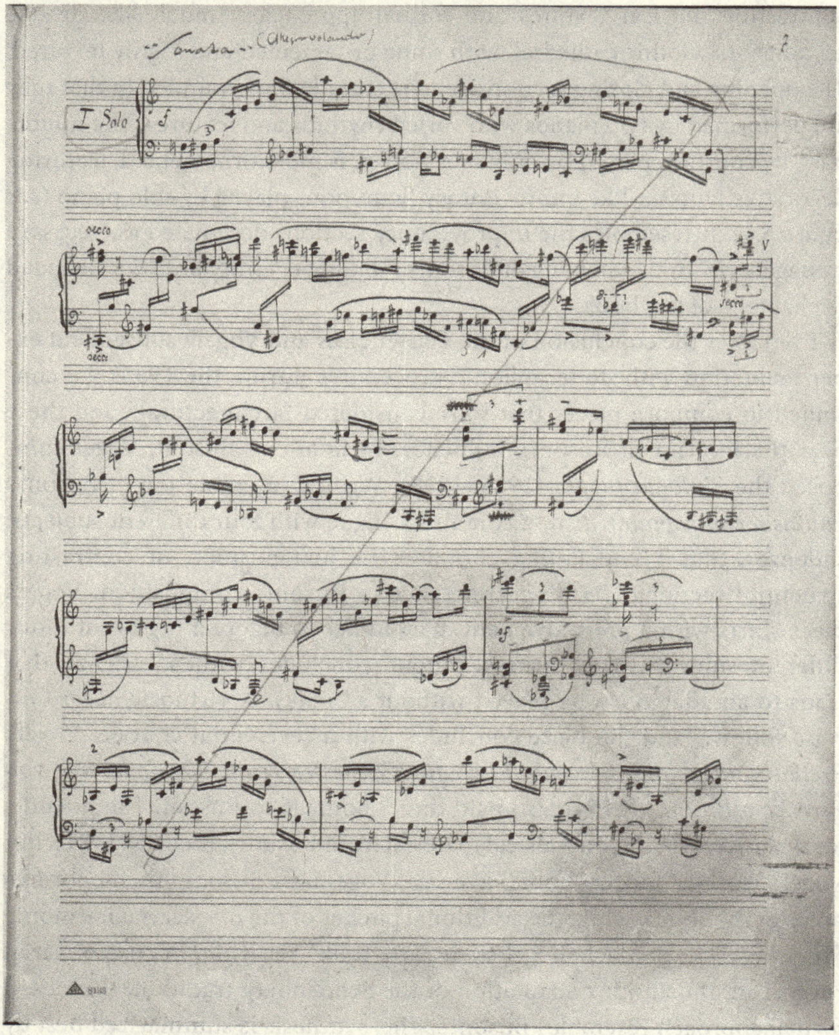

Figure 5.5. Vogel, Sonata für ein und zwei Klaviere. Wladimir Vogel Nachlass, Zentralbibliothek zu Zurich, MUS_NL_116_52_1_1, p. 7. These pages illustrate the textural difference between the two-piano and solo piano writing.

> classicality, even my own language, which later turned to the discipline of dodecaphony.[45]

Vogel maintained that his approach was timeless and widely applicable regardless of the compositional method or musical language employed: "According to Busoni's definition, classicism can be achieved in every epoch and in every musical language, not by adopting the traditional small and large forms, but by casting today's musical language into clear and balanced proportions and forms; 'freedom of form, not formlessness.'"[46]

Busoni's influence on Vogel extended beyond varied formal structures and included the evocation of space with texture, sonority, timbre, and register. Tamara Levitz notes that Vogel was impressed by Busoni's teachings about orchestration, including that:

> every instrument in an ensemble should complete its own musical line, that two voices which were consonant should always be in the same instrumental group, while pitches which did not belong together should be in different groups, and that a vocal line should always be composed a fourth or fifth above or below the instrumental part to assure textual clarity.[47]

In addition to ensuring clarity, such an approach also invokes senses of space and multi-dimensionality. Vogel looked to Busoni's *Doktor Faust* as a model in this regard. He describes the Sarabande movement, in particular, as possessing depth and height as a result of the orchestration. In

45 [Was ich vom Aesthetiker und Theoretiker Busoni als für mich fruchtbar annahm, waren seine Ansichten über die Form, die inneren und äusseren Proportionen in der Musik. Seine dies bezüglichen Thesen, die veröffentlichte und in den Meisterkursen immer betonte, waren u.a. die Einsicht, dass der Subjektivismus in der Musik und der übertriebene Expressionismus seinem Ende entgegen gingen und einer jungen Klassizität weichen wurden.... Für mich war das Prinzip, die Elemente der neuen Musik in neue Formen einzufügen, ein Wegweiser, jede Musiksprache de Kriterium der Klassizität zu unterstellen, also auch die Meinige, die sich später der dodekaphonischen Disziplin zuwandte.] Vogel, untitled essay, Wladimir Vogel Nachlass, Zentralbibliothek zu Zurich, MUS_NL_1146_14_15, pp. 1–2. This essay was later published in Vogel, "Der Weg meines musikalisch-kompositorischen Werdens," in Vogel, *Schriften und Aufzeichnungen über Musik*, 207–8.

46 [Nach Busonis Definition kann Klassizität in jeder Epoche und in jeder Tonsprache erreicht werden, nicht indem man die traditionellen Klein—und Grossformen übernimmt, sondern jene der heutigen Tonsprache in klare und ausgewogene Proportionen und Formen giesst, "Freiheit der Form, nicht Formlosigkeit."] Vogel, untitled essay, Wladimir Vogel Nachlass, Zentralbibliothek zu Zurich, MUS_NL_1146_14_15, p. 2. This essay draft became Vogel, "Der Weg meines musikalisch-kompositorischen Werdens."

47 Levitz, "Teaching New Classicality," 175.

short, he thought of it as a combination of depth, height, color, texture, and shape:

> A peaceful, prolonged consecration, a round of voices which alternate and are woven into each other with the greatest mastery.
> Violins—Flutes—Clarinets
> Measured depth—Striding . . .
> Heights—Lightly suspended . . .
> A wailing middle . . .
> A plucked end—unresolved cadences . . .
> Without a gesture . . . unemotional, never self-indulgent.
> Everything clearly on the surface, nothing hidden . . . once one grasps the core, one
> never loses it . . .
> Architecture which strives for the height of transcendence.[48]

Vogel also built upon Busoni's teachings on the spatial aspects of music through his own explorations of acoustics and staging. In an article written in 1930, he, like Busoni, claimed that reform of opera and other staged pieces, such as oratorios, should be linked to considerations of architectural design. As noted in chapter 3, this topic had previously fascinated Busoni and others at the Bauhaus, such as Walter Gropius. Vogel similarly stated: "The redesign of the opera, last but not least, involves capturing the architecture of the stage, the spatial dimension, as an element acting indirectly."[49] In particular,

[48] [Ein ruhiges, gedehntes Weihen, ein Reigen der sich abwechselnden, mit höchster Meisterschaft ineinander geflochtenen Stimmen.

> Geigen—Flöten—Klarinetten . . .
> Gemessene Tiefe—Schreitende . . .
> Höhen—leicht schwebende . . .
> Klagende Mitten . . .
> Zupfende Enden—ungeendete Schlüsse . . .
> Ohne Geste . . . unpathetisch, nie schwelgend.
> Alles klar auf der Oberfläche, nichts Verdecktes . . . einmal erfasst, verliert man den Boden schon nie . . .

Zur Höhe der Transzendenz strebende Architektonik]. Vogel, quoted in Levitz, "Teaching New Classicality," 295. Vogel, "Über das Rassenhafte, Aesthetische und Ethische in Ferruccio Busonis Kunst: Anlässlich einer Gedächtnisfeier für Ferruccio Busoni im Hamburger Stadttheater," *Der deutsche Rundfunk* (August 1924), 221–22; republished in *Schriften und Aufzeichnungen über Musik: "Innerhalb—Ausserhalb,"* 161–62.

[49] [Neugestaltung der Oper heisst nicht zuletzt Erfassen der Architektonik der Bühne, der räumlichen Dimension als mittelbar agierendes Element.] Vogel, "Die Funktion des Räumlichen, in

he urged changing the boxy quadrilateral theatrical openings, citing their artificial divisions between actors and spectators. Instead, he praised the new open architectural designs of Gropius and Erwin Piscator.[50] In terms of space, Vogel also considered new approaches toward the placement of the orchestra and the use of the stage for scenery and action:

> Certainly, these efforts will be combined with those of the architects in the design of the new theater space. The updating of the opera in the future will not only be a matter of updating the subject, but also of acquiring and using new spatial and temporal dimensions through the means of operatic gesture.[51]

He also encouraged exploration of staging experimentation within traditional theatrical space, for which he praised Mozart in *Die Zauberflöte* for exploring the possibilities of height and depth in the staging. This reference to *Die Zauberflöte* is especially noteworthy, as Busoni upheld it as the highest ideal of theater and encouraged his students to study it in detail.[52] In terms of more contemporary pieces, Vogel specifically praised the works of those in the Busoni circle, such as Weill's stage works, including *Der Protagonist* (1925) and *Die Dreigroschenoper* (1928), pieces, he maintained, that reduced the distance between spectator and actor.

Vogel's concern with space and dimension extended beyond theatrical music to instrumental music as well. Like Busoni, he believed that music inherently possesses spatial qualities. In particular, he writes about what it means for music to move vertically, horizontally, and statically. In an essay from 1925, Vogel described the dimensions of music in explicitly spatial terms:

> Thematic material, line, color, and constructive framework are of course available, so that the individual lines have their substructure and support.

Das Kunstblatt XIV (Dec. 1930)," 248–49. https://magazines.iaddb.org/issue/DKB/1930-12-01/edition/14-12/page/39?query= (accessed Sept. 23, 2022).

50 Vogel, "Die Funktion des Räumlichen," 248–49.

51 [Sicher werden diese Bestrebungen sich mit denen der Architekten in der Gestaltung des neuen Theaterraums verbinden. Die Aktualisierung der Oper ist in Zukunft nicht nur Frage der Aktualisierung des Sujets, sondern Frage der Gewinnung und Ausnutzung neuer räumlicher und zeitlicher Dimensionen durch due Taktik der Operngeste.] Vogel, "Die Funktion des Räumlichen," 248–49.

52 For more information, see Knyt, *Ferruccio Busoni and His Legacy* (Bloomington: Indiana University Press, 2017), 27–28.

> If you want to see details, you linger when looking at a floor—but the whole requires movement as an experience of musical architecture.[53]

Although Vogel's instrumental music exhibited architectural tendencies beginning with his Busoni master class compositions, it was in his mixed-genre drama oratorios that his exploration of space and music are synthesized most fully. The first of these pieces, *Wagadus Untergang durch die Eitelkeit* (1926–1930), represents a synthesis of speech theater and oratorio without scenery.[54] Vogel stated that the relationship between the spoken word and the sung word began to fascinate him, leading to a new genre in which the dramatic and the epic-oratorio elements bind together.[55] Featuring two main sections, the piece is also composed of numerous smaller movements ranging from choral numbers, to speech recitative, to instrumental numbers. Vogel paid specific attention to the possibilities of timbre and range by featuring a spectrum of sounds from the lowest rumbles of basses to the highest strains of the sopranos. Vogel described his innovations, including of sonorous masses of sound that threaded in and out of the complete texture:

> The instrumental ensemble should be able to cut through the choral setting (from the low to the high registers), have a full sound, be in balance with the choir masses, as homogenous as possible in the tone colors, and like the vocals, be carried by human breath. . . . A wood-and-brass chamber choir orchestra from deep bass to high soprano appears.[56]

[53] [Thematik, Linie, Farbe, und konstruktives Gerüst sind selbstverständlich vorhanden, damit die einzelnen Stockwerke ihren Unterbau und Halt haben. Will man Details sehen, verweile man bei der Betrachtung eines solchen Stockwerkes—das Ganze aber fordert *Mitbewegung* als Erlebnis einer Musik-architektur.] Vogel, "For the Komposition für Ein und Zwei Klaviere" (1923), in Vogel, *Schriften und Aufzeichnungen*, 235.

[54] For more information, see Friedrich Geiger, *Di Dramma-Oratorien von Wladimir Vogel, 1896–1984*, Musik im "Dritten Reich" und im Exil 5, ed. Hans-Werner Heister and Peter Peterson (Hamburg: von Bockel Verlag, 1998). Vogel also wrote an article about his connections to Kurt Weill, whom he was close to during the master class. Vogel, "Kurt Weill," in *Schriften und Aufzeichnungen*, 193.

[55] Vogel, "Wagadus Untergang durch die Eitelkeit (1926–30)," in Vogel, *Schriften und Aufzeichnungen*, 13–18.

[56] [Das Instrumentalensemble sollte den Chorsatz stützen können (von den tiefen bis zu den hohen Registern), einen vollen Klang haben, im Gleichgewicht zu den Chormassen stehen, möglichst homogen in der Klangfarbe [*sic*], und wie der Gesang, vom menschlichen Atem getragen sein. . . . Ein aus Holz und Blech zusammengestelltes kamerorchestrales Ensembels erchien . . .—vom tiefen Bass bis zu hohen Sopran—zu wählen diese Gruppe entsprach am besten meine Forderungen und auch ihr spezifischer Klang dürfte zum Stoff passen.] Vogel, "Wagadu," Vogel Nachlass, Zentralbibliothek zu Zurich, MUS_NL_116 14_11, 5–6. He reiterated his ideas about the spatialization of music in an essay entitled: "One of the Fundamental Problems of New Music." In particular, he claimed that dimensionality is an issue that has dominated the development of contemporary music. [Nach der Auflösung der tonal bedington vertikalen und horizontalen Bezogenheiten der verschiedenen

The composer notes that when writing this piece, he was inspired by Busoni's theories and the model of *Doktor Faust*:[57] Busoni's *Arlecchino* was also a model with its spoken text in the title role. He expressed how impressed he was by the latter piece in a letter to Busoni in which he specifically mentioned aspects of the staging and praised the director, Leopold Sachse (1880–1961), for his ability to make the performances "lively and varied."[58]

Connections between Busoni's works for stage and Vogel's extended beyond plot and character representation to the textural layering and spatialization of the music. It is true that Vogel's treatment of the voice is unique in that his speech art is based on linguistic-phonetic connections. However, Vogel's choir also speaks polyphonically in canons and fugues, just as the choirs in Busoni's *Doktor Faust* featured many polyphonic sections and were also split into distinct groups, as in the Wittenburg tavern scene. Like many oratorios, Vogel envisioned the different choirs as serving different functions. Like Busoni's composition, the music explores timbre, dynamics, and register in idiosyncratic ways. Yet Vogel's singing choir supports main points and serves as a musical background, while the main action takes place in the speech choirs and soloist roles. While Busoni invoked the less common timbre of bells, Vogel decided to use the saxophone family, an ensemble he hoped would balance and support the choir without overwhelming it. He treats it like an integral part of the composition:

> The orchestra then supports the word, underscoring chanted syllables and unconventional sentence repetitions. The word rhythm is intercepted, recolored, thrown back, or further developed by the various instruments. Thus, the influence of speech music on the instrumental parts is manifold and secures the unity of the work.[59]

Stimmkomplexe und Klangebenen—beherrscht im Wesentlichen ein Problem die ganze Entwicklung der modernen Musik: vom "linearen Kontrapunkt" der 20-iger Jahre, der "atonal-nicht kontrapunktierenden" oder "durchbrochenen Polyphonie" der 30-iger Jahre, zur Dodekaphonie (Schönberg und seine Schule), und weiter zur "poetischen, inneren Schau der musikalischen Formvorgänge" bei Webern und den sterilen Skelettkonstruktionen des "punktuellen, resp. seriellen Stils" bis zu den "partiellen oder totalen Clustereffekten."] Vogel, "Eines der Grundproblem der neuen Musik," Vogel Nachlass, Zentralbibliothek zu Zurich, MUS_NL_116_14_ 15, p. 1.

57 In the Weimar Republic there were proletarian speech choirs that doubtless also influenced the genre. The speech choirs were initially founded by Albert Florath around 1920. The Rote Sprechchor was founded in Berlin in 1927.

58 Vogel, letter of March 1924 to Busoni, Staatsbibliothek zu Berlin–Preußischer Kulturbesitz, Musikabteilung mit Mendelssohn-Archiv, Mus. Nachl. F. Busoni BII 5259.

59 [Das Orchester unterstüzt dann das Wort, unterstreicht skandierte Silben und eigenwillige Satzwiederholungen. Der Wort Rhythmus wird von den verschiedenen Instrumenten aufgefangen,

In addition, he explored the unique timbral qualities of the voices, including changes invoked by the extreme registers, the possibilities of vocal glissandi, and *Sprechstimme*, as well as more lyrical singing.

Some of these vocal qualities invoke architectural structures, such as in number eleven, where each member of the speech choir (S1, S2, A1, A2, T1, T2, T3, B1, B2, B3) speaks at a fixed pitch and builds an aural pyramid of sound. Vogel staggers entrances in the opening measure ranging from the lowest pitch and voice part (E below the bass staff in Bass 3) followed in ascending pitch order to the highest (Sopranos 1 and 2) singing D and F♯ at the top of the treble clef. Vogel reinforces this dramatic shift in register and vocal quality with a sudden crescendo. The following measure features the voice entries in reverse (from highest to lowest) with a dramatic decrescendo.[60] He repeats this same pyramid effect three more times throughout the brief number (see example 5.1). In number nine, scored for a small speech choir, he also juxtaposes sharply contrasting dynamics and vocal styles that range from spoken text to whispers and hisses in imitation in contrasting registers.[61]

Vogel thought of his works in terms of space, texture, and structure. He thought about them in physical terms, related to mass, height, and depth, as he mentions in relation to a large symphonic work, *In Signum Im* (1976):

> The design is, as in other of my compositions, extremely architectonic, especially here in the "Mosso" part; architectonic—not unlike the laws of architecture [*Baukunst*]—with the categories of heavy and light, of depth and height, of space, so that the sound visual analogue of the forms and the structure allows the sections to be recognized. Thus, for example, moving through the sound spaces from the low to the high, and vice versa, through uniform rhombic elements, tempi, etc. creates a closed picture. They are form structures, not just rows. Great importance is attached to the diversity of such structures. These are all features of my compositional conception.[62]

umgefarbt, zurückgeworfen oder weiterentwickelt. So ist der Einfluss der Sprechmusik auf die gespielte Musik vielfältig und sichert die Einheit des Werkes.] Vogel, "Der modern Sprechor," Vogel, *Schriften und Aufzeichnungen*, 78.

[60] Vogel, *Wagadus Untergang durch die Eitelkeit* (Milan: Ricordi, 2003), 123.

[61] Vogel, "Der modern Sprechor," 78–80.

[62] [Die Gestaltung ist, wie auch in anderen meiner Kompositionen, meistens architektonisch, besonders hier im "Mosso" Teil; architektonisch—den Gesetzen der Baukunst nicht unähnlich—mit den Kategorien von Schwer und das Licht, von Tiefe und Höhe, von Räumlichen, so dass das "Horvisuelle" der Formen und des Aufbaus den Ablauf der Perioden erkennen last. So entsteht zum Beispiel durch Abschreiten der Ton-Räume von der tiefen zur hohen Lage und umgekehrt, durch einheitliche rhythmische Elemente, Tempi usw. Ein geschlossenes Bild. Es sind Formen-Strukturen,

Example 5.1. Vogel, *Wagadus Untergang durch die Eitelkeit*, no. 11, mm. 1–2.

Nr. 11 Sprechchor (fixierte tonhöhe) (Silben sehr genau und kurz aussprechen)
Speech-Choir (at a fixed pitch) (Syllables spoken very precise and short)
Choeur parlé à notes déterminées (chaque syllabe précise et courte)

Beim Studium dieses Stückes wird empfehlen es ganz langsam und mit voller Singstimme zu üben, dann das Tempo immer mehr beschleunigen und die Notenwerte bis zum Sprechton zu reduzieren.

We advise to study this piece at first very slowly and in a singing-voice; then to accelerate the movement and reduce the singing to a recitative accordant to the written notes.

Il est à recommander d'étudier ce morceau d'abord très lentement et en chantant, puis accéler de plus en plus et réduire le chant à un "parlé" sur les notes indiquées.

Figure 5.6. Photograph of Ferruccio Busoni in his apartment at Viktoria-Luise-Platz with some of his Berlin master class pupils (Kurt Weill, Walther Geiser, Luc Balmer, and Wladimir Vogel), c. 1923. Staatsbibliothek zu Berlin–Preußischer Kulturbesitz, Mus. Nachl. F. Busoni P I, 235.

Vogel, like Busoni, thought of himself as an architect of sound (see figure 5.6). Although he struck out on his own path, inventing the drama oratorio featuring speech choirs, his ideas were rooted in Busoni's aesthetic ideals and on the model of his compositions, which he in turn talked about with his own pupils, such as Einojuhani Rautavaara.[63]

Dissemination: Kurt Weill

Like Vogel, Weill was also impacted by his studies with Busoni, especially in his approach to form (see figure 5.6). Although he seems to have been

nicht bloss Reihen-Strukturen. Auf die Vielfältigkeit solcher Strukturen wird grosses Gewicht gelegt. Dies alles sind einige Merkmale meiner kompositorischen Konzeption.] Vogel, "In Signum Im," in *Schriften und Aufzeichnungen*, 127.

[63] As Kimmo Korhonen mentions, although Rautavaara initially went to Ascona, Switzerland, to study dodecaphony with Vogel in 1957, the longer-lasting effect was a new constructivist approach to form that first surfaced in *Praevariata* and later in the Fourth Symphony (*Arabasceta*, 1962). Korhonen, "New Music of Finland," in *New Music of the Nordic Countries*, ed. John D. White (Hillsdale, NY: Pendragon Press, 2002), 198.

less profoundly influenced by the 1923 Bauhaus exhibition than Vogel, his writings bear ample evidence of homage to Busoni's ideas, as do his montage forms. His concept of *Urform*, in particular, represents a personal interpretation of Busoni's teachings, as do his notions of gestic music and spatialized cinematic music.[64] Busoni's influence led to an interest in multi-sectional montage structures that display textural and timbral layering in response to the plots and genre mixture.

Weill, who attended Busoni's composition master class in Berlin from January 1921 to December 1923, wrote fondly of his studies with Busoni; in his memoirs, he notes the unconventionality of the instruction, which often featured abstract discussions of ideas rather than discussions about tangible technical problems.[65] In addition, he remembers the experience as collegial, leading to long-lasting friendships with other students, including Vogel:[66]

> He called us disciples and there were no actual lessons, but he allowed us to breathe his aura, which emanated in every sphere, but eventually manifested itself in music. . . . It was a mutual exchange of ideas in the very best sense, with no attempt to force an opinion, no autocracy, and not the slightest sign of envy or malice; and any piece of work that revealed talent and ability was immediately recognized and enthusiastically received.[67]

Weill's lasting admiration for Busoni's ideas and compositions is also evident in his tribute for Busoni's sixtieth birthday. In it, Weill praised him for envisioning a new future of music and foreshadowing its possibilities in what he considered to be his greatest work, *Doktor Faust*:

> Busoni sought the miraculous; his music had to free itself from the narrow limits of classical forms, from the narrow range of tonal bondage. So, he forged ahead on the arduous path transforming musical production in the first 2 decades of this century. . . . Faust, which unfortunately was not quite

[64] It is worth noting that Weill was not the only one using this term at the time. Karl Blossfeldt, for instance, published a collection of plant photographs under the title *Urformen der Kunst* in 1928. It is also prevalent in Goethe's writings. However, its application to music was unusual.

[65] He simultaneously studied counterpoint with Philipp Jarnach.

[66] The two composers were still corresponding in the 1950s.

[67] Weill, quoted in Kim H. Kowalke, *Kurt Weill in Europe*, Studies in Musicology 14 (Ann Arbor, MI: UMI Press, 1979), 24. Kowalke, quoted in Hans Heinz Stuckenschmidt, *Ferruccio Busoni: Chronicle of a European*, trans. Sandra Morris (New York: St. Martin's Press, 1970). Stuckenschmidt does not indicate a source for the quote.

> completed, represents the most perfect expression of all the life and art views of the Master; it can be considered in every respect as the basis for a further development of the musical stage work.[68]

Upon Busoni's death, Weill eulogized "that with him one of the greatest artistic personalities of all time has passed."[69] At the same time, he surmised that the lasting value of his compositions would be finally recognized once people heard his *Doktor Faust*.[70] He also described him as forging a "new, future-oriented art, so every expression of man's life was designed to build a bridge between the greatest personalities of earlier times and the ideal of humanity that we are striving to achieve."[71] Moreover, he stated that he considered Busoni to be a main musical leader in Europe: "All of the recent stylistic changes were initiated or at least announced by him."[72] Weill specifically cited his ability to bring together all the stylistic experiments of the past decade into new forms as being one of his greatest innovations.[73] He also remembered him talking about architectural structure.[74]

[68] [Busoni süchte das Wunderbare; seine Musik müsste sich befreien aus den engen Grenzen klassischer Formen, aus dem schmalen Bereich tonaler Gebundenheit. So ging er stets voran auf dem beschwerlichen Wege, den die musikalische Produktion in den ersten 2 Jahrzehnten dieses Jahrhunderts zurückleite. . . . Dieser *Faust*, der leider nicht ganz vollendet wurde, stellt den vollkommensten Ausdruck aller Lebens- und Kunstanschauungen des Meisters dar; er kann in jeder Beziehung als Grundlage einer weiteren Entwicklung des musikalischen Bühnenwerken gelten.] Weill, "Ferruccio Busoni zu seinem 60. Geburtstage am 1 April [1926]," in *Musik und musikalisches Theater: Gesammelte Schriften*, ed. Stephen Hinton, Jürgen Schebera, and Elmar Juchem (Mainz: Schott, 2000), 216–17.

[69] [Dass mit ihm eine der grössten Kunstlerpersönlichkeiten aller Zeiten dahingegangen ist. Er gehörte zu jenen reinsten Gestalten, die es durch die Grosse ihrer Gesinnung so unendlich schwer hätten, deren entmaterialisiertes, erdenernes Künstlertum dem geschäftlichen Wesen ihrer Umgebung fremd und feindlich gegenüberstand.] Weill, "Todestage Bachs und Busonis [1925]," in *Musik und musikalisches Theater: Gesammelte Schriften*, 196–97.

[70] Weill, "Busoni: Zu seinen einjährigen Todestage," in *Musik und musikalisches Theater: Gesammelte Schriften*, 20.

[71] [wie sein Werk aus der bedeutendsten musikalischen Produktion der Vergangenheit den Weg zu neuer, zukunftsträchtiger Kunst fand, so war jede Lebensäusserung dieses Mannes dazu angetan, die Brücke zu schlagen zwischen den grössten Persönlichkeiten früherer Zeiten und dem Menschheitsideal, das wir erreichen bemüht sind.] Weill, "Busoni: Zu seinen einjährigen Todestage," 21.

[72] Erst jetzt, da wir ihn vermissen, wird uns klar, wie stark Busonis Einfluss gerade in diesen letzten Jahren geworden war. Ohne äusserlich mit irgendwelchen Machtvollkommenheiten ausgestattet zu sein, war er doch unsichtbarer Führer im europäischen Musikleben geworden. . . . Alle stilistischen Veränderungen der jüngsten Zeit waren durch ihn veranlasst oder doch verkündet worden. Weill, "Busoni: Zu seinen einjährigen Todestage," 21.

[73] [konnte er zu einer Zeit des allgemeinen Tumultes die Forderung nach einer Synthese aller Stilgattungen der letzten Jahrzehnte.] "Busoni und die neue Musik," in *Musik und musikalisches Theater: Gesammelte Schriften*, 27. This article was originally published in *Der neue Weg: Amtliche Zeitung der Genossenschaft Deutscher Bühnenangehöriger* in Berlin (November 1925).

[74] "Busoni himself has given sufficient information about the architecture of the work." [Über die Architektur des Werkes hat sich Busoni selbst ausführlich genug geäußert.] Weill, "Busonis *Faust* und die Erneuerung der Opernform," in *Musik und musikalisches Theater: Gesammelte Schriften*, 41. This essay was originally published in the *Oper Jahrbuch* in Vienna in 1927.

Busoni's later operas became important formal models for Weill's montage structures, especially *Doktor Faust*.[75] *Arlecchino*, which Busoni's master class pupils saw performed in Berlin, Hamburg, Dresden, and Weimar, also became a significant model. Weill claimed that "without his *Arlequino* [*sic*], an opera in which the principal actor was not a singer, but an actor, there might have been no music for *Johnny Johnson, Mahagony* [*sic*]."[76] Stephen Hinton furthermore notes similarities between Busoni's *Arlecchino* and Weill's *Der Protagonist* in terms of texture, tone, and overall melodic contour.[77]

Busoni's influence on Weill impacted his adoption of a montage structural approach and his experimentation with the spatialization of instrumental forces.[78] His first major composition after joining the Berlin composition master class was a symphony (1921). In terms of form, it displayed Busoni's penchant for multi-sectionality, much like Vogel's early master class compositions. It was also a major departure from his pre-Busoni works in its polyphonic layering of the material; it contrasts distinctly with the Sonata for Cello and Piano from 1920, which featured long and continuous movements in more consistent and homophonic textures even despite some topical stylistic juxtapositions (see figure 5.7).

Weill's sectional approach to form is also evident in his String Quartet, op. 8 (1923), which premiered on June 24, 1923, at the Frankfurt Kammermusikwoche and then was performed again on Jan 22, 1924 with the Novembergruppe.[79] Although originally drafted in a more traditional four-movement structure, Weill finally settled on three movements, in which the first two are condensed uneasily into a single movement: "Introduction." The final movement, a *Choralphantasie*, pays homage to Bach in its counterpoint, but with a metatonal treatment of the language in the manner of Busoni, and is structurally divided into several contrasting styles and sections.[80]

[75] Weill, "Busoni and Modern Music," in Kowalke, *Kurt Weill in Europe*, 462–63.

[76] Stephen Hinton, *Musical Theater: Stages of Reform* (Berkeley: University of California Press, 2012), 64.

[77] Hinton, *Musical Theater*, 64.

[78] Busoni had Weill study counterpoint with Philipp Jarnach to improve his skills in that area. As a pedagogue, Busoni focused primarily on aesthetic ideals. See Knyt, *Ferruccio Busoni and His Legacy*.

[79] As one of Weill's finest early pieces, Busoni championed it with Universal Edition, leading to its eventual publication.

[80] Like Busoni, Weill held Bach and Mozart as his main historical music examples. Weill's student pieces thus also displayed more Baroque allusions. *Sinfonia Sacra* (1922), for instance, contains a fugue and a passacaglia, as well as a chorale fantasy. They also displayed Mozartian clarity and concision beginning with *Die Zaubernacht* (1922), for which Mozart was an important model. *Der Protagonist* (1925) is a fascinating blend of Bachian and Mozartian ideals with its onstage wind octet and an idiosyncratic orchestra with two oboes, bass clarinets, three horns and trombones, percussion, and strings.

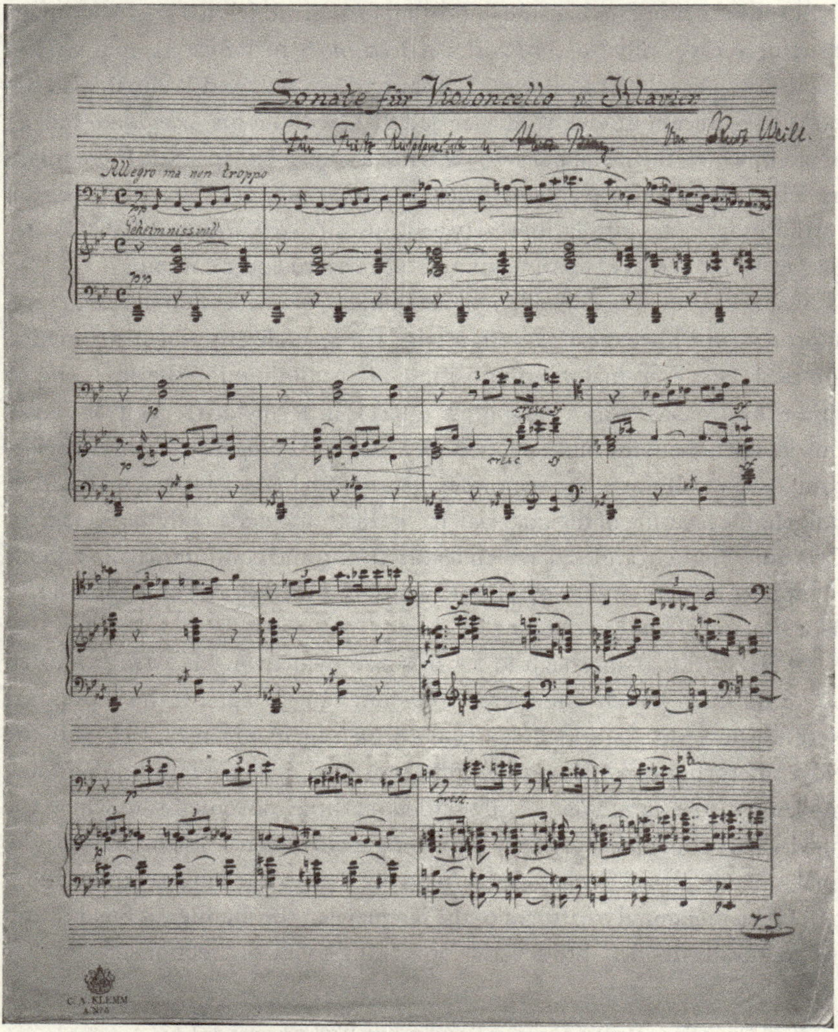

Figure 5.7. Weill, Sonata for Cello and Piano (1920), mvmt. 1, p. 1. Papers of Kurt Weill and Lotte Lenya, Mss. 30_s01F_b036_f0545. The Papers of Kurt Weill and Lotte Lenya in the Irving S. Gilmore Music Library of Yale University. Copyright by the Kurt Weill Foundation for Music, New York. All rights reserved. Used with permission. The dedication and attribution are in Weill's hand. Everything else was notated by a copyist.

Weill's theatrical music also pioneered a montage structural approach.[81] As Kim Kowalke notes, Weill's concept of the *Urform* was modeled after his perception of Busoni's formal solutions that united contrasting styles and textures that varied in relation to the subject matter—especially in his final opera, *Doktor Faust*:

> Weill made such high claims for Busoni's final opera because it exhibited an ideal union of idea and form and a perfect fusion of musical and theatrical impulse; in it Weill found a solution to the problem of formal organization: The formal idea—just as the melodic or harmonic—is subject to no other laws than that of the total idea, that of the intellectual material. This material creates the stimulus for formal construction in the first place. The symphonic idea must find itself completely fulfilled in the form of the symphony.[82]

Weill believed Faust's complicated and conflicted mind was aptly represented by multiple voices in Busoni's polyphonic forms.[83] At the same time, the structure was a montage of sound; it featured diverse and distinct sections:

> Busoni has amply expressed himself concerning the architecture of the work. What in *Arlecchino* was still a musically determined arrangement of separate numbers with linking dialogue is in *Doktor Faust* now an arrangement of compact forms of greatly expanded format, generated from the plot, whereby the recitatives are drawn into the musical progressions either as contrast or as transition.[84]

[81] It is not a surprise that architects appreciated Weill's montage structures. Le Corbusier, for instance, expressed pleasure at hearing his music. Le Corbusier, letter of December 13, 1932, to Weill, Papers of Kurt Weill and Lotte Lenya, Yale University, Special Collections, Mss_30_s04B_b048_f0044.

[82] Kowalke, *Kurt Weill in Europe*, 100.

[83] Weill, "Busoni's *Faust* and the Renewal of Operatic Form," quoted in Kowalke, *Kurt Weill in Europe*, 469–70. Originally published as "Busonis *Faust* und die Erneuerung der Opernform," *Jahrbuch Oper* (Vienna: Universal Edition, 1926), 53–56. Reprinted as "Das Problem der neuen Oper," *Vossische Zeitung* (January 22, 1927).

[84] Weill, quoted in Kowalke, *Kurt Weill in Europe*, 470. Weill's concept of structure manifested itself in several different ways, practically speaking, and evolved throughout his career. For detailed analyses of this evolution, see Stephen Hinton, *Weill's Musical Theater.* In particular, Weill's notion of an *Urform* resembles Busoni's own vision of a primordial source of music (*Urmusik*), in that it is all-encompassing, containing all styles of music, and can have many formal manifestations in relation to the subject. For more about this topic, see Knyt, "Approaching the Essence of Music," and "Ferruccio Busoni and the Absolute in Music: Nature, Form, and *Idee*," *Journal of the Royal Musical Association* 137:1 (May 2012): 35–69. He first used the term in relation to *Die Dreigroschenoper*, when he stated, "What we were aiming to create was the *Urform* of opera," yet the concept existed prior to the piece and extended to his American musicals, when he preferred to use other terms, such as

Table 5.1. Selected Theatrical or Operatic Works by Weill

Der Protagonist: Opera in one through composed act and two scenes (a comedy and a tragedy) in pantomime
Royal Palace: Opera in one act with ballet and film
Na und?: Comic opera in two acts
Mahagonny-Songspiel: Song-play in three parts
Der Zar lässt sich photographieren: Opera buffa in one act
Die Dreigroschenoper: Play with music in three acts
Happy End: Comedy with music in three acts
Aufstieg und Fall der Stadt Mahagonny: Epic opera in three acts with twenty-one closed sections
Der Jasager: Schuloper in two acts
Die Bürgschaft: Opera in three acts with a Vorspiel
Der Silbersee: Winter's tale with music in three acts
Die sieben Todsünden: Ballet with singing in seven sections
Marie galante: Play with music in two acts
A Kingdom for a Cow: Operetta in two acts

Weill's structures are usually built out of short contrasting sections and varied textures, like Busoni's, and this is often aided by genre mixture. According to Hinton, "Mozart's work mediated through Busoni inspired Weill to invent a whole series of new mixed genres,"[85] and these inspired some of Weill's creative structural approaches. Accordingly, he explored different montage structures in all his dramatic works that ranged from grouping together various dance, instrumental, and operatic forms to mime, ballet, and different genres of opera (see table 5.1).

In his mixed genre compositions, Weill juxtaposed contrasting formal elements in conspicuous ways. A mixture of opera and ballet contribute to the montage effect in *Die Zaubernacht* (1922). It brings together pantomime, dancing, and singing, as well as simple forms, such as a gavotte, a waltz, a can-can, a march, and a lied.[86] The structure consists of short numbers (mainly dances and songs) that are juxtaposed musically but linked together

"form-problems." Hinton, *Weill's Musical Theater*, 46. In the 1930s he also used the term in relation to his aspirations for a future film opera.

[85] Hinton, *Weill's Musical Theater*, 451.

[86] Weill's chamber orchestral scoring (recently rediscovered at Yale University in 2005) features string quartet, flute, bassoon, harp, piano, and percussion.

idealistically by the common idea of a nighttime fantasy in which a fairy brings toys to life.

Der Protagonist (1925), a play within a play, features a similar formal montage as well as a spatial placement of instruments. This blending of the spatial and the temporal is amply evident in the nearly through-composed single-act opera that is nevertheless punctuated by two long orchestral interludes and two theatrical pantomimes, one comic and one tragic. Set in Shakespearean England, a troupe of actors rehearsing before the Duke and his guests provides a play in mime, thereby eliminating language barriers, because some guests are foreigners. The overall framework features expressive late romantic operatic styles that accompany the main plot, while the rehearsals for the interior plays are in pantomime and in a contrasting Neoclassical style. The first pantomime, for instance, contains a repeated ground bass in the bassoon with rhythmically free writing that is followed by parallel fourths. This contrasts with the more expressive writing of the operatic sections. This montage of styles accentuates the unique structure that stems from a basic plot in which there are intersections between reality and the stage world. Symbolic of this mixture is the double role of some of the instrumentalists, as both part of the pit orchestra and the octet accompanying the pantomimes. The spatial movement between ensembles aurally embodies the fusion of the real and the imagined.

Die Dreigroschenoper (1928), by contrast, shares its basic structure with opera seria—featuring six main characters with few ensemble numbers, and three acts. Yet it contains spoken dialogue like a play, as well as instrumental interludes that are more common in operettas. Weill simultaneously described the structure as "a piece with music in one Vorspiel and eight Bildern," thus suggesting the superposition of two basic structural ideas.[87] As a parody of the 1728 *Beggar's Opera* by John Gay, the opera overture is a blend of Handelian polyphony and more contemporary writing. Its form resembles a typical opening Baroque French overture with three sections and polyphonic writing in the center, yet with harmonies and timbres of Weill's era. But the work also juxtaposes aspects of theater, film, cabaret, and comic opera in relation to the plot. Some individual movements are based on contemporary and colloquial dance types, such as the tango, foxtrot, waltz, and march. Others are composed in a religious chorale style or display influence of blues.

[87] Weill, *Die Dreigroschenoper* (Vienna: Universal Edition, 1928), 2.

An assemblage approach is also evident within movements. Weill often relied on song form (verse and refrain), rather than da capo arias, a reference to the subject of everyday people, but he disrupts the regularity of the structure with timbral, textural, and stylistic differences. The overall form results from a montage of distinct textures. For instance, the strophic "Anstatt dass" mixes French overture, ragtime, and march styles, and these juxtapositions disrupt the normal regularity of the structure. Diverse timbres and instrumental colors reinforce the structural sections. The ideas in the plot support these textural differences. Each strophe begins with dotted notes initially played by the trumpet and trombone, and then by the saxophone during the second strophe, in a manner reminiscent of French overtures (see example 5.2).

The plot supports this French overture style, as a self-righteous and pompous ("kingly") Mr. Peachum is trying to assert his authority over his daughter, Polly. By contrast, the second part of each strophe switches to march form with regular rhythmic pulsations in the piano and banjo. Offbeat interruptions in the vocal and piano part provide a syncopated ragtime feel as Mrs. Peachum sings a romantic entreaty where she talks about the moon and love, phrases that Polly later alludes to in her Liebeslied duet with Macheath. She is finally joined by Mr. Peachum in the final part of the second strophe.[88]

Sectional forms also appear in Weill's other cross-genre pieces, in particular, film operas and radio operas. An early example is *Der Lindberghflug* (1929), a radio cantata devised by Brecht and Weill for the Frankfurt Radio Stations, in which the noise of propellers, the murmur of ocean waves, and the sounds of the crowd, were projected by the radio.[89] Comprising fifteen short tableaux, the many sections reflect the dramatic action. The "Fog" movement, for instance, is a three-part invention, in which polyphony leads to an ostinato, thereby suggesting both density and continuity of the clouds, while "Sleep" is a hypnotic lullaby.

If Weill was indebted to Busoni for models of montage forms, he also adopted his interest in spatialized instrument ensembles. Weill was particularly interested in juxtaposing visual and aural aspects in abstract film. His vision of film music also included multilingualism, unusual instrument

[88] Changes in orchestration from brass to saxophone and small ensemble to full ensemble offer a change of color, texture, and meaning.

[89] There is a version in which about half of the pieces are composed by Paul Hindemith and a version in which the piece is entirely composed by Weill. I am referring here to the version authored solely by Weill.

Example 5.2. Weill, "Anstatt-Dass," *Die Dreigroschenoper*, mm. 1–5.

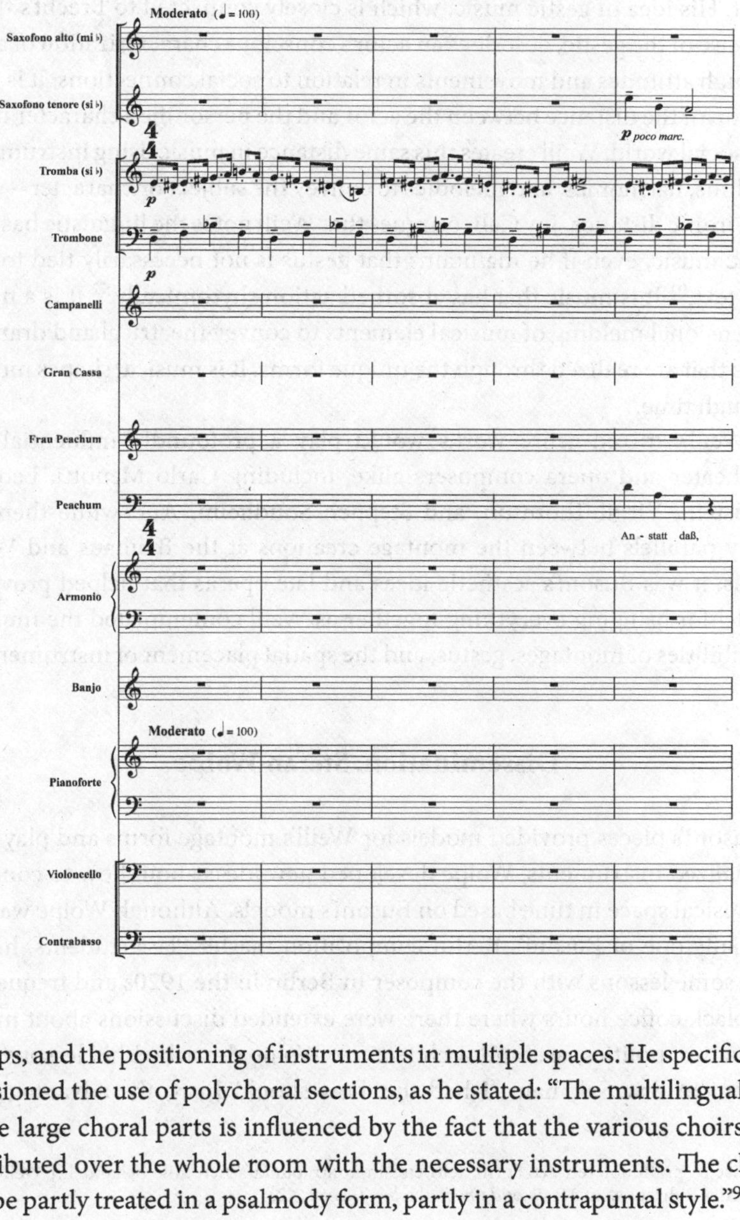

groups, and the positioning of instruments in multiple spaces. He specifically envisioned the use of polychoral sections, as he stated: "The multilingualism of the large choral parts is influenced by the fact that the various choirs are distributed over the whole room with the necessary instruments. The choir will be partly treated in a psalmody form, partly in a contrapuntal style."[90]

90 [Die Mehrchörigkeit der grossen Chorpartien wird dadurch gestützt, dass die verschiedene Chöre mit dazugehörigen Instrumenten über den ganzen Raum verteilt werden. Die chöre werden

In addition, Weill's conception of form was based on theories about movement. His idea of gestic music, which is closely connected to Brecht's theatrical use of the gestic, describes an actor's conscious characterization of a role through attitudes and movements in relation to social connections. It is a depiction of the distance between the actor and the personified character in the real social world. Weill creates this same distance in music using instruments, rhythms, harmonies, and melodies to convey the subject or character—often with ironic distance. Joy Calico argues that Weill notes the linguistic basis for gestic music, even if he maintains that gestus is not necessarily tied to specific text.[91] It is music that has absorbed action rhythmically.[92] It is a multidimensional melding of musical elements to convey theatrical and dramatic ideas that are realized through the unique forms. It is musical shapes moving through time.

Weill's mixed-genre works would play a profoundly influential role on theater and opera composers alike, including Carlo Menotti, Leonard Bernstein, Virgil Thomson, and Stephen Sondheim. And while there are many parallels between the montage creations at the Bauhaus and Weill's forms, it was Busoni's aesthetic ideas and late operas that helped provide a model for bringing everything together as Weill contemplated the multiple possibilities of montages, gestus, and the spatial placement of instruments.[93]

Dissemination: Stefan Wolpe

If Busoni's pieces provided models for Weill's montage forms and play with spatialized instruments, Wolpe developed new ideas about how to conceive of musical space in time based on Busoni's models. Although Wolpe was not officially one of Busoni's Berlin composition master class students, he did take some lessons with the composer in Berlin in the 1920s and frequented his black coffee hours where there were extended discussions about music, aesthetics, politics, art, and architecture. Wolpe described his lessons with Busoni to Eric Salzman: "I had the, how should I say, the advantage, no,

teilweise in psalmodieren der Form, teilweise in kontrapunktischen Stile behandelt.] Weill, "Zur Musik des Ruhrepos," in *Musik und musikalisches Theater*, 42.

91 Joy Calico, *Brecht at the Opera* (Berkeley: University of California Press, 2008), 50–51.

92 Weill, "Über den gestischen Charakter der Musik," *Die Musik* 21 (March 1929): 419–23.

93 The Kurt-Weill-Zentrum, founded in 1993, is located in the Lyonel Feininger house in Dessau, an abode designed by Gropius, and a commemoration of the Bauhaus in all its glory and creativity.

the pleasure, no, it's more than pleasure—I studied with Busoni a couple of times. I was invited to his sessions, and he gave me plenty of criticisms, and he supported me in many ways."[94] Yet if the lessons were few, the influence was long-lasting. Bernard Benoliel remembers that Wolpe, who notoriously struggled to find value in more traditional instruction in music at the Berlin Hochschule, appreciated his lessons with Busoni, stating that he said: "I saw Busoni six times for composition lessons over a period of a year and a half. And he added, 'I remember every word.' That's the quote that sticks in my mind. Another time he mentioned to me how important the aesthetics of composition were to Busoni."[95] Hilda Wolpe, who married Stefan Wolpe in 1952, remembers Wolpe explaining that Busoni was more than a mentor, and something of a father figure, who fed and clothed him when he was needy. In addition, he invited him to sit in his own box during a performance of *Arlecchino*.[96]

Wolpe talked frequently about Busoni to his students and colleagues for decades after his studies with him, thereby indicating the extent of influence. Irma Wolpe Rademacher, who was married to Stefan Wolpe from 1935 to 1949, recalls his admiration for Busoni:[97]

> All I heard about Busoni was that he adored him. He just had no words when he thought about Busoni, about the greatness of Busoni as a pianist. As a composer he asked Busoni for advice, and Busoni said, take the *Marriage of Figaro* or *Don Giovanni* and try to re-orchestrate a few measures, and then you learn from it.[98]

Milton Babbitt also remembers that Wolpe talked incessantly about Busoni and the spatial aspects of music:

> That is the piece [Composition for Tenor and Six Instruments] with which I can remember the most discussion about the organization—spatial

[94] Stefan Wolpe, "Conversation with Eric Salzman," *Musical Quarterly* 83:3 (Autumn 1999): 378–412.

[95] Bernard Benoliel, remembrances of Stefan Wolpe, in *Recollections of Stefan Wolpe by Former Students and Friends*, ed. Austin Clarkson https://sites.evergreen.edu/arunchandra/wp-content/uploads/sites/395/2020/08/wolpeRecollections.pdf (accessed June 15, 2019).

[96] Hilda Wolpe, remembrances of Stefan Wolpe, in *Recollections of Stefan Wolpe by Former Students and Friends*. Hilda Wolpe was Wolpe's third wife.

[97] She was Wolpe's second wife.

[98] Irma Rademacher Wolpe, remembrances of Stefan Wolpe, in *Recollections of Stefan Wolpe by Former Students and Friends*.

> organization, division of the musical space, as well as musical time, and possible analogies between the two. . . . He said something much vaguer about the unity of musical space, and this had really nothing very much to do with some notion about whatever goes up may go sideways, or something such as that. It was rather that the whole problem of how to make identifications between that which is defined linearly and that which is defined vertically. Wolpe said you must read Busoni's book on new music.[99]

Morton Feldman, similarly, remembers that Wolpe spoke about both Busoni and musical shape: "He felt that Busoni somehow was the beginning of an alternative way of making music. Some of the neo-classical aspects of Busoni meant something to Stefan in terms of the structuring of music. I know that he spoke very fondly about Busoni."[100]

Austin Clarkson and Tamara Levitz have already documented that Wolpe was also closely affiliated with members of the Busoni circle, including Vogel and Varèse.[101] Wolpe and Vogel maintained a friendship that lasted for decades. In the mid-1920s, they collaborated on pieces together in the Novembergruppe. Both were experimenting with new rhythmic principles at that time. In particular, Wolpe was pioneering *Stehende Musik*, in which rhythmic forms are foregrounded over thematic ones.[102] Clarkson has also considered similarities between Wolpe's approach and that of Varèse, who studied with Busoni in Berlin in the 1910s.[103] As he notes, one of the greatest similarities between them is a spatialized approach to sound, even if the two went about it in very different ways. Moreover, like Weill, Wolpe's structural approach is one of montage, with different stylistic and textural sections juxtaposed next to each other.[104]

99 Milton Babbitt, remembrances of Stefan Wolpe, in *Recollections of Stefan Wolpe by Former Students and Friends*.

100 Morton Feldman, remembrances of Stefan Wolpe, in *Recollections of Stefan Wolpe by Former Students and Friends*.

101 See Tamara Levitz, "The Would-Be Master-Student: Stefan Wolpe and Ferruccio Busoni," in *On the Music of Stefan Wolpe: Essays and Recollections*, ed. Austin Clarkson (Hillsdale, NY: Pendragon Press, 2003), 31–40; Austin Clarkson, "Wolpe, Varèse and the Busoni Effect," *Contemporary Music Review* 27:2/3 (April/June 2008): 361–81.

102 Levitz, "The Would-Be Master-Student," 31–40.

103 Clarkson, "Wolpe, Varèse and the Busoni Effect," 361–81.

104 Wolpe also wrote a strong letter of recommendation for one of his close pupils, Joe Livingston, to Otto Luening, who was yet another Busoni pupil. Wolpe, letter of November 28, 1955 to Otto Luening, Wolpe Collection, Paul Sacher Foundation, Basel. He also mentioned Eduard Steuermann in a letter without date to Josef Marx. Wolpe Collection, Paul Sacher Foundation, Basel. Letters between Wolpe and Varèse that extend to the 1960s indicate that Wolpe admired Varèse and looked to him to help establish connections, including for his Guggenheim applications and to speak at

Wolpe was active in the Busoni circle beginning in 1921, and he was also part of the Novembergruppe and the Berlin International Composer Guild, where he met Varèse as early as 1922.[105] As part of the Busoni circle, he attended performances of *Arlecchino* and other Busoni concerts. Wolpe also visited the 1923 Bauhaus exhibition with Weill, Vogel, Hirsch, and Busoni, and the Bauhaus experience was transformative for him, helping him understand how to realize his abstract ideas in tangible ways. Yet unlike the other figures considered in this chapter, it was not Busoni who introduced Wolpe to the Bauhaus.[106] Nevertheless, it was Busoni who showed him how to apply the Bauhaus ideas more fully to his compositions.

Wolpe's exposure to the Bauhaus predated his time with Busoni (he made his first trip there in 1919) and it extended beyond Busoni's life too. As Brigid Cohen has documented, he lived with Bauhaus students in 1921 and he participated in the preliminary course taught by Johannes Itten as an unofficial student as early as 1920.[107] His diary also indicates that he went back to the Bauhaus in 1924 as well.[108] Wolpe developed a close friendship with several of the instructors at the Bauhaus, including Lyonel Feininger, Paul Klee, Oskar Schlemmer, Johannes Itten, and László Moholy-Nagy. This is not to mention that his first wife, the painter Ola Okuniewska (married in 1927), was also a student at the Bauhaus. Irma Wolpe Rademacher, Wolpe's second wife, recalls: "[Stefan] went to the Bauhaus in search of his ideal. They were searching there for the essence, for the pure form, and at the same time, the perfectly functional. He was a great young friend of Klee, and he accompanied Klee when he played violin."[109] Wolpe also created some paintings and drawings while at the Bauhaus, and was heavily influenced by

Darmstadt. See especially Wolpe, letter of October 18, 1952, to Varèse, and Wolpe, letter of September 15, 1955, to Varèse, Varèse Collection, Paul Sacher Foundation, Basel.

[105] For more about Novembergruppe members, see Nils Grosch, *Die Musik der neuen Sachlichkeit* (Stuttgart: J. B. Metzler, 1999).

[106] Another Busoni pupil, Gisella Selden-Goth, was also involved with the Bauhaus as early as 1919.

[107] See Johannes Itten, "Material and Texture," in *Design and Form: The Basic Course at the Bauhaus* (New York: Reinhold Publishing Corporation, 1964), 45–46. The dates of Wolpe's Bauhaus attendance can be gleaned from his diaries and letters. For instance, he noted that he was there in October 1922. Wolpe, Diary I, Wolpe Collection, Paul Sacher Foundation, Basel, 8.

[108] Brigid Cohen, *Stefan Wolpe and the Avant-Garde Diaspora* (New York: Oxford University Press, 2012), 76. Lyonel Feininger sent Wolpe a letter as late as 1940, thereby showing lengthy connections with instructors at the Bauhaus: Feininger, letter of November 15, 1940, to Wolpe, Wolpe Collection, Paul Sacher Foundation, Basel.

[109] Irma Rademacher Wolpe, remembrances of Stefan Wolpe, in *Recollections of Stefan Wolpe by Former Students and Friends*.

visual artists.[110] Itten was one such influence, and he famously emphasized the wholeness of mind and body, leading students not only in texture studies, but also movement exercises.[111] He also considered correspondences between colors and musical intervals that he had developed together with Josef Matthias Hauer. Wolpe remembers that Klee and Itten also taught about texture and formal montage by encouraging students to collect everyday objects from the streets, trash bins, and drawers to combine into unified works of art that displayed proportion and balance.[112] They were taught to disregard the subjective meanings or purposes of the objects and to consider them instead from more structural mindsets.[113] Wolpe also learned about proportions in space from Schlemmer. Clarkson claims that Wolpe would listen intently to discussions about visual space, eventually transposing them into musical space.[114]

Wolpe's music changed considerably after studying with Busoni and attending classes at the Bauhaus, as evident by a freer play with form and more emphasis on timbre, register, and space. Of the pieces that survive from Wolpe's pre-Busoni years (he destroyed much of what he wrote, except for sixteen pieces from 1920), the music is already mainly bitonal, bimodal, or freely atonal with some quartal chords.[115] The *Fünf Gesänge auf Hölderlin* (1924), of which no. 2 is dedicated to the memory of Busoni, represent one of Wolpe's early attempts to create montage forms. No. 3, "Diotima," for instance, juxtaposes chorale-like and agitated styles of music. However, the most dramatic departures from what came before can be observed beginning in Wolpe's Piano Sonata no. 1 ("Stehende Musik," 1925), which expanded the timbral and spatial possibilities of the piano. As Clarkson describes, it features "constellatory pitch space organized by intervallic proportions."[116]

110 Mordecai Ardon, remembrances of Stefan Wolpe, in *Recollections of Stefan Wolpe by Former Students and Friends*.

111 See Rolf Bothe, Peter Hahn, and Hans Christoph von Tavel, eds., *Das frühe Bauhaus und Johannes Itten* (Stuttgart: Hatje Cantz Verlag, 1994).

112 For descriptions of Paul Klee's montage puppets, see Paul Klee, *Hand Puppets* (Ostfildern, Germany: Hatje Cantz, 2006). For more about his organicist aesthetics, see Ernst-Gerhard Guse, ed., *Wachstum regt sich: Klees Zwiesprache mit der Natur* (Munich: Prestel-Verlag, 1990).

113 See Stefan Wolpe, "Lecture on Dada," *Musical Quarterly* 72:2 (January 1986), 205. The original German can be found here: Thomas Phelps, *Die Ganze ist überall: Vorträge über Musik, 1940–1962* (Basel: Paul Sacher Stiftung, 2011), 150–64.

114 Clarkson, "Stefan Wolpe and Abstract Expressionism," in *The New York Schools of Music and Visual Arts*, ed. Steven Johnson (New York: Routledge, 2001), 78.

115 See the following source for an analysis of short piece by Wolpe from 1924 that was found in a guestbook of Lily Klee: Thomas Gartmann, "Stefan Wolpe und das Weimarer Bauhaus: Ein Gästebucheintrag als Dokument der Wendezeit," *Zwitschermachine* 8 (2020): 70–77.

116 Wolpe's *Stehende Musik* (1925) expanded the timbral possibilities of the piano and pioneered a spatial approach to pitch relationships based on intervallic proportions in space.

Yet this description captures only part of the spatial effect. While thematic material fades into the background, especially in the first and third movements, rhythm and register play a fundamental role as well. In the first and third movements, for instance, Wolpe creates a dramatic contrast of register on the piano with motoric toccata-like chords, thereby creating very physical soundscapes with senses of height, depth, and textural contour. In the opening of the first movement, for instance, the first three bars present dense rhythmic-thematic chordal material in low bass registers. The highest pitch being the D below middle C, and the lowest, a C just over two octaves lower. After a measure of silence punctuating the movement, a shift in register in measure 5 is shocking, as the right-hand chord rises into the treble clef (the highest pitch is G♭ above middle C) even while the left hand rises onto the bass clef staff for three bars. Ensuing middle-staff material in perpetual sixteenth-note motion beginning in bar eight presents yet another registral (and textural) contrast, with single notes, before it gradually descends back into the bass regions, where it resides beginning in measure 12, varied mainly by accents and dynamic coloristic means. Starting in measure 25, Wolpe contrasts the static middle register material with chords in contrasting registers (high and low) as well as contrasting dynamic levels. The shifts in color and register add dynamic appeal to otherwise harmonically static material. In the extended second movement, by contrast, Wolpe explores delicately unfolding linear counterpoint coupled with Mozartian textures and rhythmic variety in a Busonian manner and with many stylistic juxtapositions—yet with added emphasis on register and space, as lines move in contrary motion, thereby emphasizing the distance between them.

Claude Ballif, who met Wolpe at Darmstadt, which he attended from 1956 to 1959, described Wolpe's spatialized approach, noting his interest in register to create a sense of distance and expansiveness. He also seemed to connect the conversation about musical space to Busoni, by mentioning Wolpe's interest in Busoni and new music in the same paragraph:

> It was really interesting for me, because before Xenakis, Wolpe was very concerned with this idea of register and pitch. He explained to me his idea of taking in the middle a pitch, and after, two, four, five [pitches], and so on, like a tree. . . . Wolpe said you must read Busoni's book on new music.[117]

[117] Claude Ballif, remembrances of Stefan Wolpe, in *Recollections of Stefan Wolpe by Former Students and Friends*.

Harvey Sollberger likewise remembers that Wolpe spoke frequently about music in spatial and almost physical terms—as pitches in relation to one another in space, like constellations in the sky or various objects in a room. Their proportions and relations to each other in space were what interested Wolpe.[118]

Wolpe communicated his idiosyncratic ideas about space to his acquaintances and students. In a particularly detailed letter of August 19, 1955, to Thomas Nee, Wolpe discussed spatial levels or planes of voices and their relationships to each other. He urged Nee to write with greater variety and density, with greater "formal depth," and to establish more "elasticity" between the levels of the voices.[119]

Wolpe's interest in spatial aspects of music that begin in the 1920s persisted to later in his career even as they continued to evolve. Wolpe also detailed his notions of space in numerous essays, personal notebooks, and other documents. For instance, in his notebook on space ("Raum"), he left the following notes:

> To speak about space, to sense as existence presupposes: Distance, volume, frequency, evolution, envelopment, complete, fixity, gravity, point of departure, completion tendencies, dimension, depth, volume, matters of organization . . . the establishment of that tangible recurring proportion, set up of planes, as set up of a field of predictable reactions.[120]

Like Weill, Wolpe also described music in space as constantly moving: "The unconditional nature of music involves movement. Movement of the intervals and of 'form-contrasts.'"[121] He wrote about music as discontinuous, collapsing, and coalescing. For Wolpe, each tone happens in space and divides the space into planes, thereby creating tonal-spatial relationships.[122] He describes multi-dimensional space as an infinity that is constantly divided by through antithesis.[123]

118 Harvey Sollberger, remembrances of Stefan Wolpe, in *Recollections of Stefan Wolpe by Former Students and Friends*.

119 Wolpe, letter of August 19, 1955, to Thomas Nee, Stefan Wolpe Papers, Paul Sacher Foundation, Basel.

120 Wolpe, Notebook on Raum, Stefan Wolpe Papers, Paul Sacher Foundation, Basel. A complete essay on the topic can be found in Phelps, *Das Ganze*, 54–74.

121 Wolpe, Diary II: 1928–1930, 375, Wolpe Collection, Paul Sacher Foundation, Basel.

122 Wolpe, "On Proportions," Wolpe Collection, Paul Sacher Foundation, Basel.

123 Wolpe, "On Proportions."

Wolpe's spatialized approach to music is amply evident in his *Seven Pieces for Three Pianos*, dedicated to Varèse, which he originally prepared as a music example to accompany a lecture about space that he gave at Yale University in 1951.[124] He later reworked the pieces into his more complex *Enactments for Three Pianos*, which he considered a turning point in his evolution as a composer:

> I really found myself when I started to work on my *Enactments for Three Pianos*, which announced and indicated a new world which was bound to be delivered. And the principle of simultaneity, or the principle of a kind of futuristic jumble/futuristic puzzle of events. I mean, interspaced, interspersed, interlaced, where the same material can live on a variety of levels simultaneously—on a syntactically high elaborate level, and at the same time on a syntactically rather crude and primitive level. . . . So that kind of idea, where the ideas live within a multi-dimensional space and behave that way, behave discontinuous, behave abrupt, behave collapsing, behave cohering, coalescing. That was a new experience to me.[125]

In *Enactments*, there are wide distances between the pitches—at one point more than six octaves' difference from the lowest to the highest pitches. Extreme and sudden dynamic contrasts also help evoke a sense of space. Yet the main play with space is in the way the pitches move in relation to each other. This can be observed more clearly in his preparatory work, the *Seven Pieces for Three Pianos*, where the notes are often widely spaced, sometimes more than one octave apart, even as the texture becomes gradually denser. In the first piece, "Calm," not only is there distance in sound between the three pianos, but there is also distance in register between the three parts. None of the pianos plays more than one pitch at a time, and the middle piano remains in the middle of the other two. At the same time, Wolpe gradually expands registers by moving up one octave higher every two measures at the beginning. Comparatively, the piece descends an octave every two measures beginning in measure 14. The dynamic levels increase with the register to create a sense of climax and release. In *Aggressive*, the second piece, Wolpe

[124] The transcript of the speech was lost in a fire in the Wolpe's home. For more information, see Clarkson, "Essays in Actionism: Wolpe's Pieces for Three Pianists," *Perspectives of New Music* 40:2 (Summer 2002): 115–33.

[125] Wolpe, interview with Eric Salzman. See also Wolpe, "Lecture on Dada," and Wolpe, "On Proportions," trans. Matthew Greenbaum, *Perspectives of New Music* 34:2 (Summer 1996): 132–84.

plays with spatial relationships between the pitches as they continually take turns with voicings. An upper note becomes the middle note and the lower becomes the upper pitch, for instance. In total, the pitches reach a span of over six octaves. In *Tired*, the layers fold around each other as they continually explore new relationship in acoustic space and in time.[126]

Wolpe's journey as a composer was an unconventional one. His training in the more traditional institutions such as the Berlin Hochschule did not offer him what he was searching for. As he would later admit in his "Lecture on Dada," his studies at the Bauhaus were an essential inspiration for his art in terms of its spatialization and the reconciling of seemingly disparate elements. Yet it was Busoni's voice that showed connections between these ideas and music, and it was of Busoni that Wolpe would speak most affectionately to the end of his life. Busoni's role was not only exposing his students to a wide array of influences, but also discussing aesthetic ideals that emphasized the spatial possibilities of sound and of formal organization. In addition, he showed them his own compositions, which displayed his efforts to spatialize sound and musical form. While the Bauhaus focused more exclusively on spatial and visual aspects related to visual and physical arts, such as painting, textiles, and architecture, Busoni spoke more of the same possibilities as they applied to music. Together, these influences helped foster spatialized and montage approaches in Busoni's mentees, however diverse the end results.

Dissemination: Egon Petri

Petri, who also accompanied Busoni to the Bauhaus, similarly followed in Busoni's example to reflect ideals of an objective, large-scale, and monumental architectural conception of form coupled with an enrichment of vertical dimensions in his arrangements. Although he had known Busoni from childhood, it was during Busoni's Weimar master class in 1900 that Petri decided to become a concert pianist. The relationship came full circle in 1923, when in Weimar, an ailing Busoni selected Petri to perform his pieces at the Bauhaus exhibition. Busoni's choice of Petri for such an important exhibition is understandable.[127] Harold Schonberg called Petri

[126] Wolpe, "Seven Pieces for Three Pianos," Wolpe Collection, Paul Sacher Foundation, Basel.

[127] Petri (1881–1962) played both violin and piano, but it was after Busoni's Weimar master class in 1900 that he chose the piano as his main instrument. He helped Busoni edit the collected Bach

Busoni's "best pupil," "who inherited his master's taste for the big pieces of the repertoire."[128] Alistair Londonderry likewise concluded: "From what one can tell from records and reminiscences, Busoni's style of playing was very similar to Petri's."[129] Another reviewer noted parallels in their interpretive approach: "With an astounding and monumental performance of Liszt's mammoth sonata in B minor, Egon Petri again established his right to be considered the rightful heir of his master, Busoni, as an interpreter of that composer's keyboard compositions."[130] Like Busoni, he created liquid architecture out of the music of others.[131] It is fitting that he was one of the first interpreters of Busoni's massive "skyscraper" piano concerto, and he actively promoted Busoni's compositions. Petri performed the concerto in Amsterdam with the Concertgebouworkest and Busoni conducting on October 25–26, 1905, and then again with the Berlin Philharmonic on March 10, 1908, with numerous performances thereafter.[132] In addition, his tone was powerful, like Busoni's even if Olin Downes saw this in a negative light, describing his rendition of Bach's *Italian Concerto* as "heavy-handed" and "hard surfaced."[133] The architectural implications are obvious, as Petri was not a fluid and light pianist, but rather, played with solid toned and focused on structure.

Like Busoni, Petri created the impression of blocks of sound differentiated by pedal and touch. He was also noted for his wide range of colors and dynamics. His pupil John Ogdon specifically remembers the variety of Petri's tone: "He had strong views on how to use the instrument to the greatest advantage, and every single movement was done to draw out

edition in during World War I, and helped Busoni edit proofs for publication. Busoni, for his part, promoted Petri. Petri earned a doctorate from Manchester University, and he also taught there from 1905 to 1911, before returning to Berlin and spending World War I in Zakopane. Beginning in 1921, he taught at the Hochschule in Berlin—as such, he was close to Busoni during the final years of his life. He was the resident pianist at Cornell University from 1940 to 1946 and at Mills College beginning in 1947. He also taught at the San Francisco Conservatory of Music from 1957 until his death in 1962. His students include Victor Borge, Gunnar Johansen, Earl Wild, and John Ogdon. The author of this book studied with two Petri pupils, including Lois Brandwynne and Julian White.

128 Schonberg, "Doktor Faustus at the Keyboard," in *The Great Pianists*, 349.

129 Alistair Londonderry, quoted in "Egon Petri," *Musical Times* 103:1433 (July 1962): 489.

130 N.S., "Egon Petri Gives Recital of Liszt," *New York Times* (February 16, 1936), N9.

131 Michaele Benedict, "The Legacy of Egon Petri," *Clavier* 36:9 (1997): 19. Unfortunately, Benedict does not provide a citation for the article.

132 Marc-André Roberge, "Le Concerto pour Piano, Orchestre et Choeur d'Hommes, Op. 39 (1904), de Ferruccio Busoni: Etude historique et analytique" (MA thesis, McGill University, 1981), 191–201.

133 Downes, "Second Recital by Egon Petri," *New York Times* (February 10, 1932), 27.

the greatest variety of tone colours from the piano. He, himself, was a superb pianist, with a unique, glowing tone which I still hear in my ears."[134] In his comments to his students, Petri confirmed that he, like Busoni, used the weight of the arm for his massive tone and thought of chords simultaneously as vertical dimension and part of horizontal forms and shapes: "Chords must be thought of vertically, but also horizontally and melodically."[135]

Petri's Bach transcriptions, such as of J. S. Bach's "Sheep May Safely Graze," from J. S. Bach's cantata "The Lively Hunt Is All My Heart's Desire" [Was mir behagt, ist nur die muntre Jagd], BWV 208, also display Busoni's influence. Like Busoni, Petri enriched the harmonies vertically. For instance, if the original continuo part had only single notes and no figured bass symbols, Petri supplied block chords. He also reinforced the musical structure of the piece by making the final cadence before the da capo return firmer by placing the tonic in the soprano voice. Petri also repeated the opening four bars of the piece at the end to form a more emphatic conclusion. Petri acknowledged his deep debt to Busoni: "The manner in which my taste and judgment were developed is due to him [Busoni]. . . . I learned to see music as a whole, in its broadest aspects of both forms and periods, together with its minutest details and various relationships."[136]

[134] John Ogdon, quoted in Carola Grindea, *Great Pianists and Pedagogies: In Conversation with Carola Grindea* (London: Kahn and Averill, 2007), 127.

[135] Robert Sheldon, *Petri-Liebermann Notes on the Art and Technique of Pianoforte Playing* (Columbia, MO: R. Sheldon, 1957), 7. Other Busoni pupils, including Theodore Szántò and Michael Zadora, likewise aimed for a rich and full sound on the piano in their individual transcriptions of the same Bach organ Prelude and Fugue in G Minor, BWV 535. Szántò, for instance, fills in the chords at the end of both the prelude and the fugue to create a richer and more dramatic conclusion. In sequential passages, he also avoids repetition by varying every other measure through registral displacement and by adding diminution in the left hand (rapid sixteenth notes instead of eighth notes). Numerous programs in the Rudolph Ganz Papers at the Newberry Library reveal that after he studied with Busoni, Ganz also began to favor large-scale masterworks and to create his own monumental programs. Many of Busoni's ideas about performance, interpretation, and music in general translated into an idiosyncratic and authoritarian manner of performing for Edward Steuermann as well; Steuermann's approach often vacillated between the more massive Busonian sound and the more driven and thinner Schoenbergian linear style, even if his characteristic sound featured many colors fueled by a luminous touch and the use of the pedal. Steuermann, who attended Busoni's master class in Basel in 1910 and then later privately in Berlin, cited Busoni's emphasis on structure and color as seminal for his interpretive style. In his sketches, he stated that *Klangfarbe* was the number one concern of the interpreter. Edward Steuermann, Sketches, Eduard and Clara Steuermann Collection, Library of Congress, Box 1, folder 17.

[136] Egon Petri and Friede F. Rohe, "How Ferruccio Busoni Taught: An Interview with the Distinguished Dutch Pianist," *Etude* 58 (October 1940): 657. For more about Petri's technique, see Egon Petri, "Problems of Piano Playing and Teaching," in *Be Your Own Music Critic: The Carnegie Hall Anniversary Lectures*, ed. Robert Edward Simon (n.p.: Books for Libraries Press, 1971), 137–64.

Dissemination: Edgard Varèse

Although Busoni's Berlin composition pupils and Egon Petri were the recipients of his mature ideas about tonal expansion, form, and/or sound ideals and had the added benefit of seeing analogous ideas presented in other art forms at the Bauhaus, some of Busoni's earlier mentees, such as Varèse, adopted spatialized and montage compositional approaches as well, thereby suggesting continuity in his teachings.[137] Varèse, like Busoni's other mentees, also found models for his compositions in architecture and the plastic arts, even if he could not be present at the Weimar Bauhaus exhibition.

Varèse studied with Busoni from 1907 or 1908 to 1913 and has long been considered a pioneer of spatialized music in terms of varying densities of sound and montage forms that combine different textures. Jonathan Bernard used the term "frozen music" to describes Varèse's sound world in which vertical densities are juxtaposed to contrasting textures: "As a matter of vertical compass, of the highest and lowest pitches heard at a given time and of the fluctuating density of the parts operating within these boundaries."[138] He described the "frozen music" as when "pitch collections consisting of short phrases, of one or more chords, or combinations of the two, are repeated in varying rhythms before abruptly reverting to something new."[139]

The word "architecture" frequently comes up in descriptions of his music for that very reason. Paul Rosenfeld, for instance, described Varèse as a "poet of the tall New Yorks" and his sonorities as "majestic skyscraper chords."[140] This association of Varèse with architecture is hardly surprising. From his youth, Varèse, like Busoni, had been fascinated by architectural space. He attached importance on the architecture of the Abbatial church of Saint-Philibert in Tournus, Burgundy, where he spent a great deal of time as a child, and he stated in his maturity (to his second wife, Louise) that "if there is any strength of beauty in my music, I owe it to Saint-Philibert."[141] He described the church with affection in 1961 in a letter: "There is a small Romanesque church connected with the Prieure which Anatole France chose as the

[137] For more about Busoni's earlier composition mentees, see Knyt, *Ferruccio Busoni and His Legacy*.

[138] Jonathan W. Bernard, "Varèse's Space, Varèse's Time," in *Edgard Varèse: Composer, Sound Sculptor, Visionary*, ed. Felix Meyer and Heidy Zimmermann, Paul Sacher Foundation (Woodbridge, Suffolk: Boydell Press, 2006), 150.

[139] Bernard, "Varèse's Space, Varèse's Time," 151.

[140] Paul Rosenfeld, *An Hour with American Music* (Philadelphia: J. B. Lippincott, 1929), 160–79. See also Malcolm MacDonald, *Varèse Astronomer in Sound* (London: Kahn & Averill, 2002).

[141] Louise Varèse, *Varèse: A Looking-Glass Diary* (n.p.: Davis Poynter, 1972), 67.

setting for the death of his Abbe Jérôme Coignard in La Rotisserie de la reine Pedauque."[142]

Varèse thought of music in architectural terms of mass, planes, and volume. Likewise, he considered music to be blocks of sound, calculated and balanced against one another. Varèse socialized with artists and sculptors, collecting their art, and he also collected architectural drawings. For instance, in addition to numerous drawings of Les Villars that was so dear to him, he kept prints of Joseph Stella's five oils, including "the Skyscraper" (1921) and a newspaper clipping featuring the château à Toto, a building featuring many diverse angles and shapes. Varèse was also friends with architects, such as Le Corbusier, who famously said, "Music, like architecture, is time and space."[143] The two met in 1935 and their friendship continued in the 1950s at Darmstadt and until Le Corbusier's death; Varèse spoke at his funeral. Just as Le Corbusier conceived of architecture in musical terms, so Varèse conceived of music in architectural terms, as "blocks of sound calculated in and balanced against each other."[144] Moreover, Varèse praised the innovations he saw in architecture, and looked there for models for the music he dreamed of creating:

> Here architecture speaks the language of our time and is understood. In the construction of our modern cathedrals, our modern pyramids and cathedrals: dams, bridges, industrial plants, grain elevators, laboratories, etc., the tendency toward rigorous predecision, utilization of forces and materials has merged architect and engineer. But in music, that other art-science, we have hardly begun to make use of the discoveries of science. We have not yet given people the new musical language of their own day.[145]

In particular, he remembers being fascinated by granite and stone and considered ways they related to music as blocks of sound:

> The earlier works were what I would call more architectonic. I was working with blocks of sound, calculated and balanced against each other.

[142] Varèse, letter of July 28, 1961, to Baryl Barr, Varèse Collection, Paul Sacher Foundation, Basel.

[143] Le Corbusier, quoted in Olivia Mattis, "From Bebop to Poo-Wip: Jazz Influence in Varèses's *Poème électronique*," in *Edgard Varèse: Composer, Sound Sculptor, Visionary*, 309.

[144] Mattis, "From Bebop to Poo-Wip," 310. A contemporary project that seeks to bring all of these elements together is the proposal of an architectonics of music studio in New York. Steven Holl, "Steven Holl Architects." https://www.stevenholl.com/architectonics-of-music/studio-2018/ (accessed June 2, 2019).

[145] Varèse, "Organized Sound for Film," *Commonweal* (1940), 205.

> I was preoccupied with volume in an architectural sense, and with projection. . . . As a child, I was tremendously impressed by the qualities and character of the granite I found in Burgundy, where I often visited my grandfather. There were two kinds of granite there, one grey, the other streaked with pink and yellow. Then there was the old Romanesque architecture in that part of France: I used to play in one of the oldest French churches—in Tournus—one that was started in the sixth century and built in the purest Romanesque style.[146]

Yet if this early architectural knowledge was helpful, Varèse attributes Busoni with showing him how to apply it to music to create spatialized, architectural music. Although his first dreams about spatializing music were catalyzed by exposure to the thoughts of physicist Józef Maria Hoëné-Wroński, it was Busoni who helped him understand how to realize those ideas in his compositions beginning with *Amériques*:

> I met Busoni when I was living in Berlin before the first World War. . . . We talked at length on all the questions that were my chief preoccupation at the time—and still are. Although our views differed radically on many subjects connected with the art of music, I am convinced that it was those long talks with Busoni, during which new horizons were constantly opening for me, that helped crystallize my ideas and confirmed my belief that new means must be found to liberate sound, to free it from the limitations of the tempered system, make it possible to realize my conception of rhythm as an element of stability, and to achieve unrelated metrical simultaneity. My first physical attempt to give music greater freedom was by the use of sirens in several of my scores (*Amériques, Ionisation*).[147]

Varèse also attributed his montage formal approach to Busoni. When describing form, Varèse used the metaphor of containers and boxes to show how musical material should not be restricted to predetermined musical

[146] Varèse, quoted in Gunther Schuller, *Conversation with Varèse, Perspectives of New Music* 3:2 (Spring 1965): 34. Other helpful sources include the following: Varèse, "Ferruccio Busoni: A Reminiscence," *Columbia University Forum* 9:2 (1966): 20; Varèse, "Organized Sound for the Sound Film," *The Commonwealth* (December 13, 1940), 205–6; Varèse, "In Quest of a Melodist," *Musical America* (October 10, 1925), 227–28; Varèse, "New Instruments in Orchestra Are Needed," *Christian Science Monitor* (July 8, 1922), 18.

[147] Varèse, "Spatial Music" (from a lecture given at St. Lawrence College in 1959), in *Contemporary Composers on Contemporary Music*, ed. Elliott Schwarz and Barney Childs (New York: Holt, Rinehart, and Winston, 1967), 205.

forms. He argued that the materials would burst out of them in different directions because the materials dictated the structural space they needed to occupy. Like assemblage or montage art, Varèse argued that only soft or liquid materials could fit in prescribed molds. Varèse states that these ideas about structure originated with Busoni, who was adamant about achieving unique structures consistent with the material:

> Busoni once wrote: "Is it not singular to demand of a composer originality on all things and to forbid it as regards to form? No wonder that once he becomes original, he is accused of formlessness." This misunderstanding has come from thinking of form as a point of departure, a pattern to be followed, a mold to be filled. Form is a result—the result of a process. Each of my works discovers its own form. I could never have fitted them into any of the historical containers.[148]

Varèse described music, much like Wolpe, as pitches splitting and changing relationships, always evolving in shape, and occupying space that required structures as varied as the makeup of other multi-dimensional objects, such as crystals. However, Varèse's images and analogies are often more natural and organic than Wolpe's:

> This, I believe, suggests, better than any explanation I could give, the way my works are formed. There is an idea, the basis of an internal structure, expanded and split into different shapes of groups of sound constantly changing in shape, direction, and speed, attracted and repulsed by various forces. The form of the work is the consequence of the interaction. Possible musical forms are as limitless as the exterior forms of crystals.[149]

He also thought architecturally in the way he combined pitches in space, and those ideas can also be traced back to Busoni. The clearest early visual representation of Varèse's connection between his spatialized music and architecture is a pyramid diagram that he used to illustrate the spatialization of the chromatic scale and the interrelationships of the pitches (see figure 5.8). Using lines to connect the pitches, Varèse sketched a pyramid with a wide base that is connected at the sides by pitches forming the chromatic scale.

[148] Varèse, "Spatial Music," 202–3.
[149] Varèse, "Spatial Music," 203.

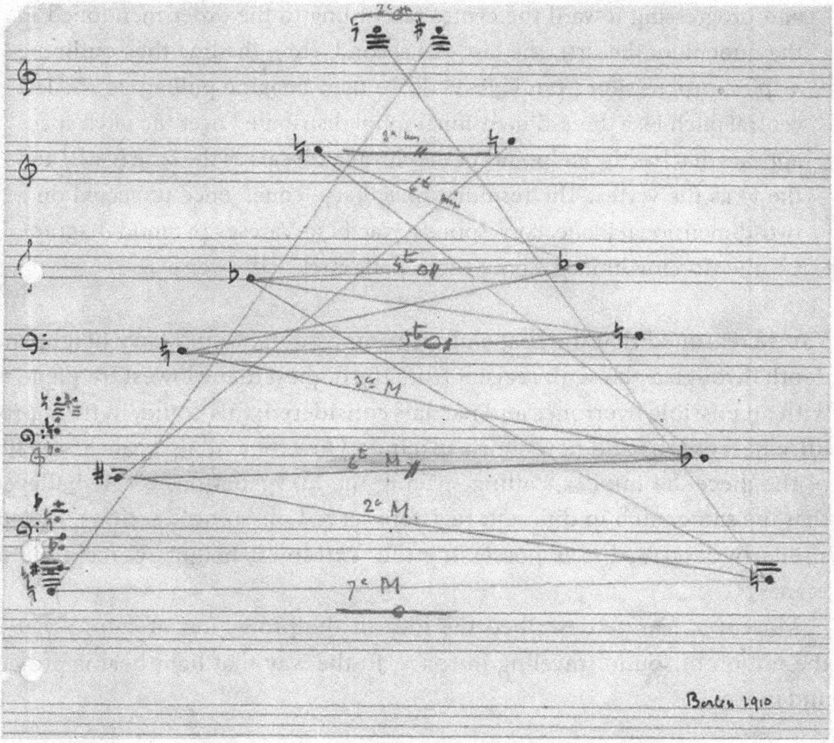

Figure 5.8. Varèse's pyramid diagram from Berlin, 1910. Edgard Varèse Collection, Paul Sacher Foundation, Basel.

Even if reconstructed later, as Felix Meyer has surmised, the diagram, which is marked Berlin 1910 at the bottom right corner, seems to represent important ideas about the spatialization of sound gleaned from the time Varèse studied with Busoni.[150] Federica di Gasbarro has described the meaning of the diagram with vividness and clarity:

> To reconstruct Varèse's "recipe" one only needs to connect the notes of a rising chromatic scale by a continuous line linking the extreme pitches

[150] Varèse, Pyramid Diagram, Varèse Collection, Paul Sacher Foundation, Basel. Felix Meyer believes the diagram to have been reconstructed sometime after 1910 due to the fluency of the diagram and the paper. However, no context has been discovered for the diagram, and as Meyer notes, Varèse was not a composer who intentionally tried to misrepresent facts. Meyer, conversation with the author of June 6, 2019 in Basel, Switzerland. Federica di Gasbarro has written in detail about the theoretical ramifications of the diagram, even connecting it to Schoenberg's

> and progressing toward the centre (according to the order mentioned in the quotation: the first, the last, the second, etc.), the line thus outlining a spiral progression from C to F♯. If we then imagine pulling up the last central pitch F♯, a three-dimensional spiral distributed over the pitch space appears that has the endpoints of the chromatic scale as the base (C–B) and the F♯ as the vertex. The resulting imaginary "cone," once projected on a two-dimensional plane, corresponds exactly to Varèse's pyramid diagram, i.e., the aforementioned "spaced chromatic circle."[151]

Varèse reasoned that the shape of his compositions would have height and depth through a play with register from the highest to the lowest frequencies with all possible overtones and partials considered; this could, in turn, produce new chords and new chord spacings. How they fill up space is the life of the piece, he implies, calling spacing the "oxygenation."[152] He believed that the same pitch in different registers served different functions. Busoni similarly described it as possessing the "extremest heights perceptible to man."[153]

Moreover, Varèse described the idea of the projection of sound that is the notion of sound traveling in space, in the way that light beams project and move:

> We have actually three dimensions in music: horizontal, vertical, and dynamic swelling or decreasing. I shall add a fourth, sound projection—that feeling that sound is leaving us with no hope of being reflected back, a feeling akin to that aroused by beams of light sent forth by a powerful searchlight—for the ear as for the eye, that sense of projection, of a journey into space.[154]

He described music in very physical manners as sound mass with multiple dimensions, including volume. He used the visual analogy of light rays

compositional practice: Gasbarro, "Sketching a New Verticality: Varèse's Atonal Sound and Its Contexts—Schoenberg, Webern and Ruggles," *Contemporary Music Review* 38:3–4 (2019): 271–315.

[151] Gasbarro, "Sketching a New Verticality," 279.
[152] Varèse, "The Liberation of Sound: New Instruments and New Music," from a lecture given at Mary Austin House, Santa Fe, 1936, in *Contemporary Composers on Contemporary Music*, 198.
[153] Busoni, *Sketch of a New Esthetic of Music*, trans. Theodore Baker (New York: G. Schirmer, 1911 [1906]), 5.
[154] Varèse, "The Liberation of Sound," 198.

with color to illustrate his points about how music occupies space: "In my works, these organized masses of sounds move against each other, varying in radiance and volume. Sound beams against each other, are like light rays projected by a reflector, . . . an extension, a journey into space."[155] These notions appear to gloss Busoni's own writings about music, who nevertheless, relied more heavily on natural imagery, as part of the vibrating universe and as traversing through physical objects in waves, even if they are invisible. The composer conjured up similar images using metaphors describing it as leaping like "the line of the rainbow" and like breaking "sunbeams with the clouds."[156] He also described the infinite possibilities of the tonal system like the sun with an infinite gradation of possibilities.[157]

Varèse, like Busoni, envisioned that different instrumental colors, like rays of light, would accentuate the differences in shape, which he described in physical terms as moveable planes and masses that collide, penetrate, or move apart. The masses create new textures and shapes even as different colors delineate the angles:

> When new instruments will allow me to write music as I conceive it, the movement of sound-masses, of shifting planes will be clearly perceived in my work, taking the place of linear counterpoint. When these sound-masses collide, the phenomena of penetration or repulsion will seem to occur. Certain transmutations taking place on certain planes will seem to be projected onto other planes, moving at different speeds and at different angles. . . . These zones would be differentiated by various timbres or colors and different loudnesses. . . . The role of color would be completely changed from being incidental, anecdotal, sensual or picturesque.[158]

A vital part of Varèse's conception of spatialized music was that of color, and he actively explored new instruments that would be able to help create the sound masses as he envisioned them. Thanks to Busoni's enthusiasm about the perceived unlimited possibilities of electronic sound, Varèse also became

155 [Nelle mie opere, queste masse organizzate dei suoni si muovano una contro l'altra, variando in radianza e in volume. I raggi sonori sono come raggi luminosi proiettati da un riflettore . . . un prolungamento, un viaggio nello spazio.] Varèse, "Music of Our Time" (Musica del nostro tempo), in Varèse, *Il suono organizzato: Scritti sulla musica Edgard Varèse* (Milan: Edizioni Unicopli, 1985), 100–1.

156 Busoni, *Sketch of a New Esthetic of Music*, 4–5.

157 Busoni, *Sketch of a New Esthetic of Music*, 23–24.

158 Varèse, "The Liberation of Sound," 197–98.

captivated by the idea of electronic music.[159] He described the theremin as having a "high pitched sound never heard before and [it] offers a whole range of possibilities."[160] His notes on the instrument include information about frequency, vibration, and range.[161] Varèse used the Ondes martenot as a substitute for sirens as early as 1929 and used it in place of the two theremins in 1961. Letters to Maurice Martenot from the 1940s discuss the range of the instrument as well as possible timbres and dynamic range.[162] He also collaborated with René Bertrand on the Dynaphone, based on electronic oscillations that he hoped would provide pure fundamentals and to extend ranges to obtain higher frequencies.[163]

In addition, he considered how partials and overtones could influence composition. In unpublished acoustic sketches, he mapped out partials and overtones while creating a table of frequencies. He also drew many diagrams of spirals to indicate the way that sound and frequencies radiate.[164]

Varèse dreamed of using and teaching new orchestration techniques that facilitated spatialized music: "The symphony orchestra strives for the utmost blending of colors. I strive to make the listener aware of the utmost differentiation of colorings and densities. I use color to distinguish planes, volumes, and zones of intensities."[165] He was also fascinated by unconventional ways of playing traditional instruments. His sketches include an undated diagram

159 See Busoni, *Sketch of a New Esthetic of Music*, 33–34. Busoni had read about the Telharmonium, which he spoke about incessantly with his pupils. When Varèse was able to play on the instrument in New York, he was disappointed, but he never stopped exploring the electronic possibilities spoken of by Busoni. He actively sought out new instrumental possibilities and met Leon Theremin at least as early as 1928, sometime after Theremin settled in New York in 1927, and he owned a copy of the concert program that Theremin gave in 1932 when he played Bach, Haydn, and Debussy. Yet Varèse had ideas about how the instrument could be used for more unconventional music as pure sound inserted into masses of acoustic phenomena with other instruments to create liquid architecture.

160 Varèse, "Music of Our Time." Varèse apparently tried to contact Theremin in the late 1930s, but his letter was never received.

161 Varèse, "Notes about the Theremin," Varèse Collection, Paul Sacher Foundation, Basel.

162 Varèse, letter of May 23, 1947, to Maurice Martenot, Varèse Collection, Paul Sacher Foundation, Basel.

163 Varèse, Lettere ad Henry Allen Moe (Fondazione Guggenheim), in *Il suono organizzato*, 80–81.

164 In addition, notes in the Varèse Collection at the Paul Sacher Foundation indicate copious and painstaking studies for producing tape music, in which he wrote out charts of pitch and speed correlations. There are plenty of diagrams of pitches with exact Hertz numbers listed beside them or underneath. Moreover, he was part of the Acoustical Society of America. The Varèse Collection even contains a call for papers for the 54th meeting of the Society to be held in Ann Arbor, Michigan, on October 24–26, 1957. Varèse Collection, Paul Sacher Foundation, Basel. In October 1959, he received a silver certificate honoring his twenty-five years of membership in the society

165 [L'orchestra sinfonica cerca il maggiore amalgama possibile tra i colori; io mi sforzo di chiarire all'ascoltatore per quanto è possibile la distinzione tra i colori è tra le densità. Utilizzo il colore per distinguere i piani, i volume è le zone di suono, non come mezzo per produrre una serie di episodi in contrasto caleidoscopio uno con l'altro.] *Varèse*, "La liberazione del suono," in *Il suono organizzato*, 76/110.

for a prepared piano that calls for the use of big screws, bolts, and rubber.[166] Moreover, he advocated for using unconventional instruments, such as type H sirens from the Sterling Fire Alarm Company.[167] Most notable is his colorful and varied use of percussion, often in sections, that create unusual densities or clusters of sonority and timbre. In his notes for *Tuning Up*, Chou Wen-chung, for instance, listed five percussion parts:

1. Tambourine, fixed
   Low Ride Cymbal (bounce), suspended
   Snare Drum
   Tenor Drum
2. High Ride Cymbal, suspended
   Low Crash Cymbal (thin), suspended
   Low Tam-Tam (shallowed rim)
   Very Low Tam-Tam
   Very Low Bass Drum
3. Xylophone
   Tambourine
   High Anvil
   Low Anvil
4. Glockenspiel
   Triangle
   2 Maracas
   High Cymbal a2
   Low Cymbal a1
5. Triangle
   Tambourine
   3 Chinese Woodblocks
   High Siren (hand operated)
6. Tambourine
   Sleighbells
   Very Low Gong (deep rim, flat face)
   Low Siren[168]

166 Varèse, "Prepared Piano Sketch," Varèse Collection, Paul Sacher Foundation, Basel.
167 Varèse, letter of March 12, 1934, to the Sterling Fire Alarm Company, Varèse Collection, Paul Sacher Foundation, Basel.
168 Chou Wen-chung, "Notes for Varèse's *Tuning Up*," Varèse Collection, Paul Sacher Foundation, Basel.

Unpublished documents also indicate that Varèse avidly studied lists of percussion instruments, such as the Carroll Drum Service Book, and made notes about the instruments he wanted to learn more about.[169] Notes for the electronically interpolated sections for *Déserts* indicate the variety of sounds he hoped to evoke, and he used graphic terms to describe the sounds he was after, such as swishing, grinding, and hammering.[170]

Varèse's ideas about spatialized music, like Busoni's, were never fully realized, except, perhaps, in his *Poème électronique* (1958), where sound, color, and architectural space merge into one.[171] As he stated: "For the first time I heard my music literally projected into space" as electronic sound was projected from hundreds of loudspeakers throughout a building designed by Le Corbusier for the 1958 World's Fair in Brussels.[172]

For this event, he finally had access to equipment that could adequately express his ideas, provided by the Phillips Studio. Prior to that event, Pierre Schaeffer's Radiodiffusion in France invited him to create tapes of organized industrial and percussion sounds that he inserted into the already composed *Déserts.* At the first performance of *Déserts*, loudspeakers were placed on each side of the orchestra, and two radio stations broadcast it, each carrying half the signal. Yet listeners had to own two radios to hear the complete effect.

In *Poème électronique*, sound is projected in a more complex manner from somewhere between 300 and 425 speakers and 20 amplifiers, so that tones would literally surround listeners as they strolled through the esophagus-shaped building.[173] Numerous sketches at the Paul Sacher Foundation indicate that Varèse studied the architectural shape of the building in detail when thinking about how the sound of his taped music could radiate in different directions. Although Le Corbusier sent him a basic scenario of the visual projections and descriptions of color projections as well on June 22, 1957, the music was to be created independently of the scenario. On July 22, 1957, Varèse responded, agreeing with Le Corbusier about fundamental

[169] Varèse, annotated notes in the Carroll Service Drum Book, Varèse Collection, Paul Sacher Foundation, Basel.

[170] Varèse, sketches for tape interpolations for *Déserts*, Varèse Collection, Paul Sacher Foundation, Basel.

[171] Their first planned collaboration was for the inauguration of the Chapel of Pilgrimage of Ronchamp, but it did not come to fruition. Letters between Varèse and Le Corbusier's secretary include images of the building and indicate that the hope was that Varèse would use sound machines. L. Hailberth, letter of January 21, 1954, to Varèse, Varèse Collection, Paul Sacher Foundation, Basel.

[172] Varèse, "Spatial Music," 207.

[173] Accounts differ as to how many speakers there were.

differences in perception between ears and eyes, and that the two should act independently.[174]

Indeed, Varèse seems to have more carefully studied the acoustic space and shape of the building than the scenario, given that there is little indication of his having even seen the images as he was composing; by contrast, he possessed multiple drawings of the architectural shape of the building.[175] Drawings indicate surface dimensions as well as height, depth, and hyperbolic curves. In notes, Varèse wrote that he planned to place high frequencies on low speakers. He also plotted out six physical points in the building (A through F) that were to correspond to different sections in the tape, each featuring different textures and acoustic properties that would correspond with the listeners' journey through the esophagus-shaped building:

1. Point A: Projection—rotation of sound
   perspectives of sound from very remote, outside—far away, coming clearer and clearer. At a certain moment its presence in the hall suddenly dims any route—coming at a chosen point (exit or entrance) and from there goes away again—disappearing
2. Point B: Projection—a certain sound, very special, one route parallel differentiated, mercurial effect, mysterious stereophonic effect, location purely individual and subjective, at a certain moment you feel the sound inside of you . . .
3. Point C—Sound in the Hall—impression of dimension of hall—same sound in which reverberation is introduced . . .
4. Point D—Jumping of sounds (loudness restricted), jumping independent of each other; Independent track
5. Point E—Echo effect—mixed with jumping and reverberation; all combination possible combination of the 3 tapes—any choice—any projection following its route
6. Point F—Rain—kind of—falling counterpoint of the 3 Tapes.[176]

174 Varèse, letter of July 22, 1957, to Le Corbusier, Varèse Collection, Paul Sacher Foundation, Basel.

175 Le Corbusier, letter of June 22, 1957, to Varèse, Varèse Collection, Paul Sacher Foundation, Basel.

176 Varèse, notes for *Poème eléctronique*, Varèse Papers Paul Sacher Foundation, Basel. Xenakis, letter of January 11, 1957, to Varèse, Varèse Collection, Paul Sacher Foundation, Basel. Xenakis indicated that he would have loudspeakers at his disposal that allowed for bass, treble, or in between as well as special mixes. Varèse recorded his music on a three-track magnetic tape. Varèse's music was accompanied by a light show and images produced by Le Corbusier.

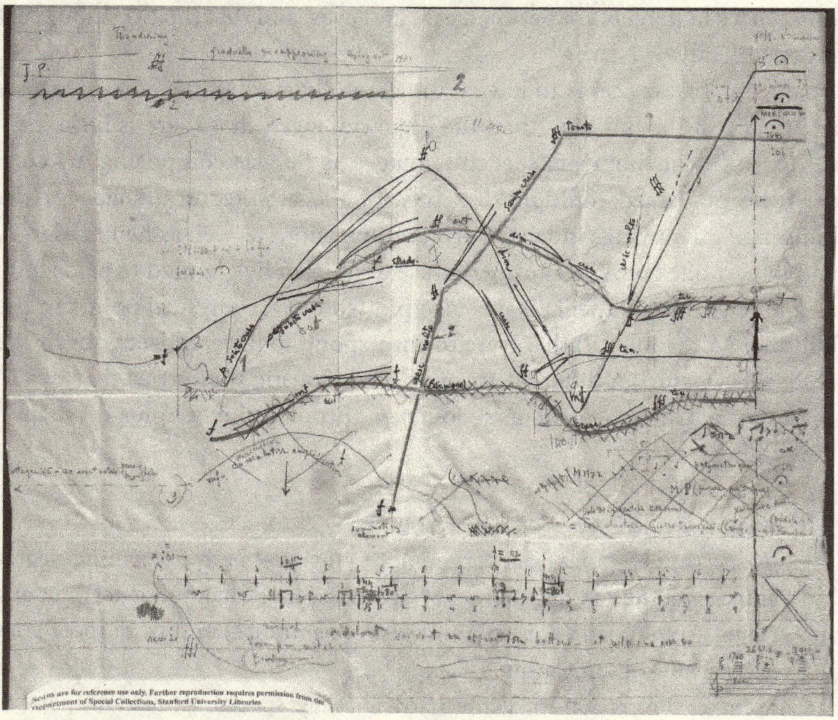

Figure 5.9. Varèse, sketch for the end of *Poème électronique*. Special Collections, Stanford University.

One obvious connection between the shape of the architecture and the music was the use of hyperbolic curves. Both Le Corbusier and Varèse were fascinated by parabolas and hyperbolic parabolas.[177] Pitch glissandi represent small segments of these curves of sound, and Varèse's diagram for the end of the piece features six such curves (see figure 5.9).

The hyperbolic parabola reconciles curved lines out of straight ones and was also used extensively in the architectural planning for the building for the Brussels World's Fair that was designed by Le Corbusier and Xenakis. That Varèse uses similar curves in his sketch of the *Poème électronique* can hardly be coincidental, even though he had used them as far back as *Amériques*.[178]

[177] It is important to note, however, that Varèse claims he already used parabolic and hyperbolic sound in *Amériques* and *Ionisation*.

[178] See Olivia Mattis, "Varèse and the Visual Arts" (PhD diss., Stanford University, 1992), 310.

Although Varèse believed that he succeeded for the first time in hearing his music set in space with the *Poème électronique*, his earlier pieces, some left incomplete, experimented with aspects of space in numerous ways. Olivia Mattis has already documented the spatial aspects of the incomplete *Espace*, calling it a "spatial symphony," that combines text, music, color, movement, and projected light or film. The text was to consist of leftist political slogans in all languages, along with "laughter, humming, yelling, chanting, mumbling, hammered declamation, and other extended vocal techniques." The composer conceived the work to be sung simultaneously from many points on the globe, so that the world could be symbolically united. The rhythms were to erupt into a final dramatic ending that increased in volume and projected into space. It was to coincide with visual images too, but the Spanish Civil War (1936–1939) interrupted his plans.[179] It is a piece that was to combine theatre, pantomime, dance, literature, and electronic sounds.

Étude pour Espace was the final draft of a reduced conception for the *Espace*. It also featured a wide variety of sounds and timbres. Main characters were to omit howls and cries, even if other vocal parts were more traditional. In addition, there are invisible choruses, lighting effects, a mime role, and sound projected in different directions from speakers. The theme of distance is evoked by the subject matter as much as the music, as the main figure is an astronomer and the plot deals with signals between a star and the astronomer. Earthly disasters are announced over loudspeakers, and the astronomer, a mute character, is eventually absorbed by the light of the star in the end.

While Varèse was undoubtedly a major influence on the way that sound developed in the twentieth century, he was not alone; there were others of Busoni's circle that were thinking about similar ideas. This book has shown how Busoni's ideas not only impacted his own compositions in terms of spatialized music and montage forms, but also many of his students as well, from his earlier mentees to those he taught in his composition master class shortly before he died. Moreover, the phenomenon of spatial music that Busoni fostered, in each case considered, was also fostered by exposure to other arts, especially architecture. Whether one is dealing with notions of multi-dimensionality or how to fill the space of a particular hall, these

[179] Mattis, "The Physical and the Abstract: Varèse and the New York School," in *The New York Schools of Music and the Visual Arts*, ed. Steven Johnson, Studies in Contemporary Music and Culture 5 (London: Routledge, 2001), 57–75.

considerations were important to Busoni, and led to the development of a group of followers interested in the physicality of sound, a montage approach to form, and an insatiable curiosity for ways the music could expand in terms of scope and possibility.

Concluding Thoughts

This book has revealed that Busoni participated in a variety of musical approaches associated with modernism in music. His indebtedness to Bach reflects a tendency toward the "Historicist Modernism" described by Walter Frisch.[180] At the same time, many of Busoni's compositions also reflected some of the contemporaneous experimentalist trends and ideals that spanned across the arts.[181] Without rejecting the immediate musical past, Busoni still envisioned a new future of music that simultaneously acknowledged what he considered to be timeless compositional techniques *and* new sounds and structures characteristic of his own generation. References to tradition and experimentation exist side by side in his compositions, as they also do in the music of some of his contemporaries as well. In that sense, this book about Busoni contributes the growing body of scholarly literature exploring a multiplicity of modernisms in music and, in the process, sheds greater light on Busoni's historiographic position and significance as a composer.[182] Even if Busoni did not realize every idea in his visionary writings, he did seek to expand tonality, to write montage forms, and to explore spatialized sound, while he simultaneously embraced counterpoint. At the same time, this book has also shown that many of Busoni's idiosyncratic approaches to music composition were informed by an understanding of architecture. He was aware of resonance, acoustics, and texture, and these influenced his creative activities.

This chapter has also demonstrated that these features were also seminal to the development of much music that was to follow. In addition to experimenting with form, sound, and musical language, some twentieth- and twenty-first-century composers also began to think of music, invisible as

[180] Walter Frisch, "Bach, Regeneration, and Historicist Modernism," in *German Modernism: Music and the Arts* (Berkeley: University of California Press, 2005).

[181] For a summary of different scholarly explanations of modernism, consult the introduction to this book.

[182] Consult the introduction for an overview of this scholarly literature.

sound waves are, in very visceral terms and in relation to space. This marks a departure from romantic metaphysical thought, where the abstractness and ineffability were celebrated. While Busoni was not connecting music to the human body as much as some recent composers, physicality of sound was nevertheless at the forefront of his musical explorations. He illustrated the physical space and forms his music occupied with visual drawings and architectural metaphors. His writings include descriptions of an ethereal and mystical realm, but that ethereal realm still vibrated in physical ways for Busoni. Rather than solely emphasizing the otherworldly and the uncanny with his references to the Gothic, Busoni responded to the physicality of the architectural spaces in his compositions. He sought to re create the resonance, reverberation, and distance. He sought realistic aural portrayals of overtones, timing, physical shapes, and ornamentation.

These trends lasted beyond Busoni and his immediate mentees. Many of those studying with or influenced by Busoni's pupils were also blending temporal music and spatialized sound as well, using montage forms and expansions of the tonal organization in response to the physical environment. In addition, many were concerned with the spatialized placement of performers, as Busoni had been.

Iannis Xenakis, for instance, who was influenced by Varèse and Le Corbusier in his architecture studio and in the collaboration on *Poème électronique*, dispersed the orchestra throughout the performance spaces.[183] For instance, in *Nomos Gamma* (1968), musicians were seated among listeners. In *Persephassa* (1969), six percussionists form a paragon around the audience. *Persephassa* has several musical layers that are simultaneously superimposed, each in its own tempo. For Xenakis, as for Wolpe, notions of space also related to the arrangement of intervals, as he describes in relation to *Metastasis* (1953–1954):

> I discovered the intoxicating effects of combining architectural elements, after having experimented with them in music. Indeed, in *Metastasis* for orchestra, which I was finishing at about the same time (1953–54), the

[183] He was given a flute at age six and was thereafter captivated by music. After earning a degree in engineering, he went to work in Le Corbusier's studio. He also enrolled in Arthur Honegger's class at the Paris Conservatoire and took classes with Nadia Boulanger and Olivier Messiaen. For more information about architecture and music in the output of Xenakis, see Xenakis, *Music and Architecture: Architectural Projects, Texts, and Realizations*, ed. and trans. Sharon Kanach, The Iannis Xenakis Series 1 (Hillsdale, NY: Pendragon Press, 2008).

> central section was constructed on a combinatorial organization of melodic intervals +1+2+3+4+5+6, *expressed in semitones.*[184]

He also conceived of cinematic stereophonics in which sound is projected to fill up multi-dimensional space even while expanding tonal possibilities through the mathematical generation of pitch sets.[185]

For Xenakis, who was both a composer and an architect, music was connected to physical spaces, as Busoni's had been. *Bohor* (1962) is one of the first eight-track compositions and explores sound immersion. *Hibiki Hana Ma* (1970) for the Osaka World's Fair utilizes 250 speakers and 800 loudspeakers and features a score for a twelve-track tape that can create cylindrical acoustic fields. In *Polytope de Cluny* (1972), the performance itself, with actions in light and sound, becomes a type of architecture as the spectators are submerged within the performance. *Diatope* (1978) was intended to span the oceans and continents with digital sound synthesis. In *The Polytope de Montréal* (1967), Xenakis created virtual architecture within the structure using webs of steel cables based on hyperbolic parabolas that coincided with the music. In the structure he created 1,200 light flashes in five colors (white, yellow, green, red, blue) even as eleven musicians played through four fixed groups of loudspeakers. Spectators moved about the space during the performance.

Feldman, a student of Wolpe and friend and follower of Varèse who greatly admired Busoni, also began creating spatialized music.[186] His *Projections* (1950–1951), for instance, feature cubist notation inspired by painters and reflects sounds that are thought of in terms of height, width, and space, but without definite pitch designations. Feldman described *Projection II* as one of the first geometric pieces, stating, "My desire here was not to compose, but to project sounds into time, free from compositional rhetoric that had no place here."[187]

Feldman also wrote compositions intimately related to physical space with unique montage structures and with pitch organization that expanded

184 Xenakis, "*Metastaseis* and the Modulor (1955)," in Xenakis, *Music and Architecture*, 64.

185 For more about Xenakis's treatment of the musical language, see Wolfgang von Schweinitz, "Iannis Xenakis' Contributions to 20th Century Atonal Harmony and the History of Equal Temperament," in *Xenakis Matters: Contexts, Processes, Applications*, ed. Sharon Kanach, Iannis Xenakis Series 4 (Hillsdale, NY: Pendragon Press, 2012), 25–38.

186 Morton Feldman, "Autobiography [1926]," in Morton Feldman, *Essays*, ed. Walter Zimmermann (Cologne: Beginner Press, 1985). Feldman was especially influenced by Varèse's notions of space.

187 Feldman, "Autobiography," 38.

tonal possibilities. The Rothko Chapel in Houston, for instance, a spiritual environment created by the American painter and Feldman's friend, Mark Rothko for people of all faiths, inspired his own composition with the same title. Feldman claims that he chose the instruments in terms of timbre and balance in response to the spatial aspects of the chapel. He also sought to mimic the physical space of the building through sound:

> Rothko's imagery goes right to the edge of his canvas, and I wanted the same effect with the music—that it should permeate the whole octagonal-shaped room and not be heard from a certain distance. The result is very much what you have in a recording—the sound is closer, more physically with you than get in a concert hall.[188]

This evocation of space resulted in antiphonal spacing of the choir on opposite sides of the building. In addition, Steven Johnson has established that Feldman employs textual layering, such as the juxtaposition of timpani ostinato and choral writing, each with its own rhythmic material.[189]

While Feldman was concerned with spatial perceptions of the music, he also, like Busoni and his mentees, tried alternatives to dodecaphony using an expanded tonal vocabulary, yet with modal inflections. The entire piece is organized around concepts of plurisignificance, with certain pitch sets around a five-note chord in measure 11 (F, G♭, A♭, A♯, B) serving as germinal material. As Dániel Péter Biro has argued, the intervals in this chord are then varied through intervallic association, interval reinterpretation, intervallic variations, and reiteration.[190] In the process, Feldman explores a whole spectrum of approaches ranging from atonality to tonality. This range is amply evident in the viola solos, for instance.[191]

In addition, the montage formal structure is inspired by the shape of the octagonal chapel and Rothko's paintings. Despite linear thematic continuity, the piece contains four widely contrasting main sections, the first featuring solos for soprano and viola, the second a more static band of sound in which isolated harmonies and motivic fragments weave in and out (with a single

[188] Feldman, "The Rothko Chapel," in *Essays*, 141.
[189] Steven Johnson, "Rothko Chapel and Rothko's Chapel," in *Perspectives of New Music* 32:2 (Summer 1994): 39.
[190] Dániel Péter Biro, "Slowly Watching Memory: An Analysis of Morton Feldman's 'Rothko Chapel'" (MA thesis, Musikhochshule-Frankfurt am Main, 1998).
[191] Johnson, "Rothko Chapel and Rothko's Chapel," 20.

chord punctuated by chimes), the third being more lyrical, while the fourth contains a modal Hebraic viola melody. Within these main sections are further contrasting segments, described by Feldman as inspired directly by architecture, rather than linear musical forms: "I felt the music called for a series of highly contrasted merging sections. I envisioned an immobile procession not unlike the friezes on Greek temples."[192]

These are but a few ways non-linear forms, an expansion of tonality, and spatialized sound became part of the twentieth-century music scene. From projected sound in some large opera halls and theaters, to electronically enhanced string quartets, and special sound effects, new approaches to sound became a dominant trend in the twentieth century. Composers today also explore the spatial properties of music from the verticalization of the overtone series in spectral composition, to the varied dimensions of textural music, to the filling in of pitch space with microtones, to the reshaping of pieces in juxtaposed montages, to the virtualization of space in online choirs and orchestra; music has become an art form that brings together the temporal and spatial in constantly evolving manners. In addition, they employ a wide range of approaches to the musical language.

While Busoni could not possibly have envisioned all these developments, in thinking about ways music could be structured spatially like architecture, Busoni was anticipating trends that would become important several decades after his death. By focusing on aspects of space and dimension that allowed for a capacious embrace of non-traditional scales, his compositional ideas included the conception of music as a spatialized art form and, in that sense, as an art form that encompassed the combinations of spaces between and with pitches. He also envisioned non-linear conceptions of form, embraced an expansive approach to the musical language that became more common in the post-tonal era, and responded to acoustics and resonances. In the process, Busoni joined numerous other contemporaneous artists in bringing together spatial and temporal art forms to reconceive artistic possibilities. In leaving behind a legacy of compositions and performances exploring the spatialization of sound and its connectedness to tangible physical spaces, he helped promote this vision of sound as part of the physical universe and, in the process, constructed durable musical masterpieces that might be more important for the development of twentieth-century music than previously thought.

[192] Feldman, Notes to *Rothko Chapel; for Frank O'Hara*, in Feldman, *Essays*, ed. Walter Zimmermann (Cologne: Beginner Press, 1985), 141–42.

Selected Bibliography

Archival Collections Consulted

Archives et Musée de la littérature (Brussels, Belgium)
Archivio storico comunale (Bologna, Italy)
Bauhaus-Archiv (Berlin, Germany)
Bildarchiv Foto Marburg (Marburg, Germany)
Edgard Varèse Collection, Paul Sacher Stiftung (Basel Switzerland)
Edward and Clara Steuermann Collection, 1922–1981, Library of Congress (Washington, DC, USA)
Goethe- und Schiller-Archiv, Klassik Stiftung (Weimar, Germany)
Grainger Museum (Melbourne, Australia).
Howard Lebow Collection, University of Massachusetts Amherst (Amherst, Massachusetts, USA)
J. Paul Getty Museum (Los Angeles, California, USA)
Kurt Weill Foundation (New York, New York, USA)
Morton Feldman Papers, 1950–1999, State University of New York at Buffalo (Buffalo, New York, USA)
Nachlass Ferruccio Busoni, Staatsbibliothek zu Berlin–Preußischer Kulturbesitz, Musikabteilung mit Mendelssohn-Archiv (Berlin, Germany)
Papers of Kurt Weill and Lotte Lenya, Yale University Library (New Haven, Connecticut, USA)
Papers of Larry Sitsky, National Library of Australia (Canberra, Australia)
Rudolph Ganz Papers, 1864–2013, The Newberry Library (Chicago, Illinois, USA)
Special Collections, Stanford University (Stanford, California, USA)
Stefan Wolpe Collection, Paul Sacher Stiftung (Basel, Switzerland)
Vogel-Nachlass, Zentralbibliothek Zürich (Zurich, Switzerland)

Books and Articles

Abell, Arthur. "Ferruccio Busoni's Great Art." *Musical Courier: A Weekly Journal Devoted to Music and the Music Trades* 59:13 (1909): 6.

Adorno, Theodor W. *Philosophie der Neuen Musik*. Tübingen: J.C.B. Mohr, 1948.

Albert-Birot, Pierre. "A Propos d'un Théâtre Nunique." *Sic* 8, 9, 10 (August–October, 1916).

Albright, Daniel. *Putting Modernism Together: Literature, Music, and Painting: 1872–1927*. Hopkins Studies in Modernism. Edited by Douglas Mao. Baltimore: Johns Hopkins University Press, 2015.

Albright, Daniel. *Untwisting the Serpent: Modernism in Music, Literature, and Other Arts*. Chicago: University of Chicago Press, 2000.

Arias, Enrique. "Wilhelm Middelschulte's 'Kontrapunktische Symphonie' and the Chicago Gothics." *The Diapason* 94:6 (June 2003): 17–22.

Aronson, Arnold. "Theatres of the Future." *Theatre Journal* 33:4 (December 1981): 489–503.

Arthur, Donald. *Malevolent Muse: The Life of Alma Mahler.* Translated by Oliver Hilmes. Boston: Northeastern University Press, 2015.

Barone, Joshua. "At the Bauhaus, Music Was More Than a Hobby." *New York Times* (August 23, 2019).

"Das Bauhaus in Weimar." *Allgemeine Zeitung* (September 2, 1923).

"Bauhaus Konzerte." *Berliner Börsen-Courier* (August 22, 1923).

"Die Bauhauswoche." *Deutsche Allgemeine Zeitung* (August 21,1923).

Bayer, Herbert, ed. *Bauhaus, 1919–1928.* New York: The Museum of Modern Art, 1938. https://www.moma.org/documents/moma_catalogue_2735_300190238.pdf (accessed May 8, 2018).

Becker, C. J. "Ideen über Baukunst und Musik [1838]." In *Music and Aesthetics in the Eighteenth and Early Nineteenth Centuries*, edited by Peter le Huray and James Day, 493–97. Cambridge Readings in the Literature of Music. Cambridge: Cambridge University Press, 1981.

Becker, John. "Wilhelm Middelschulte, Master of Counterpoint." *Musical Quarterly* 14 (1928): 192–202.

Bekker, Paul. "Kontrapunkt und Neuzeit." *Frankfurter Zeitung* (March 27, 1918).

Bergdoll, Barry, and Leah Dickerman. *Bauhaus 1919–1933: Workshops for Modernity.* New York: D. A. P., 2009.

Bergeron, Katherine. *Decadent Enchantments: The Revival of Gregorian Chant at Solesmes.* Berkeley: University of California Press, 1998.

Beaumont, Antony. *Busoni the Composer.* Bloomington: Indiana University Press, 1985.

Beaumont, Antony. "Busoni's *Doktor Faust:* A Reconstruction and Its Problems." *Musical Times* 126:1718 (1986): 196–99.

Beaumont, Antony, ed. *Ferruccio Busoni: Selected Letters.* New York: Columbia University Press, 1987.

Berger, Karol, Anthony Newcomb, and Reinhold Brinkmann, eds. *Music and the Aesthetics of Modernity: Essays.* Cambridge, MA: Harvard University Department of Music, 2005.

Berger, Karol. *Bach's Cycle, Mozart's Arrow: An Essay on the Origins of Musical Modernity.* Berkeley: University of California Press, 2007.

Blauert, Jens. *Spatial Hearing: The Psychophysics of Human Sound Localization* [1974]. Translated by John S. Allen. Cambridge: MIT Press, 1983.

Blaukopf, Kurt. "Space in Electronic Music." *Music and Technology* 2:1 (1971): 157–72.

Blondel, François, and Simon de la Boissière. *Cours d'architecture enseigné dans l'Académie Royale d'Architecture.* Paris: Paris Auboin, 1675.

Bonney, Thomas George. *Cathedrals, Abbeys and Churches of England and Wales.* 2 vols. London: Cassell, 1896.

Bothe, Rolf, Peter Hahn, and Hans Christoph von Tavel, eds. *Das frühe Bauhaus und Johannes Itten.* Stuttgart: Hatje Cantz Verlag, 1994.

Brée, Malwine. *The Groundwork of the Leschetizky Method: Issued with His Approval.* Translated by Dr. Th. Baker. Mainz: Mayence, 1903.

Brée, Malwine. *The Leschetitzky Method: A Guide to Fine and Correct Piano Playing.* Translated by Arthur Elson. Mineola, NY: Dover Publications, 1997.

Brelet, Gisèle. *Le temps musical: Essai d'une esthétique nouvelle de la musique*. Paris: Presses universitaires de France, 1949.

Brennecke, Dietrich. *Das Lebenswerk Max Buttings*. Leipzig: VEB Deutscher Verlag für Musik, 1973.

Brookshire, Bradley. "Edwin Fischer and Bach Pianism of the Weimar Republic." PhD diss., City University of New York, 2016.

Burkholder, J. Peter. "Stylistic Heterogeneity and Topics in the Music of Charles Ives." *Journal of Musicological Research* 31 (2012): 166–99.

Burnham, Scott. *Musical Form in the Age of Beethoven: Selected Writings on Theory and Method by Adolf Bernhard Marx*. Edited and translated by Scott Burnham. Cambridge Studies in Theory and Analysis. Edited by Ian Bent. Cambridge: Cambridge University Press, 1997.

Bushart, Magdalena. "Am Anfang ein Missverständnis. Feiningers 'Kathedrale' und das Bauhaus-Manifest." In *Bauhaus-Archiv Berlin/Museum für Gestaltung, Stiftung Bauhaus Dessau und Klassik Stiftung Weimar: Modell Bauhaus*, edited by Hatte Cantz, 29–32. Ostfildern: Kulturstiftung des Bundes, 2009.

Busoni, Ferruccio. *Briefe an Seine Frau*. Edited by F. Schnapp. Zurich: Rotapel, 1935.

Busoni, Ferruccio. *Entwurf einer neuen Ästhetik der Tonkunst*. Edited by Martina Weindel. Taschenbücher zur Musikwissenschaft 145. Edited by Richard Schaal. Wilhelmshaven: Florian Noetzel, 2001.

Busoni, Ferruccio. *The Essence and Oneness of Music and Other Papers*. Translated by Rosamond Ley. London: Rockliff, 1957.

Busoni, Ferruccio. *Ferruccio Busoni: Lettere ai genitori*. Edited by Martina Weindel. Rome: Ismez, 2004.

Busoni, Ferruccio. *Letters to His Wife*. Translated by Rosamond Ley. Da Capo Press Music Reprint Series. Edited by Roland Jackson. New York: Da Capo Press, 1975.

Busoni, Ferruccio. "Routine." *Pan* 1:20 (August 16, 1911): 654–55.

Busoni, Ferruccio. "Schönberg-Matinée." *Pan* 2:10 (January 25, 1912): 298.

Busoni, Ferruccio. "Selbst-Rezension." *Pan* 2:11 (February 1, 1912): 327–30.

Busoni, Ferruccio. *Sketch of a New Aesthetic of Music*. Translated by Th. Baker. New York: G. Schirmer, 1911.

Busoni, Ferruccio. *Von der Einheit der Music*. Edited by Joachim Hermann. Max Hesses Handbücher der Musik 76. Berlin: Max Hesses Verlag, 1956.

Butler, Christopher. *Early Modernism, Literature, Music, and Painting in Europe, 1900–1916*. Oxford: Clarendon Press, 1994.

Butt, John. *Bach's Dialogue with Modernity: Perspectives on the Passions*. Cambridge: Cambridge University Press, 2010.

Cage, John. *Silence: Lectures and Writings*. Middletown, CT: Wesleyan University Press, 1961.

Calico, Joy H. *Brecht at the Opera*. Berkeley: University of California Press, 2008.

Calinescu, Matei. *Five Faces of Modernity: Modernism, Avant-Garde, Decadence, Kitsch, Postmodernism*. Durham, NC: Duke University Press, 1987.

Charlton, David E. T. A. *Hoffmann's Musical Writings: "Kreisleriana," "The Poet and the Composer," Music Criticism*. Translated by Martyn Clarke. Cambridge: Cambridge University Press, 1989.

Charlton, David. *Opera in the Age of Rousseau: Music, Confrontation, Realism*. Cambridge Studies in Opera. Cambridge: Cambridge University Press, 2012.

Childs, Peter. *Modernism*. London: Routledge, 2000.

Christensen, Peter, and Marc Aurel Schnabel. "Spatial Polyphony: Virtual Architecture Generated from the Music of J. S. Bach." Advanced Study Report, University of Sydney, 2007. https://www.researchgate.net/profile/Marc_Aurel_Schnabel/publication/30868841_Spatial_polyphony_Virtual_Architecture_Generated_from_the_Music_of_JS_Bach/links/0a85e52d6195cf2301000000.pdf (accessed June 13, 2019).

Clarkson, Austin. "Essays in Actionism: Wolpe's Pieces for Three Pianists." *Perspectives of New Music* 40:2 (Summer 2002): 115–33.

Clarkson, Austin. *On the Music of Stefan Wolpe: Essays and Recollections*. Dimension and Diversity Series 6. Edited by Mark DeVoto. Hillsdale, NY: Pendragon Press, 2003.

Clarkson, Austin. "Stefan Wolpe and the Busoni Legacy." In *Busoni in Berlin: Facetten eines kosmopolitischen Komponisten*, edited by Albrecht Riethmüller and Hyesu Shin, 257–74. Wiesbaden: Franz Steiner Verlag, 2004.

Clarkson, Austin. "Wolpe, Varèse and the Busoni Effect." *Contemporary Music Review* 27:2/3 (April/June 2008): 361–81.

Clarkson, Austin, ed. "Recollections of Stefan Wolpe by Former Students and Friends." http://ada.evergreen.edu/~arunc/texts/music/wolpe/wolpe.pdf (accessed June 15, 2019).

Clifton, Thomas. *Music as Heard: A Study in Applied Phenomenology*. New Haven, CT: Yale University Press, 1983.

Cohen, Brigid. *Stefan Wolpe and the Avant-Garde Diaspora*. New York: Oxford University Press, 2012.

Cone, Edward T. "Berlioz's Divine Comedy: The Grande messe des morts." *19th-Century Music* 4:1 (1980): 3–16.

Cottlow, Augusta. "My Years with Busoni." *Musical Observer* 24:6 (June 1925): 11/28.

Couling, Della. *Ferruccio Busoni: A Musical Ishmael*. Lanham, MD: Scarecrow Press, 2005.

Crispin, Judith. "Introducing Larry Sitsky's New Ending for Ferruccio Busoni's *Doktor Faust*." In *Ereignis und Exegese: Musikalische Interpretation, Interpretation der Musik*. Festschrift für Hermann Danuser zum 65. Geburtstag, edited by Camilla Bork et al., 539–51. Schliengen: Edition Argus, 2011.

Dahlhaus, Carl. *Nineteenth-Century Music* [1980]. Translated by Bradford Robinson. Berkeley: University of California Press, 1989.

Davis, Colin. "'The New Harmony' of Ferruccio Busoni's *Fantasia Contrappuntistica*." *Journal of Musicological Research* 37:3 (July–September 2018): 239–73.

Dayan, Peter. *The Music of Dada: A Lesson in Intermediality for Our Times*. New York: Routledge, 2019.

Dearstyne, Howard. *Inside the Bauhaus*. Edited by David Spaeth. London: Rizzoli International Publications, 1986.

Dent, Edward. "Ferruccio Busoni." *The Listener* (October 16, 1935).

Doctor, Jenny. "The Parataxis of 'British Musical Modernism.'" *Musical Quarterly* 91:1–2 (Spring/Summer 2008): 89–90/110.

Dorra, Henri, ed. *Symbolist Art Theories: A Critical Anthology*. Berkeley: University of California Press, 1994.

Downes, Olin. "Egon Petri Impressive in Debut." *New York Times* (January 12, 1932).

Downes, Olin. "Petri Introduces 3 Pieces for Piano: Bach Chorale-Preludes among Works Played at Town Hall—Busoni Music Featured." *New York Times* (October 10, 1945).

Downes, Olin. "Second Recital by Egon Petri." *New York Times* (February 10, 1932).

Dreyfus, Laurence. *Bach and the Patterns of Invention*. Cambridge, MA: Harvard University Press, 1996.

Droste, Magdalena. *Bauhaus-Archiv: 1919–1933*. London: Taschen, 2002.
Dyment, Christopher. "Ferruccio Busoni: His Phonograph Recordings." *Journal of the Association for Recorded Sound* 10 (1979): 185–87.
Eckermann, Johann Peter, and Margaret Fuller, eds. *Conversations with Goethe in the Last Years of His Life*. Translated by Margaret Fuller. Boston: Hilliard Gray, 1839.
Egan, M. David. *Architectural Acoustics*. New York: McGraw-Hill, 1988.
Eimert, Herbert. "A Change of Focus." *Die Reihe 2: Anton Webern* (1955): 29–36.
Feldman, Morton. *Essays*. Edited by Walter Zimmermann. Cologne: Beginner Press, 1985.
Fergusson, James. *History of Architecture in all Countries*. 3rd ed. London: John Murray, 1893.
Fischer, Esther. "Busoni and Philipp." *Recorded Sound* 1:8 (1962): 245–46.
Fischer, Ole W. "Passion, Function, and Beauty: Henry van de Velde and His Contribution to European Modernism." *West 86th: A Journal of Decorative Arts, Design, History, and Material Culture* 21:1 (Spring–Summer 2014): 142–48.
Fleet, Paul. *Ferruccio Busoni: A Phenomenological Approach to His Music and Aesthetics*. Cologne: Lambert Academic Publishing, 2009.
Fontaine, Susanne. "Ausdruck und Konstruktion: Die Bachrezeption von Kandinsky, Itten, Klee, und Feininger." In *Bach und die Nachwelt*, edited by Michael Heinemann and Joachim Lüdtke, 396–426. Regensburg: Laaber Verlag, 2000.
Forsyth, Michael. *Buildings for Music*. Cambridge, MA: MIT Press, 1985.
Frank, Isabelle, ed. *The Theory of Decorative Art: An Anthology of European and American Writings: 1750–1940*. New Haven, CT: Yale University Press, 2000.
Friedman, Susan Stanford. "Definitional Excursions: The Meanings of Modern/Modernity/Modernism." *Modernism/Modernity* 8:3 (2001): 493–513.
Frisch, Walter. *German Modernism: Music and the Arts*. California Studies in 20th Century Music. Berkeley: University of California Press, 2005.
Frisch, Walter. "Musik and Jugendstil." *Critical Inquiry* 17:1 (Autumn 1990): 138–61.
Frisch, Walter. "Reger's Bach and Historicist Modernism." *19th-Century Music* 25:2–3 (2001): 296–312.
Galston, Gottfried. *Gli ultimi mesi di vita. Diario di Gottfried Galston*. Edited by Martina Weindel. Rome: Ismez, 2002.
Galston, Gottfried. *Kalendernotizen über Ferruccio Busoni*. Edited by Martina Weindel. Wilhelmshaven: L. F. Noetzel, 2000.
Galston, Gottfried. *Studienbuch*. Berlin: Bruno Cassirer, 1910.
Gasbarro, Federica di. "Sketching a New Verticality: Varèse's Atonal Sound and Its Contexts—Schoenberg, Webern and Ruggles." *Contemporary Music Review* 38:3–4 (2019): 271–315.
Gehring, Franz Eduard. *Mozart the Great Musicians*. Edited by Francis Hueffer. London: Sampson Low, Marston, Searle, and Rivington, 1883.
Geiger, Friedrich. *Die Dramma-Oratorien von Wladimir Vogel, 1896–1984*. Musik im "Dritten Reich" und im Exil 5. Edited by Hans-Werner Heister and Peter Peterson. Hamburg: von Bockel Verlag, 1998.
Gilmore, Bob. *Harry Partch: A Biography*. New Haven, CT: Yale University Press, 1998.
Goethe, Johann Wolfgang von. *Goethe on Art*. Berkeley: University of California Press, 1980.
Goethe, Johann Wolfgang von. *Scientific Studies*. Edited and translated by Douglas Miller. New York: Suhrkamp Publishers, 1988.

Grey, Thomas. "Metaphorical Modes in Nineteenth-Century Music Criticism: Image, Narrative, and Idea." In *Music and Text: Critical Inquiries*, edited by Steven Paul Scheer, 93–118. Cambridge and New York: Cambridge University Press, 1992.

Grimley, Daniel M. *Carl Nielsen and the Idea of Modernism*. Woodbridge, Suffolk: Boydell Press, 2010.

Grindea, Carola. *Great Pianists and Pedagogies: In Conversation with Carola Grindea*. London: Kahn and Averill, 2007.

Gropius, Walter. "Manifesto and Programme of the Weimar State Bauhaus, April 1919." https://www.bauhaus100.de/en/past/works/education/manifest-und-programm-des-staatlichen-bauhauses/ (accessed March 25, 2018).

Gropius, Walter, and László Moholy-Nagy, eds. *Bauhaus: Zeitschrift für Gestaltung*. Dessau: n.p., 1926.

Grosch, Nils. *Die Musik der neuen Sachlichkeit*. Stuttgart: J. B. Metzler, 1999.

Guadet, Julien, and Jean-Louis Pascal. *Eléments et théorie de l'architecture; cours professé a l'Ecole nationale et spéciale des beaux-arts*. Paris: Librairie de la Construction Moderne, 1915.

Guerrini, Guido. *Ferruccio Busoni: La vita, la figura, l'opera*. Florence: Monsalvato, 1944.

Günther, Herbert. *Künstlerische Doppelbegabungen*. Expanded ed. Munich: Heimeran, 1960.

Guse, Ernst-Gerhard, ed. *Wachstum regt sich: Klees Zwiesprache mit der Natur*. Munich: Prestel-Verlag, 1990.

Gutkind, Erwin. *New Building: Basics of Practical Settlement Activity*. Berlin: Verlag der Bauwelt, 1919.

Habermas, Jürgen. *The Philosophical Discourse of Modernity*. Translated by Frederick Lawrence. Cambridge, MA: MIT Press, 2000.

Hale, Jacquelyn. "Consonance, Tertian Structures and Tonal Coherence in Wladimir Vogel's Dodecaphonic World." PhD diss., University of North Texas, 2002. https://digital.library.unt.edu/ark:/67531/metadc3344/m2/1/high_res_d/dissertation.pdf (accessed June 15, 2019).

Halm, August. *Von Form und Sinn der Musik*. Edited by Siegfried Schmalzriedt. Wiesbaden: Breitkopf & Härtel, 1978.

Hamilton, Kenneth. *After the Golden Age: Romantic Pianism and Modern Performance*. New York: Oxford University Press, 2008.

Hamlin, Talbot. *Forms and Functions of Twentieth Century Architecture*. New York: Columbia University Press, 1952.

Hanslick, Eduard. *On the Musically Beautiful: A Contribution towards the Revision of the Aesthetics of Music*. Translated by Geoffrey Payzant. Based on the 8th ed. [1891]. Indianapolis: Hackett, 1986.

Harkness, John C., ed. *The Walter Gropius Archive: An Illustrated Catalogue of the Drawings, Prints, and Photographs in the Walter Gropius Archive at the Busch-Reisinger Museum, Harvard University*, Vol. 1. New York: Garland Publishing and Harvard University Art Museums, 1990.

Harley, Maria Anna. "Space and Spatialization in Contemporary Music." PhD diss., McGill University, 1994. http://digitool.library.mcgill.ca/webclient/StreamGate?folder_id=0&dvs=1533492339494~311&usePid1=true&usePid2=true (accessed August 5, 2018).

Harper-Scott, J. P. E. *Edward Elgar, Modernist*. Cambridge: Cambridge University Press, 2006.

Hartmann, Eduard von. *Ästhetik*. Eduard von Hartmann's Ausgewählte Werke. Berlin: Carl Duncker's Verlag, 1886.

Haste, Cate. *Passionate Spirit: The Life of Alma Mahler*. London: Bloomsbury Publishing, 2019.

Hauptmann, Gerhart. *Gesammelte Werke in zwölf Bänden*. n.p.: Berlin, 1922.

Heile, Björn, and Charles Wilson, eds. *The Routledge Research Companion to Modernism in Music*. London: Routledge, 2019.

Heinkel, Nicole. *Religiöse Kunst, Kunstreligion und die Überwindung der Säkularisierung Frühromantik als Sehnsucht und Suche nach der verlorenen Religion*. Frankfurt am Main: Peter Lang Verlag, 2004.

Hepokoski, James. *Sibelius: Symphony No. 5*. Cambridge: Cambridge University Press, 1993.

Herr, Christopher R., and Gary W. Siebein. "An Acoustical History of Theaters and Concert Halls: An Investigation of Parallel Developments in Music, Performance Spaces, and the Orchestra," "Souped-Up and Unplugged: Proceedings of the 86th ACSA Annual Meeting and Technology Conference," 146. n.p.: Association of Collegiate Schools of Architecture, 1998. https://www.acsa-arch.org/proceedings/Annual%20Meeting%20Proceedings/ACSA.AM.86/ACSA.AM.86.29.pdf (accessed May 12, 2021).

Hildesheimer, Wolfgang. *Mozart*. Translated by Marion Faber. New York: Farrar, Straus & Giroux, 1982.

Hinton, Stephen. *Musical Theater: Stages of Reform*. Berkeley: University of California Press, 2012.

Hollander, Hans. *Musik und Jugendstil*. Zurich: Atlantis, 1975.

Huse, Norbert. *New Building 1918–1933*. Munich: Heinz Moos, 1975.

Hutchinson, Dennis C. "Performance, Technology, and Politics: Scherchen's Aesthetics of Modernism." PhD diss., Florida State University, 2003.

Ingarden, Roman. *The Work of Music and the Problem of Its identity* [1958]. Translated by Adam Czerniawski. Berkeley: University of California Press, 1986.

Jewitt, Clement. "Music at the Bauhaus, 1919–1933." *Tempo* 213 (July 2000): 5–11.

Johnson, Julian. *Out of Time: Music and the Making of Modernity*. New York: Oxford University Press, 2015.

Johnson, Steven. *The New York Schools of Music and Visual Arts*. New York: Routledge, 2001.

Joseph, Branden W. *John Cage in Music, Art, and Architecture*. New York: Bloomsbury, 2016.

Joseph, Charles M. "Bach the Architect: Some Remarks on Structure and Pacing in Selected Praeludia." In *Johann Sebastian: A Tercentenary Celebration*, edited by Seymour L. Benstock, 83–93. Westport, CT: Greenwood Press, 1992.

Kater, Michael H. *Weimar: From Enlightenment to the Present*. New Haven, CT: Yale University Press, 2014.

Kellett, E. E., and E. W. Naylor. *A History of Pianoforte and Pianoforte Players*. Translated by Oscar Bie. New York: Da Capo Press, 1966.

Kelly, Debra. *Pierre Albert-Birot: A Poetics in Movement, a Poetics of Movement*. London: Associated University Presses, 1997.

Klee, Paul. *Hand Puppets*. Ostfildern, Germany: Hatje Cantz, 2006.

Knyt, Erinn. "Approaching the Essence of Music: Ferruccio Busoni and Stylistic Heterogeneity in *Doktor Faust*." *Journal of Musicological Research* 35:3 (August 2016): 176–99.

Knyt, Erinn. "The Bach-Busoni 'Goldberg Variations.'" *Bach Perspectives* 13 (December 2020): 74–100.

Knyt, Erinn. *Ferruccio Busoni and His Legacy*. Bloomington: Indiana University Press, 2017.

Knyt, Erinn. "Ferruccio Busoni and the Absolute in Music: Nature, Form, and *Idee*." *Journal of the Royal Musical Association* 137:1 (May 2012): 35–69.

Knyt, Erinn. "Ferruccio Busoni and the 'Halfness' of Frédéric Chopin." *Journal of Musicology* 34:2 (Spring 2017): 241–80.

Knyt, Erinn. "From Nationalism to Transnationalism: Ferruccio Busoni, the Liceo Musicale di Bologna, and *Arlecchino*." *Music & Letters* 99:4 (November 2018): 604–34.

Knyt, Erinn. "How I Compose: Ferruccio Busoni's Views about Invention, Quotation, and the Compositional Process." *Journal of Musicology* 27:2 (Spring 2010): 224–64.

Knyt, Erinn. "J. S. Bach and Metatonality in the Early Piano Pieces of Ferruccio Busoni." In *Musics with and after Tonality: Mining the Gap*, edited by Paul Fleet, 126–49. Abingdon: Routledge, 2022.

Kobb, Christina. "Viennese Piano Technique of the 1820s and Implications for Today's Pianists." *Music and Practice* 4 (2019). https://www.musicandpractice.org/volume-4/viennese-piano-technique-of-the-1820s-and-implications-for-todays-pianists/ (accessed July 28, 2019).

Kogan, Grigory. *Busoni as Pianist*. Translated by Svetlana Belsky. Eastman Studies in Musicology. Rochester, NY: University of Rochester Press, 2010.

"Die Konzerte der Bauhaus-Woche." *Das Volk* (August 24, 1923).

Kowalke, Kim H. *Kurt Weill in Europe*. Studies in Musicology 14. Ann Arbor, MI: UMI Press, 1979.

Kurth, Ernst. *Grundlagen des linearen Kontrapunkts Einführung in Stil und Technik von Bachs melodischer Polyphonie*. Bern: Drechsel, 1917.

Kurth, Ernst. *Musikpsychologie*. New York: Georg Olms Verlag, 1969

Le Corbusier (Charles-Edouard Jeanneret). *Towards a New Architecture* [1931]. Translated by Frederick Etchells. New York: Dover, 1986.

Le Corbusier. "Towards a New Architecture: Guiding Principles." In *Programs and Manifestoes on 20th-Century Architecture*, edited by Ulrich Conrads, 59–62. Cambridge, MA: MIT Press, 1975.

Leichtentritt, Hugo. *Ferruccio Busoni*. Leipzig: Breitkopf & Härtel, 1916.

Leichtentritt, Hugo. "Ferruccio Busoni." *Music Review* 6:4 (November 1945): 209.

Leichtentritt, Hugo. "Ferruccio Busoni as a Composer." *Musical Quarterly* 3:1 (January 1917): 69–97.

Leichtentritt, Hugo. *Musical Form*. Cambridge, MA: Harvard University Press, 1951.

Leslie, Thomas. *Chicago Skyscrapers 1871–1934*. Urbana: University of Illinois Press, 2017.

Levenson, Michael, ed. *The Cambridge Companion to Modernism*. Cambridge: Cambridge University Press, 1999.

Levitz, Tamara. "Teaching Young Classicality: Busoni's Masterclass in Composition, 1921–1924." PhD diss., Eastman School of Music, 1993.

Lipps, Theodor. *Ästhetik: Psychologie des Schönen und der Kunst*. Hamburg: Voss, 1903.

Lockwood, Annea. Special Section Introduction. *Leonardo Music Journal* 19 (2009): 44–45.

Lorenz-Kierakiewitz, K. H., and M. Vercammen. "Acoustical Survey of 25 European Concert Halls." Rotterdam: NAG, 2009.

Lucchesi, Joachim. "Architektonische Musik." *Berliner Börsen-Courier* (April 21, 1926).

Lucchesi, Joachim. "Brecht und Busoni: Entwürfe zu einem Theater der Gegenwart." In *Man muss versuchen, sich einzurichten in Deutschland: Brecht in den Zwanzigern*.

Der Neue Brecht 14, edited by Jan Knopf and Jürgen Hillesheim, 203–11. Würzburg: Königshausen & Neumann, 2015.

MacDonald, Malcolm. *Varèse Astronomer in Sound*. London: Kahn & Averill, 2002.

Mattis, Olivia. "Edgard Varèse and the Visual Arts." PhD diss., Stanford University, 1992.

Mattis, Olivia. "The Physical and the Abstract: Varèse and the New York School." In *The New York Schools of Music and the Visual Arts*, edited by Steven Johnson, 57–75. Studies in Contemporary Music and Culture 5. London: Routledge, 2001.

Mauvan, John. "Shoe Box: An Analysis of the Concert-Hall and Its Adaptation to Small-Scale Music Performance Space." MA thesis: University of Wellington, 2011.

McCredie, Andrew, ed. *Art Nouveau and Jugendstil and the Music of the Early 20th Century*. Adelaide Studies in Musicology 13. Adelaide: Miscellanea Musicologica, 1984.

Mersmann, Hans. *Angewandte Musikästhetik*. Berlin: M. Hesse, 1926.

Metzger, Christopher. "Die Künstlerische Bach-Rezeption bei Paul Klee und Lyonel Feininger." In *Musikwissenschaft zwischen Kunst, Ästhetik und Experiment: Festschrift Helga de la motte-haber zum 60. Geburtstag*, edited by Reinhard Kopiez, 371–85. Würzburg: Königshausen und Neumann, 1998.

Meyer, Felix, and Heidy Zimmermann, eds. *Edgard Varèse: Composer, Sound Sculptor, Visionary*. Paul Sacher Foundation. Woodbridge, Suffolk: Boydell Press, 2006.

Monson, Karen. *Alma Mahler, Muse to Genius: From fin-de-siècle Vienna to Hollywood's Heyday*. Boston: Houghton Mifflin, 1983.

Morgan, Robert P. "Ives and Mahler: Mutual Responses at the End of an Era." *19th-Century Music* 2:1 (July 1978): 72–81.

Moser, Hans Joachim. *Musikästhetik*. Berlin: W. de Gruyter, 1953.

Münster, Robert, ed. *Jugendstil-Musik? Münchner Musikleben 1890–1918*. Wiesbaden: Reichert, 1987.

"Music and the Drama." *Chicago Record Herald* (January 23, 1904).

"Musik in der Bauhaus-Woche." *Berliner Tageblatt* (August 25, 1923).

Neff, Severine. "Otto Luening (1900–) and the Theories of Bernhard Ziehn (1845–1912)." *Current Musicology* 39 (1985): 21–41.

Nerdinger, Winfried. *The Walter Gropius Archive: An Illustrated Catalogue of the Drawings, Prints, and Photographs in the Walter Gropius Archive at the Busch-Reisinger Museum, Harvard University*. Vol. 1. New York: Garland Publishing and Harvard University Art Museums, 1990.

Oesch, Hans. *Wladimir Vogel: Sein Weg zu einer neuen musikalischen Wirklichkeit*. Munich: Francke Verlag, 1967.

Oja, Carol J. *Making Music Modern: New York in the 1920s*. Oxford: Oxford University Press, 2000.

Panofsky, Erwin. *Gothic Architecture and Scholasticism*. New York: The World Publishing Co., 1967.

Perl, Max. *Bibliothek Ferruccio Busoni: Werke der Weltliteratur in schönen Gesamtausgaben und Erstdrucken, illustrierte Bücher aller Jahrhunderte, eine hervorragende Cervantes- und E. T. A Hoffmann-Sammlung, Bücher mit handschriftlichen Dedikationen, ältere und neuere Literatur aus allen Wissensgebieten, Musik: Versteigerung Montag, den 30. und Dienstag, den 31. März 1925*. Berlin: Max Perl Antiquariat, 1925.

Petri, Egon. "Problems of Piano Playing and Teaching." In *Be Your Own Music Critic: The Carnegie Hall Anniversary Lectures*, edited by Robert Edward Simon, 137–64. n.p.: Books for Libraries Press, 1971.

Petri, Egon, and Friede F. Rohe. "How Ferruccio Busoni Taught: An Interview with the Distinguished Dutch Pianist." *Etude* 58 (October 1940): 685/710.

Peters, W. F., Jr. "Mozart; an Appreciation." *Yale Literary Magazine* 610 (October 1903): 8.

Phelps, Thomas. *Die Ganze ist überall: Vorträge über Musik, 1940–1962*. Basel: Paul Sacher Stiftung, 2011.

Philipp, Isidore. *Le lettere a Isidor Philipp: "Toute supériorité est un exil."* Edited by Laureto Rodoni. Rome: Ismez, 2005.

Poggi, Christine. *In Defiance of Painting: Cubism, Futurism, and the Invention of Collage*. New Haven, CT: Yale University Press, 1992.

Poos, Heinrich. "Henrik Neugeborens Entwurf zu einem Bach-Monument (1928): Dokumentation und Kritik." In *Töne, Farben, Formen: Über Musik und die bildenden Künste—Festschrift Elmar Budde zum 60. Geburtstag*, edited by Elisabeth Schmierer et al., 45–57. Laaber: Laaber-Verlag, 1995.

Poppelreuter, Tanja. *The New Building for the New Person: On the Change and Effect of the Image of Man in the Architecture of the 1920s in Germany*. New York: Olms, 2007.

Prince, Denise Gail. "Kleinhans Music Hall: A Study in Modern Sound." MA thesis, University of Buffalo, State University of New York, 2011.

Probst, Stephanie. "Pen, Paper, Steel: Visualizing Bach's Polyphony at the Bauhaus." *Music Theory Online: A Journal of the Society for Music Theory* 26:4 (December 2020), https://mtosmt.org/issues/mto.20.26.4/mto.20.26.4.probst.html (accessed April 13, 2021).

Probst, Stephanie. "Sounding Lines: New Approaches to Melody in 1920s Musical Thought." PhD diss., Harvard University, 2018.

Ra, Julie. *Rückblick und Erneuerung: Bachs Fuge in Klaviermusik von Reger, Busoni, und Hindemith*. Quellen und Studien zur Musikgeschichte von der Antike bis in die Gegenwart 40. Edited by Michael von Albrecht. Frankfurt am Main: Peter Lang, 2002.

Rasula, Jed. *History of a Shiver: The Sublime Impudence of Modernism*. New York: Oxford University Press, 2016.

Rehding, Alexander. "(Mis)Interpreting Ernst Kurth." MA thesis, Harvard University, 1995.

Reuter, Otto. "Bauhaus-Woche: Neue Musik in Weimar." *Deutschland* (August 21, 1923).

Richter, Hans. *Hans Richter: Plastic Arts of the Twentieth Century*. Neuchâtel, Switzerland: Editions du Griffon, 1965.

Riethmüller, Albrecht. *Ferruccio Busonis Poetik*. Neue Studien zur Musikwissenschaft 4. Mainz: Schott, 1988.

Riethmüller, Albrecht, and Hyesu Shin. *Busoni in Berlin: Facetten eines kosmopolitischen Komponisten*. Wiesbaden: Franz Steiner Verlag, 2004.

Riley, Matthew, ed. *British Music and Modernism, 1895–1960*. Burlington, VT: Ashgate, 2010.

Roberge, Marc-André. *Ferruccio Busoni: A Bio-bibliography*. New York: Greenwood Press, 1991.

Roberge, Marc-André. "Le Concerto pour Piano, Orchestre et Choeur d'Hommes, Op. 39 (1904), de Ferruccio Busoni: Etude historique et analytique." MA thesis, McGill University, 1981.

Roberge, Marc-André. "Ferruccio Busoni: His Chicago Friends, and Frederick Stock's Transcription for Large Orchestra and Organ of the Fantasia Contrappuntistica." *Musical Quarterly* 80 (1996): 302–31.

Roberge, Marc-André. "Ferruccio Busoni in the United States." *American Music* 13:3 (Autumn 1995): 295–332.

Roberts, David. *The Total Work of Art in European Modernism*. Signale: Modern German Letters, Cultures, and Thought. Ithaca, NY: Cornell University Press, 2011.

Rochberg, George. "The New Image of Music." *Perspectives of New Music* 2 (1963): 1–10.

Rodoni, Laureto. "Die Gerade Linie ist unterbrochen: L'esilio di Busoni a Zurigo, 1915–1920." In *Schweizer Jahrbuch für Musikwissenschaft*, New Series 19 (1999), 27–106.

Rosenfeld, Paul. *An Hour with American Music*. Philadelphia: J. B. Lippincott & Co., 1929.

Rothe, Alexander K. "Dramaturgy of Sound: Bauhaus, Music, Technology." https://alexanderkrothemusicology.wordpress.com/2019/01/01/dramaturgy-of-sound-bauhaus-music-technology/ (accessed August 19, 2019).

Rousseau, G. S., ed. *Organic Form: The Life of an Idea*. London: Routledge and Kegan, 1972.

Salvadori, Silvano. *Arlecchino ovvero si riapra il sipario!: Il progetto di Ferruccio Busoni e l'opera grafica del figlio Rafaello*. Empoli: Ibiskos, 2016.

Sargeant, Winthrop. "Bernhard Ziehn, Precursor." *Musical Quarterly* 19 (1933): 169–77.

Scheler, Max. *Wesen und Formen der Sympathie*. Bonn: Friedrich Cohen Verlag, 1923.

Schelling, Friedrich Wilhelm Joseph. *Philosophie der Kunst*. Stuttgart: Cotta, 1859.

Scherchen, Hermann. *Aus meinem Leben*. Berlin: Henschel, 1984.

Schittenhelm, Vânia. "The Dangerous Issue of Modern Music in the Controversy Between Busoni and Pfitzner." *Electronic Musicological Review* 2:1 (October 1997). http://www.rem.ufpr.br/_REM/REMv2.1/vol2.1/The_Dangerous_Issue.html (accessed August 7, 2019).

Schlemmer, Oskar. *The Letters and Diaries of Oskar Schlemmer*. Edited by Tut Schlemmer. Translated by Krishna Winston. Middletown, CT: Wesleyan University Press, 1972.

Schlemmer, Oskar. *The Triadic Ballet*. Berlin: Druckhaus Heinrich, 1985.

Schlemmer, Oskar, László Moholy-Nagy, and Farkas Molnár. *The Theater of the Bauhaus*. Edited by Walter Gropius. Translated by Arthur S. Wensinger. Middleton, CT: Wesleyan University Press, 1961.

Schoenberg, Arnold. *Style and Idea: Selected Writings of Arnold Schoenberg*. Edited by Leonard Stein. Translated by Leo Black. London: Faber and Faber, 1975.

Schonberg, Harold. "Doktor Faustus of the Keyboard." In *The Great Pianists: From Mozart to the Present*, 366–76. New York: Simon & Schuster, 1963.

Schopenhauer, Arthur. *Parerga and Paralipomena: Short Philosophical Essays*. Vol. II. Translated by E. F. J. Payne. Gloucestershire: Clarendon Press, 2001.

Schuller, Gunther. "Conversation with Varèse." *Perspectives of New Music* 3:2 (Spring 1965): 32–37.

Schwartz, Elliott, and Barney Childs, eds. *Contemporary Composers on Contemporary Music*. New York: Holt, Rinehart, and Winston, 1967.

Schweitzer, Albert. *J. S. Bach* [1911]. Translated by Ernest Newman. Vol. 1. New York: Dover Publications, 2012.

Selden-Goth, Gisella. "Das andere Weimar." *Prager Tagblatt* (August 26, 1923).

Selden-Goth, Gisella. *Ferruccio Busoni: Der Versuch eines Porträts*. Leipzig: E. P. Tal & Co., 1922.

Sheldon, Robert. *Petri-Liebermann Notes on the Art and Technique of Pianoforte Playing*. Columbia, MO: R. Sheldon, 1957.

Sibelius, Jean. *Dagbok: 1909–1944*. Edited by Fabian Dahlström. Skrifter utgivna av Svenska litteratursällskapet i Finland 681. Helsingfors: Svenska litteratursällskapet i Finland, 2005.

Siitan, Toomas. "Muusika: Elustunud arhitektuur?" In *Tekste modernismist. II: Muusika ja arhitektuur*, edited by Gerhard Lock, Maris Valk-Falk, and Saale Kareda, 11–18. Tallinn: Scripta Musicalia, 2008.

Sitsky, Larry. *Busoni and the Piano: The Works, the Writings, and the Recordings*. Distinguished Reprints 3. 2nd ed. Hillsdale, NY: Pendragon Press, 2009.

Solie, Ruth. "The Living Work: Organicism and Music Analysis." *19th-Century Music* 4:2 (1980): 147–56.

Sponheuer, Bernd. "Reconstructing Ideal Types of the 'German' in Music." In *Music and German National Identity*, 36–58. Chicago: University of Chicago Press, 2002.

Starr, Lawrence. *A Union of Diversities: Style in the Music of Charles Ives*. New York: Schirmer Books, 1992.

Starr, Lawrence. "Charles Ives: The Next Hundred Years—Towards a Method of Analyzing the Music." *Music Review* 38 (May 1977): 101–11.

Stenzl, Jürg, ed. *Art Nouveau, Jugendstil, und Musik*. Zurich: Atlantis, 1980.

Steuermann, Clara, David Porter, and Gunther Schuller, eds. *The Not Quite Innocent Bystander: Writings of Edward Steuermann*. Translated by Richard Cantwell and Charles Messner. Lincoln: University of Nebraska Press, 1989.

Stevenson, Ronald. "Busoni-Doktor Faust of the Keyboard." *Piano Journal* 1:1 (1980): 14–15.

Straus, Joseph N. *Remaking the Past*. Cambridge: Cambridge University Press, 1990.

Stuckenschmidt, H. H. *Ferruccio Busoni: Chronicle of a European*. Translated by Sandra Morris. New York: Saint Martin's Press, 1967.

Taruskin, Richard. *The Danger of Music and Other Anti-Utopian Essays*. Berkeley: University of California Press, 2008.

Taruskin, Richard. *Music in the Early Twentieth Century*. Vol. 4 of *The Oxford History of Western Music*. New York: Oxford University Press, 2010.

Tatlow, Ruth, *Bach's Numbers: Compositional Proportion and Significance*. Cambridge: Cambridge University Press, 2015.

Till, Nicholas. *Mozart and the Enlightenment: Truth, Virtue, and Beauty in Mozart's Operas*. New York: W. W. Norton, 1992.

Tushinsky, Joseph. "Ferruccio Busoni Radio Documentary." November 16, 1969. https://www.youtube.com/watch?v=64KupE4NcmM (accessed July 27, 2019).

Van de Velde, Henry. "A Clean Sweep for the Future of Art [1894]." In *Symbolist Art Theories: A Critical Anthology*, edited by Henri Dorra, 117–24. Berkeley: University of California Press, 1994.

Van de Velde, Henry. *Die drei Sünden wider die Schönheit*. Zurich: Max Rascher Verlag, 1918.

Van de Velde, Henry. *Geschichte meines Lebens*. Edited by Hans Curjel. Munich: R. Piper and Co., 1962.

Van de Velde, Henry. "Ein Kapitel über Entwurf und Bau Moderner Möbel." *Pan* 4 (1898): 260–64.

Van de Velde, Henry. "Das neue Ornament [1901]." In *Zum neuen Stil*, edited by Hans Curjel, 94–104. Munich: R. Piper, 1955.

Van Elferen, Isabella. "The Gothic Bach." *Understanding Bach* 7 (2012): 9–20. http://www.bachnetwork.co.uk/ub7/UB7_Elferen.pdf (accessed May 8, 2018).

Van Elferen, Isabella. *Gothic Music: The Sounds of the Uncanny*. Gothic Literary Studies. Cardiff: University of Wales Press, 2012.

Varèse, Edward. "Ferruccio Busoni: A Reminiscence." *Columbia University Forum* 9:2 (1966): 73–74.

Varèse, Edward. "In Quest of a Melodist." *Musical America* (October 10, 1925).

Varèse, Edward. "New Instruments in Orchestra are Needed." *Christian Science Monitor* (July 8, 1922).

Varèse, Edward. *Il suono organizzato: Scritti sulla musica Edgard Varèse*. Milan: Edizioni unicopli, 1985.

Varwig, Bettina. "Beware the Lamb: Staging Bach's Passions." *Twentieth-Century Music* 11:2 (September 2014): 245–74.

Vischer, Friderich Theodor. *Das Symbol* [1887]. *Kritische Gänge*. 4th ed. Munich: Meyer und Jesser, 1922.

Vitali, Christoph, ed. *Paul Klee und die Musik: Schirn-Kunsthalle Frankfurt, 14 Juni bis 17 August 1986*. Berlin: Nicolaische Verlagsbuchhandlung, 1986.

Vogel, Wladimir. "Impressions of Ferruccio Busoni." *Perspectives of New Music* 6:2 (Spring–Summer 1968): 169.

Vogel, Wladimir. *Schriften und Aufzeichnungen über Musik: "Innerhalb-Ausserhalb."* Zurich: Atlantis, 1977.

Volkelt, Johannes. *Der Symbol-Begriff in der neuesten Ästhetik*. Jena: Hermann Dufft, 1876.

Waliszewska, Wanda. "Recollections about Egon Petri." *Ruch muzyczny* 9 (May 1969): 13–15.

Walkowitz, Rebecca. *Cosmopolitan Style: Modernism beyond the Nation*. New York: Columbia University Press, 2012.

Walton, Chris. *Othmar Schoeck: Life and Works*. Rochester, NY: University of Rochester Press, 2009.

Watkins, Holly. *Musical Vitalities: Ventures in a Biotic Aesthetics of Music*. Chicago: University of Chicago Press, 2018.

Watkins, Holly. "Towards a Post-Humanist Organicism." *Nineteenth-Century Music Review* 14 (2017): 94–114.

Weill, Kurt. *Musik und musikalisches Theater: Gesammelte Schriften*. Edited by Stephen Hinton, Jürgen Schebera, and Elmar Juchem. Mainz: Schott, 2000.

Weill, Kurt. "Über den gestischen Charakter der Musik." *Die Musik* 21 (March 1929): 419–23.

"Die Weimarer Bauhauswoche." *Allgemeiner Anzeiger für Stadt und Kreis Erfurt* (August 21, 1923).

Weindel, Martina, *Ferruccio Busonis Ästhetik in Seinen Briefen und Schriften*. Veröffentlichungen zur Musikforschung 18. Wilhelmshaven: Florian Noetzel, 1996.

Weindel, Martina, ed. *Ferruccio Busoni: Lettere ai genitori*. Rome: Ismez, 2004.

White, John D., ed. *New Music of the Nordic Countries*. Hillsdale, NY: Pendragon Press, 2002.

Williamson, John. "The Musical Artwork and Its Materials in the Music and Aesthetics of Ferruccio Busoni." In *The Musical Work: Reality or Invention?*, edited by Michael Talbot, 187–204. Liverpool Music Symposium. Liverpool: Liverpool University Press, 2000.

Winckelmann, Johann Joachim. "Reflections on the Painting and Sculpture of the Greeks." London: A Millar and T. Cadell, 1767.

Wingler, Hans M. *The Bauhaus: Weimar, Dessau, Berlin, Chicago*. Cambridge, MA: MIT Press, 1969.

Wolff, Christoph. "Die Architektur von Bachs Passacaglia." *Acta Organologica* 3 (1969): 183–94.

Wölfflin, Heinrich. *Prolegomena to a Psychology of Architecture* [1886]. In *Empathy, Form and Space: Problems in German Aesthetics, 1873–1893*, edited by Harry Francis Mallgrave and Eleftherios Ikonomou, 149–90. Santa Monica, CA: Getty Centre for the History of Art and the Humanities, 1994.

Wolpe, Stefan. "Conversation with Eric Salzman." *Musical Quarterly* 83:3 (Autumn 1999): 378–412.

Worringer, Wilhelm. *Form Problems of the Gothic*. Authorized American Edition. New York: G. E. Stechert and Co., 1910.

Wright, Frank Lloyd. "The Architect" [1900]. *Essential Text*. Edited by Robert Twombly. New York: W. W. Norton, 2009.

Wulfrank, T., and R. J. Orlowski. "Acoustic Analysis of Wigmore Hall, London, in the Context of the 2004 Refurbishment." Proceedings of the Institute of Acoustics (May 2006). https://www.researchgate.net/publication/257361623_Acoustic_Analysis_of_Wigmore_Hall_London_in_the_Context_of_the_2004_Refurbishment (accessed May 12, 2021).

Xenakis, Iannis. *Music and Architecture: Architectural Projects, Texts, and Realizations*. Edited and translated by Sharon Kanach. The Iannis Xenakis Series 1. Hillsdale, NY: Pendragon Press, 2008.

Yearsley, David. *Bach and the Meanings of Counterpoint*. New Perspectives in Music History and Criticism. Cambridge and New York: Cambridge University Press, 2002.

Zilkens, Udo. "Romantische Interpretation: Carl Czerny, Ferruccio Busoni, Samuel Feinberg . . ." In *Johann Sebastian Bach: Zwischen Zahlenmystik und Jazz—Die Eröffnung des Wohltemperierten Klaviers im Spiegel ihrer Interpretationen durch Musiktheoretiker und Musiker, in Kunstwerken und Bearbeitungen*, 24–31. Köln-Rodenkirchen: P. J. Tonger Musikverlag, 1996.

Zuckerkandl, Viktor. *Sound and Symbol: Music and the External World*. Translated by W. R. Trask. New York: Pantheon Books, 1956.

Index

Tables, figures, and examples are indicated by *t*, *f*, and *ex* following the page number